Alpha Boys' School:

Cradle of Jamaican Music

By Heather Augustyn
and Adam Reeves

Half Pint Press

Cover image: Jean-Christophe Molineris, *Alpha Boys' School.* Oil on canvas, 100 cm X 120 cm, 2017 (courtesy of the artist). Musicians, clockwise from top, Lester Sterling, Rico Rodriguez, Don Drummond, Leroy "Horsemouth" Wallace, Yellowman, and Sister Mary Ignatius Davies.

Cover design: Chris Sick

Manufactured in the United States of America.

Half Pint Press, Chesterton, Indiana, www.skabook.com

For our families
and all of those who shared their stories with us.

Table of Contents

Foreword
By David 'Ram Jam' Rodigan

You are about to be taken on a journey to the heart of one of the earliest and most unlikely bastions of Jamaican popular music, Alpha Boys' School. It was in the 1940s, 1950s, and 1960s in the now hallowed halls of the Alpha Boys' School in Kingston that a group of young boys would set out on their journey of discovery—a journey that would eventually lead them to be recognised as iconic music maestros, responsible for creating a new world sound—ska, rocksteady, and reggae.

It was at Alpha that musicians like Don Drummond, Eddie 'Tan Tan' Thornton, and Tommy McCook received their earliest formal music tuition. These so called 'wayward boys' were taken under the wing of Sister Ignatius and her fellow sisters, who had devoted their lives to Christ and in turn to the needs of young children who were often helpless, unloved, and even without a proper home. The list of future stars who attended as young boys is something to behold; little did they know that in years to come they would exercise such a profound influence over the birth and development of Jamaican popular music. It was only when they left the school and began playing in various orchestras in Kingston that they would perhaps realise how important (and enjoyable) playing music could be. I say this as a father who knows only too well how difficult it can be to get young boys to practice their instruments every day. With the eventual progression towards professional sound studio recordings in the 1960s, these young Alpha Boys would become the young men who formed the backbone of the earliest band sessions both before, and after, some of them had formed the greatest ska band of all time—the legendary Skatalites.

Heather Augustyn's unswerving devotion to documenting this vital part of Jamaican history has already been reflected in her portrait of Don Drummond in her book *Don Drummond: The Genius and Tragedy of the World's Greatest Trombonist*, and now she goes even deeper (if that seems possible) to discover the importance of Alpha Boys' School and Sister Ignatius and the Sisters of Mercy. She has also written a number of other books on Jamaican music that chronicle the half that has never been told.

Adam Reeves has been integral to bringing the story of Alpha to the world as a co-producer on a forthcoming Alpha Boys documentary. Having interviewed many of the surviving Alpharian legends he came together with

Heather to create what they hope will be the definitive document on Alpha. Jamaican music is now revered throughout the world, with thousands of devoted fans avidly collecting and trading 'doubles' from their precious record collections. It is to them that this book will have a special purpose as it unveils even more about the music for which we all have such a deep love and affection and the establishment that was to have given the young musicians such a vital start—Alpha Boys' School.

David Rodigan
Rome 2016

Trades at Alpha: Printery
Photo by Adam Reeves

Introduction

By Heather Augustyn

I have always considered myself more of a storyteller than a writer. I've called myself a conduit, through which people's tales of life flow. As a storyteller, I have come to realize that people's stories are not singular, not simple, and sometimes they are contradictory to others and even to reality. But this is what makes these stories, in my opinion, more beautiful. One person's perspective is just as meaningful as the facts themselves, maybe even more so, because it can tell much about that person or culture or situation. The more perspectives, the richer the milieu. It is with this philosophy that I try to approach all of my work. As a newspaper journalist I never interview one person for a story and instead I seek at least three or four sources. As a book writer I try to be as exhaustive as possible, to talk to as many people connected to the story and utilize as many articles and materials as I can locate. And it gets overwhelming at times, but it is a necessary approach, I believe.

When I came to write this book on Alpha Boys' School, I kept that same method in mind. I recognized that each individual boy who walked barefoot on the blue tiled floors of the band room would have a story different from the next. For many boys, their story of Alpha is that it literally saved their lives. For other boys, it gave them a career. For others, it was hurtful. Alpha has too many facets to be captured by a single point of view, and so this book is an attempt at telling Alpha's story through the many stories of some of its most notable band members. It is important to consider that there are hundreds of boys who became brick makers and tailors and farmers and woodworkers and even today, barbers and printmakers and computer technicians, whose stories we may never know. The complexity is mind boggling. Alpha is a galaxy within a universe.

I had been to Alpha twice before I was approached by my co-author, Adam Reeves, to help write this book. I came the first time in my research for my biography of Don Drummond, and so it was with Drummond in my head that I viewed Alpha, telling this one story. I came back again, with a film team from Australia, helping to advise on a documentary on Drummond, so again I walked the grounds with one story in my mind. But I knew that there were hundreds more stories, and each one of them had a different view of these grounds—each one had seen it differently, experienced it differently, been inhabited by it in a way that only their own individual life could. So when I came to Alpha for the third time, I prepared to tell that story—those stories.

I had thought about writing this book years ago and pitched it to officials at Alpha, asking them to work with me and even have the boys print the book in their print shop and bindery, but they had much bigger missions, such as raising and educating hundreds of boys while trying to obtain funding to keep their doors open. It was shortly after this that they closed their residential program and became Alpha Institute instead of Alpha Boys' School. They had even larger concerns than I, or perhaps anyone, realized. The timing just wasn't right. But when Adam contacted me to say that he had a number of interviews with Alpharians from his work as a filmmaker, and would I like to co-author a book with him, I knew that the time was now right. There were many stories available, interviews with a number of musicians who have since died, and combined with my own that I had conducted over my years of researching ska and rocksteady music, I felt this galaxy could be explored. Over the past three years, Adam and I have been hunting stories and finding them, but like a hydra, we cut off one head and two grew back. It has been impossible to tell every story, but I feel we get as close as possible to providing a view of some of the lives of Alpha Boys' School.

Throughout this process of researching and telling stories there have been too many discoveries and meaningful realizations to elucidate properly here, but among them were the discoveries of a handful of musicians associated with Alpha incorrectly, so I hope to set the record straight on a few. First, Desmond Dekker did not attend Alpha. Dekker's long-time manager Delroy Williams says that Dekker, or Desmond Aldolphus Dacres, as was his birth name, attended school in St. Thomas where he was raised by his father before coming to Kingston to learn welding in the same shop as Bob Marley. Milton Moore and Eddie "Tan Tan" Thornton, both contemporaries of Dekker who attended Alpha at this time, corroborate that Dekker did not go to Alpha. Staff at Alpha has been unable to locate any records to prove he was a student there, though they have displayed his name on a wall of alumni. This is likely simply an error of perpetuating what has somehow slipped into historical accounts, rather than any overt attempt to claim credit for his fame.

Additionally, Dalton Browne never attended Alpha, though he erroneously appears on some lists of Alpharians. "It was Arlene Gardens," said Browne of the neighborhood that he and his brothers grew up in. "My dad build houses all over the place. We went to Jamaica College and I played in the band and people heard about this guy who could play guitar and I started recording at 14." Another guitar player, Winston "Bo Pee" Bowen, also never attended Alpha. Bowen grew up in Clarendon and he taught himself to play after watching a man in his village play guitar and building his own from a pan and strings. When he moved to Kingston to live with his mother, he attended St. Andrew Tech. "I wasn't one of those who were in Alpha. I give guitars to the school, to Sparrow Martin. I donated because Sparrow Martin is a good teacher and he do a lot for the kids. I see many of my good friends who come out of Alpha and I take my hat off to Sister [Ignatius] because she was a mother and a father to them." Additionally, Noel "Skully" Simms did not attend Alpha. He attended Ebenezer School near Coronation Market. And Winston Francis never attended Alpha. He told me in 2014, "I attended St. Aloyisius in Kingston but all of the nuns from Alpha were in attendance at St. Aloyisus."

Also discovered during this process were a number of musicians who attended Alpha, but little to no information exists on them. This is not surprising considering two social factors of the early to mid-1900s. First, though it may be respectable to be associated with the Alpha Boys Band today, this is a relatively new phenomenon. For most boys in the past, to have gone to Alpha was to be labeled as poor, "wayward," disobedient or rude, a ward of the state, or in the case of guitarist Janet Enright's father who forbid his upper class daughter to perform on stage with them, "prisoners." So the opportunities available to boys from Alpha had to be earned through exceptional talent—talent beyond those with means and access.

This leads to the second factor why there may be less known of some musicians from Alpha. The prominent Jamaican newspapers rarely covered music at all, let alone a feature or article on a "wayward boy." The largest newspaper in Jamaica, the *Gleaner*, or as it was known prior to December 7, 1992, the *Daily Gleaner*, was founded in 1834, established by brothers Joshua and Jacob deCordova, British colonizers and land owners. Jacob went on to become a senator in Texas and he established the city of Waco, Texas. Founded in wealth and privilege, the *Gleaner* avoided coverage of unsavory topics such as slavery and emancipation, socialist politics, Rastafari spirituality, and music which was a manifestation of the lower class. "The paper was very English-oriented and focused on the business, political and social interests—and amusements—of the local white ruling class," said the *Gleaner* itself in an article on their 180th anniversary on September 13, 2014. This explains well why there was little coverage of music in the *Daily Gleaner*, especially the music produced by Alpharians, given the colonial and patrician nature of the publication's ownership and editorial direction.

One of the other newspapers in Jamaica during this era, *The Star*, was called "the people's paper." It was founded in 1951 and today is owned by the Gleaner Company. It did cover music and entertainment and had a special weekend section that featured articles on musicians and it also had a column, "Vere Johns Says." Vere Johns, as one may recognize, was the same as the originator and host of the Vere Johns Opportunity Hour, that talent competition that launched so many musical careers. Despite these connections to music and coverage of numerous musicians, some Alpharians escaped publicity and recognition. Though they may have appeared on recordings, proper documentation of which musicians played on which tracks is always an issue. Some of these other Alpharians of which little is known include Irvin "Allah" Lloyd, organ, guitar, and piano; Ansel Johnson, bass; Lloyd Williams, bass; Winston Turner, trumpet; Derrick Stewart, drums; Felix Taylor, trombone; Frank Aird, trumpet; Charlie Clarke, music tutor; Winston Graham, trumpet; Arthur "Bucky" Buchanan, bass, and his brother, Jocelyn "Blu Blu" Buchanan; Norris Ridguard, trumpet; Harold Williams, bass; Chester Power, trumpet; and Sam Bernard, alto saxophone, Everol Wray, Whippa Demus, Richard "Dirty Harry" Hall, and others. Granted, some musicians were simply better or more successful than others and so they may have garnered less, or no, newsprint. There are also plenty of musicians from Alpha who are young and just emerging, like Travis "Trombone" Wedderburn and Kemar Miller, as well as those whose attendance at Alpha is just coming to the fore, and those we simply missed. We hope to be able to include these musicians in future editions of the book.

I would like to take this opportunity to thank Adam Reeves who I first knew as a fan of ska via social media. He helped me to source photos for my previous books and then when he asked me to write this book, I had known we would make good work partners since we had similar taste in music, similar world views, and similar work ethics and sensitivities. It has been an absolute delight, every step of the way. I wish all work relationships were so easy, and perhaps this is due in large part to the fact that this did not feel like work at all. It is, as the cliché goes, a labor of love. We never once had a battle, though we did have different thoughts on approaches or edits, but because we each respected each other, it resulted in better writing. Ideal. This book is a yin and yang in many ways. Those Adam claimed as his artist to cover, I gladly relented, and vice versa. I preferred the older artists, he chose the younger. And so we had thought at one point we would edit our styles together, to merge them into one big tome with two names. We soon found that our own voices were important enough to us that we would leave the styles alone and so our name appears on each chapter we authored. The length we devoted to each musician is in no way correlative to their value, talent, or popularity. There were several factors that determined length, most of which were subjective. We attempted to keep the lengths of each entry the same, but that proved a futile effort. Additionally, American and British English spellings and conventions are kept by each author, rather than adapting to one system or the other. We hope this will not be a distraction to readers, but will further bring home the message that there are many stories, told my many authors, about many lives and places and music. This is what makes Jamaican music history as rich as it is, flowing like the Nile River and its various tributaries, to fertilize lands near and far.

Albert Hird, bandmaster of the Jamaica Defence Force and a 1987 graduate of Alpha Boys' School, conducts at Hope Gardens, 2015.
Photo by Heather Augustyn 2015

A trombone student at Alpha Boys' School in 2013
Photo by Heather Augustyn

Introduction

By Adam Reeves

A diminutive, bespectacled Roman Catholic nun who spins the hippest 45 records of the day at parties she throws with her own bass-heavy soundsystem? Who runs a musical education program for sixty four years, the graduates of which give birth to one of the greatest musical genres of the 20th Century? Talk to Jamaicans, and the story of Alpha often seems like nothing too out-of-the-ordinary to them. The school is simply part of the fabric of their society, with ex-Alpha boys taking positions in sectors such as the military, police, the print industry and pretty much every area of working life. Talk to anyone from outside of Jamaica and they can't quite believe what they're hearing. How this nun taught boxing, cricket and athletics and knew everything worth knowing about the sporting heroes of the day. How she owned a record collection that most collectors would die for. Throw into this mix the story of her 'golden boy,' the genius jazz trombonist who forms the greatest ska band in history, succumbs to mental illness, takes the life of his true-love then spends the rest of his days in a mental asylum until his own light is extinguished in mysterious circumstances, aged just thirty five—at this point people are usually asking why there hasn't been movie made, or at the very least a book. The Alpha story is simply too powerful not to be told. Up until now there has been no comprehensive account available but we have attempted to set that straight.

I never set out to write a book on Alpha Boys School—far from it, but events led me here. I certainly would never have considered myself qualified for such an undertaking and I don't consider myself to be any kind of academic reggae historian or musicologist, just someone with a love of the music and some simple storytelling skills.

I first came across the story of Alpha sometime in the early 1990s when UK jazz saxophonist Courtney Pine made a TV documentary about his Jamaican heritage, which incorporated a visit to Alpha and an encounter with Sister Ignatius. As a dedicated reggae fan, the story grabbed me. Over a decade later, in February 2007 I was given an opportunity to film a one-off Alpha Boys reunion concert in London, hosted and promoted by Milton Moore of The Alpha Old Boys Association UK Chapter. Twelve living legends of Alpha came together to put on a three hour concert in honour of Sister Ignatius on the fourth anniversary of her passing. During the two day rehearsal period I interviewed all of them about their time at Alpha. It was a dream come true to be right at the heart of this once-of-a-lifetime gathering, meeting such fabled characters as Horsemouth, Tan Tan, Rico, Deadly Headley and Karl 'Cannonball' Bryan, names I'd been seeing on record covers since I was a teenager. Some of these guys hadn't crossed paths for over forty years and the sense of camaraderie was infectious. Old stories came pouring out, recounted with much hilarity, often teasing each other in such a way that only those who have known each other as children can do. The atmosphere in the rehearsal room was smoking hot, with some killer spontaneous jams. During the interviews, each and every one of them spoke with deep reverence and gratitude about Sister Ignatius, how she had recognized something inside them that they had not known themselves was even there, how she gave them an opportunity, encouraged them, with fierce discipline and love to reach the standards of professional musicians. Several told us that if it wasn't for Alpha they'd either be dead or in prison. Some of them had kept in touch with her for many decades after leaving, keeping her updated with their progress via letters or occasional visits. It struck me that she was one of the most important people in their lives and they loved her almost like a mother. I realized that Sister Ignatius really was the Godmother of Jamaican Music.

Six months after the London reunion show I found myself in Kingston, walking the grounds and the classrooms of Alpha along with a small documentary film crew. Having obtained some initial seed funding we were assessing the viability of a full length-feature documentary. Ultimately such a project proved too complex and costly an undertaking (although I hope it may one day materialize). It took a further seven years to connect the dots and realize that the material I had accumulated in the process was enough to form the beginnings of a book, but there was still a long way to go. I was fortunate enough to know of an ideal prospective co-author, Heather Augustyn, who had just recently published her book on Don Drummond. I say 'know,' but in actual fact, at the time of publishing we have still not met in person, based as we are on different continents. Happily, Heather jumped at the chance. Working with someone who was able to hold the vision for the bigger picture and seemed to be on the same page as me from the outset has made it possible to bring this work to completion. It is an example of what is possible in today's digitally global village, whereby we can connect with like-minded people via social media to form working partnerships based on mutual trust and respect. As Heather states, we managed to work closely together with our quite different approaches, without cramping each other's styles or offending each other with our honesty. I hope our distinct writing styles work to complement each other. We have signed each chapter to distinguish our styles.

The approach we took was largely to step out of the way and allow the Alpharians to tell their own stories themselves. Without their willingness to open up and share with us how Alpha impacted their lives, our task would have been impossible. For us to appreciate the full reach of Alpha's influence upon Jamaican music, a Who's Who of Alpha musicians was needed, to line them all up side by side and examine their individual contributions and reflect upon their collective achievements as a whole. As you work through the chapters (or randomly dip in) gradually a picture is built up of a school with such an immense impact that it is hard to think of anything else comparable anywhere in the world. Which is why it is not unreasonable to state that this small boarding school run by Sisters of Mercy nuns is quite simply the greatest musical school anywhere on Earth. Well, if you happen to know of a better one—or at least a more influential one then we definitely want to hear about it!

One question that Heather and I have debated and have differing opinions on, is whether ska and reggae music would have been possible without the input of Alpha Boys. Would this music we love have evolved regardless? The answer remains open to debate, but there is no doubt that their immense contribution in studios like Treasure Isle and Studio One enabled ska to happen and later on rocksteady and reggae. Certainly, there were plenty of terrific non-Alpharian Jamaican musicians around who were eager to make their mark. But as highly disciplined young players, Alpharians brought a level of professionalism—in reading, composing, arranging and improvising music to a bourgeoning local music industry that many of the other musicians around that time just didn't have. Above and beyond their discipline, the Alpha boys could really swing. They had metronomic timing, but they also had a spontaneous, soulful expressiveness that reached new heights as far as Jamaican musical standards were concerned. I am of the belief that reggae was an inevitable conclusion to ceaseless musical innovations driven forward by sound system operators who were on the lookout for whatever made people dance and bawl out for more. Quite simply, if something worked, a soundman would milk that groove for what it was worth, cutting tunes in a similar vein until they hit upon the next thing. But it was often Alpha Boys who would be the driving force enabling these new innovations in the studio, as they had the confidence to reach out into unknown territory, to try out new rhythmic structures. They helped to create something distinctly Jamaican with the birth of ska. In this respect, it can be boldly asserted that Alpha Boys' School players were the ones who were at the rockface, carving out new musical seams and bringing about each significant change in style. They are the geniuses behind the scenes, or in the case of some like Yellowman and Johnny Osbourne, spearheading the scene. We are sure you will agree, Alpha is truly the cradle of Jamaican music.

The garden at Alpha
Photo by Heather Augustyn

To experience the musical legacy of the artists whose stories are told in the following pages, visit Alpha Boys' School Radio, a streaming radio station showcasing decades of jazz, ska, rocksteady, and reggae recordings by current and past students at alphaboysschoolradio.com.

Photos on the wall at the Lennie Hibbert Music Hall in 2013
Photo by Heather Augustyn

History of Alpha Boys' School and the Alpha Boys' Band

Since Alpha's official foundation on May 1, 1880, the institution has morphed as the needs of the island dictated. Alpha began as a small shelter for a single orphan, a girl, and over the decades has included both girls and boys schools, a banana plantation, a business school, a school for infants, a primary school, a convent, a training home for domestic servants, and a school that taught trades such as printing, brick making, gardening, tailoring, and of course, music. It is this last trade that produced the wealth of stellar musicians who shaped Jamaican music and subsequent music forever. To fully understand the scope of the Alpha Boys Band, it is important to first consider the institution from which the band was created.

A photo of the Alpha Boys Band hangs in the Lennie Hibbert Music Hall, 2013

According to a *Daily Gleaner* article, September 11, 1936, the formation of Alpha came through the efforts of women who made helping Kingston's children their mission. "Long the foundation of the Cradle of

Alpha, many devoted young ladies of Kingston had zealously cooperated with the Rev. Father Hathaway, S.J., in organized relief work for the poor and suffering. Regular meetings were held. Miss Anne Llado was the president and Miss Jessie Ripoll the secretary, while Miss Josephine Ximenes, Miss Louise Dugiol and several others had charge of various districts. Not merely philanthropists, but truly devoted religious workers, they came in contact with distressing examples of poverty and misfortune; and as time went on, the wail of many a homeless child touched the hearts of these angels of mercy. They appealed to the Very Rev. Father Porter, S.J., representing the evident need for an orphanage, and the good Father assured them that he would do all in his power to help them. Soon, under his able direction, a lowly shelter was erected on the property known as 'Alpha,' then a country estate outside the city proper, and Miss Jessie Ripoll left home and dear ones to take care of the poor and neglected."

The article continues, "Viewing to-day the hundreds who comprise the population of Alpha, it is almost incredible to think that the institution came into being on May 1, 1880 with Miss Ripoll, one servant and a single orphan. But sublime was her trust in Divine Providence and firm her belief in the work which she felt that she was called upon to perform as her mission in life. Miss Josephine Ximenes and others who could not leave home immediately came every day to help. Before a month had elapsed, fifty orphans had been admitted. With no material resources, one of the daily duties of the now-called Sisters was to go to the town begging. To these refined ladies that was, humanly speaking, no easy task, and they were not spared rebuffs by some who got tired of their daily cravings; but the generous support and kind encouragement of the majority made up for the thoughtlessness of those who could not fully understand. After two years, Father Porter was firmly convinced that the finger of God was in the work, and having tested the disposition of those engaged in it, he permitted them to wear a distinctive black habit, and on May 1, 1882, to their great delight, he allowed them to make temporary religious vows, which they renewed every three years. In the year 1881, the community had grown to such proportions that the small cottage was found to be entirely inadequate. As a result, Fr. Porter succeeded in having a new two-storey building erected on the ground. Thus far, the sole source of income were the alms which the four ladies in charge secured by begging. To provide more ample funds for support, a large vegetable garden was begun and the products sold in the city.

The pasture lands were leased to nearby farmers, and generous families made donations to assist the struggling enterprise. A Government grant, which Fr. Porter was seeking for some time was also finally secured, and thus the little community could be assured of a small but certain financial aid."

Further, "In 1890, Rt. Rev. Bishop Charles Gordon, S.J., was appointed to Jamaica. His first efforts were directed towards introducing here a religious Community of Sisters to take up the work which was rapidly becoming too great for the original four laywomen. He was finally successful, and on December 12, 1890, the first group of Sisters of Mercy arrived from Bermondsey, England. They were six in number, five professed Sisters and one Novice. Three of the four ladies who had charge of the community of Alpha immediately applied for admission to the Order. On the very day of thc arrival of the Sisters, Bishop Gordon began preparations for the expansion of Alpha by breaking ground for the Boys' Industrial School. A few weeks later this new school opened with an enrolment of nine."

It continues, "In the year 1891, on February 2, Miss Ripoll, Miss Ximenes and Miss Dugiol received the religious habit or dress of the Order of the Sisters of Mercy, and became Sister M. Claver, Sister Margaret Mary and Sister M. Joseph respectively. That same year, the Sisters opened the East Branch Elementary School with an attendance of fourteen children. To-day the average attendance is over five hundred. The next direction in which the Sisters turned their attention was in the establishment of an Academy to provide a secondary education for girls. The Academy School was originally intended to care for Jamaican girls, but a glance at its enrolment list shows that it now receives pupils from Cuba, Haiti, Panama, Costa Rica and South American countries. The Academy has a Branch School which claims high scholastic standing, and the building serves as a local centre for Cambridge Examinations. Following rapidly on the establishment of the Academy came the new Alpha Elementary school and Infant School."

A drawing of Sister Ripoll hangs on the wall at Alpha today
Photo by Heather Augustyn

The article further states, "Towards the close of the year 1891, the Rev. Mother procured some band instruments from England. Many boys soon showed a talent in music, and a Sister was appointed to train them. With years they improved, and soon the Alpha Band was in popular demand to aid musical engagements. Many a well-known musician has received his early training at Alpha. The late West India Regimental Band, with its unique record, numbered many an old Alpha Boy in its ranks. When on the disbandment of the Regiment a number of years ago popular feeling cried out against the dispersal of such a fine and talented body of musicians, the Jamaica Military Band came into existence, and old Alpha Boys are helping to carry on the excellent musical traditions which the Band inherited. In addition there is scarcely a band or Orchestra of any distinction or ability in the city that does not contain an old Alpha Band boy. In an open Dance Band Competition held in the city, the prize was by popular acclaim awarded to a band led by one of these. This young man has since left for England to pursue his musical career place in a wider field which offers more scope for his ability. In this, he is following in the footsteps of another who has won a proud name after obtaining the best of the musical world in England, and is the holder of a medal from the Kneller Hall School of Music. In the early days of the Band one boy was sent to England to the Royal Academy of Music where he was presented with a gold medal by Her Majesty the late Queen Victoria."

Mother Mary Claver Ripoll's grave at Calvary Cemetery
Photo by Roberto Moore

It continues, "The establishment of a House of Mercy for training servant girls was provided shortly after the arrival of the Sisters of Mercy from England, and this has proved an invaluable help not only to the girls themselves, but to the ladies who sought well-trained and respectful servants. From 1894 until 1906 an Orphanage was conducted in Spanish Town; but eventually the place proved unhealthy for the work. In 1901 schools were established at Alva and Murray Mount in St. Ann and in 1905 at Falmouth; but they had to be closed in 1909 as the Bishop wished the Sisters to take charge of the large elementary school in Spanish Town and the work in Kingston required more Sisters. In 1904 the best building on the property had been destroyed by fire; and slowly but surely through the generosity of the people, new edifices arose on the ashes, just in time to be shaken to the ground by the Earthquake of 1907. Only the Chapel stood its ground; but there was no time to think of self; the whole city needed mercy's help. In spite of the fact that two Sisters were seriously injured and the days of poverty were renewed, the many appeals for assistance spurred them on to more deeds of self-sacrifice. Not until 1910 did the Sisters have a real Convent home. In 1917 a poor school was started at Gordon Town."

The article concludes, "Through many trials this school has prospered and is still progressing; and in 1920 another school for the poor, and an Academy were opened in Port Antonio. In 1932 the Sisters began educational work in Seaford Town where they now have one hundred and sixty-five pupils, and in 1933 a splendid Academy was opened at Mandeville which at present has an enrollment of thirty-two students. Meanwhile a calamity happened when a new building at the Boys' School was reduced to ashes. Once again, the co-operation of the good people of Kingston was remarkable. Even at midnight they came from all directions to help the Sisters and the children. In two weeks enough money had been subscribed to rebuild. His Eminence Cardinal O'Connell of Boston, Mass., U.S.A. sent a donation of one thousand dollars. During the last few years a spacious dormitory has been added to the Boys' School. A new Printing Shop and various other improvements which have elicited the admiration of the Members of the K.S.A.C. and manifest the constant growth of this department. The former Alpha Club has been converted into use for the Infant Section of the Boys' School...."

It is worth noting that the orphanage in Spanish Town referenced briefly in the article was in fact called St. Claver's Orphanage and the Roman Catholic Agricultural School. It was similar to Alpha Boys' School in many ways. It housed boys in need of shelter and provided them with food, and it also provided two hours of school during the hottest hours of the day, because the remaining hours were meant for cultivating bananas and breaking up and removing stones from the land to prepare the soil for planting. There were 73 acres managed by Father Mulry, but the concept for the "self-supporting institution" was the idea of Bishop Charles Gordon. The boys tended to every aspect of the plantation which was owned by Gordon, including weaving their own straw hats to wear in the fields to shield them from the sun. This orphanage also housed a band. In addition to the calamities and disasters referenced, there was also Hurricane Charlie in 1951 which killed four Alpha boys after a dormitory collapsed on them, Hurricane Gilbert in 1988 which destroyed many trees and damaged buildings at the school, and Hurricane Ivan in 2004 which also caused destruction on campus. Additionally, the Spanish Flu and typhoid epidemic in 1918 infected 200 Alpha boys, killing one, and a disease called Alastrin in 1920 spread to many boys on campus, though none died. In 1920 a fire destroyed the refectory, and in 1987 fire destroyed the woodwork shop.

The *Daily Gleaner* on September 1, 1939 also provided information on the history of Alpha and it included detail the daily activities of the students. The article, entitled, "A Great Institution Alpha, 'An Island within an Island' Doing Valuable Work for Boys & Girls: Two Hour Tour Of Industrial Section," by J. W. Taffe, was featured on the front page, just beneath a story on WWII whose headline read, "The German Army. Who Are Its Leaders? What Can It Do?" Taffe's article stated, "The boys are trained, as only to be expected, in a larger, and more varied sphere. They are trained in printing, tailoring, basket and hat making, carpentry, shoemaking, cabinet making, music, according to their choice, but every one of the 370 boys must take the agricultural course which is consistent to an institution of that kind and in a tropical agricultural island. DAILY ROUTINE. Irrespective of their various lines of occupation, all the children of the Institution attend school for half of each day and the instruction of their class work is based entirely on the requirements of the Code for our Elementary Schools. Before making my tour and seeing the various aspects of Alpha, I interested myself as to the routine work there day by day, and so I made enquiries of one of the good sisters in charge as to just how each day was spent there. I was informed that on rising at 6.30 each morning they prepare, after prayer, for the day's task and their first compulsory indulgence of each day is bathing. After this is done, under their house captains and assistants and the supervision of the two sisters in charge of both sections respectively, they launch out on their various occupations. At 8 o'clock, after an hour's work, the bell is rung and in lines, according to the system there, they march to the refectory for the first meal of the day—breakfast. An hour after this they are all in the class room neatly attired in their attractive uniforms, and 12 o'clock finds them again at the dinner table. After the various games and pranks over the campus they prepare themselves at 5 o'clock for supper and an hour and a half after finds them on their knees, under the guidance of the good sisters, thanking God for the blessings of the day, after which they retire for a good twelve hours rest. TWO HOURS TOUR. My first route in going through the industrial section of Alpha on Monday, was through the girls' section. There the majority of the girls were engaged in their class work—others in one of the main halls engaged in sewing, knitting and hat making. It was a very impressive spectacle from two points of view—the serene quietude of the entire place and the studiousness which characterized the period. I was taken around by the sister in charge who explained, in very gracious manner, the details of each section, and their undertakings then and prior to my arrival. Under the supervision of this good sister and another, this section of industrial Alpha carries a far-reaching aspect. There is that touch of feminine gentleness, artistry and industry which is driven home forcibly even to the casual visitor, as ranging from tender ages to around sixteen years, this assembly of girls gives the genuine impression of culture and thoroughness as a whole. Unfortunately I could not spend as long a time in this section as I intended because classes were in session. But I did want to see more of the practical indulgences of the girls and promised both myself and the sister who took me around to pay another visit, so after the girls filed out in orderly and quiet manner and posed for a press picture, I left for the boys section. BOYS' SECTION. Indeed, the boys' section presented a far more striking impression, under the circumstances, than was the case with the girls. On entering St. Joseph Avenue—the principal section of this side of the 'island' of Alpha, the immensity of the industrial work that is being taught here is clearly revealed. I was met by one of the sisters in charge, who, apart from explaining the various phases of work conducted there, personally conducted me around. We first entered the printery where the boys were busy at work compiling matter for their second publication of the 'Alpharian,' their magazine. After spending some time here, we left and passed swiftly over to the carpentry, tailor and shoemaking shops and had a glance at one or two other units of the place. Under a group of palm trees, stood Mr. George Neilson, musical director, and his band of musicians at practice, while gathered here and there in groups were happy companies of boys, on the oval—the big play centre—enthusiastically in pursuit of their favourite pastimes. It was indeed a wonderful revelation, going over this section of the area of Alpha in particular; but admittedly, while I was carried away with the great industrial activity carried on, I was more so with the agricultural work which in carried on at the eastern section of the place which not only reveals great success in this line, but shows, most of all the soundness of the instruction given the boys and by their work their potentiality for agricultural pursuit. PILLAR OF SUCCESS. Three hundred and seventy boys of ranging ages are, in the ordinary course of events, a problem to handle; and on completion of my tour, I enquired how was it possible for just the two sisters stationed in this section and who are really the supervisors of the boys to handle their problem of management. 'This is a simple matter,' sister informed me, 'for the boys are all specially trained in principles of discipline, and show the expected respect to who are set over them as their house captains and leaders, who assist greatly in the work, and they all show the same to us, in the slightest given order.' This is one of the pillars of success on which the industrial institution Alpha is based upon...."

In celebration of Alpha's Golden Jubilee, their 50th anniversary, the *Daily Gleaner* on April 8, 1930 featured an article on the institution's "Upward Struggle." The article mentioned the Alpha Boys Band when it stated, "Here the boys were taught agriculture, shoemaking, tailoring, and carpentry, and that very useful attachment to institutions of the kind—to play in a band. From that beginning in 1891, the Alpha Cottage Band has grown into prominence, and from year to year has entertained thousands of persons in various parts of the island—as late as Sunday night, there was a splendid concert given in support of the Band in the Theatre at Winchester Park, and in which they were heard to great advantage."

On August 29, 1965, a *Daily Gleaner* article on Alpha Boys' School's Diamond Jubilee, or 75th anniversary, featured photos of the boys in various settings of their daily life, including in the classroom, in trades, and in the band. The section on the Alpha Boys Band stated, "All students take part in cricket, football, track athletics, baseball and boxing. The school, which has prepared outstanding sportsmen, places much emphasis on athletic prowess. The 'ALPHA BOYS BAND' can be called 'the cradle' of Jamaica's musicians. The band has had a remarkable record of accomplishment since it was formed in 1892. In its early years it was known as the 'Drum and Fife Corps.' Over 60 past members of the band have joined the Jamaica Military Band, Jamaica Constabulary Band, and Jamaica Regiment Band. Former Alpha musicians can be heard on the Continent, in the U.S.A. and the Caribbean islands."

The Alpha Boys Band was featured in an article in the *Daily Gleaner* on November 30, 1992 for their 100th anniversary. The reporter wrote, "In the many areas in which Jamaica's name is internationally recognized, music is one area in which there is one institution which can claim to have been a vital force in developing Jamaica's musicians. It has yielded such names as Tommy McCook, saxophonist of Skatalites fame; Cedric Brooks, flute and saxophone player; Don Drummond, a world rated trombonist; Lennie Hibbert O.D. who was noted for jazz and his teaching of music; Eddie Thornton, who played with Boney M and Aswad Band; Oscar Clarke who toured with Louis Armstrong's Band and Leslie Thompson who became the first black conductor of the London Symphony Orchestra. [Editor note: There is no proof of this, nor does Thompson mention it in his own biography, not to minimize his importance. The first black conductor of the LSO was in fact Guyanese clarinetist and composer Rudolph Dunbar at the Royal Albert Hall in 1948, photographic evidence of which can be seen in Lloyd Bradley's book *Sounds Like London*]. The list goes on and on but these names are only an indication of the calibre of musicians who have emerged from Alpha Boys' School.... Alpha Boys' School is renowned for its brass band. This year, the band celebrates 100 years of outstanding contribution to music in Jamaica. The band started out as a drum and fife corps, under the wing of a soldier from the nearby Up-Park Camp, who volunteered to assist the children to learn to play music. Today, it is the nursery for the Jamaica Regiment and Jamaica Military Bands, as well as many popular groups...."

<u>Alpha's Drum and Fife Corps</u>

The earliest mention of the Alpha Drum and Fife Corps comes in the *Daily Gleaner* on November 3, 1894. According to most historical accounts, the band had been in existence for two years at this point. This article chronicled a "Children's Fete" at Trafalgar Park in which the Drum and Fife Corps performed. It stated, "The Alpha Cottage children were in the charge of Sisters Claver and Xavier. The Alpha Cottage Drum and Fife Band were also present in uniform, and played as they marched from the Cottage to the cars [trolleys from Jamaica Street Car Co.] and from the cars to the grounds." There were over 1,600 children in attendance at this event which featured performances from a number of student bands from various schools in the Kingston district. On April 23, 1896, the *Daily Gleaner* noted the band's performance at a "Garden Party and Fancy Fair" along with the band from the "Cadet Corps." The paper on July 26, 1897 wrote that the "Alpha Cottage Orphanage with fife and drum band under Father Mulry" performed at a celebration of the royal family in Spanish Town. The *Daily Gleaner* on May 25, 1906 wrote of their performance during Empire Day. "After the demonstration the children marched backed to their schools and those from Alpha cottage were accompanied by the drum corps." They performed at a garden party at Winchester Park held by the Roman Catholic Church for Easter. The *Daily Gleaner* on April 21, 1908 stated, "The Alpha Cottage drum corps supplied the music until the band of the W.I.R. [West India Regiment] arrived and the boys acquitted themselves admirably." They also performed at a ceremony of the laying of the corner stone of Holy Trinity Cathedral in Kingston on December 10, 1908 at which both Bishop Collins and Father Patrick Mulry were present. These two were crucial in the foundation of Alpha as well as the early band. The *Daily Gleaner* wrote, "The gathering was a very large one indeed, about four thousand people being in attendance. At 3.30 p.m. a mammoth procession started from Winchester Park. It was headed by the drum corps of Alpha Cottage playing the well-known hymn, 'Faith of Our Fathers.'"

ALPHA COTTAGE BAND.

The Alpha Cottage Band played on the Myrtle Bank hotel lawns on Saturday afternoon, going through a big programme in a very creditable manner.

From the *Daily Gleaner*, 1911

While there is no more reference to the Alpha Cottage Drum and Fife Corps in the *Daily Gleaner*, nor of a donation or acquisition of brass instruments in 1908 as some accounts of Alpha histories note, the next mention of the band in the newspaper after this late 1908 account of the drum and fife corps is one that contains a reference to brass instruments. The *Daily Gleaner* on May 25, 1910 with the title, "Monster Picnic" and the subtitle, "Alpha Cottage Brass Band," states, "A monster picnic in aid of St. Anne's Church, North Street, was held at Cumberland Pen yesterday. A most enjoyable day was spent by the thousands of people who attended, two bands of music being in attendance. The chief attraction was the Alpha Cottage band. The boys are now attired in uniform resembling that worn by the soldiers of the West India Regiment, and are all supplied with brass and reed instruments. The band at present consists of about 17 boys and they are being trained by Mr. Knibbs [sic Nibbs] late band sergeant of the 1st battalion West India Regiment. The boys acquitted themselves excellently yesterday and showed the result of careful and skilled tuition on the part of Mr. Knibbs [sic Nibbs]. The programme they rendered at Cumberland Pen and on the train yesterday was highly appreciated." Sometime between the end of December 1908 and spring of 1910, the Alpha band had acquired brass instruments, uniforms, and their first bandmaster.

Throughout the decades, instruments were obtained through a number of fundraising performances and solicitation for donations, but it is likely that the first donation which is normally attributed to a bishop came from Lieutenant L. E. Ottley who was staff officer of the local forces. A *Daily Gleaner* article on August 4, 1931 recalled, "Fr. Williams here referenced the assistance given by Lt. Ottley, a former S.O.L.F and Bandmaster Owen of the then W.I.R. in procuring Alpha the instruments they had.... And so when they did get their instruments through the instrumentality of Lt. Ottley and Bandmaster Owen, they marched up through the town playing them for all." Lt. Ottley left the island to go back to England in 1916, so Fr. Williams' memory is one from this time period, during the birth of the band. A number of articles in the early 1900s mention Lt. Ottley's attendance at Alpha band performances. Perhaps the attribution of instrument donation from a bishop comes because Lt. Ottley was close to the Roman Catholic Bishop Collins. Lt. Ottley was a member of the congregation and served as a sponsor for boys during their confirmation under Bishop Collins.

Alpha Boys' School sign that used to hang in the school refectory

Photo by Seb Carayol

Bandmasters of the Alpha Boys' Band

The bandmasters during the early years of the Alpha Boys Band frequently rotated in and out of their duties as need dictated. As a result, there is some overlap in their tenures. They were sourced from the West India Regiment or Father Patrick Mulry stepped into this post from time to time. Sergeant H.W. Harrison served throughout the decades as a drill sergeant for the band, helping with their maneuvers and form. Harrison was a drummer with the West India Regiment First Battalion and he also served as an officer with the Alpha Old Boys who at one time had their own club house on the campus. The band uniforms the boys wore were patterned after the same uniforms worn by the West India Regiment and the two bands frequently performed together at a large number of public performances throughout the years, including government events, garden parties, and holiday concerts.

The first bandmaster for Alpha Boys' School was Uriah Nathaniel Nibbs (born in 1876 and died on November 5, 1927) who served in this post in 1910 but it is not known for how long. He served as a band sergeant in the First Battalion of the West India Regiment. He married Albertha Josephine Tavares and he had at least one daughter named Alice Adina, and two sons, Fitz Herbert and Arthur Sullivan, the latter of which was also a musician. Nibbs led the band during a performance of Rip Van Winkle in November 1912, functions at St. George's College, and a May Pole Dance at Winchester Park where the boys performed a march called "The Boy's Brigade," that was arranged by Nibbs.

The Alpha Boys' School Band under the direction of H.W. Harrison, 1920

A number of leaders with the West India Regiment then continued to assist the Alpha Cottage Band, including William Wilson who was also chairman of the Jamaica War Contingent Committee, Lt. Ottley, and others. Sgt. Harrison also continued to work with the band. In 1914, the Alpha Cottage Band performed "sweet music" for Her Highness Princess Marie Louise of Schleswig-Holstein and other dignitaries who traveled the island and visited the school.

In 1915-1917, William Ernest Beek (born in 1887) served as bandmaster at Alpha and he too was a sergeant with the West India Regiment where he was trained at the Royal Military School at Kneller Hall in London and played clarinet with the band. He also came back to assist the band again in 1931. Beek served as bandmaster in his early years, then went on to become an accountant, as well as the foreman of engineering and foreman of roads and works for Kingston. He was married to his wife Helene Leontine Stuart who died at age 45 and together they had at least four sons and a daughter—Cecil Eric who died six days after birth, Stanley Joseph, Dudley Anthony, Victor Leslie, and Hazel Eugenie Cecelia. In late December, 1915, the *Daily Gleaner* wrote, "The Alpha Cottage Band which supplied a fine programme of music throughout the afternoon, was at its best under the conductorship of Band Sergeant Beek of the West India Regiment." A midsummer performance at a Shakespeare festival in 1916 was well received by audiences as the *Daily Gleaner* stated, "The splendid playing of the Alpha Cottage Band, under Bandmaster Beek, the excellent acting of the youthful artistes, and the gorgeous costumes displayed all went to make the time delightful and elicited the applause of the audience." A *Daily Gleaner* article on July 25, 1931 tells how he came to serve with the band during his last tenure. "Thanks to the great interest displayed by the Rev. Father J. J. Williams, S J., in the Alpha Band it has made great improvement during the past few months. Mr. Ernest Beek, a former Band Sergeant of the old West India Regiment Band, was engaged by Father Williams (on his visit to Jamaica towards the end of last year) to give instruction to the members of the band on certain evenings, and under his direction the boys are showing commendable advancement with their instruments. Persons who have heard the band recently have observed the improvement which has been made and Father Williams is also pleased with the progress of the Band," states the article.

William Ernest Beek died on April 16, 1940 at the age of 53 from "shock and cardiac compression and we are unable to say how the injuries were received," according to his death certificate. Masses turned out for his funeral. "Ample testimony was borne to the popularity and esteem enjoyed during his life-time when over 150 motor cars joined in the funeral procession yesterday afternoon of Mr. William Ernest Beek, who came to his death on Tuesday morning under tragic circumstances. Hundreds lined the route from the residence in Norfolk Lane, Franklin Town, to the Roman Catholic Cathedral, North Street, where the obsequies were held. And there were hundreds, who could not hold in the Cathedral, outside. Following a short service at the home by the Rev. Fr. Muollo, S.J., shortly after 4.30 o'clock, the procession left for the Cathedral, headed by the band of the West India Regiment, under Band Sergeant Stewart. At the Cathedral, another very impressive service was held, the full choir of Alpha boys in attendance, and accompanying Mr. Chevolleau at the organ were members of the orchestras in which the deceased played from time to time," stated the *Daily Gleaner* on April 18, 1940. Also in attendance at the funeral was Samuel Vincent Tulloch, the bandmaster at Alpha at the time of Beek's death.

Between the tenures of Beek and Tulloch, Leyland W.J. Palmer served as bandmaster of the Alpha Boys Band from around 1914 to 1920 with some periods of overlap with Beek. Palmer's first name is sometimes listed as Leland, but this is likely incorrect. In September, 1914 the band performed a concert at the Palace Gardens in which they played a march arranged by Uriah Nibbs entitled "Alpha," and another entitled "Brass Head Jimmy," along with the "Panama Rag" and other tunes. The program for the band's performances under the direction of Palmer frequently appeared in the newspaper and commonly featured waltzes, two-steps, overtures, marches, valses, gavottes, foxtrots, serenades, and even a "skipping rope dance." Each program listing was signed the same: "God Save the King, Leyland W. J. Palmer, Bandmaster, Alpha Cottage Band."

In 1920, clarinetist Samuel Vincent Tulloch (born in 1902) became bandmaster at Alpha Boys' School where he remained until 1935 (although Ernest Beek did lend his support in 1931 during Tulloch's tenure) and again from 1940 until 1945. He married his wife Rhea Teresa Henriques on October 30, 1928 at the Alpha Chapel where Leyland W.J. Palmer served as an usher and the band performed Mendelsohn's wedding march. Tulloch and his wife had a number of children including sons Karl Ignatious, Horace Aloysius, Vincent Paul who died just after birth, and Francis who became a member of Jamaican Parliament. Sgt. Harrison continued to serve as drill sergeant while Tulloch was bandmaster, and so articles in the *Daily Gleaner* reviewing the band's performances also make note of the boys' "interesting movements" and maneuvers. During Tulloch's reign the band performed at holiday concerts, garden parties, football (soccer) matches, carnivals, dignitary visits, church processions, Christmas programs at the Union Poor House, a memorial service for the president of China at the Chinese Benevolent Society, and alongside Canadian Grenadiers Band. In January of 1927 the Alpha Cottage Band directed by Tulloch performed during a visit from the Duke and Duchess of York and their royal entourage. A *Daily Gleaner* article on May 3, 1930 revealed that in addition to the Alpha Band performing under the direction of Tulloch, so too did the "fife band of the institution." It is to be noted that the original fife band still performed at this point and was still in existence.

MARRIAGE OF POPULAR BANDMASTER

L. to R.—Lieut. F. A. Bradley, the Misses [illegible] and [illegible] (flower girls with baskets) the Misses Sybil and Carmen Prevost, bridesmaids, the bridegroom (Mr. and Mrs. Samuel Vincent Tulloch) Mr. C. C. Campbell and Miss Hazel Saunders, chief bridesmaid.

***Daily Gleaner*, November 1, 1928**

In the summer of 1935, the Alpha Boys Band was involved in a vehicular accident that resulted in half of the traveling group to be hospitalized. It may have been traumatic for Tulloch, as just three months later he left his post as bandmaster, although he did return five years later. Of the accident, the *Daily Gleaner* on June 4, 1935 wrote, "Alpha Lads Are Hurt in a Truck Accident. A party of boys and the Alpha Band numbering about 16 under the charge of Bandmaster Samuel Tulloch whilst on their way in a motor vehicle to Montego Bay on Sunday afternoon last met with an accident at Bengal Hill, near Rio Bueno, which resulted in several members having to be sent to the Hospital at St. Ann's Bay. It was near on to 4.30 o'clock when the trip, which had up to then been a happy one, ended in serious injury for two members of the party, and injuries of a more or less serious nature for several others. The party set out from Kingston to play for Rev. Fr. Becker at Montego Bay, at a Carnival held there yesterday. On taking a curve at Bengal Hill, the truck inclined a bit towards the high bank and the weight of the boys on that side helped to send the side of the vehicle more over with the result that it gave way, and fully half the party were thrown out (The right hand side of the body of the truck gave way). As soon as was possible, word was sent to Rev. Fr. Raymond Sullivan, S.J. of Brown's Town, St. Ann, and he set out at once for Rio Bueno, and found the boys there. One was seriously injured and Fr. Sullivan anointed him. In the meantime some passers-by had taken the others on to the Hospital at St. Ann's Bay, and Fr. Sullivan then hurried on there to attend to them. At the Hospital he anointed another boy who was also seriously injured. Rev. Father Becker at Montego Bay got word of the accident and he hurried out to Rio Bueno and had the truck and other members of the Band who were not injured sent on to Montego Bay...."

The Alpha Boys Band in April 1924 under Tulloch's direction

It is unknown how the boys recovered from the accident, but on September 28, 1935 the *Daily Gleaner* reported on Tulloch's departure, though it is not evident if these events were related. "Mr. C.V. [sic S.V.] Tulloch, the popular Bandmaster of the Alpha Boys' Band, has relinquished his connections with the Band after fifteen years of unbroken service. Bandmaster Tulloch as he is known by his boys as well as his many friends and admirers, has turned out a number of musicians who are holding their own in the musical art, not only in Jamaica, but in other countries as well."

Even when he left Alpha, Tulloch continued to keep one foot firmly planted in music. In early 1960 he performed clarinet at the George Good Music Festival at the Kingston Parish Church. Samuel Vincent Tulloch died in 1961 of apoplexy, high blood pressure, and arterial sclerosis. He was 59 years old.

In 1927, the band's moderator during Tulloch's leadership left the island for America. The moderator, Rev. Fr. O.B.A. Oates, was responsible for the boys' education in music and the business aspects of the band, while Tulloch was responsible for their performance and instruction. "During the three years of Fr. Oates' management, the band has made marked progress. Many old instruments have been replaced with new ones, and the band boys have been constantly supplied with clean smart uniforms. As a proof of the musical estimation which the band enjoys under Fr. Oates it can be stated that during his period of office no less than 286 engagements have been satisfactorily filled throughout the island," stated the *Daily Gleaner* on August 12, 1927. The appearance of the band during Tulloch's tenure was of utmost importance. A performance during the Easter season in 1923 featured the Alpha Cottage Band in their new uniforms, though the *Daily Gleaner* did not reveal anything about the appearance of these uniforms. A decade later in June, 1933 their uniforms were described as "sailor suits." In 1940 while under Tulloch's direction the band members were described as "cream clad."

The connection between the Alpha Boys Band and the military band during Tulloch's tenure, as well as throughout the course of the band's history, was strong. Sgt. Harrison was also a part of the boys' performances,

Postcard of the West India Regiment Band, Jamaica, circa 1930s, a band where many Alpha Boys found work after graduation

and most of the headmasters had at one time been a member of the West India Regiment and subsequent military and constabulary bands, and certainly these military bands were large employers of Alpha boys after their graduation, but there was an additional connection. The bands frequently performed together. Many times the bands performed on the same program, while at other times they quite literally performed together. A *Daily Gleaner* article on October 3, 1933 describes a performance at the All-Jamaica Industrial Trade Exhibition and Fair at the Kingston Race Course. "The

Alpha and Jamaica Military Bands were early in arriving on the grounds and treated the gathering to very fine programmes of music, sometimes both bands playing at the same time, the Alpha youngsters under the direction of Bandmaster Tulloch in the grand stand and the Jamaica Military Band under

The Alpha Boys Band in the 1930s
Photo courtesy Leslie Thompson/Jeffrey Green

Lieut. Bradley taking up position in the court of the Kingston Industrial Garage, their exhibits having been removed. The Alpha boys showed up much better on Saturday afternoon than they did during the previous days and at that they had been receiving commendation on all sides. The Jamaica Military Band was of course A1, treating the people to the popular old Jamaica airs."

After Tulloch, George Henry Neilson (born in 1885) took over as bandmaster and was a musician his entire life. On July 18, 1925 he married Mabel Iona Carr. They had one adopted son, Howard DeLeon. Neilson was musically trained at Kneller Hall where he won the Cousins Memorial Medal in 1905. He played both the cornet and the violin. According to the *Daily Gleaner*, October 7, 1961, "During his stay at Kneller Hall, King Edward VII visited the school and Mr. Neilson was selected by Professor W. O'Keefe to play for the King. Mr. Neilson joined the band of the 2nd Battalion of the West India Regiment in 1901 and left for Sierra Leone in 1903. As band

Sergeant in the West India Regiment, he returned to Jamaica in 1919. He went to the Canadian National Exhibition with the Band and to Wembley Exhibition, England in 1924. He retired from the Army in December of that year, serving for 34 years and became a co-founder of YMCA Band, and played the Palace Theatre bands in the twenties. Mr. Neilson was a member of the Jamaica Philharmonic Society and served on its executive [board] for several years." Neilson's brother Edward was also a musician who played clarinet in the West India Regiment. Edward relocated to Panama where he performed with their Government National Band. They also had a brother and two sisters. During his five years with the Alpha Boys Band they continued to perform at garden parties and Catholic Church functions at Winchester Park in a hall that had been constructed and named for Father Mulry who had been a religious leader at Alpha since the days of inception. The band during Neilson's term as headmaster also performed during the opening of a rectory and ceremonial blessing at Holy Cross Cathedral. In April, 1940 Neilson suffered an illness, though it is not known what it was nor if it contributed to his departure from Alpha, which coincides with this year, though it is likely as he was hospitalized for several weeks. G.W. Neilson died on October 4, 1961 at age 76 of acute cardiac failure.

The Alpha Boys Band in 1936 under the direction of George Henry Neilson

S.V. Tulloch returned to lead the band from 1940 until 1945 and then on November 1, 1945, Reuben Delgado took charge. Delgado was brought to Alpha by Sister Mary Ignatius Davies because he was a former Alpha boy himself, and he had served in the West India Regiment for 23 years, during which period he was a solo clarinet player with the band. After the West India Regiment disbanded in 1926, and after a short leave, Delgado returned in 1927 to the Jamaica Military Band, where he served as band sergeant. Reuben Leopold Delgado was born in 1904 and on June 5, 1930 he married Myrtle Isaline Palmer, a dressmaker who was 18 years old. Delgado was 26. Together they had at least two daughters, Daisy Loraine and Rose Pansy.

One of the first acts of business for Delgado after he took over the band was to raise funds for much-needed instruments and "to fit the youngsters out with more serviceable uniforms. The boys of the band are from families representing almost every type of denominations in the island, and the training given them to be bandsmen is in furtherance of the regular schooling they get at Alpha. Their ages range from 11 to 16 and those who have heard them—their latest broadcast was over ZQI on Wednesday night last—feel that bandmaster R. Delgado is going a good job," stated the *Daily Gleaner* on October 15, 1947. During Delgado's tenure the band performed at a large number of events including holiday events, garden parties, church processions, a hospital groundbreaking, mayoral engagements, and events for dignitaries.

Trumpeter Johnny "Dizzy" Moore remembers Reuben Delgado as a motivator and a good teacher and Sparrow Martin, drummer and bandmaster, says that Delgado was "strict." Trumpeter Eddie "Tan Tan" Thornton says, "Mr. Delgado was a good man. He was an old Alpha boy. Maybe he was in Alpha in the teens or 20s or something like that, or maybe 19th century or so. He learned clarinet. He was the best clarinet player in Jamaica. So he joined the military band in Jamaica. He was in the military band for all his life and then he leave the military band to come and teach us at Alpha. Sister get him from the military band so it was like a blessing in disguise because before he came we have a band leader named Buchannan, he was one of the old boys who leave school but he was not a good teacher, didn't teach music for nothin' you know? He was an old boy too, he leave school and he play bass. He was just a temporary until Sister could get Mr. Delgado. So when Mr. Delgado come, everything change, musically, because we get better and all that and so forth. Mr. Delgado was doing the same music as what the military band was doing. So we was at the top level with all the classical bands in Jamaica, because Mr. Delgado come from the military band and play classical music all the while. He bring all the classical music arrangement, come to the school, so the standard of our music went high, because we were playing Beethoven and Mozart and all those great classical composers. The Jamaica Military Band, all they play is great composers from Germany, Russia, and Vienna. All those American tunes they play in the army, that's what we used to play. So I know all the American tunes. So the boys get a good experience that when they leave Alpha they can play in any band because they can write and they come from classical music, which is the foundation. He was a nice man. He was one of us. He always encourage everybody and he teaches really good, really good. There is no better teacher in the world than Mr. Delgado."

Other students remember Reuben Delgado fondly as well and recognize that he was crucial to their learning, perhaps because he was so strict and disciplined. Trombonist Ronald Knight recalls, "Mr. Delgado, the band master, was quite handy with whacking a boy with his baton if a wrong note was played. We did mostly classical music and marches, overtures and a medley of calypsos which we were more than happy to play rather than marches. Mr. Delgado wasn't keen on dance and jazz music. He wanted us to join the Jamaica Military Band instead of going to dance bands. He used to say things like, 'Look how pale and sickly these dance hall band men look.' He went to the Royal School of Music London [Kneller Hall] so he thought we should all be like him." Despite his view on dance hall band men, Delgado himself performed in dance halls while serving as bandmaster at Alpha. In

Reuben Delgado leads the Alpha Boys Band.
Rico Rodriguez, far left, 1950

May 1949 he was billed as "Reuben Delgado and His Swingsters" for "Dancing at Doncaster On Sea," a club that was located on Windward Road. He also continued to perform as a solo artist at church functions such as a St. George's College Centenary mass in April, 1950.

Trombonist Rico Rodriguez says, "Reuben Delgado, he used to teach the sessions. Sometimes when you have time you should go write the answers up on the house staff [the chalk board for writing music], you know? This is the ones he would try to ask us, to write it on top of the house staff, and when you go he cannot see you lookin' up, you know? You got to be very clever, you know? He'll say you're not really concentrating, you're only watching what's written up there. Very strict man, very strict man, very strict. One day we were playing a song, 'Ol' Rotten Joe,' you know that song? (Sings) And the drummer wasn't concentrating, and he touched him with his staff [baton], touched [whacked] it. He wasn't playing with sincerity. You must play the music with more sincerity, more meaningful."

In October, 1955 Delgado left Alpha on sick leave for an operation, though it is not evident the nature of the operation. He was replaced by Charlie Clarke, an understudy of Delgado who was an assistant organist at Holy Trinity Cathedral, and Delgado's leave was intended to be temporary, but it proved to be permanent as Lennie Hibbert took over this same year. Delgado recovered and went on to live a long life, continuing his involvement in music as a judge for drum corps competitions. Reuben Leopold Delgado died on August 21, 1986 at the age of 82. The cause of death was "asthenia," a debiltating condition characterized by weakness.

Leonard Aloysius Hibbert was born on November 12, 1928 and was one of five children. His mother, Fuphemia Stewart, sent him to Alpha Boys' School in 1940 where he learned to play both the drums and the vibraphone. He could also play the organ and the piano. After graduation he joined the Jamaica Military Band before serving as bandmaster at Alpha Boys' School. While at Alpha, one of the world's most well-known jazzmen visited the school where he was hosted by Lennie Hibbert. "Strains of music in the true Birdland style filled one of the classrooms at the Alpha Boys' School for a few minutes when Dave Brubeck paid a short visit there in Monday afternoon," stated the *Daily Gleaner* on March 17, 1959. "Mr. Brubeck and his son Christopher played an improvisation on 'St. Louis Blues' and another short piece with local musician Lennie Hibbert. Mr. Brubeck later listened to the Alpha Band play 'Old Comrades,' 'Slide Mongoose,' and a vibes solo 'On the Track' by Ezekiel Nelson. Mr. Brubeck who was presented with the music for 'Slide Mongoose' by Glen DaCosta, was met by the Social Welfare Officer of the school, Mr. Garfield Clarke and Mr. Lennie Hibbert, who conducted the band. He was shown around the school by Sister Marie Therese, who is in charge, and Sister Mary Ignatius, her assistant."

Lennie Hibbert on vibraphone with Sheila Rickards, vocalist, in the early 1960s

According to the *Daily Gleaner* on September 10, 1984, Hibbert was active in music during his entire life. "In 1960 he left Alpha Boys Band and formed his own group 'The Lennie Hibbert Combo' at the old Myrtle Bank Hotel. He returned a second time to lead the Alpha Boys' Band two more times before finally leaving in 1966. Lennie Hibbert played at the Courtleigh Manor Hotel for some time and then went to the Shaw Park Hotel where he also stayed a number of years before going onto other hotels such as Mallards Beach, Jamaica Hilton, and finally Plantation Inn.... His most popular hit tune was with [Don] Drummond when both teamed up to produce 'Reload.' Lennie Hibbert also wrote several musical scores for plays and pageants during his career. Some are 'March to Nationhood,' 'Jamaica Way,' 'One Solitary Life,' and 'Jezebel.' The first three were produced by the Sisters of Alpha Boys' School and Mr. Leo Oakley, a former teacher at the school and the music was played by the Alpha Boys Band. He also released two albums, 'Creation' and 'More Creation....' Hibbert's last visit overseas before illness struck was to New York where he played with The Skatalites at Love People Disco Club for the Alpha Boys' School 100th Anniversary Celebrations. Lennie Hibbert held several positions in his lifetime. He was a member of the Alpha Boys' School's Advisory Board, Chairman of the Alpha Centenary Plan Committee, Vice-President of the Kiwanis in Ocho Rios, bandmaster and teacher of Ocho

Rios Secondary School, and organist and choir master at the Ocho Rios Catholic Church."

In 1967, Lennie Hibbert served as the president of the Jazz Association. He strongly defended jazz and stated, "The people rave over rock 'n' roll and Ska, but when it comes to good music they just turn up their

Lennie Hibbert, far right, with Lloyd Knibb, drums; Steve Lauz, bass; Jerome Walters, congo; and Aubrey Adams, piano

Jamaica Journal, March 1970

noses." He performed at a number of jazz concerts throughout the years including Jazz '57 alongside Don Drummond, Carlos Malcolm, Foggy Mullings, Sheila Rickards, Baba Motta, and Totlyn Jackson; as well as sessions at the Ivory Club, the Victoria Pier Lounge, the Lemon Tree in Harbour View, Hotel Flamingo, Johnson's Drive-Inn & Club, the Terra Nova, and as the Lennie Hibbert Aggregation in north shore hotels throughout the 1970s.

While serving as bandmaster at Alpha, Hibbert also assisted as coach of the school's cricket and football teams for a number of years. In addition to scores for the plays listed by the *Daily Gleaner*, he also wrote "The Mock Trial of Theophilus Ramzaka" and "The Doctor and the Mad Dispenser" which were performed by the Alpha Old Boys Association. In 1976, Lennie

Lennie Hibbert on vibes with fellow Alpharian Don Drummond on trombone in 1957

Hibbert was awarded the Order of Distinction by the Government of Jamaica for his contributions to music. It is Jamaica's highest honor.

Lennie Hibbert died on September 18, 1984 in Content Gardens in Ocho Rios at age 56 of cardiac arrest, renal failure, hepatic failure, and carcinoma of the liver. A funeral mass was held in his memory in the chapel of Alpha Boys' School. He had one son, Joseph, and an adopted son, Patrick Henry. His nephew was Oscar Delgado Hibbert, better known as Junior Delgado, reggae vocalist. In 1987, Ocho Rios Secondary School began a fundraising campaign to build an auditorium named for Lennie Hibbert, and today at Alpha Boys' School, the band room is named Lennie Hibbert Hall in honor of this incredible musician, mentor, and teacher. Just six months prior to his death, Hibbert was in New York performing with The Skatalites with Sister Mary Ignatius Davies in the audience. The *Daily Gleaner* on March 29, 1984 wrote, "Former bandmaster of the Alpha Band and Jamaica's leading vibes player, arranger and composer, Lennie Hibbert O.D. opened with 'I'II Remember April' which got the crowd roaring as his fingers

Lennie Hibbert on vibes in 1963 with Sheila Rickards

seemingly flew all over the vibes, coaxing all manner wondrous sounds from the instrument. Lennie maintained his commanding mood and shocked all who saw him, they never having seen a musician play the vibes so fast."

A number of individuals led the band after Lennie Hibbert. Reuben Delgado stepped back in to help, Ron Wilson took over in 1972, another bandmaster with the last name Moore served in the 1970s, Gerald Reid was bandmaster during the early 1980s, and Jackie Willacy served in 1984 until the post was taken over by Winston "Sparrow" Martin in 1988. Martin's own days as a student at Alpha Boys' School, and his strong musical career touring with legendary bands, recording on crucial tunes, made him the perfect leader for the next generation of musicians. What Sparrow is able to bring to his students though is something that cannot be chronicled in a resume of performances and accolades or measured in matrix numbers in a record catalog. Sparrow is a leader by example, the ultimate motivator. Read about Winston "Sparrow" Martin in his subsequent chapter.

--H.A.

Lennie Hibbert Hall at Alpha

Photo by Heather Augustyn

Alpha Boys Band, 1950s

Jackie Willacy leads the Alpha Boys' School Band 1970s

The Alpha Band

ANOTHER MILESTONE in the history of the Alpha Band has occurred on their road "upward and onward", as their school motto encourages them. The band has been commissioned by the Mayor of Kingston to give a series of public concerts in the city, starting next month.

The band was one of the very first projects for students at the approved home when it was established [illegible] years ago. Boys selected for the band have always been very keen and many have brought credit to their alma mater by distinguishing themselves in the field of music. Many a prominent Jamaican bandsman is a graduate of Alpha—in fact, almost every local orchestra of worth has among it Alpha graduates. The following pictures were taken—with the permission of Sister Marie Therese, Asst. Supt. in charge of the Boys' School—by Carl McDonald for the STAR.

The band, under the direction of 15-year-old Daniel Simpson, who is seen at upper left, were rehearsing The Contemplation by Lon Stanley when the Dudley Taylor. For public performances etc. Bandmaster is Mr. Leonard Hibbert of the Jamaica Military Band.

A SECTION of the wind instruments is pictured here. In the band, there are five clarinets, five trumpets, two trombones, three saxophones, one bass, two horns and three drums. There are also a flute, a piccolo, a pair of cymbals and a set of bells.

MAKING A MELODY is this representative group of musicians. Left to right are Frederick French, 11, on bells; Harold Wilson, (13) on trombone, Ronald Wilson (14) and Zekiel Nelson (13), on drums, Staf-

Star Newspaper 1955

A member of the Alpha Boys' School Band in 2013 practices in the Lennie Hibbert Music Hall, playing a composition of fellow Alpharian Don Drummond, "Addis Ababa."

Photo by Heather Augustyn

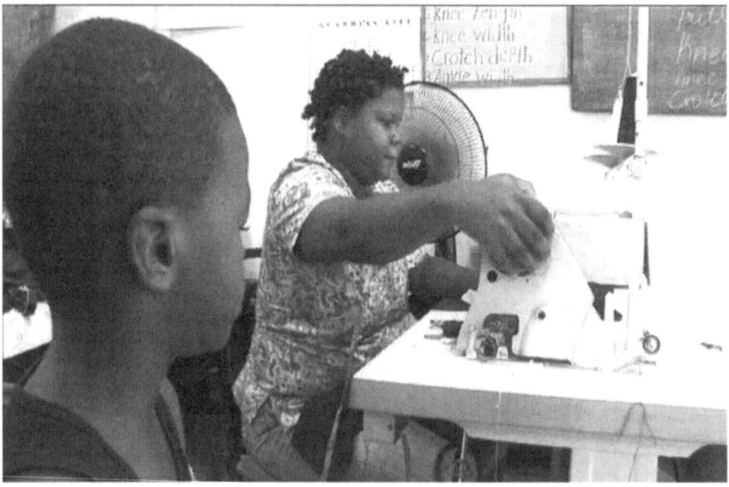

Trades at Alpha: Tailoring

Photo by Adam Reeves

Sister Mary Ignatius Davies

Without the life of Sister Ignatius, Jamaican music wouldn't be the same. In fact, it is arguable that without Sister Iggy, as she was affectionately known by her students, reggae, rocksteady, even ska may not have seen its genesis through the horns and drums of the boys in her care. The music world owes a great debt to Sister Mary Ignatius Davies—a nun, a leader, a mother of sorts who truly embodies the spirit behind the Jamaican phrase "likkle but tallawa," small but mighty. It's not that Sister Ignatius was small. In fact, she was tall, as the Alpha Boys remember her, shrinking a bit later in life due to her age. But she was always skinny, delicate, bird-like even—so thin that Johnny "Dizzy" Moore and other boys referred to her affectionately as "Bones."

Sister Mary Ignatius Davies, or as her boys called her, Iggy, was born in Jamaica on November 18, 1921 in Innswood, St. Catherine. She was born Marjorie Agnes Davies to John Robert Davies and Ethel Davies, nee Starege. Her mother was a native of Demerara, Guyana and died in 1935, so father John was left to raise the three children alone, two boys and Marjorie who was the youngest. John seemed unable to raise a 14-year-old girl and called on Marjorie's Aunt Ivy to care for her. Marjorie was enrolled at the high school run by the Sisters of Mercy at Convent of Mercy Academy, which was the girls section of Alpha. According to Sister Mary Bernadette Little who wrote the exhaustive story of Alpha, *You Did It Unto Me*, Marjorie excelled at business classes while in high school—classes such as shorthand, accounting, and typing.

Shortly after graduation from school, Marjorie, who then became Sister Mary Ignatius Davies, became a member of the Sisters of Mercy, a community of Roman Catholic women who take vows of poverty, chastity, obedience, and service, in 1939. She said she felt a calling to the convent after she visited Mother Magdalen, the superior at her high school who encouraged her spiritual devotion. Marjorie was only 17 years old when she started her life at Alpha Boys' School and she stayed there her entire life (except for a couple of years when she helped to establish the St. John Bosco Children's Home in Manchester, Jamaica opened by the sisters at Alpha Boys' School). When Marjorie joined the sisterhood, she adopted the religious name Ignatius

Sister Mary Ignatius Davies, 1940

You Did It Unto Me: The Story of Alpha and the Sisters of Mercy in Jamaica, Sister Mary Bernadette Little

after Saint Ignatius Loyola who founded the Jesuits, a congregation of the Catholic Church. "To all outward appearances, there was nothing dramatic about that time or her involvement in ministry; hers was the humdrum experience of supervising dormitories at night, every one of her charges was provided with the attire that was appropriate for each occasion that presented itself, and that each young boy and/or teenager had the required nourishment for his wellbeing and development," writes Sister Little of Sister Ignatius's quiet devotion to her tasks. Sister Ignatius had services, vision, and expertise beyond these day-to-day responsibilities as she rose through the ranks with her quiet commitment to her boys. Always skilled in sports, having played cricket and soccer in high school with a natural love for competition, Sister Ignatius encouraged her boys to play sports at Alpha and she even played alongside them on the field, showing them how to kick the ball and swing a bat. "Ignatius was the one who train you, tell you how to play, what to play, and at that time she was a young, beautiful person and she used to teach the boys a lot. She wanted them to be the best," remembers Winston "Sparrow" Martin, band director at Alpha Boys' School and former student. "She would teach them how to box because she loved boxing. She would have movies of boxers and she would take us down to the convent and show us these movies of great boxers, Rocky Marciano and Sugar Ray Robinson and all these guys. The guys who do boxing, she would tell them, 'When you look at the movie, you should watch his foot and see his hand how he punches.' She would teach boxing also, she show you how to jab, how to throw a punch. How to throw a left hook and then a right cross and she says, 'If you jab twice and then you throw your left hook, then your opponent must be down.' She would tell us about the great English cricketers. She would show us how to bat and all this. She like games. She could play table tennis. She would come around and we'd say, 'Sister, can you play a game?' and she'd say okay and she'd play table tennis and we'd try to beat her. She'd smash everything, she always beat the ball, always beat the ball. She would go to football. She show you how to shoot the ball. Everything she would do. If we sit down, she always sit with us, the boys. For spiritualness, she would sit with them," says Martin.

Sister Mary Bernadette Little says in her book that part of the reason that Sister Ignatius taught the boys about sports was for character building. "It was an interesting and awesome experience to see this nun, fully clothed in habit, don boxing gloves to demonstrate to the boys how this sport could be more deftly or skillfully performed.... And she could play cricket, football (soccer), hockey, baseball, and she was also a swimmer. With the game, there naturally came the qualities of discipline and good sportsmanship and these fundamental elements of good character building were ever in the forefront of her instruction to the boys," writes Little.

Sister Mary Ignatius Davies
Daily Express

Charles Simpson, a student at Alpha Boys' School from 1953 to 1960 and a trombonist in the band, recalls his memories of Sister Ignatius and her love for sports which she passed on to the boys. "The ability about her, and maybe why she is loved by all the boys, is that if boxing is going on, she'll be a part of it. She would put on her gloves while in her habit. She was never in any other thing but her habit. Earlier in the day it was black and white, full black all the way down to the ankles and shoes. They had a white breast plate that ran across the chest. She was always playing. She was a complete sports person. She was a fan of the great Sugar Ray Robinson and they were pen pals. She was a tremendous cricket fan. She loved Collie Smith and love Garry Sobers, but when it came to cricket, Collie Smith was her favorite," says Simpson. He says that as a result, the school excelled at sports like cricket, boxing, soccer, and baseball, winning many national championships. She nurtured a number of Jamaican boxing champions that came from Alpha including Alan Harmon, Roy Lee, and Kid Bassey and soccer player Owen "Ital Stew" Stewart. She founded baseball and cricket associations for the private school league. "The boys know me because I talk to them a lot about sports and other things," Sister Ignatius once said.

Lester Sterling also recalls her love for sports. "Sister Ignatius introduced me to boxing and she used to tell me about the great Sugar Ray Robinson, so she get me interested and show me pictures of him. And so she say she going to teach me to box. So she take me behind the chapel and she put on her boxing gloves and I put on mine and start to spar! And in the evenings she teach me how to jab and slip and all that. It never appear funny to me because I never really been in that game. I and Sister was close. When she think I am ready she tell me I mus' go in the ring and box," he says.

Sister Ignatius also had a love for world affairs, literature, and history and she was especially fond of Nelson Mandela, Martin Luther King, Jr., and Jomo Kenyatta. But Sister Ignatius is perhaps most well-known by those outside of her boys for her great love for music. It was because of her passion for all kinds of music that the band program prospered. It is quite a sight to imagine "Bones" in her full habit, spinning records at a DJ's turntables, music pumping from the huge speakers for the boys who danced to the hits, but that's exactly

Sister Mary Ignatius Davies' Gerrard turntable
Museum of Pop Culture

what Sister Ignatius did on many occasions at Alpha Boys' School. Sparrow Martin recalls his days as a student when they all listened to her tunes. "So she would come on Saturdays and she would have a whole lot of record, you name it, classical, jazz record, pop record, all kind, Latin, American, European music, Cuban music, and mento music, and she would say, 'Okay today we are going to listen to classical music,' and she would take out Beethoven, Bach, and she says, especially to the band boys, 'Listen to your classical music.' Then she'd say, 'Okay, I'm going to play jazz for you today,' and she'd play jazz music. Then she'd play Cuban music. Now we don't speak Spanish but she would take Spanish music from Cuba and she'd say, 'Listen to the drums, listen to the bass, listen to how they play saxophone.' She would sit down with you so you have the interest," says Martin. And Sister Ignatius even took up her instrument from time to time. Owen Gray says, "Our teacher, Sister Ignatius, she was a musician herself because she could play the saxophone, she could play the flute, and she was very strict." Owen Gray says, "Sometimes I go on the piano and I make a wrong note and she comes and taps me on the finger, she says, 'No, this is it.' Because she could play the keyboard too."

Sister Ignatius on saxophone

Tony Greene remembers her spinning records for the boys and said she had a fine ear for popular music. "She know everything that was going on outside on the street. She could tell you what song was number one what song was number two, anywhere in the world. She used to amaze us! We'd say, 'How she know that? How she interested in that?'" Why did Sister Ignatius spend so much time, resources, and effort on training boys in music? Obviously she had a great love for music, that is undeniable, but she also recognized the potential of the music for her boys. Music was an occupation. It was a way of earning a living. Sister Ignatius had the vision to see that music was a viable living, a fruitful living, and one that would grow. Of the music that would soon develop in Jamaica and take over the world, largely the result of the talent at Alpha Boys' School, Sister Ignatius once said, "I knew it was not going to stay in Jamaica only."

Sister Ignatius helped her boys get employment with the popular orchestras in Kingston after they left Alpha. She gave band leaders permission to scout the boys' band for talent, including Ernest Ranglin, guitar player who recruited boys for Eric Deans directly from Alpha by working with Sister Ignatius. One of those boys was genius trombonist Don Drummond. Ranglin says, "I have a lot of friends there at Alpha and a lot of friends at Stony Hill School also, so I always pass through and sometimes rehearse with them also. Alpha and Stony Hill were the two main places that train new musicians. And I was neighbors with a lot of musicians that go to those two schools which is how I get that association. I would come there and Sister [Ignatius] really get to know me and she gave me permission [to recruit] which is how I got Don Drummond, Blu Buchanan, Reuben Alexander, and Edward Tan Tan. We play at the Colony Club in Cross Roads and we went to Haiti. We were the first group from Jamaica that play the merengue there," says Ranglin with a little laugh. Virtually every orchestra in Jamaica employed Alpha alumni, and many boys left the island to perform worldwide. "And if you go to England, or Germany, the Scandinavian countries, or France in Europe, to many of the States in our northern

Sister Mary Ignatius Davies with Coxsone Dodd at the Alpha Boys' School.

neighbor, and across the Pacific to Japan, you can be sure to find an Alpha Old Boy playing in concert halls, on stage shows and in night clubs, or recording in studios," wrote journalist Hartley Neita in the *Daily Gleaner.*

Alpha Boys were not only employable though, they were also innovators. The education they received at Alpha, and the possibilities they were shown by Sister Mary Ignatius Davies who exposed them to a world-wide repertoire of music, allowed them to create, to expand the boundaries of Jamaican music. They weren't just performing the standards in the clubs—they were generating their own form, their own genre, by blending what they learned with what they loved. And so when the rhythm and blues of America combined with the calypso and mento of the islands and the jazz of the schools, it was Alpha, and more specifically Sister Ignatius, who made that combination possible. She was the cook stirring the pot to produce a delicious blend known as ska, without which there would be no rocksteady and no reggae. They entered the studio when the recording industry ignited, performing the instrumentals behind the vocalists who would propel the island to fame. Alpha Boys helped launch the careers of Bob Marley, Jimmy Cliff, Alton Ellis, Toots Hibbert, Desmond Dekker, Millie Small. Alpha boys helped launch and sustain the recording industry by producing hit after hit for Coxsone Dodd, Duke Reid, Prince Buster, Leslie Kong, Vincent Chin, Justin Yap, and Sonia Pottinger. Through their recordings, Alpha Boys reached the people of the island who flocked to the dancehalls and yards to dance to the sound systems that played their compositions. The music of the Alpha Boys reached the people of the world as their sounds spread to other countries through immigration and inspired countless others to create their own versions. In short, Alpha Boys gave all who listen, the joy of their imagination and talent, none of which would be possible without

Sister Mary Ignatius Davies
Photo courtesy Edward Thornton

Sister Ignatius. To conceive how Jamaican music would be changed without the impact of Sister Ignatius, Charles Simpson says it is "Impossible. It could not be." Tony Greene says, "In my opinion she IS Alpha."

The reach of Sister Mary Ignatius Davies goes beyond music. She gave thousands of boys not only a means of employment through learning a trade at Alpha Boys' School—gardening and agriculture, tailoring, printmaking and binding, brickmaking, and woodworking—but she also gave them a roof over their heads, food on their plates, clothes on their backs, character skills, and love. She truly cared for her boys and she was even able to reach the tough ones. Simpson says, "She is one of the greatest persons, to take what you would call a troublemaker, and she fall in love with that troublemaker and she had a means, a way, of getting to them and to like them. She would give them a special little pet name. We had a fella one time, she gave him the name Sly Fox because he was tricky. There was a fellow that played with Byron Lee, Uriah Johnson was his name, and he was the split image of Sammy Davis Jr. and she named him Little Sammy." Sparrow Martin also received his nickname this way, given to him by Sister Ignatius.

Sister Ignatius was a teacher, a leader, a mother to her boys. Sister Little says, "When they were ill, she nursed them back to health. The band boys would always know that their uniforms would be ready for an engagement, nor would they have to be anxious about transportation, since this was also a given at the Alpha Boys' School; their meals would be reserved for them when they returned from an engagement and Sister, good listener that she was, would willingly share in their success as they recounted them." She gave them vocational support, emotional and psychological support, spiritual support, and most of all, love. She was one of them. Leroy "Horsemouth" Wallace says, "To her we didn't see her as a white person. You don't have that mentality at that time. Being a Catholic there was so much laws and rules and regulations on how you

Sister Ignatius and Edward "Tan Tan" Thornton
Photo courtesy Edward Thornton

have to be and Sister Ignatius she break down a lot of that. Sister Ignatius, she blends in, she break down the barriers, and she blends in with what you are, and what she want you to be and then she makes a mixture. And for that I really respect her. She don't make you feel to be a Catholic you have to do that."

Sister Mary Ignatius stayed in touch with her boys all through their lives. She grew them into young men, she sent them off into the world, and she stayed with them every step of the way. Sparrow Martin tells the story of when some of the musicians went overseas to try to find success in Europe. "She try to arrange for them to go to England to stay at somebody's house. They live in England ten years and come back with their wife and children. She used to say, 'How many children you make?' and you'd say, 'Four, sister,' and she'd say, 'And those that you don't know about?' (laughs). She would treat you like a human," says Martin. Greene concurs, "She remember everything about everybody. She can tell you about everybody and have it perfectly right. She keep in contact with everybody, send cards to them, and she always calls at birthday and Christmas. She's amazing. She keep the link with every past student who leave the school. When you do an interview, she'll listen and she call you and say, 'That was a good interview.' I love that. And of course when you mention Alpha she would give you the thumbs up! When I was putting out my first album, I came over here and give her a copy and she say she follow everything and keep all the clippings. And I was just freaking out, I could not believe it, she keep up with every interview I do. She could tell me everything, what date, and she would show you the clippings and say, 'Oh this was a great interview,' and she like it. She say she proud of me, god bless her soul. I love that sister very much."

on right, New York, March 1984, seeing snow for the first time.

Photo courtesy Charles Simpson

It is well known that Sister Ignatius cared deeply for Don Drummond. She saw his potential by ushering him into the band and she helped him to grow into a successful musician. She also loved the music he produced and "Eastern Standard Time" was her favorite song of his. But Charles Simpson says that she also had such a connection with Drummond that after he murdered his live-in girlfriend Margarita and died in Bellevue Mental Hospital, Sister Ignatius felt a responsibility. Simpson recalls, "She told me one day after Don Drummond died, she said, 'I feel like I am supposed to be blamed for Don Drummond.' I'm telling you straight, you're getting it from the horse's mouth. She told me that because she said, 'I think I send him out to the wolves too early.' In other words, she let him leave school too early and she send him out into a big man world. And I never forget the way in which she said it, like she was taking blame for what happen to him." He adds that Drummond's brilliant talent made it easy for Sister Ignatius to think he was ready. "The military band always play at Victoria Park in downtown, the last Sunday of each month, and there was a discussion. Mr. Delgado, the bandmaster, went down there and told the bandmaster of the military band, 'I have a little boy at Alpha who can play better than all of them.' And he thought he was just boasting about it. So they decided to send Don Drummond down there one Sunday when the military band was playing. A likkle boy at Alpha, he went there and stole the show! Stole the show! And that was when everybody start to be aware of him, from that time, and his name start to spread across Jamaica, while he was still a little boy at Alpha. So his name start to become a household name before he even left school.

A photo of Sister Mary Ignatius Davies hangs on the wall of Lennie Hibbert Hall.
Photo by Heather Augustyn

And he was in demand. And I think that is why Sister Ignatius blame herself because she said she send him out before time, she send him to the wolves that aim to destroy. So she took it personally. If you listen to her you could see she was emotional about it because she did love her boys," he says. Drummond left Alpha Boys' School on October 31, 1950, six weeks before graduation. He returned frequently to visit with Sister Ignatius.

"She loved them like they were her child," says Simpson. "There was a gift she had there because she could respond to them in a loving way. She was just a beautiful, sweet human being. If you talk to 100 Alpha Boys, 95 percent of them would refer to her as their mother. And that speaks volumes. When you leave the school, she never leave you. She know where you are. She keep on top of all her children. Leaving school wasn't the end of it. She know where they were and the boys would keep in touch with her. I think she was a living saint, you know? Maybe we could not detect, but she was just a living saint," says Simpson. Eddie "Tan Tan" Thornton says, "I always say to her, I don't know about saints, but you're my living saint. And she laughed at that. I call her mum." Saxophonist Bobby Gaynair says, "Sister Ignatius was a saint. What more can I say? She was a living saint. She was not an ordinary type of saint. I love her more than a mother. Sister Ignatius help me to bury my mother. My mother died in the poor house and Sister Ignatius contact my wife and told her that my mother died. I had to leave Florida, I was day laboring and I lose my job, and I went to bury her and Sister Ignatius help me through all of that. I say, 'Sister, how can I give you thanks for what you are doing?'"

The Sister Mary Ignatius Davies Hospitality Room at today's Alpha Institute in honor of her legacy

Thornton still carries Sister Ignatius with him through his life, all these years later. He explains, "Sister Ignatius gave me this rosary in 1965. Everywhere I go, I go with this rosary. When I die, this rosary go with me.

It's like a blessing from my adopted mother. Her favorite tune was 'One Scotch, One Bourbon, One Beer.' So every time I go to Jamaica, I go to the cemetery to look for her, and when I get to 20 yards from where she buried, I start singing 'One Scotch, One Bourbon, One Beer.'" Dizzy Reece says, "She's great. I think she bought 'Blues in Trinity,' one of my first records. She used to have all my records."

Sister Mary Ignatius Davies died on February 9, 2003 at the age of 81 of a heart attack after ailing from heart disease for three years. Her funeral was held at Holy Trinity Cathedral on North Street in Kingston and she is interred at Dovecot Cemetery in St. Catherine. She has not been awarded with the Order of Distinction, although she certainly has earned it. She was, however, awarded the *Jamaica Observer*'s Award for Outstanding Community Service on February 25, 1997. "Sister Ignatius never wants to be in the spotlight, preferring to be in the supporting role, yet being the strongest pillar of the foundation," wrote Dr. George Phillip, CEO of the newspaper. Perhaps the most poignant statement of her impact comes from *Jamaica Gleaner* columnist Gordon Robinson who wrote, "If Clement Dodd is the father of Jamaican popular music, Sister Ignatius is the mother." Upward and Onward.

--H.A.

Sister Ignatius, center, with Sisters Madeline Sophie on left and Sister Thelca on right in 1992

You Did It Unto Me: The Story of Alpha and the Sisters of Mercy in Jamaica,
Sister Mary Bernadette Little

Leslie Thompson

"You had to get away from Jamaica to stand a chance," said Leslie Thompson in his book *Swing from a Small Island* which he co-wrote with Historian Jeffrey Green. At the time that he observed this truth, and for decades to come, it did seem that a musician had to leave the small Caribbean island to have any real chance at success, unless they intended to play jazz standards to tourists for the rest of their days. Playing in Kingston clubs could give a skilled brassman a few coins to rub together, but for those who dreamed of more—composing their own works, innovating a new style, standing on stage with the big guns—well that required leaving home.

Leslie Thompson
Photo courtesy Leslie Thompson/Jeffrey Green

Home for Leslie Anthony Joseph Thompson was Kingston, Jamaica where he was born on October 17, 1901 to Charlotte and Emmanuel Thompson. He was one of five children. Times were tough and so his mother traveled to Panama in 1911 for work opportunities while his father stayed in Jamaica to work. His father sent Thompson to Alpha Boys' School in 1912, and by the time he was done, little Leslie could play "all the instruments and read the sheet music for all the instruments," he said.

After Thompson completed his education at Alpha, he joined the West India Regiment Band. He was trained as a bandsman and also as a soldier. "I wasn't keen to join the army but I was told that promising musicians had that chance of studying in Britain, so I joined," said Thompson who officially joined in October, 1917. Before he had the opportunity to go to Britain to study, he performed in Kingston with the army, playing quadrilles, marches, and two-steps for tourists. Thompson performed with the army during the day and for special engagements, and during the evenings he played in the orchestra pits at the movie theaters such as the Palace Theatre to accompany the silent movies. He was able to make a living.

In May 1919, at the age of 17, Thompson caught a ship to England along with three other colleagues, aiming to study at Kneller Hall which housed the Royal Military School of Music. Here he joined 500 other soldiers and he honed his skills on the euphonium while playing for the public at concerts throughout London. Thompson also continued his education on other instruments, including all of the brass instruments, cello, violin, cornet, clarinet, and percussion. At the end of his time at Kneller Hall he was awarded a Silver Medal by his commander for his strong talent and was lauded by his fellow soldiers and bandmates.

Thompson returned to Jamaica on Christmas Day in 1920 with the hopes of becoming a bandmaster but was not able to because he was black. The King's Regulations required that anyone in a rank above third class must be European. Although he regretted not returning to Alpha to teach, he continued to perform with the West India Regiment and traveled to Canada in the summer of 1922 and England in 1924. He was made a corporal in 1925 and he also continued to perform for movie theaters, but in 1926 when the West India Regiment band was broken up and the Jamaica Military Band was formed, Thompson left. He worked full-time for the movie theaters as a music director and here learned to anticipate the action of the film in coordination with a cue sheet, a true skill indeed. In 1929 when talking movies were invented, Thompson was forced out of work, and so he returned to London, seeking work as a musician.

Thompson's first job in London was with a 16-piece Jewish orchestra. He was lucky to find this small amount of work in a society where racism was rampant and limited one's opportunities. Later in life, Thompson would study the work of Marcus Garvey whom he credits with his "awakening." Shortly thereafter he met Spike Hughes who was composing avant-garde music and he recruited Thompson to perform for his recordings. Through Hughes, Thompson met Charles Cochran and Noel Coward who provided him with the opportunity to perform in the films *Revue* and *Cavalcade*. In June 1933, Thompson performed with Duke Ellington in

Brighton, and in 1935 he recorded and toured with Louis Armstrong throughout Europe. In 1935 he also performed in a pit orchestra for Josephine Baker. "She made me feel as important as the star of the show," remembered Thompson.

At the request of his friend Ken "Snakehips" Johnson, who was not a musician but a great dancer, Thompson put together a "coloured band." Snakehips was born in British Guyana in 1914 into a wealthy family. His

Leslie Thompson, far right, on upright bass in 1924 with the West Indian Regiment band at Wembley

Photo courtesy Leslie Thompson/Jeffrey Green

father, a doctor, sent him to England to the William Borlase School in Buckingham. While in England he developed a love for dance and he studied under Buddy Bradley who had taught such legends as Lucille Ball and Fred Astaire. In 1934, Snakehips traveled to the United States where he worked in cabarets and appeared in film. But it was during this trip that Snakeships first heard the music of Harlem, seeing the great Cab Calloway and Fletcher Henderson perform. He was captivated and brought this style of dance and showmanship back to London, proposing the idea to Thompson for a similar orchestra. Thompson was the bandleader, while Snakehips served as a mock conductor and Cotton-Clubesque performer extraordinaire. Trumpeter

Leslie "Jiver" Hutchinson who was also from Jamaica and a member of the West India Regiment Band, and fellow Alpharian Bertie King on tenor sax also performed in the band. They toured before settling into a residency at the Old Florida Club in Mayfair and they called themselves the Emperors of Jazz.

After six months at this club, Ken Johnson left the band to strike out on his own, double crossing the other members for his own fame. Thompson was heartbroken. Here he had put together the talent of the group, shaping it to bring the playful energy of Harlem, the lush essence of the West Indies, and the talent of the most skilled performers in the country, and Snakeships had proven himself a snake indeed. As a result, Thompson resisted putting together another band. He was stung. But Thompson persevered despite the act of betrayal. His devotion for the music was stronger than the animosity he felt toward a traitor. In 1936, Thompson recorded with the great Benny Carter and his orchestra for Decca, playing both the trumpet and trombone. As the music changed from jazz to swing, so did Thompson's performance styles. He performed with other orchestras including with Edmundo Ros from Trinidad with whom Thompson played upright bass. It was with this conglomeration at the Mayfair Hotel and on BBC that Thompson says they "started Latin American dance music in London." On March 8, 1941, at the height of WWII, Ken "Snakehips" Johnson was tragically killed with other members of his West Indian Orchestra when a bomb fell on the Café de Paris in London during a performance.

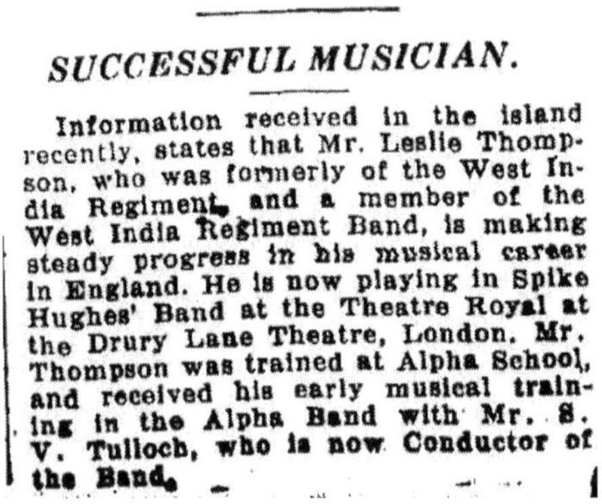

SUCCESSFUL MUSICIAN.

Information received in the island recently, states that Mr. Leslie Thompson, who was formerly of the West India Regiment, and a member of the West India Regiment Band, is making steady progress in his musical career in England. He is now playing in Spike Hughes' Band at the Theatre Royal at the Drury Lane Theatre, London. Mr. Thompson was trained at Alpha School, and received his early musical training in the Alpha Band with Mr. S. V. Tulloch, who is now Conductor of the Band.

***Daily Gleaner* March 18, 1932**

In 1942, Thompson was called up to serve in WWII at the age of 40 despite his petitioning magistrates. He led an eight-piece band while playing trumpet for dances in Devizes, England to boost soldier morale. Thompson was also a lance bombardier and he served with the artillery, shelling German planes flying over England. After the war, Thompson joined a group called Stars in Battledress and toured Germany and Norway entertaining military personnel. In 1946 he returned to civilian life and performed in nightclubs, including one called Ciro's where he played for Queen Elizabeth II when she was still a princess. Thompson enrolled in the Guildhall School of Music and studied conducting during the day, while performing at night. He never did conduct any orchestras and by 1954, Thompson had ceased performing for a living due to the difficult hours. He became warden of a residential home for undergraduates at the Alliance Club for nine years. In 1963 he was employed by the probation service in London and in 1966 he worked for the Pentonville Prison where he had a career both in probation service as well as in education.

Thompson was married though they divorced in the 1930s due to the stress from a musician's work hours. They had one son, Anthony Christopher Thompson in 1937, although Historian Jeffrey Green writes that Thompson also had a daughter about whom he did not speak. His son, Tony, was also a musician with the Royal Artillery, but he struggled with drugs, overdosing at the age of 18. This resulted in his dismissal from the army. Tony returned home to live with his dad but stole many of his father's personal items including instruments and books to sell for his habit. He ended up in prison a number of times and died of an overdose, homeless, living shoeless in the streets of London.

Leslie Thompson died on December 26, 1987 in London. He says his days at Alpha were critical to his life. "I remembered my childhood at Alpha and that atmosphere—how happy I had been, believing and trusting in God, which I did as a child does, without thinking. But the outcome of that trust and belief was that I had got my profession."

--H.A.

Leslie Thompson in 1985
Photo courtesy Leslie Thompson/Jeffrey Green

Leslie Thompson's trumpet on display in the Lennie Hibbert Music Hall at Alpha Boys' School, 2013
Photo by Heather Augustyn

Bertie King

Most Jamaican musicians either stayed in Jamaica or immigrated to the United Kingdom, but Bertie King did both. King established his own hugely successful jazz band in Kingston, Jamaica, then went to London for a number of years where he also enjoyed a fruitful career, and he returned back to Kingston to record and play on stages throughout the country until reggae took over.

Albert "Bertie" King

Albert "Bertie" King was born in Colon, Panama on June 19, 1912. His family moved to Jamaica when King was still young and he became a student at Alpha Boys' School where he learned to play both the tenor saxophone and clarinet. Upon leaving Alpha, King formed his own orchestra called Bertie King and the Rhythm Aces. The band was formed by King in 1931 and the group quickly put Jamaica on the jazz map. "This outstanding orchestra comprised of all local jazz aces needs no introduction to the public and their efforts to realise funds to maintain and increase their efficiency to a higher standard should meet with wholehearted support from every one of us," stated the *Daily Gleaner* on March 2, 1935. It continues, "Why, the United States of America boasts of Guy Lombardo and his Royal Canadians, and England of Jack Payne and his band. Then why should Jamaica not boast of Bertie King and his Rhythm Aces? Their recent performances in winning the Henriques Cup for a second time in two successive years is enough to support the argument that Bertie King and his Rhythm Aces is Jamaica's foremost dance orchestra. This was decided in January, 1934, when this band won the dance music competition, and to have won the same again in 1935 in a keener contest adds not only laurels, but a crown to their heads."

The orchestra played at clubs throughout the island including Murcott Lodge in East Race Course that entertained upper class guests. On Boxing Day, 1934, Bertie King and the Rhythm Aces performed at the Murcott Lodge to "perhaps the largest multitude ever to attend a single dance in Jamaica," reported the *Daily Gleaner* on December 28, 1934. Attendance was placed at over 1,000. His band returned in the spring of 1935 to perform here again. The *Daily Gleaner* on April 30, 1935 previewed King's performance with his band at this location to celebrate King George's 25th anniversary on the throne and said that the performance "promises to be a big affair, bright and snappy ... the orchestra with a crooner who inspires will make Murcott Lodge a spot one seldom sees even in a dream." They performed for festivities that holiday season at the Kingston Parish Church Young Men's Club. "One of Jamaica's leading orchestras will be working their hardest to give you the world's latest and most tuneful melodies. ...Leaden feet will grow light," proclaimed a *Daily Gleaner* article on December 19, 1935. He performed for numerous holiday celebrations at clubs like New Forrester Hall for Valentine's Day in 1935, social organizations, and inaugural events. On May 31, 1937 Bertie King performed at the Ward Theatre for the International Jazz Orchestra Contest in a competition that was billed as "Panama vs. All Jamaica." It wasn't the first time King had performed at this contest, and won. "Patrons of these contests will remember former occasions when Ward Theatre was the mecca for jazz-hounds and Bertie King and his Rhythm Aces used to carry off the honours, holding their own against the cream of local orchestras. Memories of Bertie King himself leading the way home with his golden saxophone," stated the *Daily Gleaner.*

Then, in January, 1936, Bertie King left Jamaica for England, sailing on the S.S. Erin with his friend and trumpeter Leslie "Jiver" Hutchinson to "take up position in one of London's leading coloured orchestras," according to the *Daily Gleaner*, January 18, 1936. He worked for Happy Blake's band and then performed with Leslie Thompson, Louis Stephenson, and Yorke de Souza in Ken "Snakehips" Johnson's band, prior to his betrayal of Thompson as mentioned in an earlier chapter. Johnson had heard King perform with Thompson, Stephenson, and de Souza and recruited them for his band, along with Abie "Pope" Clare, Joe Deniz, Arthur Dibbin, Robert Mumford Taylor, Harry Tyree, Tom Wilson, and singer Winnie Cooper. They were called the Emperors of Jazz. In 1937, they took up residency with a high-class establishment in the West End of London called the Old Florida Club for four months and King proved himself to be one of the finest jazz musicians in London, despite the prevalent racism of the time.

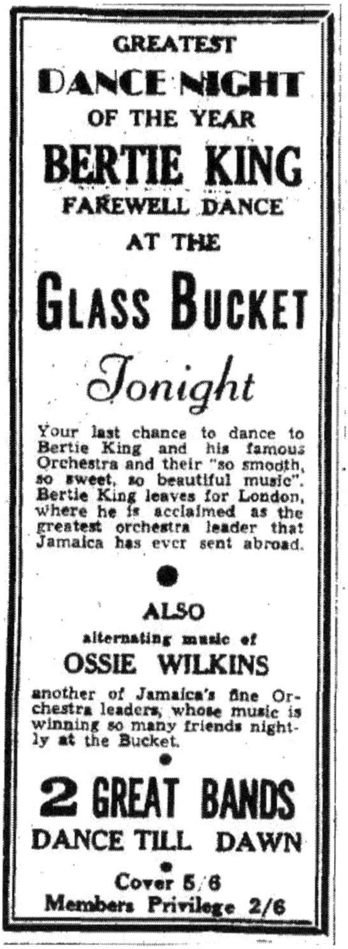

Daily Gleaner
June 16, 1952

But in 1939, King left music to join the war efforts in the Royal Navy where he served until 1943. He stayed in London after his service and he returned to the stage, building upon his reputation as one of Europe's best jazz musicians. The *Daily Gleaner* on July 18, 1947 touted his selection for the International British Jazz Team. The article stated, "The first time in history that musicians have been picked by musicians to 'play for their country' found a Jamaican among what 'Melody Maker,' British music paper terms 'the greatest international team of British Swing Musicians ever to be brought together.' That Jamaican is Bertie King who as top-man of King's Rhythm Aces gave Jamaica standard syncopation in the days when jazz was a fad and a hep-cat, something of a cross between a dope-eater and a lunatic. Bertie King, who went on to the 'old country' to climb pinnacle to pinnacle in the 'down-beat' world, was selected as one of the alto-sax men in the aggregation, which met before an audience of over 1,000 in the huge No.1 studio of the E.M.I. recording studios, London, on Sunday afternoon, June 25, to be formed into little 'jam' groups, everything they played was recorded. It was a hep-feast! Copies of their records were rushed to the United States in answer—for this swing-war—to the all-star bands assembled by 'Esquire' and 'Metronome' magazines. In other words, the Jazz Rally, as it is called, was to put British Jazz music firmly on the world map, and for this purpose it was most important to ensure the selection of representative instrumentalists, and this was made by the most competent people. Bertie King's selection was not only a tribute to his virtuosity on the alto-sax, but a feather in the cap of all Jamaican exponents of music on the ball."

King continued to work with Leslie "Jiver" Hutchinson until 1946 when King left to perform with a group of instrumentalists that formerly had played with the George Melachrino Orchestra. This aggregation, called the Blue Rockets, toured throughout Europe. On October 30, 1954, the National Jazz Federation held their inaugural British Jazz Festival at Royal Festival Hall in London. The performance was recorded and released as a full-length album on the Decca label. The record sleeve stated of King that he was "one of the few jazzmen in England at the moment who has had the opportunity to play with people like Fats Waller, Benny Carter, and Coleman Hawkins.... He last played at the Festival Hall in 1952. Since then he has been in Jamaica playing with groups led by George Shearing, Nat 'King' Cole, and Cab Calloway." King also recorded with Nat Gonella and his Georgians, in Paris with Django Reinhardt, and he appeared on a broadcast of BBC Jazz Club leading a 10-piece all-black band.

For a number of years, King performed both in Jamaica and in London and he toured Singapore, India, Australia, and New Zealand. In 1952 he returned to Jamaica and played with his orchestra. The *Daily Gleaner* on April 8, 1952 states, "Falmouth will give its welcome to Bertie King, noted Jamaican bandleader, at an Easter Ball to be held at the Town Hall on Easter Monday from 9 p.m. 'The Maestro,' as Bertie is now known since his return from a successful tour of the United Kingdom, will present popular tunes, old and new, in his own inimitable style conducting his Casa Blanca Orchestra." The following month, Kitty Kingston in her Personal Mention social column wrote, "More dancing in night clubs here.... Jamaica is one of the most beautiful and restful places in the world. I have always looked forward to coming back and I am glad to be here,' said Jamaican band leader Bertie King when he paid a visit to the Gleaner on Wednesday accompanied by his daughter Lorraine of 'Body Beautiful' fame. Mr. King has been in Jamaica since November last, after an absence of sixteen years abroad. During his travel he visited not only the neighbouring European continent, but Africa, India, and other far-away places. He estimates the 90% of his musical engagements took him outside of London. He thinks that Paris has the best night-clubs and the most varied night life and that France is the most democratic country he has yet visited. He thinks Jamaican night-clubs are bigger than their English counterparts and that we do more dancing in our clubs that the English do.... Mr. King will return to England sometime in June, but he expects to be back in the island by the end of the year. While here, he has been busy fulfilling musical engagements especially at the Casa Blanca Hotel in Montego Bay and when he returns he hopes to resume his activities there."

***Daily Gleaner*, November 18, 1960**

King performed at the Silver Slipper, the Glass Bucket, and other clubs throughout Kingston in the 1950s. When the Jamaica Broadcasting Corporation established a permanent studio band, King was selected to lead the 14-piece orchestra called Bertie King's Royal Jamaicans or the JBC Studio Men. Carlos Malcolm and Sonny Bradshaw were also crucial to the development of the JBC studio and other members included Ernest Ranglin, Lennie Hibbert, Baba Motta, and Taddy Mowatt. The orchestra recorded songs for programs and performed background music when guests visited the studios. They worked five to six days a week, from 8 a.m. to 5 p.m. King played with this orchestra, the West Indian Swing Stars, and his own orchestra, including a performance at The Little Theatre to celebrate the nation's new independence in 1962. Also performing with "The Maestro" at this event were fellow Alpharians Lennie Hibbert, Tommy McCook, and Don Drummond. King performed with his orchestra at subsequent independence celebrations, including one that required King to decline performing for Sammy Davis, Jr.'s tour of Jamaica in late July, 1962. He also performed on a number of calypso and mento tunes, namely with Mapletoft Poulle's Orchestra for Lord Fly.

Although King played on at least one recording each year between the mid-1930s and the late 1960s, in 1967 he left music behind and moved to New York. He died on September 3, 1981 while working as a manager of a apartment in Redwood City, California. The San Mateo coroner report stated his cause of death as "apparent homicide, gunshot wound." The *Peninsula Times Tribune* reported, "An apartment house manager was shot and killed and his wife was perilously wounded Wednesday night in an 'unprovoked attack' by two men … Albert A.S. King, 69, was pronounced dead just after 8 p.m. … he apparently died from gunshot wounds in the head and chest … Jailed for the shooting are Timothy Lee Watts, 24 … and James Settles, 19 . . . The killing occurred about 6:30 p.m. after two men climbed over the rear fence of the Kings' apartment … They walked into the home through a rear sliding glass door that was open . . . Mrs. King told investigators she and her husband were sitting in the living room, watching television, when the intruders appeared and ordered her and her husband to lie on the floor. The couple was starting to do so when one of the men suddenly opened fire with a handgun." Bertie King was shot four times and was unconscious, bleeding on the floor when police arrived. His wife sustained a gunshot wound to the wrist. The article says that there was no apparent motive for the murder, though investigators suspect "the intruders may have wanted to rob the Kings of rent money collected around the first of every month." The article describes King as "an artist who did portraits and landscapes" and he was well loved by the community. Bertie King had four daughters with Alice May "Massie" Young including Joan "Mitzie" King who died in 1977; Lorraine King who was named "Miss Jamaica Body Beautiful" in 1952, was a city secretary, and married Austrian-born advertising executive Dietrich Ulrich Baum in 1960; Barbara, and Armis. His second wife, Kathleen King, was shot in 1981 and recovered. --H.A.

Advertisements from the *Daily Gleaner*, from left to right, April 11, 1953; November 17, 1951; and October 26, 1935

Sonny Grey

Sonny Grey is not a household name—not even for those who may know a name or two in jazz. But Grey was leader of his own 18-piece band in Paris, he was invited to perform at international jazz festivals, and he blew his trumpet for vinyl and film with some of the best in Europe. "If you're a big band fan that wants swing with style, get a load of this guy," writes George W. Harris in *Jazz Weekly* in 2016. Even all these years later, Grey's music is relevant and moving.

Sonny Grey

Trumpeter Sonny Grey was born in Jamaica in 1925 and he attended Alpha Boys' School as a member of the band with Joe Harriott, Dizzy Reece, Harold McNair, Don Drummond, and Wilton Gaynair. Little is known of his early years, but one of his first appearances of note came in 1950 when Sonny Grey performed with the All-Star Band for a "big musical extravaganza" at the Progressive Hall on Duke Street. He performed along with "top-flight musicians drawn from the island's leading orchestras" including Baba Motta, Ken Williams, Sonny Bradshaw, Billy Cooke, Wilton Gaynair, Joe Harriott, Bobby Gaynair, Ossie Stewart, Vernon Möller, and others, according to *the Daily Gleaner*, October 30, 1950. The following year he traveled to England with a number of these musicians, including Joe Harriott, as a member of the Jamaica All Stars." Like those of his era, Grey then left Jamaica for Europe, making Paris his home in 1953. He lived there for ten years and performed in a number of orchestras and with fellow jazz musicians on vinyl. In 1957, Grey performed with "Jazz Wizard" Sidney Bechet in France on Christmas Eve in an operetta called *New Orleans* that included 72 actors and actresses and a bevy of musicians. In 1962, Grey performed during the opening credits of the French-Italian mystery film, *Le Glaive et la Balance (Two Are Guilty)* along with drummer Kenny Clark, organist Lou Bennett, altoist Sonny Criss, and vocalist Mae Mercer. Grey also performed in Paris with organist and pianist Larry Young in the studio and live from 1964 and 1965. These recordings, made initially for French radio, have recently been released by Resonance Records.

"His greatest triumph would come in 1963," writes the author of liner notes for the album, *Sonny Grey and His Orchestra in Concert at the II Festival Internacional de Jazz de Barcelona 1967,* "when he organized and led his own Big Band. It had verve and spirit, reflecting a leader able to get the best of his men. His fame grew rapidly despite the continuous personnel turnover, and the band generally swung effectively, aided by a diversified book, vibrant soloists, the ensemble's all-embracing warmth and the general sense of good feeling it conveyed. In November 1967, Grey received an invitation to play at the II Festival Internacional de Jazz de Barcelona, where his full-strength band delivered a fervent performance—before an enthusiastic audience—in the only album they ever recorded. In these recordings Sonny Grey's big band shows the vitality and wild, joyous abandon of all the best American orchestras, with its leader conducting and soloing with effervescent intensity throughout."

Charles L. Sanders reported on Grey's big band in the "Paris Scratchpad" column in *JET Magazine*, March 2, 1967. He writes, "JET fans down in Jamaica ought to be proud that their trumpetman Sonny Grey is doing so well here that he's put together an 18-piece jazz band and has taken over at Buttercup Powell's old Club Boheme." In that same column in *JET*, November 27, 1969, columnist Art Simmons wrote that Grey appeared as a mainstay at the Lugano Jazz Festival in Switzerland along with Art Taylor, Charles Tolliver, and Stan Cowell, and he was the featured artist with the F.D.R. Radio band in Hamburg, Germany during four days of recording.

Grey released *Skippin'*, an album of four songs, though some as long as 10 to 12 minutes each, with Kenny Clarke, Alain Hatot, Mal Waldron, and Gus Nemeth. It was recorded in 1971 in France though also released in 1974 in Japan. In 1973 he recorded *Parisian Concert* with Dexter Gordon and the George Arvanitas Trio in Paris. The album was released in 1976 in the UK where Michael James wrote in the liner notes that Grey is "gifted with a technical expertise that enables him unfailingly to translate into musical terms the faired melodies he draws from the harmonic infrastructure, he very occasionally reminds the listener of his compatriot Dizzy Reece, but is

essentially his own man within the broad bop trumpet tradition. Nor should one make the mistake—perhaps after recognizing that quote from Goin' to Minton's in Dexter Leaps Out—of supposing that his adherence to a style that has been in existence now for upwards of thirty years in any way detracts from his individuality."

Sonny Grey continued to perform and record and in 1977 he recorded two songs in Hiversum, Holland, guesting with a quartet that included Gijs Hendriks, Siegfried Kessler, Bert van Erk, and Micheal Baird. Over the years he performed with French jazz players such as Fred Gérard, Rene Thomas, Henri Renaud, Jacques Diéval, Jimmy Woode, Guy Lafitte, Jean Louis Chautemps, and Jacques Hélian along with countless others. He performed with numerous orchestras including The Jazz aux Champs-Élysées All Stars with Woody Shaw. Sonny Grey died in 1987.

--H.A.

Jamaica All Stars in 1948. Front: Wilton "Bogey" Gaynair, Tommy McCook, Bobby Gaynair, Harold "Little G" McNair, Joe Harriott. Back: Promoter Count Buckram, Ben Bowers, Vernon Möller, Sonny Grey, Sonny Bradshaw, Ken Williams, and Baba Motta

Dudley Farrier

Dudley Anthony Farrier was born on January 12, 1925 in Kingston and was just seven years old when his father, David Farrier, passed away, leaving his mother, Lucy Farrier, nee Hall, to care for their seven children. As a result, Dudley and his other brothers attended Alpha. "It was because his dad died early," says Miriam Farrier, Dudley's wife. "His dad went to work, came home, and he started to throw up blood. He had a heart attack. All of the children went to Alpha," she says. Dudley's daughter Margaret adds, "Because his mother knew an education at Alpha Boys' School would provide her son with a strong foundation and discipline, she sent him to the school. He always talked about everything he learned there as a boy. He always talked about the school and when he was a boy and how he learned to love jazz. He was a jazz man. He said they set high standards at the school and that went in line with how he was raised. He learned there and would write music. His discipline came from Alpha Boys' School."

Dudley Farrier
Photo courtesy Margaret Farrier-Mba and Miriam Farrier

It was here that Dudley learned to play the tenor saxophone as a member of the band, and Margaret says that his mother nurtured his talent for music, though at the time, Dudley may not have seen it as such. "His mom forced him to learn the saxophone," Margaret says. "She wanted her children to be musical. He told me that all of the other kids got to do lots of fun things and he had to take his saxophone practice. He said that rather than hate the instrument, because his mother gave him a hard time, he said 'I'm going to put my mind to it and learn.' And he fell in love with the instrument." Miriam adds, "His mom also sent him out and pay for him [to have music lessons] but he started it there [at Alpha] and he could manage to play it [saxophone]. He also played the piano—not outside, just home." When asked if Dudley liked Alpha, Miriam says, "I don't think so, but he didn't have a choice because the father died suddenly and his mother couldn't manage."

Dudley Farrier with the Eric Deans Band, front center, saxophone

Photo courtesy Margaret Farrier-Mba and Miriam Farrier

In 1948, at the age of 23, Dudley married Miriam Rose, age 18. His occupation listed on the marriage certificate was "laborer." But Miriam says he found work in the local orchestras. "He was part of one in Montego Bay and Tower Isle Hotel and up on Crossroads, the club, the Glass Bucket, with Eric Deans and there were two more but I don't have them in memory. But after he left Eric Deans he had his own band," says Miriam. Margaret says that the name of this band was the Dudley Farrier Orchestra. An article in the *Nassau Guardian* on July 4, 1954 with a photo caption titled, "Jamaican Ensemble in Nassau," states, "Dudley Farrier Orchestra wows patrons of the Zanzibar with music tempos from latest calypso tunes to light classics. Only three months old, the band is already placed among the name bands of Nassau." The musicians identified with his band in Nassau include Ralph Williams, vocalist; Raymond Cico, trombone; Frank Anderson and Calvin Patterson, trumpet; Arthur Buchanan, bass (Alpharian along with his brother

Dudley Farrier, saxophone, with the Eric Deans Band
Photo courtesy Margaret Farrier-Mba and Miriam Farrier

Jocelyn "Blu Blu" Buchanan); Papa Son, drummer (former tap dancer); Sam Bernard (Alpharian), alto sax; Tommy McCook (Alpharian), tenor sax;

Linton Thomas "Midas Touch," piano; and Dudley Thomas performed on clarinet. Felix Johnson was listed as the club proprietor and manager.

In the early 1950s, Miriam says he had the opportunity to play in the United States. "He happened to join a musician's union and they would call him they needed him to play. There was someone who heard the band play, but he didn't send for the whole band, he just sent for Dudley. He would appear and he came back to Jamaica and we spend some more time in Jamaica and then we came back," says Miriam of their relocating to New York where they resided for 51 years. Dudley found work as a musician and other employment. "He played during the big band era in Harlem, New York," says Margaret. "He played with some of the jazz greats. He played in Harlem at the Apollo, and he did other work as well. He was a shipping manager in New Jersey for 26 years and he played at night. He had five children and one of his daughters died before he died," says Margaret.

Miriam worked as a hat designer in New York while raising the family. She explains, "He sent me to school for that. His mom used to make straw hats and I used to sit and watch her with the baby in my hands. So, I learned to make real dress hats. Dudley's father made hats and he was also working in an office and he teach Dudley's mom to do the hats." Even though she was involved in hat design, Miriam was also a musical woman, says Margaret. "My mother used to sing and he played the saxophone. He was a church deacon and he played at his Baptist church until he passed away. But he would always play for us at home as kids—we always heard him blowing his saxophone. From when I was a little girl, he would always play for us and he was always with his saxophone, more so than his clarinet because he loved his saxophone. He always played for churches. He was in the church orchestra," she says.

In addition to being musical and hardworking, Margaret says that her father was talented in many other ways. "He was a very learned man, very intelligent. He had a love for languages. He could speak three languages—Italian, Spanish, and French. His father was a French man, Farrier, who married a Jamaican-Indian and he promised his dad he would learn French. He traveled for 10 consecutive years to Montreal and have the people talk to him in French. He studied French and integrated among the people so they can speak to him in French. Same with Spanish, he learned in Mexico. He was a very educated person. He taught himself a lot of things. He loved geography. You could ask him any country in the world and he would tell you where it's at, and he loved to read maps. People always loved talking to him because he loved history. He knows a lot about historical people, like past presidents, and he was an historian. He read a lot," she says.

Dudley Farrier
Photo courtesy Margaret Farrier-Mba and Miriam Farrier

To Margaret, her father was greater than the sum of these parts of his life. Choking back the tears, she says that she will miss him terribly until the day she dies. "He was very compassionate. He was a great man, a great father and musician. Studying music at Alpha gave him perseverance, discipline, and hard work and these qualities influenced his life." Of his high expectations of the people around him, Margaret notes that four of Dudley's children went to college and one is a painter and business owner.

Dudley A. Farrier, 89 of Oviedo, Florida passed away on Friday, January 2, 2015. He was survived by his wife, Miriam Farrier; children, Donald A. Farrier, Margaret E. Farrier-Mba, Pauline Farrier-Ortiz, and Dudley Farrier, Jr.; 15 grandchildren and 13 great-grandchildren. He was also preceded in death by his daughter, Yvonne T. Farrier-LaGonterie. Margaret concludes, "He is probably playing some kind of music in heaven and learning some kind of new instrument."

--H.A.

My Father

By Margaret Farrier-Mba, 6/7/94
Daughter of Dudley A. Farrier, Sr., Musician

My father is a musician.
His mother gave him a horn at a tender age,
As his friends played outside, he played inside,
the Saxophone, clarinet, flute and piano.
From woodwind to brass he learned and burned the midnight candle as the horn he handled. The reed instruments captured his soul and he played on.

He fell in love and flew like a dove,
From bars to measure and staff to treasure, he blew and grew
Grew and blew melodies in the air and to the ears of music lovers
He dared to mix the sounds from calypso to jazz.

From show to show, Island to Island
He played in the Alpha Boys Band and then formed his own bands and played in many lands.
Then he met a beautiful lady who fulfilled his life and became his wife.

Five children later he crossed the ocean and seas.
With his loves, he knew no boundaries and played on
big bands, little bands he subbed in different clubs.
Forgetting the babes, he blew away
He earned and learned in his new land.

As his love grew, he never buried the brass in the past,
But moved on to different heights, cultures and lifestyles
Getting to know his five new treasures that turned into big pleasures.

Thomas "Tommy" McCook

Tommy McCook's catalog of recordings and compositions span the history of Jamaican popular music itself. Jazz, ska, rocksteady, reggae, dub—Tommy played it all, as bandleader, headliner, and pioneer. His body of work alone, with dozens of instrumental albums and hundreds of recordings behind well-known singers, makes McCook a legend. One of Jamaica's true tenor titans, Thomas Matthew McCook (Tommy) was born in Havana, Cuba on March 3, 1927, though his parents, Alfred Alexander McCook and Ivy Ann Hutchinson McCook, were both Jamaican. They were married on June 30, 1921—Alfred was 29 and an ex-police constable, and Ivy was 19 and a domestic. They gave birth to Tommy's sister, Inez Duretta McCook, in Kingston on May 4, 1923. There are no birth records in Jamaica for Frank McCook, Tommy's older brother, so it is likely that he was born in Cuba as well, since their father had taken a job to work at the Panama Canal and they established a family home in Havana. Tommy was born last of the three siblings and was named after his paternal grandfather.

Passenger lists from Havana in early February 1931 reveal that Ivy, Inez, Frank, and Tommy returned to Jamaica and there they continued to establish their family with father Alfred. Though records indicate that Tommy's mother Ivy died on October 8, 1965 at their home, 4 Slipdock Road, of congestive heart failure and hypertension at the age of 65, the same records show his father, Alfred, as still alive at the time of her death.

FROM HAVANA.

Andraw deLasser, Mrs. deLasser, Fred P. Thomas, William Steeper, Juan M. Suarez, Loy Ann McCook, Frank McCook, Ines McCook, Thomas McCook, Jane Burke, Sofia R. Richerson, Wilherrmina Lorde, Edward Arthur Bramwell, Lena Bramwell, William Thompson, Charlotte Thompson, Ruperto T. Thompson, Blanche Nicholson, Felix Francis, Ruby Davies. Fatnai Huntley, Rose Huntley, Sarah Thompson, Walter Miller, Matilda E. Sealy, Edith Hylton, Elelyn Cumming, Mrs. C. M. Cumming, Herman Wade, Harold Dixon, Adolphus William, Edith Arscott, E. S. K. Porter, Richard Cooper, Gladys Cooper, Gloria Huntley.

***Daily Gleaner*, February 4, 1931**

Frank McCook enrolled at Alpha Boys' School, though it is not evident why—out of need, or for a musical education. Frank made a name for himself in subsequent years as a vocalist, winning the Vere Johns Opportunity Hour and headlining as "Local Sinatra." Frank also sang with Roy Coburn and His Orchestra when they played at the Bournemouth Club where his mother, Ivy, worked in the kitchen. He also performed with Jack Brown's orchestra and at the Rock Garden Club and Colony Club throughout the late 1940s and early 1950s. Tommy was influenced by his older brother and he too wanted a career in music. His mother Ivy approached Alpha to see if there was room for Tommy with the school band. "I was 11 when I started and it was on tenor sax," says Tommy of his entry into Alpha Boys' School in the liner notes for the "Tribute to Tommy" album. "Mr. Neilson [George, bandmaster] said they needed a sax player and I jumped in. I took over the school sax and sat next to Bra [Wilton] Gaynair when the band rehearsed and played."

FRANK McCOOK who won the first prize in the opening series of Mr. and Mrs Vere Johns' "Opportunity Hour" presented by the Rialto Theatre. He sang "Ole Man Riber"

***Daily Gleaner*, July 16, 1948**

In Howard Johnson's *Deep Roots Music* documentary which aired on Channel 4 in 1983, Tommy McCook discusses his history and how he helped to shape the course of Jamaican music. "I went to school in '39, started learning in '40. I left around '43," he tells Johnson. When asked what kind of music they played he responds, "Mostly march music, classics, symphonic style of music. And while I was in school I had an offer to play with a dance band, started at Bournemouth with Eric Deans, yuh know?" Indeed it was with Eric Deans that Tommy McCook first found employment, as Deans regularly scouted Alpha for musicians to fill his orchestra seats. His mother was there, working at the Bournemouth, when Tommy took his first solo as a professional musician on the stage. She applauded his performance, "tears of joy" on her face, according to the "Tribute to Tommy" liner notes. With Eric Deans, Tommy learned to play the music he loved—jazz. "I listened to Illinois Jacquet; Coleman Hawkins, I loved his ballads; Lester Young; Arnette Cobb; Ben Webster; Charlie Ventura—'Dark Eyes' was a special favorite of ours; James Moody. Jazz is my first love," McCook told Lee O'Neill in *Reggae Report* in 1994.

Tommy McCook next performed in Don Hitchman's sextet. This combo frequently performed at the Sugar Hill Club at Red Gal Ring in St. Andrew and also featured fellow Alpharian Raymond Harper on trumpet. Hitchman was not only a professional guitarist and leader of the group, but he also was a chemist for the blood bank in Kingston, according to Hedley Jones. In 1950, Hitchman migrated to the United States to work for the Ford Motor Company, but before he left he recorded with his group at ZQI, the newly established radio station in Jamaica. According to music historian Roberto Moore, Hitchman had his own radio program at the station, so when ZQI first acquired recording equipment in 1947, the Don Hitchman Sextet made one of the country's first local recordings, but that pressing was likely a one-off test of a popular song. Tommy next performed with Roy Coburn's Blu Flames which also included Alpharians Eddie "Tan Tan" Thornton and Vernon Möller. In 1952, the Roy Coburn Blu Flame Band was voted Jamaica's second most popular band by *Ivory Magazine*'s annual popularity poll.

In 1954, Tommy McCook was invited, along with a small group of other musicians, to perform at the Zanzibar Club in Nassau, Bahamas. Though the other musicians, including guitarist Ernest Ranglin, came back to Kingston the following year, McCook stayed. He explains to Howard Johnson, "I left around '54 to go to Nassau in the Bahamas to join a Jamaican band there. We played dance music, big band, swing music. I spent about eight years there. I came back in '62." By 1962, the musical landscape in Kingston had changed—from jazz to ska. "When I came back, Don Drummond was the man on the scene. He had this hit tune, 'Schooling the Duke,' out at the time. I listened to the music, but I was playing jazz at the time, yuh know? I was at this likkle jazz club and while I was there Coxsone came to me and he ask me to do some recording. Ska recording. Well I didn't move right way. This was '62. Well he approached me again in '63 and I decided I would try it. So I got involved with the ska."

Though McCook performed as a studio musician for Coxsone, he left for more steady work with pianist Aubrey Adams, performing nightly at the Courtleigh Manor Hotel, though he soon was approached by a fellow Studio One musician, Lloyd Knibb, who suggested they form their own group led by McCook. "I couldn't form it at that time because of my contract with Aubrey Adams. This went on for several weeks. After my tenure with Aubrey Adams was up, I went back to being a studio musician. Then, after we decided to form a group, we had a meeting at the Globe Theater near Crossroads. We were looking at the name Satellites—satellites being the thing those days because of the Americans and Russians. I decided to call it Skatalites and everyone agreed it was better," says McCook in *Reggae Report.* The members of The Skatalites had already been playing together for many months, but not as an organized group. Together they simply continued recording, though this time credited as The Skatalites, as well as performing live together at clubs around the island. McCook tells Howard Johnson, "While we were recording with The Skatalites in '63, they weren't together as a band, they were just a recording outfit. Then people kept asking who played these various tune, yuh know? Then Coxsone asked me to feature a tune for him, 'Exodus.' That was my first hit during the ska time with Coxsone. After that I did other tunes like 'Road Block,' which is my composition, which I compose; 'Freedom Sound.'" The Skatalites officially came together as a band for their first live performance on May 16, 1964 at the Hi-Hat Club, 4 Hannah Street in Rae Town, according to the *Star Newspaper* on the same date. The group was comprised of McCook and Roland Alphonso on tenor sax, Lloyd Knibb on drums, Don Drummond on trombone, Johnny "Dizzy" Moore on trumpet, Lester Sterling on alto sax, Jackie Mittoo on piano, Jah Jerry Haynes on guitar, and Lloyd Brevett on bass. There were also four singers who regularly performed with the group—Doreen Shaffer, Tony DaCosta, Lord Tanamo, and Jackie Opel.

***Star Newspaper*, July 18, 1962**

"In the beginning, I asked Dodd to manage the group. He said, 'No way.' He told me that I didn't know these guys like he knew them. He said they were undisciplined, not punctual, etc., etc. He had nothing good to say about them. So I went it alone," McCook told Greg Robinson for *Windplayer Magazine* in 1993. Robinson says that McCook rented sound equipment, booked the band into clubs, and paid for advertising for The Skatalites, all out of his own pocket and the result was a success. McCook says, "The crowd ate it up. We were playing all the clubs, and all the clubs were jammed. We started making some good money."

The June 27, 1964 issue of the *Star Newspaper* ran the headline, "Skatalites Go Into Orbit" and author Lloyd Davis discussed their performance at the Bournemouth Club. "For the past few weeks, the band have taken over Bournemouth and have kept the place alive. Roland Alphonso on tenor sax, Don Drummond on trombone (when he sits in), leader Tommy McCook on tenor sax, Lloyd Brivett [sic Brevett] bass, Lloyd Knibbs [sic Knibb] drums, Johnny Moore trumpet, and Lester Sterling, alto sax and trumpet combine to produce a sound that's great." Adjacent to this

Tommy McCook and The Skatalites. McCook, bandleader, appears in a white shirt with saxophone. Jackie Opel on mic.

article was another that claimed, "Tommy McCook is the man who launched them." It stated, "In 1962 a young musician returned to his island home after spending a few years in England and the United States [sic Bahamas]. This young man, having wide experience in jazz music, linked up with a local group of jazzmen and started to make a name for himself. He was Tommy McCook. Tommy, who was then an authentic jazz musician and an increasingly popular artist, was invited by Messrs. Coxon [sic Coxsone] and Randy [Vincent Chin], to do recording for them, but for McCook, jazz was not to be given second place for SKA (which at the time was of very little significance). Roland Alfonso [sic Alphonso], who was doing recording for Coxon [sic Coxsone] and Randy left the island and also a vacant space for a recording artist which could only be filled by someone as proficient as Tommy McCook. It was at this stage that he decided to enter the recording scene and he did so with terrific force. One of his first record releases was 'DOWNBEAT' which was a hit, and he then went on to make his next hit 'Road Block,' a Ska instrumental. This release projected McCook to the front rank of leading recording artists where he was in constant demand by Ska Lords like Randy, Tip Top, Duke Kid [sic Duke Reid], and Prince Buster. Today Ska as it should be played is produced by the talented musicians who are not attached to any particular band. Tommy McCook is one of these musicians. He realised that the Ska boom was being heard all over Jamaica and in other parts of the world and he organised his fellow musicians and formed a new group called The Skatalites. The Skatalites have made four public appearances so far and have made a good impression."

***Star Newspaper*, January 29, 1965**

Though The Skatalites recorded for a number of producers and they performed throughout the island, they were together only a short time. One of the leading reasons for their breakup was the loss of Don Drummond. Drummond had been a headlining name in Kingston for 15 years, so when he stabbed his live-in girlfriend Anita "Margarita" Mahfood to death on January 2, 1965, he was never to play publicly again and ultimately died at Bellevue Mental Hospital four years later. Drummond was the main composer for The Skatalites, was a draw for audiences, and was a genius-level musician who elevated the performance of the other musicians. The Skatalites were never the same, though they tried to continue. "We never used a substitute for Don—we left his space open. There was nobody around who could fit his space," McCook said. Plus, McCook and Roland Alphonso were at odds about Coxsone and management of the band. "One night Roland confronted me before the show and said, 'I want to let Coxsone manage the band.' I said, 'Roland, Coxsone didn't tell you that I asked him to manage the band and he refused. He said you all were no good,' I told him that right in front of Coxsone. Coxsone didn't like that, so he tried to break up the band," says McCook. The band did break up, splitting into two factions that reformed as the Supersonics, led by McCook, and the Soul Brothers, led by Alphonso. "The Skatalites broke up because Dodd and Roland, who were very close, decided to form the Soul Brothers using members of the band. Jackie Mittoo, Dizzy Moore, and Roland told me they were leaving the group to form the Soul Brothers. I decided I wasn't going to continue with the group. I wanted to leave the scene being popular rather than play to empty houses. Don was locked away and wasn't going to come out for a long time, and with the guys leaving for the Soul Brothers, it didn't make sense to continue," he said.

From
Swing Magazine

In addition to taking a different direction organizationally, McCook also took a different direction musically. He explains to Howard Johnson, "The dancers got tired of the ska, it was too fast, and they figured they wanted a slower beat. It was really Duke Reid, that I heard, while at Treasure Isle that said, this was around '65, '66, said that he wanted to slow down the music a bit because his fans was saying that they got tired too easy. Now they were getting old. They were growing older. So we decided to slow down the ska a bit so we got a beat called rocksteady. You must have heard of it." McCook recorded frequently for Duke Reid during this period of his career. He says, "Duke Reid came to me about playing for him. I said I needed a rest because with The Skatalites I did every damn thing. I was the manager, I did the advertising, rehearsed the group. Reid told me, 'You don't have to do anything but deal with the music.' Then he said, 'Name your salary.' All I had to do was play. This was late September, early October of 1965" [sic August].

McCook performed rocksteady with the Supersonics, though he adapted well to the next evolution of Jamaica's music as reggae slowed down the tempo and fervor still. He had long been participating in the rhythms of Count Ossie's drums in the Wareika Hills as a regular participant at the camp's grounations that inspired the rhythms of reggae. "The Rastas at that time had to hide to play because the police would come to mash them up. At times they chopped up the drums and beat up some of the players. So the Rastas had to go further back in the hills so it would be harder for the police to get at them," says McCook of the sessions.

Tommy McCook, left, with Richard "Dirty Harry" Hall

Still from the movie Rockers, courtesy Blue Sun Film Co.

Tommy did not slow down at all, at any point in his career, and in the 1970s he returned to the studio as a session musician—this time for Channel One along with Sly Dunbar and Robbie Shakespeare as a member of The Revolutionaries, as well as freelance for the Mighty Diamonds and others. In 1975 he recorded for Bunny Lee and King Tubby with fellow musicians Robbie Shakespeare, Santa Davis, Vin Gordon, Earle Smith, Tony Chin, Bernard Harvey, Ansel Collins, Bobby Ellis, and Lennox Brown. Together they formed The Aggravators and recorded the album *Brass Rockers*, followed by a number of additional albums such as *Cookin'*, King *Tubby Meets the Aggravators at Dub Station*, *Show Case*, *Disco Rockers,* and *Instrumental Reggae*. Tommy recorded a number of other albums throughout the 1970s such as *Green Mango* and *Blazing Horns*, both with Bobby Ellis, *Reggae* and *Reggae II* both with US jazz flautist Herbie Mann, two albums with Yabby You, and record-ings with the Ja-Man Allstars, The Professionals, and The Tommy McCook All-stars. He also performed in the annual Jamaica Festival Song Compe-tition in 1979 and during this decade performed a number of songs in dub and disco genres. On October 20, 1975, Tommy McCook was awarded the Order of Distinction.

Tommy McCook
Photo courtesy David Corio

In 1983, Tommy McCook and the remaining members of The Skatalites came together for a reunion at Sunsplash, the reggae festival in Montego Bay. In September, 1985, Tommy immigrated to the United States where he reunited with Lester Sterling and Roland Alphonso, soon to be followed by Lloyd Brevett. Together they reformed The Skatalites with original vocalist Doreen Shaffer. The veterans augmented the group with guest trumpet, keyboard, and trombone players and they recorded a number of new albums including *Skavoovie*, as well as *Hi-Bop Ska* and *Greetings from Skamania* which were both nominated for Grammy awards. Their tours with young ska bands re-ignited another generation and version of ska music across the globe.

Tommy McCook had double-bypass heart surgery in 1995, after which he was always in ill health. He died in Conyers, Georgia on May 5, 1998 at the age of 71 from pneumonia. He was survived by his wife of seven years, Iris; five daughters, three sons, and one stepson. A funeral was held at the National Arena in Kingston, attended by hundreds of mourners, including Sister Mary Ignatius Davies and Prime Minister P.J. Patterson. A performance was given by members of the Alpha Boys' School Band.

--H.A.

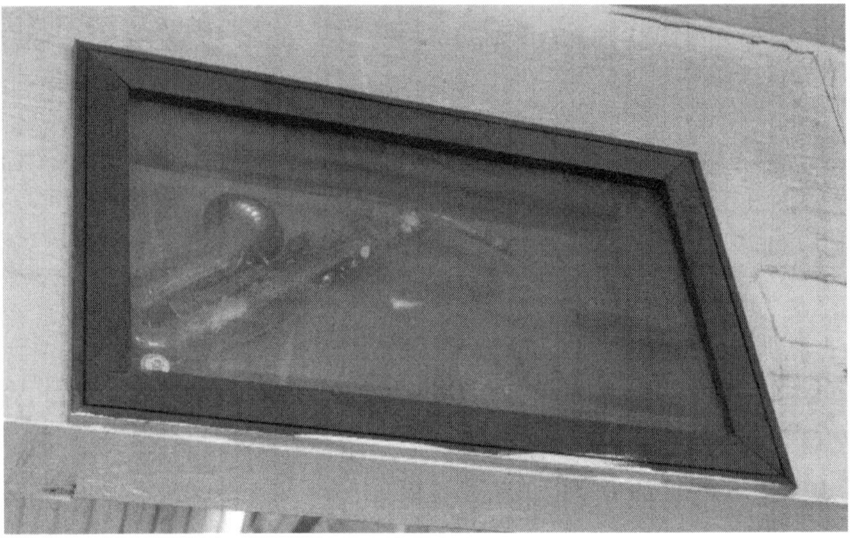

Tommy McCook's saxophone on display in Lennie Hibbert Hall in 2013

Photo by Heather Augustyn

Wilton "Bogey" Gaynair

It's not unusual to confuse Wilton "Bogey" Gaynair with his younger brother Ferdinand "Bobby" Gaynair. Interchangeably they use the nickname "Bra," a term for brother. Both play the saxophone. Both are graduates of the Alpha Boys' School band, and they both played together in the Jamaica All Stars Jazz Band. But both boys had very different careers and styles, though both were successful in their own right. Wilton began on the same instrument as his little brother, the alto saxophone, but he made the switch to tenor and according to musicologist Herbie Miller, he was the "best tenor saxophonist this country has produced," though it was in Europe that Bogey made his mark.

Born in Kingston, Jamaica on January 11, 1927, Wilton Gaynair learned to play the saxophone as a member of the Alpha Boys' School Band under the tutelage of bandmaster Samuel Vincent Tulloch. It was here that he gained a rigorous education while his style as a musician grew. Throughout the course of his life, Gaynair was able to influence others, teaching them while in Jamaica as well as during his life abroad. Sonny Bradshaw recalls, "Gaynair was our saxophone idol. After receiving new songs he would say to me, 'Let's go to the garden [Bournemouth Gardens] and play.' For example, he would say, 'Come, let's go practice the bridge on 'Body and Soul.' He was what we called in those days a Beardman [a Rastafari]; he kept a picture of [Haile] Selassie in his sax case but did not wear locks or anything like that. He was also never one for angry expression, at least not in my presence. He was a neat dresser at all times, not a fancy dresser, a gentleman nonetheless. The continental suits and ties came with his residency in Europe." It is because of his Rastafarian faith that Miller contends he was nicknamed "Bra," slang for brother, though others have claimed that Bobby received that nickname as Wilton's brother. Whatever the origin, both have been called "Bra" interchangeably, and "Bogey," Wilton's more commonly used nickname, may have been a version of "boogie."

Guitarist Janet Enright was close to Gaynair when the two performed together, along with Don Drummond, in the Eric Deans Orchestra. "Those two, Wilton and Don, just took a musical liking to me," said Enright. They got to know each other after Enright, who was selected to perform with Deans' all-female orchestra, found herself playing with the all-male orchestra due to her talent and tenacity, much to her father's dismay. After that initial performance, her father, espying Gaynair and Drummond

Wilton Gaynair taking a solo with Sonny Bradshaw and his band in 1954. Janet Enright appears on guitar in lower left corner, Sammy Ismay smiles behind Bradshaw, and Jackie Willacy sits back left.

on the stage with his daughter, sabotaged her performance. "He had unplugged the guitar because he sent his nice little middle class daughter to play with some nice middle class little girls and naturally he would come to pick me up and take me wherever and he came and he saw his daughter in the middle of two prisoners. Uptown people at the time were snobbish. And he was so mad. Because there were all nice middle class girls and then I am sandwiched, was his word, between two prisoners, which he was referring to Alpha. He said, 'You're in punishment. You're not going to play the guitar for two years,' or something like that. Wilton knew about it because they befriended me and I don't remember how we would keep in touch, but we kept in touch, Wilton and Don, and they got Mr. McMillan and they all talked to my father. McMillan was the owner of the Colony Club and he had one of the top, leading advertising companies in Jamaica. They let me continue but

I did not go back to the Eric Deans Band." It was at this time that Wilton Gaynair and Don Drummond had also left the Eric Deans Orchestra. With Janet Enright, they formed a combo of their own. "Wilton Gaynair left the band and formed Wilton Gaynair & The All-Stars. It had Drummond now on the trombone, myself on the guitar, and Foggy Mullings on piano, Cluett Johnson on bass, Donald Jarrett on drums—a hot little group with a bunch more, about seven," Enright says.

Gaynair also performed with Redver Cooke and His Royal Jamaicans along with schoolmate Sonny Grey, as well as Roy Coburn and His Blue Flames with Alpharians Don Drummond, Tommy McCook, and Harold McNair. He played with Sonny Bradshaw's group, and also backed international artists when they visited Kingston to perform, including Carmen McRae and George Shearing. Herman "Woody" King, himself a musician who attended the late-night jam sessions in the Wareika Hills, says that Wilton Gaynair honed his free-form jazz skills here. "He was also as melodic a player as any on the scene, whose heartfelt lyricism worked well with the horns and drums concept—that was being innovated at Ossie's camp—perfectly. To hear the sound of Rasta drumming with Bra, Don, Rico, Johnny, and the other horns present is, even to this day, unbelievable," King says. Though the clubs and the hills were home to Gaynair and other jazz musicians of the 1950s, there were those who had the vision and opportunity to relocate to what they saw as a land with an attractive promise of prosperity—Europe.

Wilton Gaynair, 1961

Wilton Gaynair left Jamaica in 1955, as many jazz musicians during his era did, to pursue opportunities in Europe. Carlos Malcolm says, "They had to go away. I know when Wilton Gaynair went away, he didn't want to see Jamaica again. Not that it did anything to him, it's just when you graduate to the wider sphere of consciousness you tend to leave it behind." Tony Hall, in the liner notes for the album *Blue Bogey* says that Alpha colleague Dizzy Reece had encouraged him to relocate to London where he and Joe Harriott, another Alpha chum, helped to bring Gaynair into the club circuit. "I well remember Dizzy saying; 'Wait till you hear this Bogey. Man, he's a bitch!'" writes Hall. Gaynair played with Dizzy in a group called the Hall-Stars, and he guested at Royal Festival Hall before moving permanently to Germany. Hall writes, "Then, because the work scene in town [London] was far from lucrative, Bogey cut out for the Continent where he has played almost continuously ever since." But in August, 1959, Gaynair came back to London for three weeks, during which time he performed with Joe Harriott at the Down Beat Club, and with Dizzy Reece at the Flamingo Club and the National Film Theatre. During this trip, on August 26, 1959, Gaynair recorded his debut album, *Blue Bogey.* Musicologist Herbie Miller says of the album, "This recording helps to fill a huge gap in the chronological history of popular Jamaican music during the formative years—the period between jazz and its transformation through Count Ossie's Nyabinghi music to ska." The album was recorded on Terry Hall's Tempo label at Decca's West Hampsted studio. Gaynair, a bit of a perfectionist, claimed of the album, "I can do so much better than that!" but perhaps this comment was more an indication of the potential that he saw in himself.

Gaynair claims as his influences Coleman Hawkins, Sonny Rollins, Coltrane, Johnny Griffin, Don Byas, Lucky Thompson, Charlie Ventura, and of course, Charlie Parker. "I think he was the greatest musician of all on his instruments," Gaynair says of Parker in the liner notes to "Blue Bogey." Not only did he study these greats, but according to Terry Hall, he also studied technically, obtaining a degree in arranging, composition, and advanced harmony while in Germany. Miller writes, "In Germany he had further immersed himself in the study of music, expanding his theoretical facility, solidifying his methodology, fortifying his technique and clarifying the rational that underpinned his creative impulse." Miller describes Gaynair's playing like a sommelier describes a fine wine, with a "full-bodied tone, even touch, and a mellowness of sound that lingers on the finish of his notes."

In 1960, Gaynair recorded his album "Africa Calling," and it is this title that reveals the unique approach of Bogey to his playing. Miller espouses, "This Jamaican musician shared with other home-bred masters of his time ... who emerged during Jamaica's colonial period, a period of cultural imperialism coalesced into a school of likeminded artists who understood Western technique but superimposed them on African diasporic musical form." He performed regularly with the prestigious Kurt Edelhagen Orchestra as well as for visiting artists such as Gil Evans, Shirley Bassey, the Manhattan Transfer, Freddie Hubbard, and in 1972 at the opening ceremony of the Munich Olympics. He was a featured artist on the Third Eye album *Connexion* in 1977 released on a German label. It wasn't until 1982 that Gaynair would release his next and last album, the appropriately titled *Alpharian.* Gaynair did return to Jamaica from time to time to perform but in September, 1983, Wilton Gaynair suffered a stroke while performing at a concert and he never fully recovered. The stroke left him partially paralyzed and though he was unable to play the saxophone again, he did still teach music. He died on February 3, 1995 in Germany.

Wilton Gaynair

--H.A.

Wilton "Bogey" Gaynair
***Jamaica Journal*, March, 1970**

Ferdinand 'Bobby' Gaynair

Those familiar with the name Bobby Gaynair may be surprised to hear that his birthname is actually Ferdinand Hangerfield Gaynair. His wife today, Anne, jokes that the first time she heard it she couldn't hide her surprise. "I said my merciful Jesus, what did your mother do to you? Where did that come from? The first name is bad enough!" she says with a laugh. As a result, most people call the legendary tenor saxophonist Bobby, or "Little Bra," since he was little brother to Wilton "Big Bra" Gaynair.

Born in Kingston, Jamaica on August 15, 1928 to Mary Foster and Fitz Henry Herbert Gaynair, Bobby was the baby of the family. His brother Wilton was the middle child, while sister Joyce Veronica (pet name Blossom) was the oldest. "We were so happy as a family. We loved each other," he says. Fitz Gaynair was an engineer on a ship so he was frequently gone at sea, but the family was close and there was always music in the home. "He was working so we didn't so much see my father. It was just when the boat comes in, he visit us. It was like he was a musician on tour! But the love was there, that was the main thing. My father and my mother loved music. They passed it on to their kids. In those days we used to listen to the Salvation Army Band that plays at the meeting and we used to dance. There were other places like Coney Island that was a place with a band and guitar players and singers. All the great musicians end up in Coney Island. We always want to go and learn music and my brother was born a gifted musician. He played the mouth organ. He was so good, he was like a Stevie Wonder and so progressive. My mother said if it was the last thing she do it would be so we know music. But my father wanted him to be a professional fighter and me to be a doctor, but we wanted music. We were born with the love of music in us. One time, my dad brought home a gramophone, the days before radio. That was such a beautiful gramophone, a Victrola with his master's voice. Everybody, the neighbors, was so excited. He traveled to America, Canada, all over Europe. We didn't know that we would turn out to be a traveler also," he says.

When Bobby was just seven years old, his father died which meant that his mother was left unable to properly care for the three children. Bobby explains, "He died on his bed peacefully. That was on Princess Street. Before he died, he teach me my five senses. When I was in school, I got the message he died. Diabetes. He was diabetic. He was a young man, in his 30s. After my father died, we were so poor, poverty, that my mother had to go and get work to survive and she found out about Alpha and she got us in there. You go to Alpha because of misbehavior, or you go to Alpha because of poverty, or you go to Alpha for whatever reason but it is negative reason. We went to Alpha because my mother was poor and we want to learn music." Bobby Gaynair entered Alpha Boys' School in 1937 at the age of 10. His brother, Wilton, was 12 years old and entered at the same time. "We went together. My sister was taken away by my relatives. She was about 15," he recalls.

Bobby Gaynair
Photo courtesy Bobby and Anne Gaynair

Alpha was tough for Bobby, different than what he and Wilton were accustomed to. He says, "Good, bad, and indifferent. When we went to Alpha, these were the boys we were confronted with. It was a different world. We had never been in a school like that. The boys either like you or they hate you." Fortunately for Bobby, he was befriended by a trumpeter in the band, Carlton Willacy, who helped to welcome him to the school and make the transition easier. But the treatment from the "overseers" and those in charge at Alpha was harsh to say the least. Anne says, "When Bobby told me his stories as a boy growing up in that system, I was, tears, because it was so vicious. It wasn't what everybody think, wonderful little nuns running around. They were violent. I said, 'Did you get beat up?' He said, 'I got beat up every week.' I said, 'Why you? You don't even get into a fight,' and he said, 'I was innocent. When you're innocent you get hurt.' It was from boys until he retaliated. They're called the overseers, in charge of the boarders. And some of the nuns." Bobby adds, "If I talked about my punishment, you would never believe me, however I'm still alive."

Because of his love for music, Bobby was immediately drawn to the band. "I was allowed to listen in the evenings to the band practice. They had a little bungalow and the band practice there. The music was so nice. They were playing classical music, overtures. The leader of the band was a very good musician, and a former member of the military band, Mr. George Neilson. They practiced in the evenings, every day. I listened to them and I was so amazed hearing the sousaphone and the trombone and clarinet and trumpet. I was a rookie and Mr. Neilson asked me how old I am and if I like music and he said I was one year too young, I have to wait. I was so disappointed. But he said, what else can you do? I said I can do dancing. He said if you can do dancing that means you've got music in your head. So I make a couple movements, dancing, and everybody, the bandleader, like my movements and they give me a pet name that never leave me. They call me Go Go Walk," he says with a laugh.

Wilton was old enough to enter the band, and due to his proficiency on the harmonica, he had knowledge of music as well. "My brother got the opportunity. The senior guys pick him and teach him to play the clarinet. First he was a clarinet player. He didn't take long. He was so progressive." Soon Bobby was old enough to join as well. "My first instrument was a clarinet too, just like my brother. But I got sick with a bad foot. We were playing a ball game and I had damage and I couldn't go to band practice for a while. They had engagements out and I had to stay home. So during that time, we got another bandmaster, Tulloch come in. When I was able to move around and was good enough to practice, him say now you go and pick up that baritone saxophone. It was a baritone saxophone I learned on. Everybody thought it was too big for me. I had to learn from the rest of the guys in the band and I was self-taught. After Alpha I played an alto sax. I play the clarinet, the saxophone, the piano, the guitar, and I can play the flute. I'm versatile," he says. While still at Alpha, Bobby began performing outside of the school, as did many members of the band. He says that while still a student he performed with Carlyle Henriques's band, a large 18-20-piece orchestra comprised largely of Alpha Boys. The band played every Friday night at the Carib Theatre, which Bobby describes as like "Carnegie Hall" in that one had to be very good to play there. Henriques, whose nickname was Tuby because he was "short and stubby," was not a musician, says Bobby, only a manager, a booker, and an organizer of the band. He says that Henriques frequently came to Alpha to hear the band, loved them, and took them out to play. Not only did this conglomeration of boys play at the Carib, but they also, according to Bobby, played at Vernam Air Force Base, an

American military airfield during World War II. Here they played at the base's club, entertaining US soldiers.

When Bobby graduated from Alpha, his first job was with the Redver Cooke Orchestra. He says that he stayed with this band for "several years" and performed all over the island. He also performed at the Palace Theatre with The Commandos, an orchestra led by Delroy Stephens. Bobby also performed for other bands, filling in for his brother when Wilton left Jamaica for Europe. "He followed in his brother's footsteps," says Anne. "When Wilton went off to Germany, Bobby moved into his position as a horn player with all the best bands. Tower Isle, all the hotels up and down the coast. Wherever Wilton went, Bobby was next in line. They would audition other musicians like Tommy [McCook] and when they got to Bobby, he got the job." Bobby performed with guitarist Fitz Colash, Don Drummond & His All-Stars, Baba Motta, Cecil Lloyd and His Orchestra, and others.

Bobby Gaynair made a number of recordings including "Blockade" with Johnny "Dizzy" Moore and Rico Rodriguez; "Schooling the Duke" with Don Drummond and Johnny "Dizzy" Moore; and "First Gone (Going Home)" with Count Ossie and Rico for producer Harry Mudie. Wife Anne says, "That song 'Oh Carolina,' Don Drummond was really instrumental in writing that, from what I can gather from Bobby. Bobby was the one that was with them doing the repeater drum." He performed on a number of Skatalites tunes and was a member of Clue J & His Blues Blasters, playing on songs like "Milk Lane Hop" with fellow Alpharians Dizzy Moore and Rico Rodriguez, and for Prince Buster on "My Queen." He says, "I played music to survive with the different bands, on and off because it wasn't regular. You get a job when there's an engagement. With all of that, I survived." Gaynair was also a member of Lynn Taitt's band, The Sheiks, but not before he left the stage for the hills for a number of years.

"I spent seven years in the camp. I went in the hills, the bottomless pit. If you are in the camp, in the Wareika Hills, you are in the bottomless pit, way below poverty. There were plenty of people who were displeased with me. Because of my profession, they felt I should join society. But you have to live like a beast in the wilderness. Most people would say I was crazy, I didn't have to go that far, to go off on his own in the bush. I was in my shack, my little squat I make in the bush, in the wilderness in the Wareika Hills with my friend who played the drums— his name was Count Ossie. You never get any food and you had to be hungry for days. It was like you were in famine. There were times when we would get certain things to eat. But we had wisdom, knowledge, and understanding. I had to experience all that and I didn't complain. There was nobody to complain to," he says, noting that there were a good number of times the camp was raided by police and soldiers with guns, but he was largely left alone since he had a friend on the police force who had admired his playing.

While still living in his shack in the Wareika Hills, Bobby says that one day he was approached by a manger of The Sheiks in front of all the bredren. He recalls, "One of my friends, the manager of The Sheiks, came in the camp and asked me if I could come to the Teachers Convention to entertain the teachers. But they had to go through government and make sure we weren't subversive. Me, who was in the bottomless pit, was the most dangerous, because I was a drug user—that is what they call marijuana, a drug. So they had problem taking me through immigration and I had my beard on so I couldn't hide, I had my full-grown beard. But he liked me and he asked me to come and I look at the brothers and it was like the Father, without any warning, was just taking me out of the bottomless pit to a paradise. The Father is so great. I didn't even get a break to make the proper arrangement because I had to leave everybody, just went. You couldn't get a passport in those days with beard on your face, but I was passed through so quickly. All I had to do was be civil and quiet and humble when they question me. The time was so short to leave Jamaica, I didn't even get the time to take a good shower. Coming from out of the dirt, I was like a little worm. There was a lady I left in Jamaica and she was pregnant with my last daughter. I have three

Bobby Gaynair and Jo Jo Bennett at Club Carabana in Toronto, early 1970s
Photo courtesy Bobby and Anne Gaynair

daughters, two in America and one in Jamaica. Before I went in the bottomless pit, I had a bit of a social life. I had women who fall in love with me. Sometimes I have to be careful because sometimes their husbands were jealous of me. That makes things difficult for me." Bobby Gaynair left Jamaica in July, 1964 to tour as one of 228 people, the majority of them members of the Jamaica Women Teachers Federation, for a tour of Canada, the United States, and Mexico. "We were entertaining them. We almost toured the whole of America, started from Miami, New York, Washington, Philadelphia, Chicago, to Utah, California to Los Angeles, San Francisco, and to Canada. We went up to Ottawa, to other parts of Canada," he says. The *Daily Gleaner* on August 18, 1964 writes of The Sheiks' performance in San Francisco during this tour stating, "So great was the response to the music of the Ska that later when the audience was asked to dance, they joined in with enthusiasm." The tour ended in Toronto and Bobby Gaynair decided to stay for good with the other members of the band. "When we came back, I didn't come back to Jamaica. We were in the Sheiks at that time. We went into a West Indian Federation Club by the name of WIF Club, it was for West Indians in Toronto. It became popular knowing that the Sheiks were playing there and from there we had to move around and learn to live in Canada. That was in August 1964. I applied for a working permit to stay and work in Canada. The opportunity, I wanted. The guys that were managing the group made arrangements with some politicians who

Bobby Gaynair, Florida, 1983
Photo courtesy Bobby and Anne Gaynair

Bobby Gaynair, Florida, 1985
Photo courtesy Bobby and Anne Gaynair

were Canadian and fall in love with the band and gave us an invitation to get a working permit to enter Canada and we become Canadian," he says.

In the subsequent years, Bobby Gaynair rarely performed, though he did have a stint with the band Earth, Roots & Water in the late 1970s. He met his wife Anne in Toronto and they married. Anne had two children from a previous marriage which Bobby helped to raise, and Bobby has a total of four children—Annette, Rose, Paul, and Jacqueline. Anne and Bobby have been married for 45 years and they live in Sydney, Nova Scotia near where Anne was born in Cape Breton. Bobby remained close to his brother Wilton throughout his life and even helped to raise Wilton's son. But the allure of touring never appealed to Bobby, only the music. Anne says, "Bobby didn't want to travel. He said, no, I've had enough of that. Bobby's radical with the system. He always got away from it, he couldn't stand the politics. He just wanted to play his horn." Bobby still performs regularly, every day. He says, "It's too late to turn back now!" Bobby Gaynair received the Order of Distinction on October 16, 2017.

--H.A.

Bobby Gaynair with his Order of Distinction, October 2017
Photo by Roberto Moore

Bobby Gaynair at home in Nova Scotia, 1997
Photo courtesy Bobby and Anne Gaynair

A classroom at Alpha Boys' School with the school motto, *Upward and Onward*
Photo by Heather Augustyn

Trades at Alpha: Gardening
Photo by Adam Reeves

Joe Harriott

While many associate the origins of free jazz with saxophonist Ornette Coleman and his quartet at the Five Spot Café in New York in 1959, others argue that it was not Coleman who pioneered this innovative sound that allowed for collective improvisation. The rightful inventor of free jazz, contend a number of well-researched scholars, is Joe Harriott who began his musical education at Alpha Boys' School before immigrating to England, which is precisely why it may be that he has not been given proper recognition. Harriott, although able to leave Jamaica to seek greater fame, spent years of his career in England, a country whose jazz musicians were never acknowledged on par with American jazz musicians. Even the epitaph on his headstone reflects this notion and it was a phrase he uttered a number of times during his lifetime in reference to the master, Charlie Parker, a man who was a great inspiration to Harriott who also provided a mold from which to break away. "Parker? There's them over here can play a few aces too." Perhaps only today, without such pigeonholed and elitist views, are listeners able to appreciate Harriott's true genius and contributions that forever changed the landscape of jazz music.

Joseph Arthurlin Harriott was born in Kingston, Jamaica on July 15, 1928 to Muriel Scarlett and Rafael Garfield Harriott, both of whom died when Joe was very young, and so on July 6, 1938, he went to live at Alpha Boys' School. Joe had three siblings and one half sibling, one of which, Ivanhoe Harriott, also attended Alpha four or five years after Joe. Although Joe was assigned to other trades at Alpha, like bookbinding and printing, he had a gift for music and he studied clarinet under the instruction of Bandmaster Vincent Tulloch. He worked hard and performed with the Alpha Band at functions throughout Kingston. Later during his tenure with the band he was able to move to tenor, baritone, and then alto saxophone as the instruments became available. During the last years of his time with the band, he learned to play swing music by the likes of Benny Goodman and Lionel Hampton, which added to his repertoire of classical music learned early on.

At the age of 15, Joe Harriott began working with Carlyle Henriques's Orchestra, even before he graduated from Alpha. It wasn't until 1945 that Harriott left Alpha and with his education and experience, he began immediately working with local orchestras such as Jack Brown's swing band, and the band where many Alpha boys got their start, the Eric Deans Orchestra. He also performed with the Jamaican All Stars, the Silvershine Band, and Sonny Bradshaw who first introduced Harriott to jazz arrangements. It was when Harriott worked for Ozzie DaCosta that he traveled to Europe, and with that taste of greater fame and success, Harriott, despite having a live-in girlfriend named Edith Grant and a 13-month-old daughter, Pauline Theresa, he made the move permanent and never looked back.

Joe Harriott
Star Newspaper

In 1951, Joe Harriott arrived in London and he immediately made contact with fellow Alpharian Dizzy Reece who had been in Europe since 1948 when he immigrated on the Windrush. Harriott began performing the bebop jazz of Americans Charlie Parker, Dizzy Gillespie, and Bud Powell, as well as New Orleans-style jazz and even blues, in clubs with groups all over the city. Straight away, audiences recognized Harriott's saxophone as something distinctive. Harriott was a professional, serious about his art. He was a tall man and always wore a suit with a white shirt, dark necktie, and folded handkerchief in his breast pocket, according to Alan Robertson who penned the superb biography, *Joe Harriott: Fire in His Soul.* Harriott was neat, tidy, and popular with the ladies. He never married but had relationships with a number of married women. He was a womanizer and had five known children, but was also violent with women and was the subject of a number of paternity and child-support lawsuits. He was a heavy smoker, a heavy scotch drinker, and he loved to gamble, but he vehemently stayed away from drugs after seeing a number of his friends suffer the effects of heroin. He was a member of the Rosicrucians, a mystical order popular during this era that taught the use of meditative and visualization techniques to reach personal desired goals.

Harriott's music, like his relationships and emotions, demonstrated deep passion and a strong voice, so after establishing himself as a talented saxophonist with a variety of bands, he made his first recording, *Cool Jazz*

Joe Harriott on sax with fellow Alpharian Dizzy Reece on trumpet, Tony Crombie on drums, and Lennie Bush on bass

with Joe, an EP on Siggy Jackson and Emil Shallit's Melodisc label in 1954. Harriott was a member of Tony Kinsey's trio and they went on to make a number of recordings and perform throughout England as well as in Paris. He also performed with Ronnie Scott's orchestra, and although the large group of musicians never fully gelled, it did lead to a relationship with Scott and other musicians as Harriott continued to make guest appearances over the years with a number of bands. In March, 1958, Harriott established a group of his own, the Joe Harriott Quartet, which became successful. The members of this aggregation changed from time to time as musicians rotated in and out. Musicians that were part of the Joe Harriott Quartet at one time or another include trumpeter Hank Shaw, trumpeter Shake Keane, pianist

The Joe Harriott Quintet. From left: Pat Smythe, Joe Harriott, Shake Keane, Bobby Orr, and Coleridge Goode

Pat Smythe, drummer Phil Seamen, drummer David "Benny" Goodman, drummer Bobby Orr, drummer Tommy Jones, bassist Lloyd Thompson, bassist Coleridge Goode, pianist Harry South, and others. They performed at the Marquee in London each week and over the years they played in Frankfurt, Belfast, Switzerland, Edinburgh, Glasgow, Germany, and all over England.

It was in August, 1958 when Harriott first experienced health problems after collapsing from pneumonia, a lung infection, and pleurisy. He spent three months in the hospital before recovering further at his girlfriend's home. During this time, Harriott was able to spend time thinking and composing music that would become the foundation of free jazz. Drummer Frank Holder recalled, "The idea of this free form stuff … Ornette Coleman hadn't come on the scene, really. It wasn't a question of where Joe had heard anything ... from him or anybody. He just created this thing. He said to us, everybody in a way would be soloing, in that you're not playing the changes as everybody plays. You know what the changes are, but you're playing your own line. The others are listening to that line and playing their own line. Mind blowing, I'm telling you!"

Just as Don Drummond and others would go on to create ska from the classical and jazz standards they learned at Alpha Boys' School, Joe Harriott created free form, or abstract jazz, from the classical and jazz standards he learned at Alpha Boys' School. Harriott not only called on his Alpha foundation, but also the world of art and literature. After visiting a Pablo Picasso exhibition, Harriott concluded, "That's what I'm trying to do. Paint pictures." Robertson states, "Something entirely new had arrived in jazz and Harriott was its inventor. While Coleman allowed the soloist free rein over a more formal backing, Joe's music let the whole ensemble experience free simultaneously, all the time listening to each other and allowing influences to pass between them." But Harriott's new genre of jazz wasn't easily accepted at first and so his recordings and performances typically featured a healthy balance of free jazz with bebop styles. "It is a big break from the regular formula ... it is abstract music, not relying on chordal structures and not affected by harmonic sequences. It is the most free and easy form of music possible and I predict that, eventually, it will be the type of music heard a lot in the clubs. It is so unrestrictive. I cannot dismiss the standards, but I want to create a new type of music," Harriott said. "I am not thinking of jazz at all, not in the known sense. I'm thinking of an artist, a musician, free to paint sounds, colours and effects as the ideas come to him."

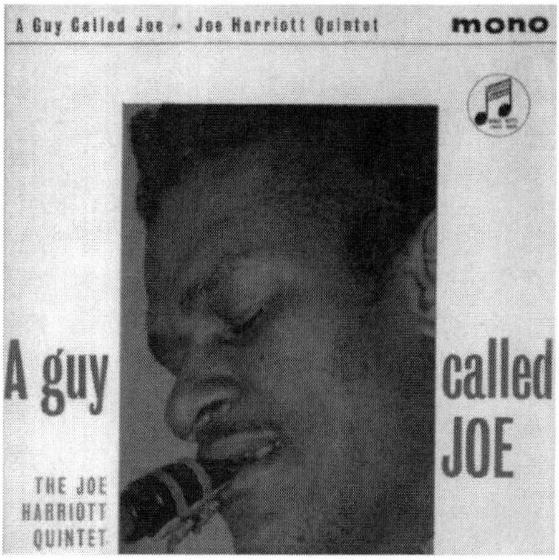

In 1960, Harriott recorded his first work of free form jazz, an album appropriately titled *Free Form.* In 1962, Harriott received a five-star review from *Down Beat Magazine* for his free-form album *Abstract*," a first for a British jazz group. The next album, *Movement*, was a mix of free form and traditional styles. After *Movement*, however, he seemed to have abandoned his belief in free form jazz. In 1962, Harriott mixed genres again, this time sharing the music world with the world of poetry for a recording called *Blues for the Lonely*, which was an EP. He partnered with pianist and composer Michael Garrick who conceived of the jazz and poetry fusion with his Jazz and Voices program at the Royal Festival Hall. Other recordings of this nature were *Promises*, *October Woman*, and *Black Marigolds*, as well as a live recording called *Poetry and Jazz in Concert.*

Another jazz fusion in which Harriott was involved was the fusion of jazz and Indian raga music with composer and musician John Mayer from Calcutta. It was, as Robertson writes, the "first time in the history of music that you had Western musicians and Indian musicians playing together from a written score." The result of this collaboration was the "Indo-Jazz Suite" which featured Harriott on alto sax, Mayer on violin and harpsichord, and others on sitar, tamboura, flute, bass, trumpet, and flugelhorn. "Obviously I don't follow the format as strictly as the Indian players do. What I try to do is paint a picture with the symbols given to me. I try to create something with raga—you know, create something over the top," said Harriott. There were subsequent recordings including "Indo-Jazz Fusions I" in 1967 and "Indo-Jazz Fusions II" in 1968, and numerous performances throughout Europe, but the results of this east-west blend are even more significant. Robertson opined, "World music began here."

Over the years, Harriott performed with a number of notable musicians. In 1965, Harriott participated in a recording session with Sonny Boy Williamson II, an American harmonica player and blues singer. This recording also featured guitarist Jimmy Page and it was released in 1968 by Marmalade Records. In 1969 Harriott performed with the Indo-Jazz Fusions on the same bill as Bob Dylan at the second Isle of Wight Festival. He performed with Dave Brubeck in 1961 and that same year was turned down by Dizzy Gillespie who refused to perform with Harriott because of his "damn weird music."

As the popularity of jazz music waned in the 1970s, Harriott's opportunities for work dried up. As music critic Duncan Heining writes, "The last three or four years of Harriott's life were dismal and depressing. He was, for all intents, destitute, often homeless and ... depended on the kindness of strangers." Heining contends that Harriott suffered from racial prejudice as well as prejudice over being a jazz musician from a colony in Britain, not from America, which may have altered his success entirely since his skill was on par with, if not greater than, his American contemporaries. Harriott could be proud, difficult, and caustic, and in the end, poverty, combined with continued lung maladies, resulted in Harriott's death on January 2, 1973 at the age of 44. Not only is the world left with his bounty of recordings in a variety of innovative genres, but Harriott also left a legacy by elevating others to perform to high standards. "He could often lift the other musicians to a higher level of performance and his influence made some play better than they believed possible," wrote Robertson. Undoubtedly that influence continues in a whole new generation of musicians.

--H.A.

Joe Harriott

Photo courtesy *Jamaica Gleaner*

Vernon "Von Mullo" Möller

Many lads who wound up at the Alpha Boys' School found themselves at the "school for wayward boys" because a mother or father had suddenly died, leaving the family without a source of income or a means of daily care. Such was the case for Vernon Möller whose father died when Von Mullo, as he would come to be known, was just three years old. However, few boys came to Alpha because their mothers worked at the school, and this too was the case for Von Mullo, whose mom was a house mother, tending to the physical care of the young students.

Vernon Möller was born on January 6, 1928 to Otto Möller, a German, and Gladys Möller, a Jamaican. "Their father was a merchant seaman," says Donna Möller, Vernon's widow, "and he died at sea of appendicitis. They buried him at sea. Vernon was a baby, maybe three years old at the time, and so that left Gladys alone to take care of the two boys that were still living. How she did it was she went to work at Alpha." Vernon was the youngest son, and his brother Aston was six years older, but there had been nine boys born to Otto and Gladys, seven of which died in infancy. "It was just the times," Donna says, noting that the family had a hard life in Trench Town where they lived. After their father's death, the boys went to live at Alpha since their mother found work at the school. Donna says that Gladys was "what they called a bush doctor. It wasn't obeah, but she knew how to boil certain leaves to make remedies and so she took care of babies. The boys were lucky because they got a fantastic education, a no-nonsense education, and it gave him the music education he needed to have a career." Gladys never remarried and she lived to be 98 years old.

VERNON MULLER
Trombone

Brother Aston was also a musician who performed with the Alpha Boys' School Band, says Donna. She says, "He played the flute and the

Vernon Möller

piccolo and then he went into the Jamaica Military Band, but he was also a soldier." Donna says that Aston died in his late 20s after gangs entered his mother's home and shot him in front of her.

Vernon enjoyed Alpha Boys' School, says Donna, though life could sometimes be tough. "He said they had uniforms and they'd get a big chunk of soap each week and they had to wash their own clothes, wash with that and their hair with that, and nobody got shoes unless they were going on a band concert, then they got shoes. He was very athletic. He played soccer and tennis and cricket. But he had no toenails because they played with no shoes." Vernon would go on to become a member of the Bahamian cricket team, Donna says.

After graduating from Alpha in the 1940s, Von Mullo found work as a trombonist with George Moxey's Orchestra, the Eric Deans Orchestra, Roy Coburn's Blue Flames Orchestra, and he even headlined at the Colony Club. He also was a member of the All Stars Big Band, an annual aggregation of the island's top musicians organized by Count Buckram, a dance promoter. This large group contained fellow Alpharians Joe Harriott, Harold McNair, brothers Wilton and Bobby Gaynair, Sonny Grey, and Tommy McCook. Möller also performed trombone for another notable singer, Frank McCook, Tommy McCook's older brother, at the Colony Club, and in July, 1956, Möller performed as a member of the Jamaica All-Stars Band with Sonny Bradshaw, Carlos Malcolm, and Don Drummond during two famous performances at the Tropical and Ward Theaters backing up Sarah Vaughan on her tour from the US.

Prior to his work with most of these orchestras, Von Mullo started a family. On June 17, 1945, Vernon married his first wife, Norma Wisdom.

***Daily Gleaner*, August 29, 1953**

"He ended up getting married young and they had a son, Jack. Everett was his name but his nickname was Jack. Vernon was only 16 years old when his son was born. He had a family and he had responsibilities," Donna Möller says. One year later the couple had another child, a daughter named Donna. It would be 10 years before Vernon had another child with Norma—another daughter named Noella. Daughter Donna Lyn explains, "My dad went to the Bahamas. He spent 25 years or more in the Bahamas. He went to Nassau with the same band that Tommy McCook played in. My mother stayed in Jamaica because there was a little bit of a rift. But he came back and Noella was born," she says.

When Von Mullo returned to Jamaica he found work with Byron Lee & the Dragonaires and toured extensively with the band. Daughter Donna says that she and her mother would go to his performances to hear him play. "When he was in Byron Lee's band, my mom and I would go and hear. He played very well, very very well. He played with Byron Lee's band at my graduation dance, the ball, for Alpha Academy. Not only could he play, but he wrote music as well," she says. One of these compositions is "Noella," a song for his daughter that appears on the album, *The Many Moods of Lee.*

When Norma and Vernon split for good, he returned to the Bahamas where he found solid work as a musician, and it was here in the Bahamas that Von Mullo made his mark, helping to put Bahamian music on the map. Widow Donna says, "He was quite successful there. He played with Freddie Munnings' band." That band, The Beginning of the End, was tremendously popular

***Daily Gleaner*, August 18, 1953**

in the Bahamas, as well as throughout the Caribbean. Their song "Funky Nassau" was a massive hit in 1971 and it featured Möller on trombone. It reached #7 on US R&B charts and charted in the UK. A year later, Toots & the Maytals came out with "Funky Kingston," perhaps inspired by Von Mullo's tune?

After a period of time, Von Mullo moved to Freeport, Grand Bahama Island and he took a residency at the famous Xanadu Hotel, a resort that was popular with the Rat Pack and owned by Howard Hughes who lived on the penthouse floor for the last four years of his life. "He was in Freeport for the beginning of it when the music was taking off," says Donna. "They were building the hotels and the hotels employed live bands. So he had his own band, and his was called The Explorers. They played in the lounges and the bars," she says. It was here at the Xanadu that he and Donna met in 1980. They were married in 1986.

Vernon Möller on upright bass
Photo courtesy Donna Möller

After a life of heavy smoking, Von Mullo's health suffered and he was prevented from blowing his horn. As a result, he played the electric string bass. In 1987, he and Donna moved to her hometown, Avon, Massachusetts where Von Mullo switched careers entirely, leaving music behind for good. He became a worker in a factory bakery to earn a pension and health benefits which Donna says made him proud. Additionally, the couple took guardianship of Donna's niece, Vanessa, when she was eight years old, and they had a son of their own, Brian.

In the late 1990s, Von Mullo's health continue to decline. After having two-thirds of his lung removed, as well as battling leukemia and emphysema, Vernon Möller died of heart failure on January 30, 1999. But the legacy of Von Mullo continues, and Donna says that he had an impact on one of the greatest musicians to come from Jamaica. "He actually gave a lot of advice to Bob Marley. They lived in the area that Bob Marley lived in, Trench Town. He knew Bob Marley and they did a lot of musical stuff together. Bob Marley was younger but they were all into that same movement then."

Vernon Möller
Photo courtesy Donna Möller

Von Mullo also left his mark through the music he created while alive, and in the music that continues after his death. "He loved to play," Donna says, remembering his performances. "The music was his soul. You could just see when he played how much he enjoyed it. It brought him alive. He loved all kinds of music and would have music on all the time. He was a good man, hard working. He was a good man," she says. Though virtually all of Von Mullo's Bahamian musical contributions have been live and have never been recorded, his impact on Bahamian music and Jamaican music is still significant. Additionally, much of his musical contribution continues in ways that cannot be easily measured, through the love of music he instilled in others, especially his children. His youngest son Brian, who was only 11 years old when his father passed away, works today in the music industry as a DJ and host on two radio stations in Boston. "I think he got the love of music from his dad," Donna says. Brian remembers learning to play the saxophone as a young boy. "I'd be sitting in the living room trying to struggle through some notes and he would be lit up like a Christmas tree. You could see that being involved with his kid and music was a huge thing. That's why now, I'm still involved, but in a different way," he says.

--H.A.

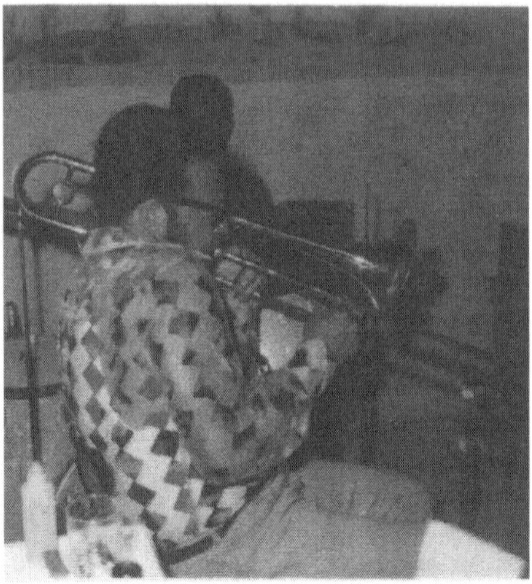

Vernon Möller on trombone
Photo courtesy Donna Möller

Vernon and Donna Möller
Photo courtesy Donna Möller

Vernon Möller's trombone on display at the Jamaica Music Museum
Photo by Heather Augustyn

Harold "Little G" McNair

Donovan strummed his guitar on stage, peaceful, wistful, singing "la dee da" in a white flowing kaftan, sleeves like clouds. The folk singer warbled as the television camera panned along the neck of his guitar, past his fingers wrapped around the frets to the musician just to his left as the lens zoomed in for the flourish between refrains. Flautist Harold McNair, pensive, eyebrows raised as he accented the song, "Lalena," in 1968. It was but one of Donovan's songs that McNair would embellish with his talent, a talent he learned at Alpha.

Harold Alexander McNair (spelling on his birth certificate is McNair, but some spellings, including recordings, show MacNair) was born in Jamaica on May 11, 1930 to father Ronald James McNair, a planter and a salesman, and mother Myrtle May McNair, nee McCadden. Ronald and Myrtle had married in May of 1928 and two months later a son, Karl Anthony McNair, was born. The family lived in Franklin Town and it is not evident if there were other children born, besides Karl and Harold, to the couple. It is also not evident why Harold came to be a student at Alpha. However, McNair studied music with the band at Alpha during a time when Vincent Tulloch was bandmaster and Joe Harriott and Wilton Gaynair were fellow musicians. The three remained close colleagues and friends throughout their entire lives. The liner notes to his album, *Bahama Bash*, on the US-based Top Rank label gives more information on his formative years. "McNair grew up on a country farm outside Kingston. While in high school, at the age of sixteen, he was given a saxophone by his uncle, and pretty much taught himself," writes Nat Henthoff with no mention of Alpha, Tulloch, or McNair's fellow bandmates.

After graduating from Alpha Boys' School, Harold McNair became a member of the Jamaica All Star Jazz Band in 1948 along with Joe Harriott, Bobby Gaynair, Tommy McCook, Wilton Gaynair, Baba Motta, Ken Williams, Sonny Bradshaw, Sonny Grey, and Vernon Möller. He found work with the local club orchestras and began to make a name for himself, or better yet, a nickname for himself in Kingston. "Little G," as he was called, played tenor saxophone with such groups as Baba Motta and the Mococo Band in 1949, headlining at the Wickie Wackie Club's Band as a "Singing Saxophonist" in 1950, and at the Shady Grove Club with Billy Cooke & His Band in 1951 on the "Sweet Sax." He performed at a number of special events such as a New Year's Eve Dance in 1956 at Melbourne's Cricket Club as director of his own group, and an Anniversary Dance at the Silver Slipper in 1955. He performed at this show with Lord Flea, as he did in 1950 at the Wickie Wackie as a member of the All King's Combo with Joe Harriott.

Performing in clubs and for local events was a way for McNair to hone his skills. Nat Henthoff writes, "After three years as an amateur, he went into music full-time at nineteen and gained a variety of experience in night clubs, hotels, and forays into 'the bush' where the listeners often react with instant action if they're not satisfied. The band usually plays in the open on a stilt-supported platform, and one time, as 'Little G' recalls, they barely got away before a group of discontented fans with a saw reached the stand. 'Little G' began to gain confidence as a jazzman through several years of meeting visiting jazz players in Jamaica. He worked in the pit bands of traveling American shows or during intermission opposite American musicians. In time, he was featured himself as a local jazz celebrity."

Harold McNair on saxophone
Jamaica Journal, March 1970

Though he was frequently playing jazz, McNair also had a love for calypso. He recorded in the 1950s for Stanley Motta's Calypso Time label, playing clarinet with Baba Motta and the Saint Jago Dons for a Sir Alfred tune called "Mama What You Done to My Papa," and another with the same label and group but playing tenor saxophone on the song, "What A T'ing 'Pon Lucy." But it wasn't until he moved to the Bahamas that Harold McNair recorded his first calypso tune as a vocalist rather than an instrumentalist, this time going not by "Little G," but as "Digby." The liner notes for a recording of the album *Flip Calypso* on the Miami-based ART Records' label, a Caribbean music label founded by American entrepreneur Harold Doane, state, "One night he put aside his sax and stepped to the microphone to sing for the first time, the song 'Digby.' 'I started with an old calypso melody from Trinidad,' reminisces McNair, 'rearranged it, changed the words, added some West Indian 'scat'—and out came 'Digby!'" On the ART Records label McNair likewise recorded the classic calypso ditty, "Zombie Jamboree," also known as "Jumbie Jamboree" or "Back to Back, Belly to Belly," a mento song made popular over the years by such artists as the Kingston Trio, Harry Belafonte, Peter Tosh, and even Lord Charmer, better known as Rev. Louis Farrakhan.

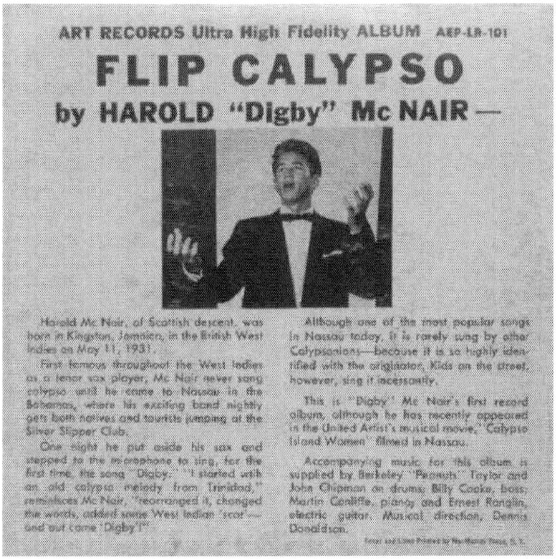

McNair lived in Nassau, a home base of sorts, for ten years, during which time he appeared in the 1958 film *Island Women*, directed by William Berke, performing as a "Bahamian Calypso Entertainer." In 1959 he recorded the album, *Bahama Bash*, whose cover features kitschy photos of the handsome McNair playing maracas, sitting on a conga drum with a Beach Blanket Bingo style design. Henthoff says of McNair's time in the Bahamas that he can be "found heading his own unit at Blackbeard's, The Junkanoo, The Silver Slipper or the Nassau Beach Lodge. Although he continued to play mainly commercial material, calypso, and meringues on the job, he maintained a vigorous interest in jazz, collecting whatever records he could and listening to the American jazz musicians who came to Nassau." Through these connections, McNair recorded the album in Miami, Florida and

he traveled to Europe to perform over the years. In 1962 he performed saxophone in the first James Bond film *Dr. No* which was largely filmed in Jamaica and featured Byron Lee & the Dragonaires as well as Count Prince Miller. He also spent periods of time performing in Cuba, Florida, New York, and London where he performed for Ronnie Scott's famous club. He toured Paris with Quincy Jones's band, and he performed with Charlie Mingus who greatly admired McNair's talent.

By 1965, Harold McNair had moved to London where he recorded the first album to truly highlight his talent as an instrumentalist. *Affectionate Fink* was recorded by Chris Blackwell for his Island Records label, which was only one year old at that point. The album featured Ornette Coleman who headlined the album with McNair, Alan Branscombe, David Izenzon, and Charles Moffett. Charles Fox states in the liner notes, "Two Americans, one West Indian and one Englishman get together to produce music that is quite simply, jazz—without any qualifying label, geographical or otherwise. The opportunity came when Harold MacNair [sic] made a business trip back to Europe. MacNair is, of course, a Jamaican. Indeed, he got his very first lessons on the alto-saxophone from a musician who played in the same band as Joe Harriott back in Jamaica. MacNair took up the flute, the instrument on which he probably shines brightest, soon after arriving in Paris at the end of the Fifties. It was in Paris too that he became a member of the orchestra which Quincey [sic] Jones took out on tour. Various trips across the Channel in Britain resulted in his appearing in a film, All Night Long, more or less an off-beat version of Othello, with a cast of musicians headed by Charlie Mingus and Dave Brubeck—and the formation of his own quartet, which included the trumpeter Ian Carr. Nowadays, MacNair lives in New York after a spell in the Bahamas. He has also forsaken the alto saxophone in favour of the tenor."

Harold McNair on flute, his signature instrument

While in England, McNair also performed as a session musician, most notably on Donovan's *In Concert* album which was recorded live when the pied piper McNair toured with the troubadour in 1967. McNair also arranged and performed on Donovan's "There is a Mountain" with a distinctive flute accompaniment. He performed on Donovan's "Hurdy Gurdy Man," as well as his most famous tune, "Mellow Yellow," along with a handful of others. McNair also performed as a session musician for Nick Drake, Davey Graham, Quincy Jones, and in the jazz-rock fusion band Ginger Baker's Air Force. The group, comprised of drummer Ginger Baker, bassist and vocalist Steve Winwood, and jazz drummer Phil Seamen who had also worked with Joe Harriott and Dizzy Reece. McNair performed on both of the albums recorded by the group in 1970.

In 1968, McNair recorded a self-titled album on the RCA label with Bill Le Sage, Spike Heatley, and Tony Carr and then in 1970 he recorded two albums—the whimsically titled *Flute and Nut* and *The Fence*. The following year, 1971, Harold McNair died tragically of lung cancer. His schoolmate, colleague, and confidante Joe Harriott was distraught over the loss. Harriott biographer Alan Robertson writes, "Harriott was, unusually, visibly distressed at the funeral in March 1971 of his lifelong friend Harold McNair who had succumbed, aged thirty-nine, to lung cancer after a long, brave struggle. Sharon Atkin said, 'I had never seen Joe so upset by

anything before.' He had tutored McNair, three years his junior, back in Alpha Boys' School. The two had a closeness born of their love of music and performing and Harold had been like an adopted younger brother. Sharon described Harriott's playing at the funeral as, 'searing' and 'raw.'"

--H.A.

Members of the Alpha Boys' School Band on flute in 2007 in the Lennie Hibbert Music Hall

Photo by Adam Reeves

Alphonso "Dizzy" Reece

"In Jamaica the big jazz movement started in 1954 when the first large scale Jazz Concert was presented at the Ward Theatre in Kingston. Our jazz men at that time were young and enthusiastic but restless and some left the island shortly after to seek their fortunes in other islands. We lost the best men in the persons of Joe Harriott, Harold McNair, Wilton Gaynair, Dizzy Reece, Sonny Grey, and Noel Gillespie among others," said Sonny Bradshaw in his liner notes for Coxsone Dodd's *Jazz Jamaica: From the Workshop* album. By 1954, Dizzy Reece and the others were long gone from Kingston. They had emigrated to England, Germany, France, and America in search of fruitful careers in music and opportunity. Reece had left many years earlier, in 1948, the same way that others had, on the Empire Windrush, the liner that brought 492 passengers and one stowaway from the West Indies to London after WWII. It was the beginning of an era for Jamaicans in jazz, and the start of a life-long career in music for Dizzy Reece.

Alphonso Son "Dizzy" Reece was born in Kingston, Jamaica on January 5, 1931. In 1943, at the age of 12, Reece was sent to Alpha Boys' School because he was wandering the streets instead of attending school. "I was bad. I used to run the streets during the revolution and such, so I was wayward in that sense," he told Christopher Porter in *JazzTimes*, October 2004. The "revolution" he speaks of was the labor strikes led by Alexander Bustamante during the late 1930s and though Reece was attracted to them as a participant, they were bloody, violent, and no place for a child. Being sent to Alpha was not objectionable to Reece who says that going to school was a way for him to become a musician. At the age of 11 he had acquired and learned to play the baritone horn, but he longed for something more. "My thing was to get a trumpet," he said of his being sent to Alpha. Reece was drawn to music and there was music on the radio as well as plenty of records in the home. His father was a pianist during the silent-film era when theaters hired musicians to perform in the orchestra pit to accompany the film. His mother encouraged his talent, recognizing in her son his musical ability. It was she who put him on the Empire Windrush, a ship from the West Indies to England, after he had left Alpha and encouraged his work with Jack Brown and His Honey Drippers, one of Jamaica's earliest swing bands, a 12-piece orchestra. Reece was 16 years old.

At the age of 17, Dizzy Reece left Jamaica for the UK, though he would return at times to perform. "I left home in May 1948," Reece told Dermot Hussey in the *Daily Gleaner* on January 19, 1964, "and went to London. The modern jazz scene in London was just about getting started. Charlie Parker had just come to Europe for that festival in Paris." Reece was soon followed to Europe by fellow Alpharians Joe Harriott in 1951, Wilton "Bogey" Gaynair in 1955, Harold McNair in 1960, and Rico Rodriguez in 1961. Reece was playing the style that Charlie Parker had brought to England in 1948—bebop. His style was called "minimalist" by critics who touted his use of the trumpet's "tonal qualities" and his "virtuoso technique" that was "never employed for its own sake, only as a means to express the full gamut of his emotions." For a decade, Reece traveled throughout Europe while making London his home base. "I made a lot of trips to Europe, Germany, Switzerland, most of Scandinavia and North Africa," he told Hussey. During this time, Reece made a number of recordings including those with Kenny Graham's Afro Cubists, Tony Crombie and His Orchestra, the In Town Jazz Group, Vic Feldman Modern Jazz Big Band, New Jazz Group, The Jazz Couriers, Dexter Gordon and Slide Hampton Sextet, and with his own groups, the Dizzy Reece Quintet and the Dizzy Reece Group. He recorded *Changing the Jazz at Buckingham Palace,* a compilation with tenor saxophonist Tubby Hayes on the Savoy label; two albums for Tempo Records, first with tenor saxophonist and owner of one of the most renowned jazz clubs in London called *Ronnie Scott Blows with the Dizzy Reece Quartet*; and his own album, *Progress Report*, also for Tempo

Dizzy Reece in *Jazz Monthly*, 1959

Records. His final recording in the UK was for the Decca imprint Blue Note, the classic, *Blues in Trinity*. He would go on to record a total of four LPs for the Blue Note label.

While in London, Reece also got married to an English woman and the couple had a daughter. They moved with him to the United States in October, 1959 in search of better opportunity, settling in New York, though the cultural climate for a bi-racial couple in the early 1960s was difficult to say the least. He relocated at the behest of Miles Davis whom he had met in 1958 and because he felt his skills would be better utilized and recognized by jazz clubs and fans in America. "Musically the States enhanced me quite a bit. But that was to be expected. That's why I went to the States. The musicianship in the States is very high and the competition is very keen. It's a lot of inspiration," Reece told Hussey. But racism was still prevalent in America during this time and Reece and his family felt the effects. "When I came here with my wife, I got negative feedback. A lot of people took umbrage at an integrated marriage. Struggle. That seems to be the theme of it," Reece told Porter who writes that the "couple had another daughter, but soon split up due to the intense pressure. Reece's wife moved back to England and she took the kids with her." Reece also experienced discrimination from the African-American community, says Porter, due to his West-Indian heritage.

Dizzy Reece

New York in the 1960s was a fertile time for jazz musicians who collaborated with one another, learning new styles of improvisation and technical variations. "All over the streets you'd hear music, and it was a different thing," Reece said of his new home. He continued to record in New York. In the liner notes to Reece's album *Asia Minor*, recorded in 1962,

Dizzy Reece from the cover of his album, *Soundin' Off*

Robert Levin wrote, "'When Reece emigrated to this country from England in Autumn of 1959 his coming was preceded by the enthusiastic support of a considerable body of musicians, among them Miles Davis, who is reported to have said of Reece upon hearing tapes that 'he has soul, originality and above all he is not afraid to blow with fire.'" Reece recorded *Nirvana: The Zen of the Jazz Trumpet* in 1968, *From In to Out* in 1970, *Possession, Exorcism, Peace* in 1974, *Manhattan Project* in 1978, and *Blowin' Away* in 1978 before going relatively silent, prompting *Downbeat's* Susan Ruel to claim in April 2007 that "sightings of Dizzy Reece, a titan of hard-bop trumpet, have been nearly as rare as Halley's Comet." He surfaced from time to time to perform in New York, though performances were rare.

In addition to his vast compendium of recorded music, Reece has also written a number of books. He was well read as a child, devouring everything from the poetry of Keats to the plays of William Shakespeare. He has written a number of books himself, though none have yet to be published. Still, they have taken years to research and produce, and one was a lengthy biographical history of jazz saxophonists. He is a deeply philosophical man and is also a prolific painter and a lover of film. In 1958 he produced the jazz background score for the film, *Nowhere to Go,* a British film noir from MGM Studios, and in 1961 he produced a score for the Canadian television show, "The Quest." He even created a documentary in 1967 called *The Pressure Cooker by Night*, a snapshot of the vibe and street of Harlem and Manhattan during this era, for which his quintet provided the soundtrack. He also wrote children's stories, poetry, musical publications, and screenplays. No wonder he has been described by many as a Renaissance man. "Dizzy Reece has kept a low profile in some ways," he says of himself, "but it's there, you know. I'm here, the substance, and I'm fortunate to still be here with my music. I'm still strong."

--H.A.

The Skatalites

Ska, Reggae, Rocksteady: It All Began With The Skatalites. Thus declared the official T-shirt of the debut tour by the re-born Skatalites in 1990. It boldly stakes their claim to history and frankly, who's arguing?

In spring of 1964 the nine members of The Skatalites coalesced to form what their first manager (and future Jamaican Prime Minister) P.J. Patterson has described as 'the greatest aggregation of musicians ever assembled on this land.' The Skatalites primary goal in coming together was to perform ska live. They had been playing together in various forms throughout the 1950s and early 1960s among the jazz bands like the Sonny Bradshaw Band, Eric Deans' Orchestra and Clue J and His Bluesblasters as well as around Jamaica's small burgeoning studio industry. As musicians they had developed the sound of ska over the previous few years and used to incorporate some ska numbers into their shows with various big bands. The next logical step was to form their very own pure ska combo as a way of showcasing this uniquely Jamaican form. Initially named The Satellites, as a nod to the burgeoning space race which was one of the big stories of the day, McCook had the novel idea of adding a 'k' to more succinctly define their mission. 'Someone suggested the Satellites. I said no. Skatalites was better since we were playing ska,' was a favourite line Tommy McCook would tell journalists.

The nucleus of the line-up was four Alpharians: Tommy McCook (tenor sax), Lester Sterling (alto sax), Don Drummond (trombone) and Johnny 'Dizzy' Moore (trumpet). The rest of the band comprised of Roland Alphonso (tenor sax), Lloyd Knibb (drums), Lloyd Brevett (bass), Donat Roy 'Jackie' Mittoo (piano, keyboards) and Jerome 'Jah Jerry' Haynes (guitar). Other non-official members would make great contributions such as Ernest Ranglin (guitar), Lynn Taitt (guitar), Baba Brooks (trumpet) and singers including Jackie Opel, Doreen Shaffer, Lord Tanamo, Tony DaCosta and Tony Gregory. Lynn Taitt was invited to be band leader but declined because he was Trinidadian and strongly believed a new Jamaican musical form should have a Jamaican at the helm. So the band approached Tommy McCook, recently back from an eight year stint trying to make it as a serious jazz player in the Bahamas. At first McCook didn't take ska at all seriously, to his ears it was a gimmick, a passing fad. However he acquiesced to become the band's official leader and photos of the day show the name Tommy

McCook And His Ska-talites on the bass drum and band-headers at the front of stage. Making their live debut on June 27th 1964 at the Hi-Hat Club in Rae Town, the band took Kingston's audiences by storm and quickly gained a reputation as the hottest act on the island. Allegedly 'Jah' Jerry only played one live show as he got stage fright so was replaced for live shows by Harold McKenzie. Sadly there are no live Skatalites recordings of this era, just fifteen seconds of silent footage of them on a parade float on Jamaican Independence Day, August 8th 1965.

The Skatalites

The band became the in-house band for the newly opened Studio One complex on Brentford Road and according to legend once word got out a huge crowd formed on their first day outside the studio gates just to hear them rehearse. Each of the nine players represented the very best in talent in Jamaica, mostly seasoned professionals, aside from the fifteen-year-old keyboard prodigy Jackie Mittoo. Longtime Skatalites manager Ken Stewart explains: 'They played everything, especially the older guys. If they played the hotel circuit, especially back in the earlier days, if you played a hotel gig you might have to play cha-cha, rumba, merengue, salsa, reggae, ska, rocksteady, Motown, funk, you name it. Anything could come up and you were expected to be able to do it. And if you can read well you can play anything.' Although only four out of nine were Alpharians, The Skatalites represent the very essence of Alpha Boys' School. The years of grueling musical study and practice from a very young age meant it was second nature for them to sight-read, arrange and compose. Alpha's training gave them a broad musical vocabulary that allowed their inventiveness to shine through, enabling them to enter a studio and turn out top-notch tunes at a dizzying rate. They had all soaked up be-bop jazz by the likes of Charlie Parker, Herbie Hancock, Sonny Rollins and Dizzy Gillespie, so ska became a medium for them to express themselves as serious jazz improvisationists. While a three minute single would only allow for short, succinct solos, onstage they could allow themselves to really stretch out. The Alpharian influence would often show up as bite-size phrases within their solos, referencing military marches, the classics, hymns, folk songs, nursery rhymes—the kind of things they would have had drilled into them in years of school band practice. There was a certain level of friendly competition that enabled them to all push each other further and further in the soloing. 'We were friends in a sense, Dizzy, Tommy, Roland and Don, but it was competition at the same time. Everybody wanted to outdo each other,' remembers Lester Sterling fondly. Their brilliant musicianship elevated The Skatalites from being a small-time local band-for-hire providing a soundtrack for what might have been merely a flash-in-the-pan localized dance craze, to being an immortal, era-defining act with near God-like status all around the world half a century later. It can be legitimately argued that without The Skatalites, Jamaican music would not have evolved in the way that it did and become the ubiquitous force it is in the world today.

SKATALITES GO INTO ORBIT

Star Newspaper, June 27, 1964

The Ska-talites to tour Island

Star Newspaper, August 20, 1964

The group's biggest name was Don Drummond, who had already made his name as the brightest star of Jamaican jazz throughout the 1950s. Having him in the band would prove a massive live draw, as his reputation for sending audiences into near-religious rapture was already well established as leader of the Don Drummond Four. Drummond's other-worldly, evocatively far-eastern trombone style sounded like no other, and although unknown outside of the island, he was rated by serious jazz fans and musicians (including British pianist George Shearing) as one of the finest trombonists in the world. He was also a prolific and hugely talented composer, constantly coming up with new tunes for the band. Also crucial to the sound was the tight rhythm section of Lloyd Brevett on upright acoustic bass and Lloyd Knibb on drums. The pair had played together with Eric Deans' Orchestra and had a sympathetic musical rapport. With Knibb's instantly recognizable crashing-and-rolling drum syncopation, and the loping, 'walking' style Brevett played on his home-built upright bass, the duo were the true architects of ska, between them innovating and evolving the foundations of the rhythm that would define this new Jamaican form. Knibb and Brevett were the first of the great Jamaican drum and bass stylists, paving the way for the Barrett brothers, Sly and Robbie then later on Steelie and Cleevie. Quoted in his 1998 obituary by Pierre Perrone in *The Independent* (UK), Tommy McCook further explains The Skatalites sound: 'It's the drop, the second and fourth beat where the drum dropped was the key to it. In rhythm 'n' blues, it was the same drop but ska was a little faster, with the guitar playing a different thing and the piano keeping the music lively. It was a good vibe and the singers used to show their appreciation of the beat, so we used to fire hard on that beat. When the horns weren't riffing, we would come in on the 'ska' and add more weight to it.'

***Daily Gleaner*, Sept. 2, 1964**

During this brief 'golden' period The Skatalites recorded an astonishing amount of music for a variety of producers, turning out song after song all day (and often all night) long. Literally hundreds of singles were released, either as The Skatalites or as solo artists under name of key players such as McCook, Drummond, Brevett or Alphonso but essentially the same band. As well as their regular Studio One work, they recorded with producers such as Vincent 'King' Edwards (appearing as The Upcoming Willows), Justin Yap at Top Deck, Duke Reid at Treasure Isle, Lindon Pottinger at Gaydisc, Vincent Chin at Randy's, Leslie Kong at Beverly's and Prince Buster (as Prince Buster's All Stars).

As well as their phenomenal recorded output, the band were in high demand as a live act and held a residency at Kingston's Bournemouth Beach Club on Wednesdays, Fridays and Saturdays as well as the Orange Bowl Club on Orange Street on Sundays. On top of these ongoing commitments they could be seen all over Kingston at such venues as the Odeon Theatre, the Hi-Hat, the Silver Slipper, the Yacht Club, the Wickie Wackie, the Blinking Beacon and Club Havana. Outside of Kingston they took bookings at Club Calypso in Falmouth, the Wooden Spoon, the Embassy and the Cellar in Montego Bay. With this amount of live and recorded work, it's hard to imagine how they had time for anything else other than playing ska. It can be a near-impossible task for music collectors to piece together the sheer volume of work from this period, as there is no definitive volume but rather a sprawling amount of album re-issues and compilations that make it virtually impossible to map the story. The music ranges from frenetically hypnotic be-bop to cheesy, soporific muzak, but all with an underlying pulsating ska hiccup provided by guitar, piano and horns on the second and forth beats of each bar. As well as their many original compositions, the band covered film themes of the day ('Guns of Navarone,' 'James Bond,' and 'Exodus') and jazz standards (Herbie Hancock's 'Watermelon Man,' Duke Ellington's 'Caravan' and Sonny Rollins' 'St. Thomas'—renamed 'Musical Communion'). They also covered several of Afro-Cuban rumba percussion maestro Mongo Santamaria's hits ('El Pussy Cat Ska,' 'Funny Money '—retitled as 'Bridge View' and 'Hammerhead'—retitled as 'Phoenix City'). As house band at

The Skatalites

Studio One they provided the musical foundations for many upcoming stars, including The Wailers, Jimmy Cliff, Delroy Wilson, Alton Ellis and Toots and the Maytals.

Some of their greatest work was for Justin Yap, a Chinese-Jamaican music producer who took a different approach to the more ruthlessly business-minded producers of the day by paying the band double the going rate in order to allow for adequate arrangement and rehearsal time. Whereas most producers expected them to record a track in just one take, Yap would also allow for up to three or four recorded takes, enabling them to keep reaching for perfection. He figured he needed to allow them to relax and express themselves if he was to get the best out them. This he did by providing an ample supply of ganja to smoke in the studio and by holding late night sessions after they had finished their day's work jobbing around various studios. Allowing The Skatalites to let off steam in this way resulted in some of their most inspired and highly charged recordings. One epic 18-hour all night session with Yap at the controls makes up the best part of their Top Deck LP *Ska-Boo-Da-Ba.* Recorded in late 1964, shortly before the calamitously abrupt end of his career, it represents some of Don Drummond's very last and finest works.

Stills from the July 31, 1965 parade

The group disintegrated soon after Don Drummond's breakdown and subsequent incarceration for murder in Bellevue Mental Hospital. They did continue for some months without him, but without the brilliance of his composition it would never be the same. By mid-1965 the band had split into two camps, each going to work for different studios. Roland Alphonso and Jackie Mittoo formed The Soul Brothers, working mostly for Studio One, later becoming The Soul Vendors. Tommy McCook and The Supersonics formed to play primarily at Duke Reid's Treasure Isle Studio on Bond Street. Both of these outfits oversaw the evolution from ska into the more relaxed rocksteady style, both with equally as prolific outputs as they had in The Skatalites, giving further credence to that T-shirt slogan, *It All Began With The Skatalites*. Horns would now become less dominant in the music and work was harder to find, causing some of the original members to seek opportunities overseas. The curtain was closed on the first chapter in The Skatalites history. To their minds it must have seemed like a fading memory, a glorious moment in time that would never be repeated. Their legacy, however, was too great to be forever put to rest.

A group of six original Skatalites members, along with jazz guitar maestro Ernest Ranglin, mystic melodica pioneer Augustus Pablo and reggae guitar wizard Earl 'Chinna' Smith were in 1975 brought together by original double bassist Lloyd Brevett, aided by Jackie Mittoo, for the very first loose regrouping of The Skatalites. Lloyd Knibb's trademark ska drumming was replaced by the contemporary reggae rhythms of both Horsemouth Wallace and Benbow Creary. They set about recording an album's worth of tunes in a roots reggae style with a heavy emphasis on the kind of Nyabinghi and Burru percussion Brevett had absorbed since he was a young man in all night marathon drumming and chanting sessions called Groundations, up at the Rasta camps in the hills above Kingston, like Wareika Hill and Bull Bay. As a radical departure, the set included a flute-led slice of raw percussive funk

TOGETHER AGAIN: The three former Skatalites saxophonists, from left to right: Roland Alphanso, Lester Sterling and Tommy McCook caught during their appearance at the Swing Magazine's "People's Ball" Wednesday night at the National Arena, Wednesday night.

The Skatalites reformed

Daily Gleaner, January 3, 1976

called 'Fugitive.' Produced by Brevett and mixed by King Tubby, the LP has been released variously as The Legendary Skatalites, *African Roots* and *Rebirth.* A King Tubby dub mix of the LP was released, *Heroes of Reggae In Dub* which may possibly be the only ever dub album to feature upright acoustic bass, providing a deeply funky, organic groove throughout the entire record.

The Skatalites would not play together again until 1983, when the full original line-up briefly came together (minus Drummond) for a show at Reggae Sunsplash in Montego Bay. They played a gig in Herbie Miller's Blue Monk Jazz Gallery as a warm up for Sunsplash which was recorded for posterity as *Stretching Out.* Originally only released on cassette, this live LP is as close as it gets to hearing The Skatalites live in their 1960s heyday. The band deliver a frenzied and hyperactive set, playing like their very lives depend on it. Perhaps it was the indoor club environment that fired them up, because the live album resulting from the Reggae Sunsplash show is an altogether more laid-back affair. This could be in part due to the absence of the band's engine house, in the form of drummer Lloyd Knibb. The Sunsplash date clashed with a live residency Knibb held in a hotel band, regular paid work which he was unwilling to forgo, so drum duties were filled in by Roland Alphonso's son Noel.

The Skatalites recorded two albums during this period. The first, *Rolling Steady* was recorded at Music Mountain Studio, funded by producer Tony Owens who had just scored a UK number one with his protégés Musical Youth and had money to invest. The album did not initially make it to the release stage. Allegedly, a disgruntled Jackie Mittoo made off with the masters. These tapes would eventually emerge two decades later, deteriorated almost beyond repair. Through painstaking digital restoration work by London-based Motion Records the nine tracks were brought back up to an acceptable standard. Motion released it in 2007, much to the delight of Skatalites fans worldwide. These introspective, meditative ska and rocksteady workouts provide a snapshot of a moment in time that would never be repeated—the very last studio recording with all living members present and correct. After Sunsplash the band played with Prince Buster at south London's own Reggae Sunsplash at a packed Crystal Palace football stadium. A year later they recorded the sublime *Return of the Big Guns*, a one-off album for Island. Mittoo and Moore did not appear on this record as they had quit due to disagreements with Tommy McCook—ironic since they were the two who had actually reunited the band. Island Records boss Chris Blackwell saw huge potential in the born-again Skatalites and wanted them to be part of what was happening with his studio Compass Point down in Nassau, Bahamas. 'Island offered them a salary and a whole huge big deal, which they ended up turning down,' recounts manager Ken Stewart. 'For whatever reason, they said no. To me that was the biggest mistake the band ever made. Bob Marley had just passed away, Chris Blackwell had just signed U2. The Compass Point thing was happening in a big way with Grace Jones, Sly and

Robbie. It would have been perfect timing to get those guys to Nassau into that studio. God knows what they would have ended up playing on. But none of it happened, they never went to Nassau, they recorded it in Jamaica and the whole thing was lackluster.' Due to internal disagreements and old resentments resurfacing the group soon disbanded and did not reconvene for another three years. Tommy McCook attempted to start his own band called The Skatalites featuring a bunch of New York-based Jamaican musicians but when he attempted to get a record deal with US reggae label Heartbeat, they showed no interest unless there were more original Skatalites involved. It was at this point that McCook got back in touch with Brevett and Knibb and arranged for them to come to New York. Lester Sterling and Roland Alphonso were already living in New York, which made five. According to Lester Sterling, McCook reached out to him with the notion to reform. 'Tommy McCook called me later and asked, "Where are you based?" "New York", I said. So he finally came down and we played together.' Having the original rhythm section of Knibb and Brevett made it much easier to create authentic sounding ska. They started gigging in New York with a week's residency at renowned jazz venue the Village Gate. Jackie Mittoo also appeared at these shows but would be so drunk on stage it was detrimental to both the band's sound and their credibility. His favorite stunt was to tear off his socks and shoes, throw them across the stage over the heads of the horn players and proceed to play his keyboard with his bare feet. If he hadn't have been so drunk he may have carried it off, but according to Ken Stewart it was excruciating to watch and did not do the band any favours with the cool Village Gate crowd and at a time when they were trying to re-establish themselves as a credible live act.

This New York based version of The Skatalites heralded the beginnings of their bid to finally take the ska they had originated to the wider world. Ken Stewart was invited to become The Skatalites' manager at this time as well as play keyboards. He says that ever since his becoming involved, Alpha Boys' School was always close to their hearts. 'It came up all time,' he says. On the first ever Skatalites tour supporting Bunny Wailer in 1989, Dizzy and Lester could often be found reminiscing about Alpha on the tour bus. Later on there would be new additions to the band from the ranks of Alpha. 'When Cedric joined the band there was a lot more conversation about Alpha. Then when Karl Bryan came into the band and Vin Gordon at the same time we had a lot more Alpha stories then too.'

The Skatalites hit the road and enthralled audiences all across the US, Europe and Japan, often with 'third wave' ska bands in support. Few people had actually witnessed the full force of a live Skatalites show before and their reputation as a formidable stage act quickly grew. That this mythical band from a bygone age could have arisen like a phoenix from the ashes as a fully operational touring concern was almost too good to be true. There was a palpable sense of witnessing some kind of messianic second coming. Many ska-punk bands began incorporating horns and generally got more jazzy as a result of their encounter with the real-deal be-bop jazz-ska. A run of three acclaimed studio albums for the Shanachie label was recorded, between 1993 and 1996: *Ska Voovie*, *Hi-Bop Ska* and *Greetings from Skamania.* The latter two of these were both nominated for Grammys. Their thirtieth anniversary album *Hi-Bop Ska* featured a host of special guests including Toots and the Maytals, Prince Buster, Jamaican jazz pianist Monty Alexander and Art Ensemble of Chicago trumpeter Lester Bowie. Tommy McCook stepped away from the band in 1997 due to ill health. Lester Sterling was invited back into the fold, keeping the torch alive for the Alpharian influence. The new line-up recorded the *Ball Of Fire* LP for Island's brief subsidiary label Island Jamaica Jazz, yet another highly polished and accomplished album. Whilst the high musicianship on these latter-day Skatalites records was undisputed, many fans did feel that the crisp, clean sound arising from both modern recording techniques and the compact disc format meant that the kind of rough-and-ready urgency evoked by their earlier recordings was lacking on these newer recordings. The inherent charm of three minutes of mayhem recorded in just one take with rudimentary equipment had given way to something more refined, mature and professional at the expense of one of the key ingredients to their magic: that raw, rough, backstreet sound. Which is not to say that there isn't listening and dancing pleasure to be had, it's just that for many die-hard fans it was something of an adjustment, and not everyone was fully on board. Also, much of the new material was played at a relentlessly fast pace, whereas their two 1980s albums had showcased a slower, more contemplative ska-reggae fusion sound, allowing Knibb and Brevett to really prove their worth as a rhythm section. According to manager Ken Stewart there were two major reasons for this. 'First of all you had a Skatalites that had been performing with every third-wave ska band in the United States.' Being supported on tours by bands who played at 100 miles an hour meant that to follow on as the next act, The Skatalites had to keep the audience jumping. 'Most of those kids were playing super-fast punked-out stuff and Tommy felt they should pick up the pace to keep up, but I was always against it, I would say, "no that's supposed to be the difference between us and them, man! We're the original, they're the copy, c'mon!"' The other reason for the frenzied speed was to do with McCook's health. 'Also, McCook had motivation to keep playing fast because of his emphysema,' says Stewart. Having breathing problems actually meant it was harder to play slow than fast. 'Because if the songs played faster, that's less time he had to hold a note. His breathing was definitely becoming an issue.' Being at the heart of the new ska scene across America and also Japan, meant as older musicians and originators of the sound, they became mentors to many of the younger players. Rather than taking an aloof kind of stance towards their young emulators, they would openly share their musical wisdom and would always make themselves available to whoever would be supporting them on a tour. 'They had plenty to do with the success of that scene,' explains Stewart. 'They were so accessible and so open and personable. You could ask them anything and you immediately found out that you could sit there and talk to Roland Alphonso about what reed he used or what horn he used to use, you know, all kinds of musical tips, knowledge, they were quite open to sharing all of that. And they would be right there in the dressing room, usually fairly early for a sound check and they would be sitting chilling and smoking herb. You know, all those kind of relationships and ways to bond with them were right there, readily available and they were quite open to it.'

1998 was a watershed year, in which Tommy McCook and Roland Alphonso both died within six months of each other. Two immense talents and stage presences at the heart of The Skatalites were now gone forever. The void was filled by Alpharian Cedric 'IM' Brooks whose immense talent and experience made him the perfect person to step into Alphonso's place. The band recorded the *Bakasha* album in 2000 with a return to the far-eastern, gyspy-esque sound on many of the tracks. A performance at Glastonbury festival in 2003 was featured in British director Julian Temple's 2006 documentary on the history of Glastonbury.

The Skatalites

After Cedric Brooks left due to ill health, Karl 'Cannonball' Bryan stepped in and not long after Vin Gordon would also do an extended stint in The Skatalites fold, further consolidating their status as an Alpharian band. Through sheer determination and against all odds, The Skatalites managed to conquer the world with ska. There are now Skatalites-style instrumental ska band in cities and towns all over the world. A band led by their long-time manager and keyboardist Ken Stewart calling itself The Skatalites still continues to tour and record, albeit with no original members in the line-up other than singer Doreen Shaffer. Throughout the band's 50-year history, there were always at least two Alpharians in the band keeping that connection going, but now there are none. The 2016 album, *Platinum Ska* features two lesser-known but important reggae musicians, drummer Trevor 'Sparrow' Thompson and bassist Val Douglas who have played together since they were youths in the 1960s. Some feel that The Skatalites brand name should be returned to its country of origin to showcase a new generation of both Alpha players and other Jamaican jazz virtuosos. But with a top-drawer line-up that plays with obsessive reverence to its forebears and with audiences worldwide still demanding to hear the authentic sound of ska, The Skatalites looks to be continuing on its global odyssey for a few years yet.

--A.R.

"Deadly" Headley Bennett

Standing in the studio in the back of an ice cream parlor at 135 Orange Street in 1962, Headley Bennett pulled his alto saxophone from its case, wetted the thin reed, and got ready to blow. There was no way Bennett, nor producer Leslie Kong, nor Bob Marley himself, could have foreseen the messianic rise that this song would set into motion. That sax solo performed by "Deadly" Headley Bennett, as he would come to be known, was Deadly indeed, helping to launch the career of Bob Marley on one of his very first songs, "Judge Not," just as Bennett did for countless other artists over the course of his long musical career. But Bennett was more than a mere backup instrumentalist—he was a musician in his own right.

Headley George Bennett was born in 1931. His father was an accountant but died when Bennett was just four years old. His mother was a store clerk and sent her son to Alpha at the age of five so he could have a Catholic upbringing. "I went to Alpha at the age of five year old and went to the age of 17. My father died at the age of 24 and my mother got pregnant at the age of 17 and he told her he would like me to go to Alpha, to grow up in Alpha. He wanted me to have a Roman Catholic education and thought Alpha would be the right place. When my mother was alone, she couldn't really look after me. She was too young to. So it was kind of rough," he says. He had a liking for music before he ever came to Alpha though. Bennett told Steve Barrow in an interview in the mid-1990s that his family introduced him to music. "We used to go to garden parties and she used to dance with me. I never forget that. My mother teach me to dance. So I would be motivated from very early. And my grandpeople, they were Pocomanian and they used to lick the drums and tings," he says. Though this African-based spirituality, Pocomania, was contradictory in many ways with the Catholic upbringing he had at Alpha, as Bennett says, it was an introduction to music.

While at Alpha, Bennett was able to further develop his love for music although it did take a few years. He says, "When I was around 7 or 8 years old I found myself humming a lot of American pop music. I went to join the band at the age of 10 year old and the bandmaster, which was a man named Sir Tulloch, said I'm too young, I have to come back. I went back when I was 14 years old and they said that was the right time for me to learn the music. They gave me the clarinet and said make a note and I make a wonderful sound and they said that is your instrument, you sound very good in it. That was a man named Reuben Delgado." Bennett says he began his tenure with the band by bringing instruments to the older boys, carrying their music stands, learning by observing and listening.

The Alpha band provided Bennett with a solid foundation that allowed him to gain employment after graduation. "Alpha is like a musical university in Jamaica. They teach you to read it, they teach you to write it, and they tell you what it mean. You grow up on European classical music, Beethoven, Tchaikovsky, Brahms, Mozart. At Alpha we used to play all of them guys' music," he says." Bennett left Alpha in 1950 at the age of 15 and after working in photography for two years, he returned to music, switching instruments, from the clarinet to the alto saxophone. "When I was at Alpha they teach me the clarinet. But when I leave Alpha and go out into the new world, I went and saved my money and buy an instrument. I teach myself the saxophone, which is a family of the clarinet, and from there I never turn back. When I joined Alpha band we used to play classical music. After you leave Alpha as a classical musician, you have to learn to play pop music in Jamaica before you can get a little work. You have to read the music." Bennett worked for two years with Tony Brown & His Orchestra and then he found work with one of the top bands in Jamaica. "I get involved with a band by the name of Eric Deans Orchestra and he used to come at Alpha. I was lucky enough. He

Headley Bennett
Stills from Steve Barrow's interview in the mid-1990s for Palm Pictures

has a contract to play at some of the hotels. I did love that because I could get a weekly salary," Bennett says. He performed at the clubs in the hotels on the north coast, but then he returned to Kingston where the music scene had changed from the jazz standards to ska. He says, "After a while I have to come back to town. When I came to town, someone says to me the music changed. It's not the pop music no more, it's something called ska. You have to learn it. I listen for about three months and what I learn is that at Alpha, ska music has something to do with the American military music, the beat. American march music. So when I change to the ska, they hire me because I really have the beat in me and the music was invented by the people in Alpha, people like Tommy McCook, Don Drummond, Rico Rodriguez, Edward Tan Tan, so it was like a family. I used to love it. We went from the American rhythm and blues type music, to the Jamaican style, which was the ska. The march, band music, is the upbeat, you know? And the ska is the upbeat, yeah mon. You have to feel it. It's not learned. You have to hear the beat and know what to do with the beat and the rhythm. The opportunity we got at Alpha is we would play a lot of this American march music, so when ska beat came it wasn't far, it was near to this style. It's ska."

Bennett in 2007

Headley Bennett
Jamaica Gleaner, August 26, 2016

After working in a number of the local clubs, Bennett, like most other musicians during this time, began recording ska as the industry took over. He started recording for Duke Reid as a member of the Drumbago All Stars. "The first tune I record was for Duke Reid, a tune called 'Joy Ride,' and I don't know if he put out that music on 45, I think they do some dub plate. When I do that recording for him, I never hear it again," he says. He also performed in a group called the Mercy Mercy Boys with Lloyd Delpratt, Lloyd Williams, and Roy Panton; and was a member of the Soul Vendors with fellow Alpharians Jackie Mittoo, Vin Gordon, Lester Sterling, Rico Rodriguez, David Madden, Tommy McCook, Johnny "Dizzy" Moore, and Leroy "Horsemouth" Wallace, among other non-Alpharians like Roland Alphonso. In 1962, Bennett was a member of The Sheiks with Lynn Taitt, Bobby Gaynair, and Jackie Mittoo and together they performed at the Palisadoes Airport for Princess Margaret when she visited the country for the independence ceremonies. The day of the ceremonies, on August 6th, Bennett performed the song "Independence," recorded for Studio One.

It was this same year that Bennett performed the solo on Derrick Morgan's "Forward March," causing a misunderstanding, and resulting song war, with Prince Buster. Also in 1962 for Beverley's, Bennett performed on Bob Marley's first song, "Judge Not," a song that has gone down in the annals of history. He says he also performed on "One Cup of Coffee" during these pioneering sessions and he thanks Alpha for giving him the foundation. He explains, "Bob knew music, he was a real composer and know what he want, and with the Alpha Boys it was easy for him to impart what he want. When you were working with Bob, and Bob take the guitar and hum out the lyrics and he tell you to hum out the part you want the horns to play, it was easy for us."

Bennett in 1985

Bennett also performed on Bob Andy's hit "I've Got to Go Back Home," along with trumpeter Bobby Ellis and the Wailers—Bunny, Peter Tosh, and Constantine "Vision" Walker, at Studio One. He performed the solo on Delroy Wilson's "Dancing Mood," a number one hit for Studio One that today is considered one of the great classic songs of this era. Additionally, Bennett blew sax on the Abyssinians' classic song, "Satta-A-Massagana," considered an anthem in roots reggae. Other notable tracks include "Honor Your Mother and Father" for Desmond Dekker, and "Man in the Street" and "Eastern Standard Time" for Don Drummond. Bennett says of the latter, "My part was saxophone. I remember the lick man. That was a classic man."

In 1969, Bennett relocated to Canada where he lived for eight years, though he would travel back to Kingston to record. He says that it was during this time that he acquired his nickname, "Deadly." Bennett recalls, "I went to Canada from 1969 to 1977. Sly and Robbie just start recording. They heard about me and they were doing an album at Channel One. They put me on some tracks, some solos on some tracks. One special track I start to lick and one of them bawl out, 'Deadly!' Percussionist Sticky bawl out, 'That sound Deadly! That was a Deadly sound man,' and the name stuck. And they said 'Deadly Headley. That is your name now.'"

Headley Bennett in 1983
Photo courtesy Beth Lesser

In 1977, Bennett returned to Jamaica and continued to perform and record with such groups as the Roots Radics, the Mighty Diamonds on "Pass the Koutchie," and for Gregory Isaacs. He also recorded his own albums, *Poolside Reggae*, *Victory*, and *35 Years from Alpha.* The latter album was recorded for Adrian Sherwood's On-U Sound label and features two vocal contributions from Bim Sherman. In October, 2005, Headley Bennett was awarded the Order of Distinction, Jamaica's highest honor, for his contribution to Jamaican music. But, like most of the Jamaican musicians of this era, Bennett never was able to earn royalties off of his music and so in 2013, an article in the *Jamaica Gleaner* revealed that Bennett was in need of assistancc with his mcdical bills. Music producer Clive Pringle who organized a fundraising concert for Bennett observed, "This man is a part of Bob Marley's success." Bennett says he is thankful for the life that Alpha provided him in music. "I have nothing to regret, you know? I love it. I feel good about it. Financially it's not that strong, but I thank God for the strength." Bennett passed away on August 21, 2016 at the age of 85.

--H.A.

Headley Bennett working for London based experimental reggae producer Adrian Sherwood's On-U Sound label, probably taken in 1982, the year he recorded his solo LP *35 Years From Alpha* for the label.
Photo courtesy Kishi Yamamoto

Headley Bennett in a break from rehearsals for the London Alpha Boys reunion show, 2007
Photo by Adam Reeves

Edward 'Tan Tan' Thornton

In a converted garage studio in Acton, West London, Eddie 'Tan Tan' Thornton scans his memory then attempts to recite a tune he hasn't played in a long, long while. After several decent tries he almost nails it, then puts his trumpet aside as the precise musical phrasing eludes him. It's been over 45 years since the recording session, so the effervescent octogenarian can be forgiven for being a bit rusty. The tune in question is The Beatles' 'Got To Get You Into My Life' which sits midway on side two of their 1966 *Revolver* LP. It is the only ever Beatles record to give a credit to a session player—not even Eric Clapton or Billy Preston were acknowledged for their contributions—but there on the back of *Revolver* is Edward Thornton's name. The man universally known as Tan Tan seems relatively unfussed about having played on one of the standout tracks on one of the greatest albums of all time. How a poor barefoot kid from the slums of Spanish Town landed in the epicenter of 1960s swinging London and became the 'go-to guy' for trumpet is a story of uncanny timing and sheer youthful determination.

Born in 1932, he entered Alpha relatively late. 'If mi father lived for three more months I wouldn't be here, I'd 'a been too old to go 'a Alpha,' says Tan Tan philosophically. Just three months before his 14th birthday his alcoholic father suddenly passed away, leaving his mother to cope alone. At the recommendation of the local police department he was placed in the care of the nuns at Alpha where an entirely different life path for him unfolded. The cut-off age for joining Alpha was 14, so this unfortunate turn of events in his life would not have had such a remarkable outcome had his father passed away any later. 'I could be a murderer or a t'ief,' muses Tan Tan on what might have happened. 'I was a barefoot kid, I never know what shoes is until I reach Alpha at 13. I never even know mi size a' shoe.'

As he settled in at Alpha, Thornton would secretly sneak off to visit his father's grave. It was on one of these clandestine outings that he was picked up by his aunt who mistakenly accused him of running away when in fact he had every intention of returning later that day. She carted him back to Alpha and made well sure that the nuns knew of his absence-without-leave. Again, this would have a life-changing impact as it drew him to the attention of Sister Ignatius, who promptly took him under her wing. They forged a close bond that would last almost 60 years, right up to her death. 'I love her man, she become like mi mother.' His love and respect for Sister Ignatius had a stabilising influence on him and he tried hard to stay in her good books.

'I was Sister Ignatius pet. Because I always try and please. She was always going in the church to pray and I was always going in there when she pray. Instead of playing in the playground, I always go in the church to pray with Sister Ignatius.' Being unable to read or write, he was assisted by Sister Ignatius to catch up with his literacy and improve his English.

Tan Tan performing in February 2016
Photo courtesy Derek D'Souza

Another life changing event occurred in the school carpentry workshop. Thornton holds his hand in the air and points to a faded scar. 'This is what get me a' play music. For some reason, they put me in cabinet making. And I'm sawing a board and get this. They stitch it up. Sister say to me, 'What you like to do?' And I say music.' The band at that time was full up, but Thornton's persistence soon led to a position on tuba, an instrument no other boys cared to learn. After a few agonizing weeks his lips could take no more and out of sympathy bandmaster Reuben Delgado allowed him to try out the trumpet. Despite having to learn on a damaged instrument, Thornton seized the moment and put the hours of study in, practising late at night in the dormitory. 'I learn music in three months. The guy that teach me, I soon pass him. I was better than him.'

Despite Alpha's tough discipline, Thornton thrived. He cracks up laughing remembering being forced to march barefoot over thorny brambles at the crack of dawn by ex-soldier Sergeant Harrison. But Thornton thrived on the simplicity of the routine. 'To me, Alpha is like heaven. You get up, you eat, you play music, you eat, you play music,' he says fondly. 'Alpha is the most inspirational place for me. The discipline and respect and everything.'

Being Sister Ignatius' pet had other advantages, which would also play a hand in Thornton's musical trajectory, including being given the unlikely role of being her personal shopper. Her brother ran a store on King Street, to which she used to send Thornton on a regular errand to pick up a pair of shoes. 'In 1949 she used to send me down to Mr Davies' store every month to fetch her a pair of loafers.' On his way he would always pass bandleader Sonny Bradshaw's record store, which would be packed with people, inside and on the street, listening to the be-bop jazz sounds that would shape his future. 'I always pass there. And I always see people out there listening and I wanna hear a' wha' them listen. And there I hear JJ Johnson and Dizzy Gillespie and Charlie Parker and Louis Jordan.' To this day, Thornton still only wears loafers.

Besides the heady new jazz sounds, it was the classical repertoire that would forever be ingrained in Thornton. 'Classical music, we used to play Beethoven, Mozart and Bach. Mr Delgado used to play in the Jamaica Military Band, that's where he get all the arrangements. Even now, I listen to classical music every day.'

While at Alpha, Thornton played in Alpha's semi-pro jazz band, doing little gigs for pocket money around Kingston and sometimes further afield. One time they got paid handsomely for playing at a US military base so Thornton gave the money to Sister Ignatius for safe keeping. Over time he would keep adding to it so by the time he left there was a tidy sum waiting for him. 'Sister keep it for me, and when I leave school, there's about a hundred odd quid—that's a lot of money! Buy me a trumpet, give me mother some, make me feel good. Buy a Raleigh bicycle and a cream suit and all the chicks see mi sharp-up.' Thornton would stay on living at Alpha until he was almost twenty, making him the oldest boy ever in the school's history, although the reason why is unclear. Yet again a twist of fate would shape Thornton's destiny. Sister Ignatius helped him get his papers in order to emigrate to America but the political climate against immigrants from the Caribbean did not work in his favour and his plans were dashed by a new legislation. 'President Truman bring in a bill that only allow a certain amount of Jamaican to come to America. But then if I did go to America maybe I wouldn't even be playing music. Maybe I'd be working in McDonald's or KFC or a car wash.'

After serving time with the dance bands of Kingston such as Bradshaw's, Dean's and others, Thornton decided to follow in the footsteps of his girlfriend who had gone to find work in the UK. 'When I come to

Trumpeter Eddie 'Tan Tan' Thornton, second on left, next to Alpharian and friend Don Drummond on trombone at the Colony Club, 1951

England, everything just go BOOM!' During the late 1950s he would travel over to Germany to work in dance bands, but it was in the early 1960s that Thornton would find himself in the centre of an elite group of musical friends. The most happening place in London was The Flamingo on Soho's Wardour Street, where one of Britain's first Jamaican sound systems had been installed by the great Count Suckle and was a hangout for mods, beatniks, jazzers and anybody remotely cool. It was here that Thornton was invited one night by a musician friend to 'come and have a blow,' and he sent the crowd into a frenzy. Once word of his talents spread through the scene, Thornton became the main man for trumpet in London. 'From there it's history. Everybody want me a come play with them.' Georgie Fame and the Blue Flames snapped him up into what would be a four year residency at The Flamingo. He played on many of Fame's hits like 'Yeah Yeah' and 'Getaway.' 'We was the best R&B band in England. Our band had three number ones, our album go number one. I never make no money, but I always happy. And I was the first guy from Alpha to get on radio and television.'

Tan Tan in August 2016

Photo courtesy Natty Bo

Thornton was part of circle of musicians who would all go on to conquer the world, hanging out together in hip joints like Blaises, The Marquee and The Roaring Twenties. 'So while I go to all these different clubs I always see them, John, Paul and Ringo, George Harrison. It was a kind of raving time, we all in a circle, with Jeff Beck, Eric Clapton, Rod Stewart, Tom Jones and all dem. Then they get so big that you don't see them no more.' The Small Faces clearly liked him enough to dedicate a song to him, 'Eddie's Dreaming.' Throughout the 1960s Thornton recorded with The Beatles, The Animals, The Rolling Stones, Jimi Hendrix, The Small Faces, Sandie Shaw and Paul Butterfield Blues Band. He helped form the backing for a Tamla Motown package tour of the UK featuring Stevie Wonder and Smokey Robinson.

During 1966 Thornton played a little hand in shaping rock history. Georgie Fame had recently disbanded The Blue Flames and the band's former drummer Mitch Mitchell was sharing a flat with Thornton in Knightsbridge, awaiting his next musical opportunity. The Animals had also recently broken up and their bass player, Thornton's friend Chas Chandler, had just returned from a trip to America, bringing with him a talented young guitarist, the then unknown Jimi Hendrix. Although he had little success so far in America, Chandler was certain London would be ready for Hendrix and he started auditioning for a band. Thornton took Hendrix under his wing and began introducing him on the scene in London while Hendrix searched for the right players to create his sound. 'I was the first guy to know Jimi in London. We used to walk up to Piccadilly from where we live in Knightsbridge.' Thornton suggested to Hendrix that Mitchell might be a good fit for his new band, the Jimi Hendrix Experience. 'Mi is the one who introduce him to Jimi fe get that job. When Georgie mash up the band it was like a blessing, he just get the job and from then he never looked back. The next time I see Mitch was in Brixton after Jimi dead.' Thornton says that he did record some session work with Hendrix at Olympic Studios in Barnes which never saw light of day.

Tan Tan in January 2017
Photo courtesy Natty Bo

Thornton's connection to Alpha and especially Sister Ignatius remained strong throughout these years. He would always write to her and tell her what was happening. 'I been writing to her from 1954.' When his mother passed away Georgie Fame loaned him the money for a fare home. On arrival in Jamaica he didn't have the money to pay for a funeral. 'When my mother die, Sister Ignatius lend me the money to bury my mother. She say, "Edward, you must get it back. But don't say nuttin' to Sister Martress."

As the 1970s rolled around, Thornton found work with The Roy Young Band and Boney M. He became part of UK roots reggae band Aswad's horn section alongside Alpharian Vin Gordon. He also played with King Sounds and The Israelites on the London reggae scene and joined Bunny Wailer on a 1984 tour of the US and Japan. In 1985 he released his first solo LP *Musical Nostalgia For Today*, a jazzy blend of Jamaican flavours. He has worked with numerous reggae artists including Bob Marley, Barrington Levy, Sugar Minott, Dennis Brown, Misty in Roots, Levi Roots, Frankie Paul and UK pop reggae stars Amazulu. Moving on into the 1990s and Thornton joined Jools Holland's Rhythm and Blues Orchestra and was an early member of Jazz Jamaica. He worked around the London ska scene with The Trojans, The Top Cats, Ska Cubano and Freetown. During the 2000s Tan Tan worked with dub producer Ryan Moore of Twilight Circus, Lily Allen, Super Furry Animals and industrial funk legends 23 Skidoo. At the time of writing he is touring the world well into his 80s with retro siblings Kitty, Daisy and Lewis playing Western swing and old time rock and roll. He is an irrepressible force of nature showing no sign of slowing down. 'I am very grateful to The Father for everything,' he says. 'Coming from nowhere, I'm very grateful. Travelling around the world three times—my passport is full up! And it's all because of Alpha!' --A.R.

Tan Tan and Rico
Photo courtesy Derek D'Souza

Tan Tan performing with Kitty, Daisy, and Lewis

Photos courtscy Derek D'Souza

Bobby Ellis

Sitting in the music room at Alpha, Bobby Ellis ruminates about his choice of instrument that he made in this very room over sixty years ago. Even after six decades Ellis still regrets settling on the trumpet. 'I never make the right choice. My teeth, familywise is as thin as chalk. In Jamaica I am the only trumpeter that have top and bottom plate and still blowing. I don't have a single one of my own teeth in me head! I'm not supposed to be blowing a trumpet.' It's remarkable that Ellis is able to blow a single note with two rows of false teeth, but one look at the credits on any vintage reggae LP and chances are those crisp horn lines are being blown by Bobby Ellis on trumpet, alongside his fellow Alpharians Tommy McCook on sax and Vin Gordon on trombone, one of the most ubiquitous horn sections in all of reggae. Ellis and McCook were captured in action in an atmospheric sequence from the 1978 reggae movie *Rockers* as they blow their horns together with Herman Marquis and Alpharian Richard 'Dirty Harry' Hall.

Bobby Ellis in the hat with Tommy McCook to his left, Richard 'Dirty Harry' Hall far left, and Herman Marquis on right

A still from the movie Rockers, courtesy Blue Sun Film Co.

Bobby Ellis in the hat with Tommy McCook on far left, Richard 'Dirty Harry' Hall, and Herman Marquis on right
A still from the movie Rockers, courtesy Blue Sun Film Co.

Born on 2nd July 1932, Robert Ellis entered Alpha in 1941 and left aged 16 in 1948. Ellis witnessed the Alpha band while attending a garden party in Kingston's Winchester Park with his brother Percy and knew instantly that he wanted to join. The boys' father arranged for both brothers to enroll. Although Bobby was not especially troublesome, Percy was having some difficulties at home so on these grounds he was able to enroll, and simply to stay closer to his brother, Bobby was allowed to join also. On his family situation he says, 'I wouldn't say it was tough, just ordinary. But ya know sometimes when boys growing up they start to give trouble in certain ways.' Ellis remembers his elder brother Percy being upset the day their father delivered them to Alpha for the first time, however Bobby instinctively knew he'd arrived in the right place. 'My bigger brother, when mi father was leaving he start crying but though I am little it never matter to me. I just shrug and say, "well, this is where I am going to be for a few years." At the time I was 9 years of age. So I have to make my own start and let miself be somebody.'

Ellis joined the band and was placed under the tutelage of senior trumpet pupil Raymond Harper—whose own distinct sound would later be heard with the Carib Beats and on numerous Prince Buster recordings. Ellis became swept up with music and quickly saw the potential for opening doors into new life experiences. 'I really like to see places. See, I am a Kingstonian, most of us are Kingstonians and 'nuff of the time the band goes out to the country to play. So when you go a' country ya see wide open space and ya enjoy yourself.' Later on music would be Ellis' key to seeing the wider world. 'Music carry me to places that I only used to read about in book or hear on the news.'

Bobby Ellis

A still from the movie Rockers, courtesy Blue Sun Film Co.

Ellis graduated from Alpha as both a musician and a printer but found work in the following years in a bus building plant at Rose Garden. Like so many Alpha Boys, the price of buying one's own instrument was out of reach, so music would have to wait. Ellis is proud of the time he spent at the manufacturing plant especially as the wages were far more reliable than what he would later make as a musician. 'It was six to eight years sitting around before I could buy an instrument and rejuvenate meself and start playing again.' The ska era was just around the corner and Ellis initially played with dance bands such as Val Bennett's and the Tony Brown Orchestra. Speaking to Peter-I at *Reggae Vibes Magazine*, Ellis recalls those dance band times, 'Right, it was mostly foxtrot, and you know swing, and we used to play some bolero and t'ings like that. In Jamaica, especially in those times, you had to play all various types of music. You had to play our mento, or calypso, or what you want to call it. And what you had was to play ballads, right, and play waltz—everything. You have to be well rounded, have a repertoire of all the various type of music. That's what you had, y'know, was to do all the time. So when you go into the dancehall to play, you have to play to suit everybody likeness.' Although Ellis and the musicians around him were getting fired up listening to new be-bop innovations of Charlie Parker, Miles Davis, Clifford Brown and Dizzy Gillespie, it wasn't possible to play anything at all challenging to the audiences in the hotels and dancehalls around Kingston since promoters were far too conservative. They literally would have been out of a job if they attempted it, as Ellis explained to *Reggae Vibes Magazine*, 'No, you wouldn't get any job, playing the progressive. But what we used to do, yunno, we used to kinda use the progressive stuff to broaden our t'ing deh. What we say now "broaden our knowledge of music," right, and it also help you to play. In other words the progressive stuff was the more harder music to play at the time, 'cause it take a lot of speed and all those t'ings. So when they start, when they playing the swing, it becomes more easier. Because we was practicin' mostly a harder t'ing than what you go out there and do in the dancehall, so that was the trend. Because we used to have a little thin, very thin book, with Dizzy Gillespie, "52nd Street (Theme)," "Dizzy Atmosphere," and all those tunes in it. We practice that as like a cheater, that was what it was there for, was being like a cheater. And the show, you start from like on the metronome, from that like you say, you start from 80 and from they get used to it they go up to probably 90, and then from 90 to a 100 and from 100 to a 105, until you reach 120. When you are doing it at 120 you are doing it like Dizzy Gillespie, that's how it used to do. And everybody used to try and have those likkle books, yu understan', and practice. So not only trumpeters but also saxophonists used to do it, and that's how we start develop.' When the new beat came around he says initially there was reluctance towards it among some of Kingston's musicians. 'When the ska come in, a lot of us, myself included, we turned our nose up at it.

Because that *uh-uh-uh* beat, we call it amateur. But it had something in it and after a while now, some of us start gravitating to it and start to feel it, while some of us never do.' It was backing The Mighty Vikings, who would later become Toots and The Maytals that the new ska craze really kicked off for Ellis when they were voted most popular Jamaican band of 1963.

The Mighty Vikings on JBC in 1963 with Bobby Ellis, second from right on trumpet, and Headley Bennett, first saxophone on right

Ellis would find his strength as a musical arranger and Alpha's extensive musical training enabled him to help compose horn arrangements and give musical direction in constructing many of ska's most loved tunes, most notably at Studio One. 'I think I was the first person Coxsone ever give an office as an arranger at 13 Brentford Road. Yeah, I think I was. I wouldn't say I'm the only one but I think I was among the first one to get that. And that's how it used to work. Jackie (Mittoo) did the riddim and I did the horn arrangements.' It was the Alpharian horn players like himself and Tommy McCook who were able to give the music the rhythmic structure that it needed, making it sound tighter, more polished and professional. Producers would want Alpha-trained musicians like Ellis in their sessions because they could help turn a simple song into something truly great. And by having a few top-notch players in a session, it would bring out the best in everyone. 'A lot of the other people who never come to Alpha never know music like we, so they never know how to measure out the music properly, ya understand? Eight bars or twelve bars or sixteen bars so that everything balance. They never know that,' Ellis explains. Many of the singers were coming to the studio for the first time and had no formal musical training so they had to quickly learn on the spot how to correctly time and phrase their singing to fit with the music. Ellis would encourage them to ride the song's rhythm so their vocal delivery could shine. The early ska recordings were made on the most rudimentary equipment, just single track tape with only a couple of microphones and no overdubs afterwards, so the arrangement would have to be spot-on. 'Because I also conduct guys in the studio and say "wait" and I know when to bring them in and most people now they know how to go with the riddim and get things proper.'

Bobby Ellis
Jamaica Gleaner, October 16, 2016

As for the hotly disputed subject of who actually invented ska, Ellis, like many others, points to one tune in particular that marked the turning point when Jamaican music found its own identity. Up until 1961 they had been imitating the sounds of American rhythm and blues, with varying degrees of success. Although much of what has been labeled JA boogie doesn't have the edge on the authentic rhythm and blues and some of it tends to plod rather than rock, hearing blues sung with distinct Jamaican patois has a certain compelling charm and in its day sent the dance crowds delirious. Ellis further compounds what many have claimed to be the turning point, when a slightly wonky shuffle beat became highlighted within the traditional twelve-bar blues structure, paving the way for the ska. 'The guy that really start that off-beat thing, Theophilus Beckford. Don't make nobody try to fool you! A lot of people try to claim it, but the tune that he did first and everybody really start gravitating was when he did the tune named "Easy Snappin."" A sparse, piano-led boogie shuffle, Beckford's 1960 'Easy Snappin" carries an infectious pulse throughout, which may not be as hard-driving as the later ska rhythms, but it points towards where the music would now go. There are many landmark records in Jamaica's musical evolution, but it could be argued that this one song carries the seed of what would later blossom into the reggae sound we know today. 'Easy Snappin" strips down the rhythm to simply *imply* it, leaving the dancer to fill in the blanks in their head and allow the feet to follow suit. 'The beat really coming from the boogie: *dumba-dumba-dumba-dumba*,' demonstrates Ellis phonetically, 'and we start, *dum-BA-dum-BA-dum-BA*.' This subtle difference of rhythmic syncopation was the very essence of ska.

When The Skatalites broke up in 1965, they formed two new groups, Tommy McCook and The Supersonics and The Soul Brothers headed by Roland Alphonso, the latter of which Ellis would join, shaping the sound of the late ska and early rocksteady period. He joined the other major rocksteady backing group Lynn Taitt and The Jets. During the 1970s he was in-house arranger and a trumpeter for roots producer Jack Ruby's studio band The Black Disciples, overseeing two of Burning Spear's greatest LPs for Island, *Marcus Garvey* and *Man in the Hills*.

The Black Disciples with Bobby Ellis on trumpet, third from left in back

Ellis is credited on hundreds of reggae LPs, including major works by Bob Marley, Burning Spear, Max Romeo, Prince Jammy, Johnny Clark,

Lee 'Scratch' Perry, Bunny Wailer, Augustus Pablo, Bim Sherman, John Holt, Gregory Isaacs and The Gladiators. He was recognized for his contribution by being awarded the Jamaican Order of Distinction in 2014. Bobby Ellis died on the 18th of October, 2016 in Kingston.

Despite never seeing much money from his output, Ellis is happy to have been at the heart of the action and to have shaped the history of reggae. 'I'm glad about taking music to be my carrier. It is tough but ya have to stick to what you love. The greatest thing is that you do thing that you love or like in life then life won't be a drag.'

--A.R.

Bobby Ellis in the band room at Alpha
Photo by Davis Coome

Don Drummond

The seats of the Carib Theatre were filled. The aisles, the walkways behind the seats, even the balconies and the foyer by the ticket booth were bursting with people. Outside the massive structure, in the parking lot, crowds nearly rioted with excitement, pushing for a chance to get inside to catch a glimpse of the exhibition. The iron fencing outside of the theater was bent by the feral multitude. Inside, under the heat of the spotlights, upon the wooden theater floor, Don Drummond strolled from the balcony to the stage, sauntering in his leather shoes, sharp suit, and hat tilted slightly to the back of his head. His trombone glistened, ripping from one note to the next with a strange combination of upbeat melancholy. Drummond wasn't blowing a tune like "Lady in Red," or "Full Moon and Empty Arms," or any other jazz standard as he had for seven years with other bands where he earned the right to perform at Jazz '57, a showcase of Jamaican musicians. This was his own composition, "The Message," and it drove the overflowing audience mad. They screamed, they called his name, some even wept. Don Drummond was a star.

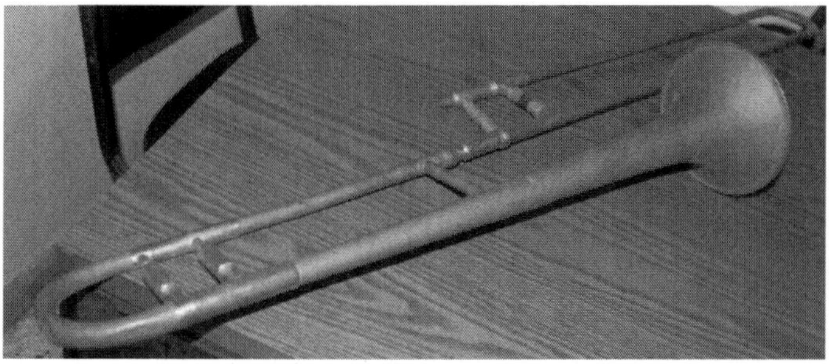

Don Drummond's trombone from his days at Alpha Boys' School

Photo by Heather Augustyn

When Donald Willis Drummond came to Alpha Boys' School on December 10, 1943, it was as a result of being sent there by the Resident Magistrate's Court for truancy. Drummond was born on March 12, 1934 to Uriah Adolphus Drummond and Doris Maud Munroe, but his father was never in Don's or Doris's life, and so Doris had to work as a domestic, cleaning homes for the wealthy. While she was away, young Don would play, roaming the streets, running through nearby yards. Consequently, he was sent to Alpha where Sister Mary Ignatius Davies became his second mother, since Doris was always close to her son.

Don Drummond entered Alpha Boys' School when he was nine years old and he was assigned to a number of different trades over the years including light domestic work, gardening, tailoring, and work in the tile factory. He was never very good at these "occupations," but it was his placement in the Alpha Boys Band where Don's record indicates that he was "very good." He was given a number of instruments to try before being assigned the trombone, including what was called a baby trumpet and a euphonium. Bandmaster Vincent Tulloch brought Don Drummond into the band and when he left in 1946, Reuben Delgado took over. Delgado recognized Don's talent and Delgado was a strict instructor, striking boys with his baton if a note was played incorrectly. Don didn't have to worry about such reprimands as he practiced incessantly instead of playing sports with the other boys. Many boys who attended school with Don during these years remember him, as if it were yesterday, practicing his trombone or reading sheet music during free time instead of playing cricket or football with the other boys. He practiced classical music, he practiced jazz music, and he performed with the band in front of dignitaries and for public events. He demonstrated incredible proficiency on the trombone, a difficult instrument to master, and even at his

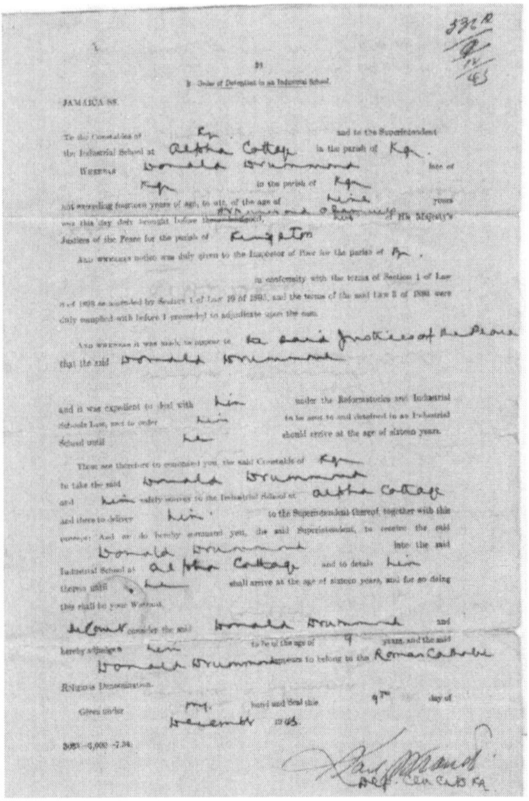

Order of Detention in an Industrial School.

JAMAICA SS.

To the Constables of Kgn and to the Superintendent the Industrial School at Alpha Cottage in the parish of Kgn.

Whereas Donald Drummond late of Kgn in the parish of Kgn not exceeding fourteen years of age, to wit, of the age of nine years was this day duly brought before [illegible] of His Majesty's Justices of the Peace for the parish of Kingston

And whereas notice was duly given to the Inspector of Poor for the parish of Kgn.

in conformity with the terms of Section 1 of Law [illegible] and the terms of the said Law [illegible] were duly complied with before I proceeded to adjudicate upon the case.

And whereas it was made to appear to the said Justices of the Peace that the said Donald Drummond [illegible]

and it was expedient to deal with him under the Reformatories and Industrial Schools Law, and to order him to be sent to and detained in an Industrial School until he should arrive at the age of sixteen years.

These are therefore to command you, the said Constable of Kgn to take the said Donald Drummond and him safely convey to the Industrial School at Alpha Cottage and there to deliver him to the Superintendent thereof, together with this precept: And we do hereby command you, the said Superintendent, to receive the said Donald Drummond into the said Industrial School at Alpha Cottage and to detain him therein until he shall arrive at the age of sixteen years, and for so doing this shall be your Warrant.

The Court consider the said Donald Drummond and hereby adjudge him to be of the age of 9 years, and the said Donald Drummond appears to belong to the Roman Catholic Religious Denomination.

Given under my hand and Seal this 9th day of December 1945.

[illegible]

Don Drummond's order of detention to Alpha.

Courtesy Alpha Boys' School

young age during his school years, Don Drummond began to compose his own music.

Sister Ignatius had a vision for all of her boys, that they would learn a trade and upon graduation be able to secure a job to earn a living. With Don Drummond, her vision was no different, although it was perhaps even stronger, given his unusual skill and talent. And so when the biggest bandleaders in Kingston came knocking on Alpha's door looking to recruit

Don Drummond, far right, with the Eric Deans Orchestra, January, 1951. Deans is second from left, Ernest Ranglin seated right of Deans, Vincent Hamilton bass, Rueben Alexander seated sax on left, Jocelyn "Blu Blu" Buchanan seated sax on right, center with tie Roy Shurland vocalist, Lester Williams trumpet, Sam Watson drums.

Photo courtesy of Lloyd "The Matador" Daley

young talent for their club bands, Sister Ignatius was proud to let bandleaders like Eric Deans or Sonny Bradshaw come and have a listen. When Ernest Ranglin, renowned guitarist and scout for Eric Deans, heard Drummond's sweet minor chords, he knew that Drummond would be a success, and so on October 31, 1950, six weeks before graduation, Don Drummond left Alpha

Boys' School to take a residency with the Eric Deans Orchestra at the Colony Club on Halfway Tree Road. He had been at Alpha for seven years.

While with the Eric Deans Orchestra, Don Drummond had the opportunity to further hone his skills, playing the jazz standards of the day for tourists, barristers, and wealthy society. The Colony Club may have only been miles away from Alpha Boys' School, but the clientele were a world away from the barefoot boys who learned to play in school rooms running

Don Drummond performs, "The Message," at the Carib during Jazz '57

with rats. Drummond performed with the orchestra alongside fellow Alpharians Reuben Alexander, Eddie "Tan Tan" Thornton, and Wilton Gaynair. The band performed as their own act and as backup for vocalists such as Diane Courtney, "The Girl with the Moonlit Voice;" Joan Gallagher, "Miami's Singing Sweetheart;" and Bea Morley, "America's Bombshell of Rhythm, The Happiness Girl Who'll Sing Your Blues Away." Drummond was cutting his chops. He was learning the ropes. He was further developing his own style by honing his musical ear, combining the jazz, blues, and Latin sounds he heard on the stage that he shared with musicians from other lands, as well as those inside his own mind and heart. Drummond left Eric Deans, perhaps because of Deans' jealousy over his girl having eyes for Drummond as "Tan Tan" suggests, or perhaps because it was simply the order of the day to move around from band to band as need or money dictated. He performed for a number of different bands, including Sonny Bradshaw's at the Bournemouth Beach Club, and The Vivian Hall All-Stars.

By 1954, Drummond was headlining his own band, the Don Drummond All-Stars and the Don Drummond Four. He had made a name for himself, and so other bands and performers sought Drummond out for guest appearances. He performed with Baba Motta, Lester Hall, Tony Brown, Roy Coburn and his Blue-Flames Orchestra, Vivian Hall, Kenny Williams, and many others. In 1956 he performed with the legendary American jazz singer Sarah Vaughan and in 1959 with great American jazz pianist Dave Brubeck and both were in awe of his talent.

Don Drummond, center, with the Sonny Bradshaw band. Carlos Malcolm, immediate right, Rupert Anderson far right, and Rico Rodriguez, left, 1957
Photo courtesy the Jamaica National Library

In the late 1950s, the recording industry in Jamaica began to pick up steam. Sound system operators like Duke Reid and Coxsone Dodd turned to their island's own talent instead of traveling to source American material for their dances in clubs and yards such as Chocomo Lawn, Forresters Hall, and Jubilee Tile Gardens, to name a few. Drummond began recording for Coxsone Dodd's Studio One in 1959 with a solo on the Owen Gray (fellow Alpharian) hit, "On the Beach." He followed the next year with his own "Don Cosmic" for Coxsone and in 1961 with "This Man is Back." It was a song he wrote after being away for some time, one of the many times he checked himself in as a patient at the Bellevue Mental Hospital.

Even at a young age, Don Drummond was described by many who knew him as quiet, strange, and of an unusual mind. As he grew older, however, these characteristics became not just descriptors for his personality, but insights into his mental condition that was finally diagnosed and treated through primitive means. With the modern benefits of an advanced understanding of mental illness, we can now speculate whether or not this diagnosis was accurate or whether his condition may have been more symptomatic of bipolar disorder or something else on the spectrum of disorders. But at the time, such behaviors as eating clay and dirt, urinating from the stage into the pit during a performance, playing the trombone without actually producing any sound during live and recorded performances, and standing cruciform in the middle of street traffic were symptoms of a disorder wrongly assigned to many black men who affiliated with Rastafarians—schizophrenia.

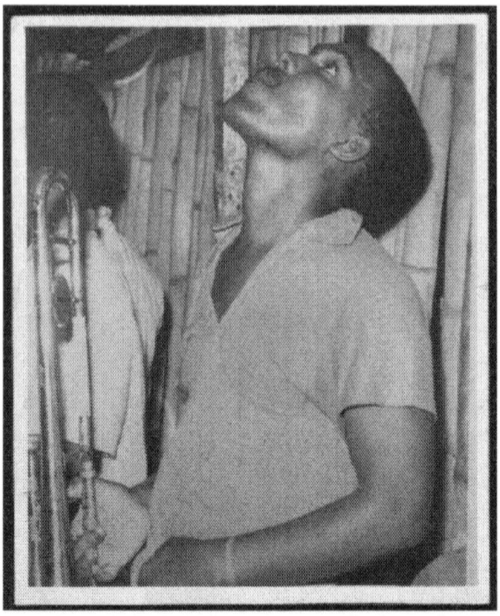

Don Drummond
Photos courtesy Clive Chin

Drummond did associate with Rastafarians, as did a number of musicians during the 1960s. After a show, musicians such as Drummond, Rico Rodriguez, Herman King, Tommy McCook, Cedric Brooks, Roland Alphonso, Harold McNair, Bobby Gaynair, Vivian Hall, Ernest Ranglin, and Johnny Moore would commune in the Wareika Hills to perform with drummers, namely Count Ossie and his bredren at the camp. They performed in a free-flowing atmosphere of creativity and spirituality. Although Don Drummond was not a Rastafarian, the titles of many of his compositions reflected the reasoning he gained from his attendance at Wareika, songs with names such as "Addis Ababa," "Marcus Junior," and "Beardman Ska." He utilized minor chords with a plaintive, melancholy feel. He employed Rastafarian rhythms in his songs. He became creator of the "Far East Sound," one upon which reggae later built.

Drummond formed a professional bond with many of his fellow musicians in the hills, as well as the musicians in the clubs and recording studios, which now began to increase in numbers with the growth of the recording industry. Musicians such as Drummond could gain work for any number of record producers who used them as studio musicians to back up vocalists like Bob Marley, Jimmy Cliff, Roy & Yvonne, and countless others. In 1964, one of these musicians, Alpharian Tommy McCook, organized a number of the studio musicians who frequently performed together during these sessions to form their own band, The Skatalites. They became known as the seminal ska band during this era, comprised of musicians who could all be leaders in their own right. They performed at clubs all over Kingston and throughout the island. They recorded numerous cover songs, as well as a number of original compositions, most of which were written by Drummond. The Skatalites were innovators and developers of ska music and therefore, the subsequent genres that evolved.

Don Drummond
Photo courtesy *Jamaica Gleaner*

Drummond continued to struggle with his mental illness, and despite seeking treatment many times at Bellevue Mental Hospital, voluntarily checking himself in for stays until he felt well enough to come out and perform, he finally broke one tragic night, January 2, 1965. After Drummond's live-in girlfriend, Anita Mahfood, came home from a performance at Club Havana where she had a residency as the rhumba dancer Margarita, Drummond became enraged. Some say he was upset for missing his performance with The Skatalites that night at the LaParisienne Club in

Harbour View, and some blame Margarita for incorrectly administering his medication, although there is no proof or logic to placing this blame. Anita was a victim and the fact is, Drummond did not receive the proper help for his mental illness that he desperately needed, and so early that morning, after a raucous argument, Don Drummond stabbed Margarita to death, four times in the chest. He was represented by P.J. Patterson who had once served as a manager for The Skatalites, but was also an attorney and later became prime minister of the country. Drummond was not immediately fit to stand trial, despondent and unresponsive. On July 24, 1966, after a one-hour jury deliberation, Drummond was found guilty of homicide and was detained to Bellevue Mental Hospital at "Her Majesty's Pleasure," meaning indefinitely. Three years later, on May 6, 1969, Don Drummond died as a result of "congestive cardiac failure and anaemia," according to his death certificate, likely the result of the uneducated and untrained staff, unsanitary conditions, and improper administration of drugs such as chlorpromazine and sodium barbital which have been since banned for causing fatalities.

Anita "Margarita" Mahfood
Star Newspaper, April 1, 1958

Don Drummond will forever be known for his genius, both in performing on the trombone, as well as his compositions which may number up to 500. He was incredibly prolific during his 35 years in Jamaica and he was never able to leave the island to pursue a career in the UK or US as many other musicians did. He was a sufferer in the true sense of the word, unable to escape the chains of poverty, but he left the world with a wealth of creativity that evolved into many other forms and inspired countless other musicians and their art.

--H.A.

Emmanuel 'Rico' Rodriguez

Surrounded by pillars of the British establishment in the regal splendour of Buckingham Palace, video footage from 12th July 2007 shows Rico Rodriguez sporting a wispy grey beard and crisp black suit, standing patiently in line as he waits to be called up. He carries an aura of dignity about him and does not look at all out of place in his current surroundings. Upon his head sits a red, gold and green woollen tam. 'Emmanuel Rico Rodriguez, for services to music' proclaims a crusty-sounding aristocratic older male voice. He steps forward from the line to accept his medal. His Royal Highness the Prince of Wales greets him with a handshake and the two exchange some private words. For a brief moment, both appear to be laughing at something. As Rico walks away, he turns back around and offers Prince Charles the hand symbol of the Rastafari faith, pressing the two thumbs and fingers of each hand together to form a diamond. It has been a long journey for Rodriguez, from the music room at Alpha to being made a Member of the British Empire (MBE), one of the highest accolades to be bestowed on a UK citizen.

Speaking about that day five years later, Rodriguez, who is universally known as Rico, still sounds in awe of his achievement. 'I can't describe it. There's a just feeling about meeting all these people, superintendent of police, lawyers and boxers, all different people are there, but in that room everyone was humble to each other. That was a very good feeling. No one was bigger than the other.' Rodriguez never knew who the person was who put his name forward for consideration for an MBE. And how exactly did The Man From Wareika put a smile on the face of England's future king that day? With a twinkle in his eye Rico admits, 'I get funny in his face. I told him I don't wanna take off mi hat because I don't want all these people round here to get scared when they see mi dreads. And he smiled at that.'

Born in Cuba on 17th October 1934, Rico's family moved to Jamaica when he was very young. He entered Alpha aged around five after being hit by a car. 'I was in the street and in an accident, a car lick me down when I was a likkle boy and my mother think the best thing for me was to put me inna Alpha, cause I been roamin' the streets, generally.' Like all Alpha boys, Rico tried out the various trade apprenticeships on offer, initially working in the gardens. But music beckoned and he fought to gain a prized place in the band, but not without proving his worth with understanding some musical theory. 'Sometime the bandmaster ask you for what you're doing and if you don't know theory then you find it difficult to explain yourself. Because with theory you can tell him what you are doing,' says Rico. 'If you make a wrong note he hits you. And because you get that hit you don't want the next one, so you always make sure you're correct next time.'

Life at Alpha was tough and highly disciplined with a fear of being punished for wrongdoing, often with a leather strap. 'We run outta school every day down to Victoria Street and down to the bakery. And if they catch ya, ya get a beatin' for that. Me get plenty beatin' man. We used to go a swim at the seaside, and come back and ya face red so they know ya been at sea. Plenty beatin' inna Alpha man, man, plenty beatin'.' This is the side of Alpha that generally does not get spoken of, that the Sisters could hand down harsh punishment which you can be sure would have hurt like hell. The ethics of beating children is highly questionable and certainly this was an entirely different era with a different set of values, but regardless, it must have been oppressive to have the fear of corporal punishment hanging over you every day, especially when it was for such petty things that nowadays wouldn't even be considered punishable.

Rico Rodriguez in his Alpha band uniform
Photo courtesy Tracey Rodriguez

With Don Drummond a few years above him, Rico was fortunate to be mentored and befriended by the young trombone maestro. Through music they developed a friendship that would continue for several years after their time at Alpha. Once Rodriguez finished his time at Alpha he made his way down to the busy seafront of Kingston where he would play his trombone to the sailors in exchange for a piece of fish for his supper. Soon enough he was in trouble with the police and placed in another school, Stony Hill where he was able to further study music.

Rico performing at the Vere Johns Opportunity Hour, 1958

It was later, while apprenticing as a mechanic that Rodriguez took the path of so many eager musicians of the day, through entering the Vere Johns Opportunity Hour and it was through his consistent winning that Rodriguez realised that a career in music was more than just a fantasy. 'I used to enter contests in places like Palace Theatre and Gaiety Theatre so when I start playing individually the crowd used to give me winnings and a lot of interest. That's how I know I can make a living out of music. I win all my contests.'

Rodriguez did stints with the various dance bands of the day such as Eric Deans and Sonny Bradshaw alongside many of the musicians who would go on to shape ska and reggae. It was around this time that Rodriguez found his spiritual home, in the Wareika Hills. Here Rodriguez further cemented his musical connection with Drummond, his trombone mentor, playing together in extended free-form jazz and African drumming jam sessions. 'When I leave school I used to go up to Wareika Hills and look for Don Drummond and play with him. He was a humble kind of man, he not tell me that you are not good enough to come and play with me. He made me feel very good being along with him.' Through studying with Drummond he found himself developing a similar sound, so had to make a concerted effort to forge his own signature sound. 'I used to go to Count Ossie and I used to listen to what he [Drummond] does and I almost try to follow him but I realise I can't be like him, I have to be myself. When I listen to some of my recordings earlier on, I was almost sounding like him. To come out of that was very good because I was making an establishment for myself.'

Rico and his mother Amy
Photo courtesy Tracey Rodriguez

By the late 1950s the supply of brand new American rhythm 'n' blues records to play on sound systems began to dry up. Black music had moved on in America as the era of soul music was ushered in. The demand in Jamaica was still high so the sound system operators attempted to record their own Jamaican style rhythm and blues. Rodriguez found himself in demand as a session player on some of these early recordings, with some rough and ready instrumentals showcasing his awesome trombone skills. For Duke Reid he recorded a clutch of tunes which became Reid's 'secret weapons,' which his competitors were desperate to find the titles of. These included 'Duke's Cookies,' 'Magic,' 'Pink Lane Shuffle,'' and 'Let George Do It.' Then, just as the ska explosion was about to get fully underway, Rodriguez left for England in 1962. 'I felt to come out of Jamaica at that time. My mother provided a fare for me to come out to England and I was very happy for that.'

Arriving in London without owning his own instrument, Rodriguez made his way to the most happening place in London, The Roaring Twenties club in Soho run by fellow Jamaican sound-man Count Suckle. Suckle knew of Rodriguez through importing records that Rico played on, so he bought Rico a trombone, which allowed him to find regular work playing with Georgie Fame and The Blue Flames in Suckle's club, alongside his fellow Alpharian Eddie 'Tan Tan' Thornton.

Throughout the 1960s Rodriguez would work at the Ford motor factory in Dagenham, all the while playing gigs around London and doing session work. He released numerous singles and two LPs under the name Rico and the Rudies, *Brixton Cat* and *Go Blow Your Horn,* featuring early reggae instrumentals, popular among the UK skinheads and mods. He also formed one of the tightest reggae backing bands of day, The Undivided, playing for Jamaican artists on UK tours and around the burgeoning UK reggae scene. After over ten years of struggling as a musician Rico was given the opportunity by Chris Blackwell at Island Records to go back to Jamaica and record an instrumental roots reggae album bearing his own compositions and utilising the cream of Kingston's studio musicians. A seriously deep jazz-reggae masterpiece, *Man from Wareika* was released in 1976 to critical acclaim and remains one of the most revered and influential reggae albums of all time. Its American release on the Blue Note jazz label is the only reggae record released in that label's 75 year history. Being an Island Records artist, alongside Bob Marley and the Wailers, Rico's band went out on the road as support act for Marley right at the point when he was exploding internationally.

Rico
Photo courtesy Pekka Vuorinen

A follow-up LP called *Midnight In Ethiopia* was shelved by Island, but a new chapter in Rico's life was about to begin. In 1978 when Jerry Dammers was searching for the right sound for The Specials, he knew he needed something that would link the new ska revival sound back to its original 1960s incarnation. He found just what he was looking for in Rico. Declining to join as a full time member, the band released the single 'A Message to You, Rudy' as 'The Specials Featuring Rico' paying homage to Dandy Livingstone's original 1969 version on which Rico also had played. Joining The Specials for shows all over the UK, Rico found himself right in the eye of the 2Tone hurricane, a brand new musical movement that swept the nation and gave him massive exposure, including appearances on the BBC weekly chart show Top of the Pops. It led to Rico being invited to support acts like The Police and Ian Dury with his own touring band featuring some of the best UK reggae players. A friendly rapport with Dury led to him being name-checked on Ian Dury and the Blockheads' 1979 UK hit single 'Reasons To Be Cheerful (Part 3)' with the rhyme, 'Listening to Rico / Harpo, Groucho, Chico,' rhyming him with the Marx brothers. 2Tone Records released two further brilliant solo albums, *Jama Rico* and *That Man Is Forward*, both recorded in Jamaica. Around this period Rico's trombone sound became in high demand in the rock and pop world and could be heard on records by the likes of John Martyn, Joan Armatrading and Paul Young, among others.

Rico and Jerry Dammers

In 1981 a malingering discontent, born out of dire urban neglect along with fraught tension between black communities and the police, saw Britain's inner cities explode in a summer of riots. It started in Brixton in the spring and spread across twelve other inner-city areas over the summer months. At the height of all the trouble The Specials held the UK number one chart spot for three weeks with 'Ghost Town.' Its bleak mood of urban decay served as an evocative soundtrack to the real-life social breakdown. Rico and Dick Cuthell's fat horns added to the song's eerie kitsch muzak feel, while the song's 12-inch mix featured an extended Rico trombone solo. The Specials' founder Jerry

Dammers spoke to James Hendicott of the *New Musical Express (NME)* after Rico's passing in 2015. 'To me his majestic solo on the 12" version of "Ghost Town" is the musical highpoint of The Specials and when I play it as a DJ it still elicits cheers from audiences, as the beginning of any Rico solo always has done live.'

After the breakup of The Specials in 1981, Dammers and several other members of the band toured Europe as 'Rico and The Special AKA.' Under this name they also released a solo single for 2Tone, 'Jungle Music,' which chopped and changed between slow reggae and high energy carnivalesque soca. The track repeats the refrain, 'What ya talkin' 'bout? Ya say ya don' like de jungle beat? Ya mus' be craaaaaaaaazy!' Possibly written as a retort to English racists who would call reggae 'jungle music,' it was to become a singalong at Rico's live shows.

Rico returned to Jamaica around 1982 where he stayed for about ten years. He returned to England in the early 1990s, invigorated and ready to reactivate his career. He briefly joined newly formed ska-jazz outfit Jazz Jamaica, recording on their first LP. After getting a tip-off that TV presenter and ex-Squeeze keyboardist Jools Holland had put together a big band not dissimilar to the ones Rodriguez played with in the 1950s, he gave Holland a call and was welcomed into the fold with open arms. Holland recounts the moment he first heard from him in his autobiography and how both Rico and his fellow Jamaican, saxophonist Michael 'Bammi' Rose brought an authentic Jamaican vibe to proceedings. For the next twenty five years he would be a rock solid member of Jools Holland's Rhythm and Blues Orchestra, giving Rodriguez regular touring and studio work as well as

Rico circa 1969 in Kingston
Photo by Vincent Chin, courtesy Clive Chin

Rico in his signature tam
Photo courtesy Tracey Rodriguez

the chance to play alongside some of the greatest artists in the business on the BBC1 show, *Later, With Jools Holland.*

'I been in Jools band a very long time,' says Rico. 'You no have no weak players, everyone is professional and to play along with them give me good feeling. That's why I've been in it so long. And I will always want to be in that band. It's the best treatment I ever get from a band.' On four separate occasions, between 2008 and 2011, Rico was given the opportunity to sing solo on Jools Holland's *Hootananny*, the big New Year 's Eve Hogmany-style party show watched by over four million all across Britain. Although not known as a singer, Rodriguez possessed a smooth rich crooner's voice and backed by Jools and his orchestra he gave wonderful renditions of 'L-O-V-E,' 'What a Wonderful World,' 'I've Got You Under My Skin' and 'I'm In The Mood For Love.' In 2103 Rico performed his masterpiece *Man From Wareika* in its entirety at The London International Ska Festival. Although he was suffering from Parkinson's disease which considerably hampered his playing abilities, he was received rapturously by an adoring crowd. Rodriguez would sometimes play with Jerry Dammers' Spacial AKA Orchestra, a 20-piece ska-infused tribute to the music of Sun Ra, formed in 2006. Dammers again: 'At the last gig he ever did, Rico could no longer play his trombone, but still continued to sing as other musicians played his music. The legendary Jamaican producer Bunny Lee said Rico was just as responsible as his fellow Jamaican trombone legend Don Drummond, in creating the iconic sound which for a while made the trombone virtually the national instrument of Jamaica, eventually playing its part in making reggae probably the most popular music in the world.'

Rico Rodriguez passed away on 4th September 2015 after being admitted to hospital in London. He was given a hero's send-off at a memorial concert in Brixton later that year, attended by the great and the good of the UK reggae scene, with Jerry Dammers playing a DJ set in his honour and his Alpharian trombone brother Vin Gordon playing a storming set with his Real Rock Band. Dammers perfectly summed up Rico's music in his *NME* tribute: 'I think it was the incredible mixture of joy and sadness at one and the same time in his playing, which gave it its power. The mournful and melancholic sound of sufferation, the humour and joy of living, and the righteous anger and defiance of the poor and oppressed people of Jamaica, all combined in a highly melodic way with no unnecessary frills. Rico said the silences in music were just as important. His playing could break your heart and make you smile and determined, all at the same time. I will greatly miss him, as will many people around the world.' As well as his MBE, Rico was awarded with the Musgrave Medal for the Arts in Jamaica, one the country's highest accolades.

--A.R.

Advertisements for Rico's recordings, 1979 at left, 1982 at right

Rico Rodriguez receiving his MBE from His Royal Highness The Prince Of Wales at Buckingham Palace 2007

Photos courtesy of Buckingham Palace Press Office

Rico telling His Royal Highness the Prince of Wales that he wore his tam so he wouldn't scare anyone with his dreadlocks.

Lester Sterling

The last surviving player from the foundation line-up of The Skatalites, Lester 'Ska' Sterling outlived all of his bandmates and continued to make the music he helped originate, enthralling audiences worldwide well into the 21st Century right up to his retirement in 2014. As one of the four Alpharians that made up the nine-piece Studio One house band formed in 1964 that became arguably the greatest Jamaican group of all time, Sterling has witnessed the initial demise and subsequent rebirth of ska as a worldwide force. With over half a century of The Skatalites behind him, Sterling sits right at the heart of the Jamaican music story. 'If I never went to Alpha, first of all I don't think I'd be known around the world,' he muses.

Lester George Sterling was born in 1936 and grew up in Allman Town, just a stone's throw away from the school that would shape his life. His father actively encouraged him and his brothers Roy, Gladstone and Keith to consider a career in music and would frequently take them to live shows. The brothers' interest in music was fueled by making connections with musicians—in particular he was inspired by his friend Frederick Brown who played in the Alpha band. Their father's determination that music should be his sons' path led to his securing places for each of them at Alpha. To get them started he bought each of them toy instruments for Christmas. All the brothers would also go on to play music—Roy played trumpet with Lynn Taitt and the Jets, while Keith played piano and keyboards with an assortment of studio bands like The Upsetters, The Aggrovators, Soul Syndicate, We the People and Sly and Robbie's Taxi Gang. Gladstone was a sax player and worked extensively in the Bahamas.

'My father encouraged me to go to Alpha. He used to take us to Coney Island in Kingston where the musicians was. And there was a Coney Island at Red Seat, he used to take us there also. I used to see the bands play there. And he preach at us that we must play music and turn musician,' says Sterling. He entered Alpha in 1945 and joined the band when he was 12 as trumpet player, alongside future musical giants. 'I started at Alpha around 8 or 9. During my time at school I met some of the greatest guys. I met Wilton and Bobby Gaynair. I met Don Drummond. I and Don Drummond was in the band at the same time. I was a little younger. I never know I was going to

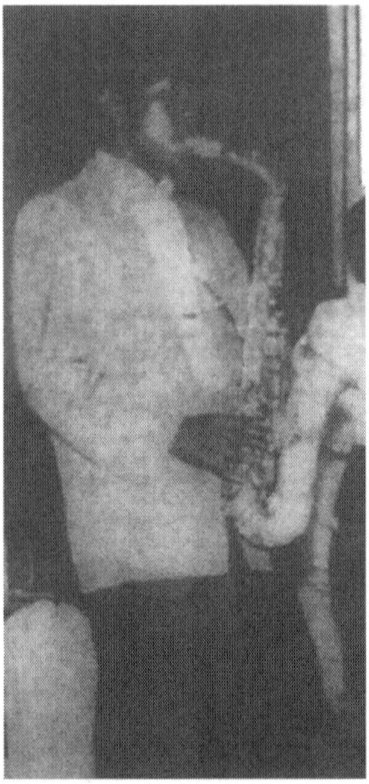

Lester Sterling as winner of the Vere Johns' Opportunity Hour
Star Newspaper, early 1960s

be great musician.' Alongside music Sterling learnt printing as his trade and like many Alpharians in the 1970s he would work in the print trade when music was unable to support him fully. 'I used to operate a 1250 press, yuhknow, an A.B. Dick. Off-set printing. So I used to work in the city of New York for years, and play music too.' While still a student at Alpha, Sterling and classmate Karl Bryan joined a local big band headed by Stanley Headlam. Upon leaving Alpha in the early 1950s, he worked in local big bands of the day such as the Luther Williams Band, The Glass Bucket Band, The Copacabana Band, Clue J and His Blues Blasters and The Val Bennett Orchestra. In this latter band he would first play alongside Ernest Ranglin and future members of The Skatalites, Jah Jerry Haynes and Lloyd Knibb. Clue J's band was also where many future band members served time, and those who were a 'cut above' would recognize each other's superior talents. Sterling also spent some time working the north coast hotel circuit, playing in a band called Eric Grant and the Montego House Orchestra in Montego Bay. At some point during this period Sterling made the switch from trumpet to alto saxophone. By 1959 he was assured enough to enter the make-or-break talent show Vere Johns' Opportunity Hour at the Majestic Theatre. He won all his rounds and came out as the final winner. 'You have to play four different songs, one in each quarter and if you win with all four then you have to play them all in the Grand Final,' he recalls in the notes to his LP *Sterling Silver*.

In 1960 Sterling joined the Jamaica Military Band for a brief spell and moved into the army barracks at Up Park Camp where he met up with Cedric Brooks and future Skatalites member Johnny 'Dizzy' Moore. Whilst in the army Sterling recorded his first single, 'Whalebone,' a rhythm and blues instrumental stomper (with audible whoops and hollers), released on the

Worldisc label under the name Lester Sterling and The City Slickers. 'I composed this on the spot at Federal Studios. We did this after Rico came to Up Park Camp in early '61 to tell me that he was going to England. I recorded it using the tenor of the Jamaica Military Band,' he says in the liner notes. When asked in 2013 by Peter Clemm of German blog *Reggae-Steady-Ska.com* to recollect what his all-time favourite band he'd played in over his entire career, Sterling answered, 'Bwoy, the best time? Well, funny enough, Luther Williams and his Orchestra at the Arawak Hotel. That was in the '50s when I was like 18. We played rhythm 'n' blues and jazz, cha cha and mambo. At that time I ran into Roland Alphonso. He got me interested in jazz. I learned a lot from Roland playing. It was good that I played in Jamaica Military Band, so I got a lot of practice.' As ska emerged as the dominant force in the early 1960s, Sterling recognized its importance as a uniquely Jamaican form and embraced it fully. 'When the music change, I really wanted it to change, because the music was *ours,* we create it. And I used to dance to it and love it,' he says. Sterling helped form The Skatalites in 1964 with four fellow Alpharians in 1964 and as the band blazed a trail until its untimely implosion 15 months later, Sterling and the band lived and breathed ska throughout that period.

Lester Sterling with The Skatalites in 1964

After The Skatalites disbanded in January 1966, Sterling went on to join Byron Lee and the Dragonaires, picking up his old trumpet again, while continuing to play sax. It was as a solo artist that he had his major breakthrough with a rocksteady instrumental for Studio One called 'Pupa Lick' which topped the Jamaican charts. A 'pupa lick' was the slang word meaning to do a graceful twist of the body while high diving. Another number one hit came the following year with 'Bangarang,' Sterling's signature tune, the title being patois for a disturbance or commotion. The tune was produced by Bunny 'Striker' Lee and featured backing vocals by Stranger

Cole, Max Romeo and Lloyd Parks with a quirky organ shuffle which became known as the 'John Crow Skank.' Bunny 'Striker' Lee often cited 'Bangarang' as the first proper reggae tune and it has since been worked over dozens of times by the likes of Lord Creator, Brigadier Jerry and Dillinger. A 1994 UK Channel 4 documentary opens with Lee in his Kingston studio, picking up a tape reel and declaring, 'Yeah, I want to tell everybody, the whole world, this is the first reggae tune that was done in Jamaica, see it? It was done in 1968 in Duke Reid's studio. I want to play it and mek the whole world hear, *"Muma no want no Bangarang."* It was Lester Sterling, Lloyd Charmers and Stranger Cole…is really the emphasis on the organ. Mek the organ go, *reggae, reggae*…this is the great "Bangarang."'

Sterling released 50 singles under his own name between 1963 and 1972, although in the tradition of Jamaican 7-inch single releases, his instrumentals would often appear as B-sides with vocal cuts as the featured A-side. He also released a solo LP in 1969 called *Bangarang* on the Pama label, released in both Jamaica and England.

In 1972 he quit Byron Lee and the Dragonaires and moved to New York City to further develop himself as a musician. Initially he played with Junior Soul and the Debonairs then later joined a big band called Jazzmobile headed by veteran hard-bop saxophonist Jimmy Heath. 'Like everybody, I wanted to be in America, become really good as a musician. I listened to Charlie Parker, Dizzy Gillespie and Miles Davis. These guys played so great,' he told Andrew Clemm at *Reggae-Steady-Ska.com.*

The first regrouping of The Skatalites took place in 1975, with an incomplete line-up, to record an album's worth of music and Sterling was present to participate in these sessions. Sterling formed his own new band in 1978 somewhat boldly naming them The Skatalites, although he was the only original member. It was a short-lived project although they did manage to release a 12-inch disco mix single, 'Devil's Triangle' on the Deep Groove Sounds label under the name Lester Sterling and The Skatalites (the tune was later re-recorded with the reformed Skatalites on the Rolling Steady sessions). Sterling took part in the first full reunion of the band in 1983, contributing to the two studio recordings and two live LPs made during this period. When McCook passed away in 1998, Sterling would then become the official band leader, touring the world extensively and recording five highly rated studio albums with The Skatalites until his departure in 2014. That he should be the last of the foundation players, alongside vocalist Doreen Shaffer, must have been something Lester Sterling could never have imagined back when The Skatalites were a uniquely Jamaican phenomena barely known outside of The Caribbean, let alone the wider world. When asked by *Reggae-Steady-Ska.com* what it feels like to be onstage, knowing he and Doreen are the last survivors, he replied: 'Strange in a sense, but then again, I have to be the one to hold up the hands and keep it going. All the music from Don Drummond and Roland and Tommy, it's always around me. Sometimes I play parts that Roland or Tommy played. I heard what Don Drummond or Dizzy played, so I play that style. It's still here!'

Lester Sterling with The Skatalites in Chicago in 1996
Photo by Heather Augustyn

In 1998 Sterling was honoured with highest accolade of the Jamaican Order of Distinction (OD) for his services to music. On his longevity in the business and his lifetime commitment to the cause, Sterling wryly remarks, 'Well, you just can't leave it.'

--A.R.

Sparrow Martin, Leroy 'Horsemouth' Wallace, and Lester Sterling perform at the Coronet Theatre, London, 2007
Photo by Adam Reeves

Lester Sterling during rehearsals for the London Alpha reunion show in 2007
Photo by Adam Reeves

Karl "Cannonball" Bryan

"It's a chilly chilly afternoon and I want to see everyone reach home safe and sound," says the man sitting on the corner of Yonge and St. Clair Streets in downtown Toronto. He is smiling and begins to play the saxophone nestled at his side, slightly swaying his elbows, his shoulders in his navy blue sweatshirt and khaki pants. He ascends and descends scales with ease, slides through trills before taking a rest to laugh and exclaim, "Music is the greatest thing." All around him busses whiz past, couriers on bikes dodge shipping vans and commuter cars, and men and women in suits cross at the light, oblivious to the fact that the man performing "Schooling the Duke" is Jamaican tenor saxophonist Karl "Cannonball" Bryan.

Carlos Malcolm and His Afro-Jamaican Rhythms in 1963 at Club Sombrero with Derrick Harriott and Alphanso Boysie Castro in front. On saxophones in back is Karl Bryan on left, and Alpharian Leslie Samuels on right, and Larry McDonald, congas.

Karl Altamont Bryan, whose name is frequently spelled Carl, more commonly goes by his nickname, Cannonball, after Julian Edwin "Cannonball" Adderley, the famous American jazz saxophonist. Bryan was born on April 3, 1937 and he had an affinity for music at a young age after listening to musicians perform all over Kingston. He was an admirer of John Coltrane, Bud Shank, and most of all, Charlie Parker. It wasn't until Bryan entered Alpha Boys' School in 1949 that he actually took up an instrument under the direction of bandmaster Reuben Delgado. He came to Alpha because, as he says, "My father died and my mother, she was very poor." His brothers attended Alpha as well, although his sister was cared for by his mother. His brother Courtney Bryan, went on to perform with the Jamaica Military Band in the mid-1960s. After trying his hand at the trade of bookbinding Karl Bryan moved to the band. He started on the clarinet before moving to the saxophone after he graduated. Delgado handed Bryan "a 'black stick' to become a clarinet player," according to a *Daily Gleaner* article on January 30, 1969. Bryan says, "When you start on the clarinet, you're on a better road to success because of the discipline." After Bryan left Alpha, he performed in an orchestra for the Coronation Tattoo in 1953, a parade and celebration for

Karl Bryan on sax, far left, in 1965 at the Regal Theater with Carlos Malcolm on trombone and Tony Gregory at the mic

the 1953 coronation of Queen Elizabeth II. "I go marching every morning and play with them," Bryan says of the orchestra.

Because Alpha Boys' School had a close relationship with the military and police bands in Jamaica, Karl Bryan found employment with military engagements, but he also had a need to survive, so he sought more lucrative ventures, giving up the clarinet and taking up the saxophone. In 1954, Bryan played the soprano, alto, tenor, and baritone saxophones with the Stanley Headlam Orchestra for one year. He then performed for a number of hotels on the north coast including Redver Cooke, Joslyn Trott, and the Jerry Bindley orchestras. After seven years playing jazz standards for tourists, Bryan returned to Kingston and he immediately took up employment with Carlos Malcolm and the Afro-Jamaican Rhythms. It was here that he earned his nickname. That same *Gleaner* article states, "He was dubbed 'Cannonball' by the fans of the band who said that his style was similar to that of the famed American tenor saxophonist Cannonball Adderley." With Malcolm's outfit, Bryan traveled to New York, Nassau, Freeport Trinidad, Puerto Rico, Miami, Barbados, Montserrat, Venezuela, Martinique, Tobago, and Antigua. Bryan's performance with Malcolm was not exclusive and he performed with a number of other groups. Bryan also became arranger for the Granville Williams Orchestra, Jimmy James & the Vagabonds, and The Zodiacs.

CARL
"CANNONBALL"
BRYAN
and the V.I.V. All Stars
featuring LASCELLES PERKINS

Daily Gleaner,
December 21, 1968

In 1962, Bryan performed for the Don Drummond's Benefit Jazz Show at the Regal Theater, performing with Drummond, Roland Alphonso, Tommy McCook, Ernest Ranglin, and a number of others in what was billed as the "greatest musical concert ever." He performed at all of the popular clubs in Kingston, including the Glass Bucket Club in 1963 with vibraphonist Lennie Hibbert who was bandmaster at Alpha Boys' School. He performed at the Myrtle Bank Hotel with Ernest Ranglin, the Embassy Club in Montego Bay with Baba Motta and Carlos Malcolm, at the Sombrero Club with the Los Caballeros Orchestra, at the Ocean View Club in Montego Bay with Cluett Johnson and Roland Alphonso, and in the later 1960s he performed with

Tommy McCook and the Supersonics. He also had his own band, Carl "Cannonball" Bryan and the Diamonds and they performed for clubs and dances. He led another band called Carl "Cannonball" Bryan and the V.I.V. All Stars featuring Lascelles Perkins (though this was likely meant to be the V.I.P. All Stars since the performance was at the V.I.P Club), as well as King Cannon and the West Indians Quintet.

Karl Bryan busking on the streets of Toronto, 2006

Karl Bryan continued to perform in the 1970s with the Jamaica Workshop conducted by Cecil Lloyd featuring Reuben Alexander and Billy Cooke, with special guest Lennie Hibbert on vibes. Even in the 1980s and early 1990s, Bryan continued to perform at jazz concerts in Jamaica with his fellow comrades in horns, such as Ernest Ranglin, Hedley Jones, Tony DaCosta, Aubrey Adams, Cedric Brooks, Keith Stoddart, and Tommy McCook, and he toured with The Skatalites from 2004 to 2007. The list of venues, the list of musicians, goes on and on, decade after decade. Cannonball performed everywhere. He performed with them all.

Bryan also performed live for vocalists and musicians who traveled to Kingston from the US and Europe. In March of 1967, Bryan performed with a handful of other musicians in Montego Bay with American saxophonist Zoot Simms. Bryan also performed with the Mighty Sparrow, Patti Labelle, Ben E. King, Sammy Davis, Jr., Jackie Wilson, and Johnny Nash during their tours of Kingston. He even performed with a fellow local saxophonist who is now a celebrity through association with his son-in-law. "I used to play with Rita Marley's father. Her father was a saxophone player and we used to play together in Jamaica in 1954. Roy Anderson. He played tenor," Bryan says. He also performed with Bob Marley himself, in 1979 at Sunsplash.

In the studio, Bryan says that performances were true to the nature of jazz—creative and innovative in style. He says, "Most of the time we just improvise. The guy who create the song maybe he tell you what he want you to play and you have to play that, or else you just come in with something and he say, 'keep that.' In those days they say, 'take one,' and the red light come on and the music was free." He recorded for Coxsone Dodd, Bunny Lee, King Edwards, Lloyd "the Matador" Daley, Byron Lee, Duke Reid, Lindon O. Pottinger, Harry Johnson, Richard Khouri, Rupie Edwards, and many others.

Karl Bryan in 2002 in Toronto for the Legends of Ska concert

Photo courtesy Greg Lawson

In addition to the clarinet and all types of saxophone, Bryan has also performed on harmonica, piano, and organ, and he was sometimes billed as King Cannon and Ace Cannon. Whatever his moniker, Karl Bryan is a master. "I can read and write it, listen and play. Alpha started me, they put me on the right track. I continued and never looked back. Alpha is great to me. You must bend the tree when it is young," he says. Today, Karl Bryan is also a husband, a father, and a grandfather. "I have ten children from one woman," he says. He has traveled the world with his music. "They love the music. They love the music, and it's Alpha, we start this music. There's so much I could say about Jamaican music, it would take me maybe five years," he says.

For the past two decades, Bryan has performed on the streets, the subways, and at the farmers markets in Toronto, busking for a few coins and performing jazz tunes for the public on his saxophone, as he has his entire life since he was a barefoot boy at Alpha. "I play in the subway, I play in the street, I don't care. I don't got no pride. And I will never stop playing," he says. "I have no regrets being a musician."

--H.A.

Cannonball with Carlos Malcolm, far right

Raymond Harper

It is said that Raymond Harper did not always use his trumpet's keys when he played and instead performed it like a bugle. Still his sound was mellow, not boastful, full of feeling and soul and he can be identified through his use of vibrato and wailing slides from one note to the next. Harper attended Alpha Boys' School during the 1940s and was a member of the school band on trumpet. When he was an older boy, Harper taught Bobby Ellis to play the trumpet when Ellis was just 12 years old, as the older boys musically mentored the younger members of the band.

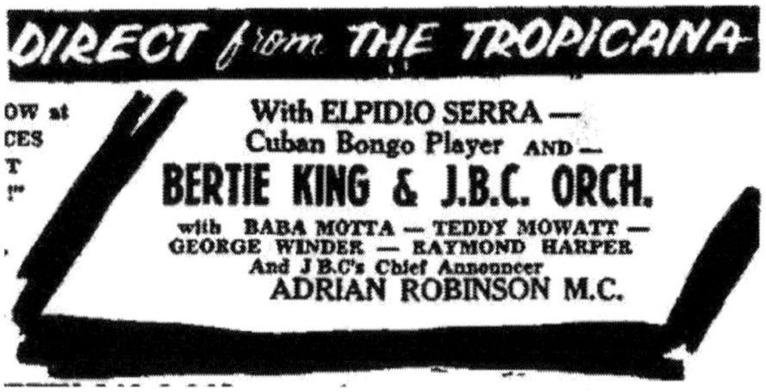

***Daily Gleaner*, October 15, 1959**

Upon leaving Alpha in the 1940s, Harper performed with a number of popular swing jazz orchestras including Eric Deans and Don Hitchman. In Hitchman's band, then based at the Sugar Hill Club in the late 1940s, Harper sat alongside a few schoolmates including tenor saxophonist Tommy McCook and drummer Ken Williams. In the early 1950s, Harper became a seminal member of a band led by elder Alpharian Bertie King who had a residence at the Casa Blanca hotel in Montego Bay, which included another Alpharian, Bobby Gaynair, then seated in the alto sax chair, according to the *Star Newspaper*, June 4, 1953.

In 1954, Harper helped to launch the career of vocalist Totlyn Jackson who made her professional debut singing "Body and Soul" with Roy Coburn and his Blue Flames at the Bournemouth Club. Later on in the decade, he appeared in the Wilton Gaynair All-Star band at the Bournemouth Club. Here he performed during the late 1940s with Alpharian tenor saxophonist Wilson Gaynair, guitarist Janet Enright, Foggy Mullings on piano, Cluett Johnson on bass, and drummer Donald Jarrett. In 1959, Harper performed with Bertie King and the J.B.C. Orchestra with Baba Motta and Taddy Mowatt.

When the recording industry started in Kingston, Harper found work in the studios as well. He performed and recorded with The Skatalites, including the tune "Tipi Tin" for Phillip Yap. Harper also recorded "Down by the Riverside" and "Shocka Shock" with Lester Sterling, "Sands of the Sea" with Alton Ellis, "Amour" and "Yours" with Bobby Aitken, "You Send Me" with Jackie Opel, "Perfidia" featuring Ossie Scott, "Bringing in the Sheep" with Theophilus Beckford, "You Were Wrong (Marjorie)" with Derrick Morgan, "Gee Baby" with Jimmy James, "I'll Always Call Your Name" with The Belltones, and "I'll Go" and "Over and Over" by the duo of Roy Panton and Millie Small, among others. He recorded with his own aggregations as well including Raymond Harper and The Melody Makers, Raymond Harper and The Torchlighters, Raymond Harper and the Carib Beats, Raymond Harper with The Drumbago Band (Arkland Parks), and when he recorded for Phillip Yap, he was Raymond Harper and the Top Deck All-Stars.

Harper worked with a number of producers like Vincent Chin and Yap, and he also recorded for Prince Buster as a member of the Prince Buster All-Stars performing on his classics "Madness" and "Judge Dread." The song "African Blood" was a ska version of Artie Shaw's "Jungle Drums" recorded for Prince Buster, and instead of Shaw's clarinet, Harper's trumpet plays the melody with the same silky style. Other producers that utilized Harper's talent include King Edwards, Delroy Dunkley (Sir Dee), Matador (Lloyd Daley), Duke Reid, and Leslie Kong, and he produced his own work and other artists along with Arkland Parks (Drumbago) for Graeme Goodall's Doctor Bird label. It was on his tune "Ska-Ta-Brain" for Goodall that he was credited as "Raymond Harper's Golden Trumpet," and his "White Christmas" also recorded for Goodall in 1967, appears on most Jamaican music holiday lists.

Harper died in abject poverty in 1997 in the Grants Pen community, allegedly under blankets of newspapers.

--H.A.

Sign at the entrance of the Alpha Boys' School in 2013

Sign at the entrance today, reflecting the name change for what is now solely a day school

Samuel "Sammy" Ismay

Rarely does one hear the name Sammy Ismay mentioned among the prodigious talent of Alpha but as both an instrumentalist and as an arranger Ismay ranks alongside the best of them. Sparse information exists on his time at the Alpha, so the focus falls on his journey through jazz and Jamaican popular music.

Samuel Lorento Ismay was born at 105 West Street, Kingston, on September 5, 1925, to Phillip and Beatrice Ismay and was the first of two siblings, his sister Nellie May making her entrance in 1928. Phillip was a tailor of standing within the community, while Beatrice was a part time dressmaker. The 1930s began in tragedy for the Ismay siblings as both parents died from ill health within four years. According to Samuel's son Tommy, the siblings "bounced around quite a bit" before becoming wards of the state at the Maxfield Park Children's Home. Both were later taken in by the Sisters of Mercy nuns at the Alpha girls and boys homes respectively. Tommy recalls his father was reverent of one particular nun, Sister Theresa. "Daddy spoke lovingly about Alpha. It was the only home he knew, and Sister Theresa was his mother."

As well as learning printing as a trade, Ismay, aged 10, began studying clarinet under the instruction of English bandmaster George Neilson and then after 1940 under Vincent Tulloch. On leaving Alpha in 1943, Ismay entered the Jamaica Military Band. Accordionist and organist Cliff Beckford led the Caribbean Orchestra, an extension of the JMB that focused primarily on dance music such as waltzes and American swing. Ismay would play gigs with Beckford's orchestra, which opened up a new world of music to the young clarinetist. The advent of jazz and swing brought greater admiration for the saxophone, driven by US giants such as Coleman Hawkins, Lester Young, Jimmy Dorsey and Ben Webster. Ultimately the saxophone overtook the clarinet, trumpet and trombone as the recognized symbol of jazz. Its appeal and popularity rose sharply in Jamaica too, especially the tenor as many emulated the styles of their American musical heroes. Ismay was attracted to the tenor's deep rich sounds and began a keen study of the instrument in the 1940s, acquiring books on the instrument such as *Jimmy Dorsey Saxophone Method: A School of Modern Rhythmic Saxophone*; and music sheets featuring the tenor sax stylings of Illinois Jacquet, Don Byas, Lester Young, and Coleman Hawkins. His proficiency on the sax attracted the attention of Sonny Bradshaw, who recruited him in the early 1950s for the Sonny Bradshaw Seven. Ismay was described as being a saxophonist from the "cool school," in the tradition of Zoot Simms, Al Cohn, or Stan Getz. He gained attention with the staging of Bradshaw's event Battle of the Saxes held at the Silver Slipper Club in 1954 and again in 1955. Here he faced off with Alpha schoolmates Wilton Gaynair, Tommy McCook, and Stony Hill Industrial School alumni Roland Alphonso. Respected jazz aficionado and promoter Harry Graham wrote, somewhat reservedly of his performance in the *Star*, April 2, 1954, "The greatest is T. McCook who blew Gaynair away again—three weeks in a row. He is definitely the best of the three...he is terrific now...Gaynair is a very good musician but too mechanical...Ismay has arrived. Coolest of the three, always pleasant but not always exciting. Lacks drive but should acquire this at such sessions as the Battle." 1954 also

Sammy Ismay, saxophone on right, with fellow Alpharian Wilton Gaynair, saxophone on right in The Sonny Bradshaw Seven at the Silver Slipper Club, 1954-1955

Photo courtesy Tommy Ismay

saw the inaugural staging of Bradshaw's Jazz at the Ward concert series. Ismay was part of a stellar cast of leading instrumentalists, among them Wilton Gaynair, Jackie Willacy Don Drummond and Cluett Johnson. Ismay supported his musical activity by to working as a printer at the Daily Gleaner newspaper from 1951 to 1956, followed by a permanent move to The Government Printing Office. Ismay left Bradshaw's Seven in 1956 to form his own five piece combo which played regularly at Vere John's Opportunity Hour. As dated music sheets in his recently discovered manuscripts show (courtesy of son Tommy), Ismay's talent as an arranger was utilized on the variety show circuit, such as those promoted by comedy duo Bim 'N' Bam. As seen on these sheets, he wrote the accompanying musical arrangements for singers including Wilfred Edwards, Owen Gray, Hyacinth Clover, Higgs and Wilson, the Jiving Juniors and Derrick Morgan.

In mid-1958, Ismay joined the newly formed sextet of dental practitioner Roy "Q" DaCosta, playing weekly at the Sugar Hill Club in St Andrew. The end of the 1950s marked the beginning of a path toward a musical identity for Jamaica. American R&B records dominated the sound system landscape in the 1950s but these lost ground to rock 'n' roll, seen by many as a watered-down imitation of R&B. As stated by Coxsone Dodd of Sir Coxsone's Downbeat sound system on Ian Boyne's *Profile* in 1991, "Rock 'n' roll didn't go over well in Jamaica." Dodd decided to make his own local rhythm and blues records for use on his sound system. The songs received favorable responses at dances, driving home a realization to Dodd, that here was a marketable product. Dodd sought aspiring singers and musicians from the talent and variety shows to launch his commercial recording venture. Thus began the march toward a national sound, and Sammy Ismay would play an essential role. Ismay was recruited to lend his deep-toned tenor to Coxsone's studio band, Clue J and his Blues Blasters, led by ex-Baba Motta bassist Cluett Johnson. Tenor sax duties were often split between Ismay and Roland Alphonso, Dodd's main man. Ismay's talent as an arranger, which had risen exponentially, was crucial to Dodd's early commercial recordings, to which Ismay was associated. With this pioneering group he recorded a number of seminal R&B tunes known as the shuffle or boogie shuffle (retrospectively referred to as JA boogie), among them "King Spinner," "Cherry," and "The Wicked," by vocal duo Bunny and Skitter; "Going Home" by Theophilus Beckford; "My Baby," and "Hard Woman Blues" by Jackie Estick, and "She Cries," by vocal duo The Mellow Larks. Ismay riffs alongside trombonist Rico Rodriguez on perhaps the most significant recording for this watershed period in Jamaican popular music, one widely regarded as the catalyst to Jamaica having a national music, Theophilus Beckford's "Easy Snappin'." As Ismay's music sheets show, he wrote the arrangements for the above recordings on June 14, 1960, with various record shop lists from the Star showing the availability of some a few days later.

Sammy Ismay with The Mighty Vikings
Photo courtesy Tommy Ismay

Dodd's fiercest rival in the sound system business, Arthur "Duke" Reid was keen on recording local R&B too and Ismay was central to his early steps in the genre. According to son Tommy, both were good friends, as he often heard his dad acknowledging the close friendship they shared. Reid was off and running with a few Ismay-arranged recordings in 1960. His tenor lights up early Reid efforts such as "More Whisky" by Laurel Aitken, "Parapinto Boogie" by Lloyd Clarke, and Derrick Morgan's first commercial record "Lover Boy." An all too familiar reality is stated by Morgan regarding Ismay, "Sammy is one of those forgotten men in this business. These were labeled as being backed by Duke Reid and His Group or Duke Reid and His Band. For Edward Seaga's WIRL imprint, he wrote arrangements for Laurel Aitken's bolero, "Stars Were Made," and "Love Me Baby;" "Rock Baby" and "Let's Sing The Blues," "Please Honey" and "Will You Dream Of Me," by The Wiggans. Ismay's sheet for these shows August 3, 1960 as the notation date.

During this period, Sammy was also playing a key role in the rapid ascent of Byron Lee and the Dragonaires. An article in the *Daily Gleaner* on June 11, 1962 affirms his importance, "Soft-spoken Sam Ismay, who plays tenor saxophone, composes and arranges most of the band's music." With The Dragonaires, Ismay backed and appeared with international acts too, such as Chuck Berry, Jerry Butler, Fats Domino, Jimmy Clanton, Sam Cooke, and Ben E. King. Lee embraced the local recording revolution with their first record being a cover of Doc Bagby's "Dumplins." Other Lee recordings with Ismay include their albums *Joy Ride in Hi Fi*, *Come Fly With Lee*, *The Many Moods of Lee*, and *Caribbean Joy Ride*. The laid-back shuffle had by 1963 had evolved into fast-paced ska and became a part of the Dragonaires fare and through it, they created a strong middle-to-upper-class following, becoming the most booked dance band of the period. Ismay's arrangements and section play are on iconic Dragonaires-backed hits such as "Sammy Dead" and "Oil In My Lamp" featuring Eric 'Monty' Morris;' "Jamaica Ska" with Keith and Ken; and Blues Buster's hits such as "I Won't Let You Go," "Soon You'll Be Gone," and "I Don't Know." His own composition, "Kukumacka," appears on *The Many Moods of Lee* LP. Band keyboardist Leslie Butler reflects on Ismay's input in the band: "he did a lot for Byron, I used to arrange a little, but Sammy was the chief arranger…he had something I think every musician should have, a distinctive style and sound…once you hear Sammy you know it's him." In addition to his sessions with the Dragonaires, Ismay frequently worked with possibly the period's most prolific recording band, that of trumpeter Oswald 'Baba' Brooks. Brooks' recording band was Duke Reid's main studio outfit during the ska era; backing vocalists for his Treasure Isle imprint, as well as recording numerous instrumentals. A few on which Ismay has solo spots include "Skalarama," "Independence Ska," "Greenfield Ska," "Guns Fever," "Teenage Ska," "One Eyed Giant," "Nightmare," and "Treasure Isle," splitting solos on the latter with trombonist Don Drummond. Vocal numbers include, "Come Bail Me," "Jump Out Of Frying Pan," and "Rub Up Push Up" by Justin Hinds and the Dominoes, and the Techniques "You Don't Know." For Ronnie Nasralla's BMN imprint, Ismay is on the Maytal's classic ballad, "Daddy." Surely a thrill for this sage arranger

Sammy Ismay with Alpha Boys' School's Sister Therese
Photo courtesy Tommy Ismay

was that a number of the records he lent his talents to made their way into the Jamaican Hit Parade; justification somewhat of their impact on the public.

Sammy was a member of three other leading bands of the mid to late 1960s. By late October 1964, he became a member of The Granville Williams Orchestra, a new 12-piece aggregation. The orchestra's popularity saw them being voted "RJR's Band of the Year" for 1965. Ismay solos on the group's rare recording, "Honky Tonk In Ska." Johnson's Drive-Inn owner, Copley Johnson, was the financier and manager of Los Caballeros, a dance band formed in late 1965. Ismay joined this band in 1966, becoming its leader a short time later. The *Daily Gleaner* on July 26, 1966 called it, "Jamaica's most versatile big band with the soulful styling of Mr. Tenor, Sammy Ismay." Another piece in the *Daily Gleaner* September 1966 proclaims, "Under the leadership of veteran saxophonist Sammy Ismay, Los Caballeros are fast becoming one of the top bands in Jamaica." Ismay and Los Caballeros made a few recordings, most notably "Keino Ska," a tribute to outstanding Kenyan athlete Kip Keino, victor in the mile and three mile event at the 1966 Commonwealth Games held in Kingston. Ismay co-wrote

Sammy Ismay presenting Prime Minister Michael Manley with a copy of his recording, "Workers of the Nation."

Photo courtesy Tommy Ismay

and soloed on this hard-driving tribute. Ismay was on the move again in 1967, joining Winston Chin Quee's Mighty Vikings. They too played the night club and stage show scene. The music by then had evolved into the slow, easy sway of Rocksteady. Ismay flashed his arranger's pen here too, and contributed to the band's recording catalog with rocksteady compositions, "Give Me Back Me Gal," and "Rockitty Frockitty," arranging also the band's 1968 album, *Jump for Days*, and penning its title track.

By the early 1970's, Ismay's professional life as a musician had scaled down significantly, as he focused more on family, work, and writing. He authored a number of songs and poems; most being religious, inspirational, or culturally based. Some were written, as indicated in his manuscripts, to be done in a reggae vein. While most remained unpublished, three works in particular were, and are projects of which Ismay was particularly proud. *Capsule Creations In Verse,* a booklet containing over a hundred inspirational quatrains, was authored and published by him in 1987. The collection was printed by the Alpha Printery. To commemorate the Government Printing Office's century of operation in 1979, and as a tribute to a former famous worker, The Right Honorable Marcus Garvey, Ismay wrote and produced for the GPO, "A Hundred Years," a centenary song. Its importance was gazetted, "Mr. Samuel Ismay, a Government Printing Office staffer, presenting a record in honour of Marcus Garvey to Youth and Sports Minister, the Hon. Hugh Small, at the Ministry on Monday. The record was produced by the Printing Office staffers as part of their centenary celebrations and will be presented to various Government Departments," stated the *Daily Gleaner* on August 31, 1979. Another recording written, arranged, and produced by Ismay was "Workers of the Nation, Worker's Marching Song," which celebrated the NWU (National Worker's Union), of which he was the chief delegate for his co-workers.

Sammy Ismay's poetry
Courtesy Tommy Ismay and Roberto Moore

Sammy Ismay was retired by the late 1980's, but continued to write poems of human upliftment, many of which have been deposited at the

Institute of Jamaica. He maintained strong ties with the Alpha, offering assistance in whatever way possible. He never forgot, or tried to hide his Alpharian roots; he sang its praises loudly, the institution that made him a consummate musician. Alpha made Sammy a man. Samuel Lorento Ismay died on February 15, 1991 at the age of 65.

--Roberto Moore

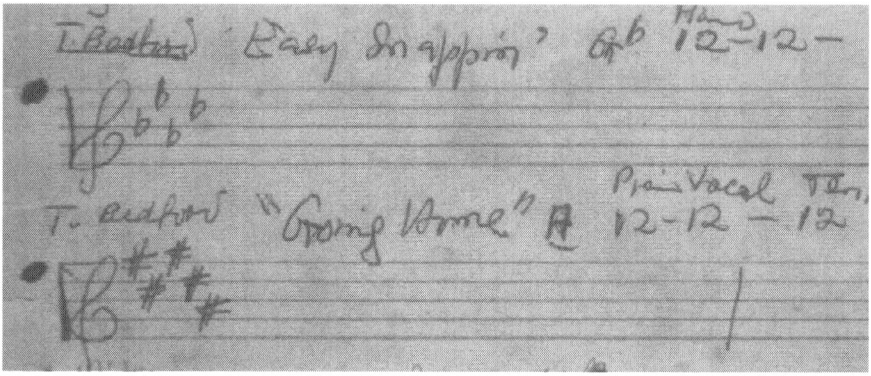

A section of Sammy Ismay's notation of "Easy Snappin'" by Theophilus Beckford, 1960

Courtesy Tommy Ismay and Roberto Moore

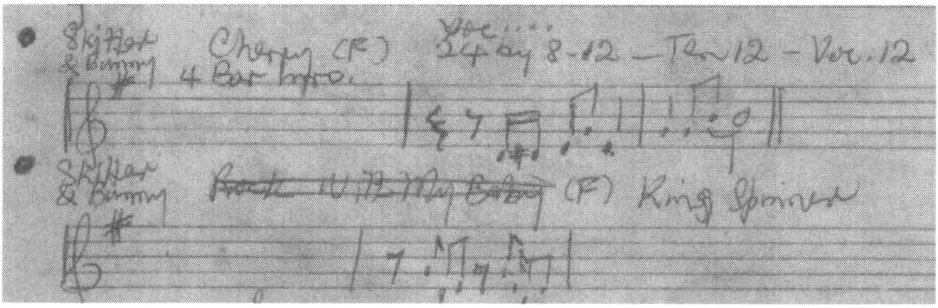

A section of Sammy Ismay's notation of "Cherry" and "King Spinner" by Bunny & Skitter, 1960

Courtesy Tommy Ismay and Roberto Moore

Johnny "Dizzy" Moore

Herbie Miller, ethnomusicologist and curator of the Jamaica Music Museum, recalls witnessing one of Jamaica's greatest musicians walk through the streets of his neighborhood on his way through to the Wareika Hills. It was a sight he remembers decades later as though it were just yesterday. "As a youth in Rockfort, I often observed Johnny 'Dizzy' Moore—the brethren with locks like a lion's mane, who wrapped his body in burlap sack while clutching a guava staff—as he trod the streets and frequented Rastafari camps in East Kingston," Miller writes in the *Daily Gleaner*, August 26, 2008, just after Moore's death. Those who knew Moore well, like Miller, describe him as a modest man, a rebellious man, and a hell of a trumpeter.

John Arlington Moore was born on October 5, 1938 in Kingston in a home where music was present, but not encouraged. In a 2005 interview with Tim Ianna while on tour in Brussels, Moore explains, "I grew up in a house with a piano there. Sadly, I wasn't allowed to touch it. My parents tried to scare me by telling me it would turn me into an alcoholic and that my backside would be out because my pants would be all torn. However, I said to my mom, 'If there's no music then nothing!'" Moore's parents, devout Seventh Day Adventists, associated music with debauchery. But Moore was determined to learn to play an instrument. He told Mohair Slim in an interview on May 11, 2000 that he "pulled a couple of pranks" so that he could go to Alpha. "I had to learn the music and ever since I was a little kid I told them [parents] I didn't want to do anything else. I used to like use the leaf of the pumpkin and make like flutes, papaya stalks, that kind of stuff there, and combs, sardine cans with elastics, anything that would make a sound. I seen some kid next door to me, beating off a mean drum. I say, 'Bwoy, where did you learn to do that?' and he said, 'Alpha.' I said, 'Where is that?' He says, 'You can't go there,' cause my folks, they weren't the worst off. They weren't the type of people, were Seventh Day Adventists.' I says, 'Whoa! I got to get to that place.' Like I said, I had to pull a couple of pranks." Those pranks, Moore tells Ianna, involved hanging around with the wrong crowd. "From that moment I chose some of the worst kids in my neighborhood to hang around with. My parents got real nervous and said,

'Oh Lord, what's going to happen to the kid? We have to get him out of here! It was all planned by me to get into Alpha and like I say, no regrets!"

At age 10, Johnny began playing the trumpet. "Why the trumpet?" asked a *Daily Gleaner* reporter on August 26, 1985, to which Moore responded, "Because it is one of the more difficult horns to play." While at Alpha, though, Moore also learned other trades, including printing and electronics. "I got a prize one time as the best electronic engineer. We were studying some type of thing from Bennett's College in Britain. But I was a bit upset because I wanted the prize for music," he said to Mohair Slim with a laugh. "I never got it." But receive a strong musical education, Moore did, under the direction of band leader Reuben Delgado. "He was very good," says Moore of his teacher. Moore was drawn to the music of trumpeters Miles Davis, Clifford Brown, and Dizzy Gillespie, the inspiration for his nickname, Dizzy.

Johnny "Dizzy" Moore on stage with Ernest Ranglin

Johnny "Dizzy" Moore graduated from Alpha Boys' School in 1955 and just a few months later he found employment with the Jamaica Military Band. He had applied for a job with the military band, as well as a job as a linotype operator for the Daily Gleaner, and was accepted for both on the same day. He chose employment with the band. For three years Moore performed at parish holiday concerts, for international dignitary visits, at horse races, as accompaniment for choirs, and for events at the Ward Theatre, Hope Gardens, King's House, and throughout the island. He performed classical music such as Beethoven's Fifth Symphony, and marches from British composers like Kenneth J.

Alford. The band also made a recording in 1957 for Stanley Motta. Conducted by Staff Sgt. E. L. Stewart, *An Afternoon at Hope Gardens* was officially released in 1958 and promoted with performances around the island. Moore was a member of the band during this time. Moore also traveled with the band outside of Jamaica. On April 17, 1958, Johnny was one of the 31 members of the Jamaica Military Band to fly to Trinidad until April 26th to play at ceremonies in connection with opening of the Federal Parliament.

Johnny "Dizzy" Moore

Moore says that he stayed with the Jamaica Military Band for three years and eight months. He performed on his trumpet that he named Annaloria, and each subsequent trumpet was given the same name and a numerically-ordered suffix (Annaloria II, Annaloria III). The original was a 1958 Bundy trumpet. But Moore says that in 1958 he was "kicked out" of the military band because he longed to play the music he heard in the clubs rather than marches and dirges. "I was messing around Charlie Parker and Dizzy Gillespie, that sort of stuff and they tell me, 'Hey, that's not what we pay you for.' I was still into that when I should have been practicing like Beethoven and Bach. I was working on Charlie Parker and Dizzy Gillespie," Moore told Mohair Slim. Johnny frequently visited his other fellow Alpharians when they performed at clubs where he could hear the music that was popular on the society stage. Moore's first job with an orchestra was with Mapletoft Poulle. "He was one of the society top bands, you know? Some lawyer by the name of Poulle. I played around for some time, until my hair start going too long and he figure it's time for me to get a haircut. I say, 'Uh uh, no more cutting,'" he says. When Moore went to play for the Eric Deans Orchestra, despite being taunted by Deans, called "little military boy," he was also asked to leave before long. The society circuit was not the place for a musician with dreadlocks, and so Moore, refusing to cut his hair, found himself, like all Rastafari during this era, cast out.

Johnny "Dizzy" Moore

Moore told Tim Ianna that he began his affiliation with the Rastafarian way of life because of his grandfather. "That is probably due to family heritage. My grandfather was a Rastafarian. His children thought he was mad then," he says. Moore told Mohair Slim, "I always was a Rasta. I was in love with Rastafari from my early childhood days. But it started coming out now. That was part of the problem in the military band too, like I refuse to shave and that sort of thing. At that time in the military you had to be clean shaven, you know? I can remember one day, the sergeant booked me for being dirty on parade, for being unshaven. So he called the corporal and says, 'Corporal, book him.' The corporal took out his notebook and pen, started writing, but something hit me. I said, 'Hey sarge, can I ask you a question?' 'Oh yes.' 'You're a Christian man sir?' 'Yes I am.' 'You believe in the Lord God Jesus Christ?' 'Yes of course I do.' I said, 'Your God nastier than me. Same beard, longer than mine.' And the whole parade cracked up. Everybody started laughing. I ran in a lot of trouble inside there, you know? Being who I am really."

It was hard for Moore to find work anywhere. "Things were not all that rosy, because in that time, nobody catered to Rastas, you know? Rastas were like outcasts in society. Even your very folks would try to get you out of sight, you know? So I went with my bredren some. We used to play around with Count Ossie with the drum and music and entertain ourselves and whoever wanted to could come listen," Moore says to Mohair Slim. And as the music of the Wareika Hills and Rastafarian rhythms became more accepted, Moore was able to emerge to find work in the recording studios. "Wha'appen is that when the hunger for the music really start eating away at me, I decide to check on Coxsone, suggested to him that he could make some local music rather than going to the states every so often to buy some music," Moore says to Mohair Slim. "Well at first he thought I was a bit crazy cause there was all those great pop musicians in America. Great musicians in general. He thought I was a nut trying to make some music that could send up against that American art form, you know?" This proposition was successful and Moore began recording. Songs like "Milk Lane Hop" recorded

Johnny "Dizzy" Moore at the Legends of Ska concert rehearsal in Toronto, 2002
Photo by Greg Lawson

in 1961 for Coxsone by Clue J & His Blues Blasters feature Moore alongside other Alpharians Rico Rodriguez and Bobby Gaynair, and with Cluett Johnson, a former member of the Jamaica Military Band, in this early shuffle tune. Moore also recorded with Rico that same year for a song called "Freeman Lane Shuffle," this time for producer Charlie Moo. Before long, Johnny was performing regularly in studios as a session musician, along with a similar cadre of others.

In a 1984 interview with David Rodigan, Moore says that a number of these session musicians eventually drew together to form their own conglomeration—The Skatalites. Moore explains, "We do a lot of works before so, this is the point, you see, we used to record in the days and everybody would go their separate ways in the nights. He would be with one group, he with another, and I was in another group and we split up in the nights. But when session we come together, so it was while we were apart, people kept asking who did this, who did that, and so we were doing all the charts but people didn't know who was who, so we said, let's form this thing and the people know who is doing the tune, so we formed the band and we started playing the tunes, understand?" Though The Skatalites performed frequently at clubs like the Bournemouth Beach Club, they have become most well-known today for their lasting legacy—their recordings. They were incredibly prolific, thanks in large part to Don Drummond's compositions, and their songs related to pop culture—film, politics, and other genres of music. Moore cites among his favorite songs on which he performed, "Ringo," "Man in the Street," and "Schooling the Duke." He and The Skatalites backed a young Bob Marley on the song, "Simmer Down."

Johnny "Dizzy" Moore
Photo by Brian Jahn

Though they were popular and prolific, The Skatalites stayed together for little more than a year before they officially broke up. Though the members tried to continue after Don Drummond killed Margarita, it is unarguable that Drummond's absence left a large void in the band. Additionally, personalities clashed, organization was tough, and as Moore explains to Rodigan, it was a just a tough conglomeration to keep together. "Frustration really. We had people who were trying to mash us up from one time you know, because you know, when you're together with one company and then you started, you don't have to depend on a studio man to give you a session, you can play, you're playing live now, and it's difficult to get everybody at the session like before, you know. I think some producers tried to break it up and another group was formed out of it, so we just called it a day." The last gig together, recalls Moore, was at the Runaway Bay Hotel Police Dance in late August 1965. He says that Tommy McCook sought greener pastures which created tension in the group between McCook and Roland Alphonso, so as a result, the musicians in The Skatalites essentially split into two bands—The Soul Vendors and The Supersonics. "When The Skatalites broke off, Roland went and joined Coxsone. Tommy took off and worked primarily with Duke Reid," Moore tells Mohair Slim. Moore eventually worked with both groups, as well as with Kes Chin & the Souvenirs.

Johnny "Dizzy" Moore
Photo by Brian Jahn

During the reggae years, however, hornsmen were in less demand than before. Fortunately, Moore says he was able to find work during this era. He performed as a member of Bunny Wailer's band, and he reunited with The Skatalites at Sunsplash in 1983. In 1984 he joined with a group of Alpharians for the 100th anniversary of Alpha in a performance at the Carib Theatre. In 2002 he joined the Jamaica All Stars and toured Europe. In 2003 he was crucial to an exhibition of Alpha Boys' School artifacts at the Experience Music Project (today called the Pop Culture Museum) in Seattle, Washington and he appeared at the opening with Sister Mary Ignatius Davies, with whom he remained close over the years. Moore was awarded the Order of Distinction on Heroes Day, 2007 for pioneering work in popularizing Jamaican music. He died on August 16, 2008 after a battle with colon cancer, leaving behind four children as well as a number of grandchildren and great-grandchildren. A funeral was held at the Ethiopian Orthodox Church and he is interred at Dovecot Cemetery.

Johnny "Dizzy" Moore's trumpet on display at the Jamaica Music Museum

Photo by Heather Augustyn

--H.A.

Owen Gray

With a six decade career reaching right back to the 1950s pre-ska days of Jamaican home-brewed rhythm and blues and with an output of over 210 singles and 45 albums, Owen Gray can claim to be a Jamaican pioneer on a number of counts. 'I am the first artist to record a bluebeat record. I am the first artist to have an album out in Jamaica. I am the first artist to make a dub-plate for a soundsystem.' This latter claim refers to his song 'On the Beach' from 1959, often cited as the first 'special' or 'dub-plate,' a song recorded and cut exclusively for a particular sound system—in this case Sir Coxsone Downbeat. It is also thought to be the first song to directly namecheck the sound operator it was made for, a feature that would become an all-important part of soundsystem culture. The song exhorts revelers to come to the dance:

Come Down to the beach!
I was dancing to the music of Sir Coxsone Downbeat, on the beach
While I was dancing, two tunes started to make my date
The girl said, 'listen to me daddy, it's getting too late.'

Bluebeat was the name sometimes given to the Jamaican style rhythm 'n' blues of the late 1950s (not to be confused with the UK record label Bluebeat, which released Jamaican blues, ska and ballads), the craze which Owen Gray claims to have kickstarted himself with his hit single 'Who Saw Lightning Flash Across The Bay.' Even more importantly, Owen Gray was the island's first homegrown star to sing in a style that wasn't mento, calypso or jazz, bursting onto the scene with a string of hits, repeatedly topping the Jamaican charts, sometimes for months at a time.

Born on 5th July 1939, Owen Gray was the son of a soldier, the oldest of six children in a strict Catholic family. He grew up largely in Trench Town, the notorious Kingston slum that has produced more world famous musicians per square foot than possibly any other neighbourhood on Earth. Gray's mother encouraged him musically and he sang first tenor in his church choir as well as learning piano, winning his first talent show aged nine. Learning to sing gospel in church at a young age would form the bedrock of Gray's musical career. He entered Alpha largely on his own initiative. Venturing into the school premises he had a chance meeting with Sister

Ignatius that changed the course of his life forever. 'She was coming out of one of the rooms. She says, "Little boy, can I help you?" And I says to her that I just come to see what's happening here, and I'd like to come to this school. And she asked me if I was a naughty boy. And I says, "no." And the same day I was signed up. And I went home and said to my mum, "I'm going to Alpha Boys' School." And my mum says, "But Alpha Boys' School is for kids who don't go to school." I says, "Not really." I says, "I wanna go, I wanna go." She says, "Ok, when are you gonna start?" I says, "next week."'

Owen Gray
Photo courtesy Trojan Records

Even before attending Alpha, Gray had won a talent contest at the age of nine and was making himself known performing drums, keyboard and guitar by the age of twelve. His decision to go to Alpha seems to have been borne out of a feeling like he could do so much better if he was given the discipline and help. "I wasn't a bad boy, I used to do a few things like throw stones, but I chose to go to this school so I could get a little more attention. I was a neat little boy in them times, very neat. And I always obey the rules, always go by the rules,' says Gray. He's keen to emphasise that Alpha is not purely for problem children, a point affirmed by several other Alpharians. 'Now, Alpha School wasn't for bad boys, no, no, no! Alpha was like an academy. You come in and you are free to go. It wasn't for the rude boy and bad boy business.' Gray would attend Alpha for three and a half years between 1953 and 1957 and it gave him the confidence he had lacked in order to make it in the music business. 'I wanted to go there to pick up what had been left off, that I never receive and by going to Alpha I receive all the dimensions that I needed: the music, the love, the respect, the understanding. That's what it's all about,' he reflects. 'The discipline they taught in the school has kept me on my toes.'

Owen Gray
Photo courtesy Trojan Records

Although Gray didn't play in the band during his three years at Alpha, he continued to study the piano at school and absorb the music that was all around him. Like so many Jamaicans he would lap up the music beaming in from US radio stations, playing the latest R&B hits of the day by the likes of Fats Domino, Smiley Lewis and Lloyd Price. Initially working in a printing and bookbinding job after Alpha, Owen Gray always had his sights set on the music business and he forged a bond of friendship with balladeer Wilfred 'Jackie' Edwards, who wrote 'Keep On Running,' a Chris Blackwell-produced international hit in 1965 for The Spencer Davis Group. The pair worked together to break into the music business. 'The two of us was like peanut and shell,' says Gray. They would back each other instrumentally in their stage shows as well as working together to create new songs. 'In the music business them time he was my very best friend, as an artist, because we lived so close together, y'know, he used to live at my aunt's place, his father was a tailor and his father used to make my clothes, and we used to ride his bicycle. The first record we made for Chris Blackwell we bought a bicycle each out of the money. He bought a Raleigh and I bought a Rudge!' As the pair had more success, the quality of their bikes crept up, eventually cruising round Kingston on handsome new Lambrettas. Gray was living in a Trench Town yard known affectionately as The Academy because it was a place where other local singers would come and practice together, such as Delroy Wilson, Joe Higgs, Roy Wilson, Alton Ellis, Stranger Cole and Ken Boothe. The only way to get recognized for your talent in the late 1950s was to enter the talent show of the day, the Vere Johns Opportunity Hour. Broadcast live on local radio station RJR, it became the launching pad for many of the early Jamaican singers and harmony groups. With an existing repertoire including songs by artists as diverse as Nat King Cole, Brook Benton and Mahalia Jackson, Gray entered the contest in 1957 with his rendition of the Leiber and Stoller song, 'Kansas City.' As a result of the exposure, he was able to make his first recording, for Simeon L. Smith's Hi-Lite label. Smith was proprietor of a shop selling hats, liquor, hardware and some records. He used to work with musicians in the back of his shop and then take them to Federal, Jamaica's one and only recording studio. Gray cut, 'Who Saw the Lightening Flash Across the Way' for Hi-Lite, which became an instant hit and Gray maintains it was the first ever Jamaican rhythm and blues record. 'I did it—just one take,' says Gray. 'And that was it. And it become big in Jamaica, and everybody want that. When the people hear that they says, *"What?"* And that's how I get started.' The '*what?*' Gray refers to is most likely the fact that the dancers were suddenly hearing the familiar sound of R&B sung in Gray's own Jamaican accent, which would have had massive impact on the crowds and it heralded a new era of new homegrown R&B. Owen Gray went on to have several more hits for Smith at Hi-Lite, including 'Hully Gully,' 'Pretty Girl' and 'Sinners Gonna Weep and Moan.' There followed a string of hits recorded for all the major

Owen Gray
Photo courtesy Jamaica Gleaner

producers of the day including Coxsone Dodd, Prince Buster, Duke Reid and Leslie Kong. Owen Gray became one of the very first artists to work with future Island Records boss Chris Blackwell. The then 23-year-old Blackwell had stumbled across Gray playing a show at the Palace Theatre and persuaded him to record for his pre-Island label, R&B Records, scoring a hit with a tune called 'Far Love' in 1960. Keen to build on their successes, Blackwell sponsored Owen Gray and Jackie Edwards to do a stint at University College of Jamaica studying musical drama where they would refine their performance skills. Also in 1960 Gray released the first ever long playing LP by a Jamaican artist in Jamaica, *Owen Gray Sings*. Produced by Blackwell at RJR Studios and featuring top musicians like Roland Alphonso and Ernest Ranglin, the LP was released on a limited press and is now something of a collector's item. Gray coached Millie Small in vocal technique until she was ready to record her first single, a duet they sang together called 'Sugar Plum.' Also in 1960 he had a number one hit with 'Please Don't Let Me Go' for Blackwell which was released in England on the Esquire label, making a name for him in the Afro-Caribbean community there.

Owen Gray
Photo courtesy Trojan Records

In 1962 Gray heard from his brother in England that he had seen some of Gray's singles for sale in a shop in Brixton belonging to a Mr and Mrs Richards. They were being released on the UK label Bluebeat without Owen's knowledge. Gray's brother explained to the Richards his connection to one of their top selling artists. The couple saw a potential opportunity and offered to pay for Gray to come to England. Gray explains. 'Yeah, they had two record shops in Brixton deh. And apparently when my brother introduced himself to those people and he mentioned my name to them an t'ing like that, they get in touch with me. And in the space of two and a half months I was in England.' A whole new European chapter of his life would begin. Gray became a regular fixture at the Marquee Club in Soho playing mainly soul music, sharing the stage with the likes of Ben E. King, Wilson Pickett, Sam and Dave, The Platters and Solomon Burke. He found himself garnering a considerable cult following on the UK club circuit as a soul artist. Gray toured Europe in 1964 and after a show at The Roaring Twenties Club was approached by a promoter to come and perform in Paris. In 1965 he relocated there, taking a residency performing at The Curosamba on Rue De Rennes then later at the Blue Note and the Billbucky. When rocksteady came around in 1966 Gray adapted to it perfectly, recording thirteen singles for Sir Clancy Collins' Downbeat label, all now collectors' items. The late 1960s saw Gray return to England to form The Rudies, who would back many of the reggae artists of the day and later became known as Greyhound, popular with the UK's burgeoning skinhead movement. Around this time Gray released records with London based label Pama, formed by three brothers Carl, Jeff and Harry Palmer, notably 'Girl What You Doing To Me?' Gray also worked with a producer called Clem Bushay on his Bushmaster label leading to a big hit in Brasil which opened up an entirely new market for him, leading to performances in San Paolo and Sao Luis. In the early 1970s he voiced records for Trojan and its offshoot label Horse, often sweetened with an overdubbed string arrangement for a more mainstream market, referred to as 'stringsing up.' Under a new contract with Island, in 1973 Gray recorded covers of

Owen Gray
Photo courtesy Natty Bo

'Tumbling Dice' by The Rolling Stones and 'Jealous Guy' by John Lennon. He relocated to New Orleans at Chris Blackwell's behest, where he recorded an LP produced by the late-great Allen Toussant. Blackwell had designs on marketing him as a New Orleans-style soul artist, but the final product remains unreleased and the tapes have since vanished. According to Gray, he was under pressure to grow dreadlocks by Blackwell to cultivate a more rootsman image, but Gray was dressing more like a 'soul man' and 'locksing up' didn't suit him at all. This he claims was one of the reasons Blackwell didn't push the album because Gray didn't want to be marketed in the way they wanted him to be. Bunny Striker Lee was his next port of call, for whom he made some excellent roots reggae including his much loved 'Natty Bongo' single although Trojan went bankrupt immediately after releasing it in the UK, stopping its progress in its tracks.

Owen Gray has continued to record and perform internationally throughout the decades but still remains one of reggae's somewhat overlooked play-ers, having missed out on the kind of international stardom of some of his contemporaries, despite an immense back catalogue of soul, ska, rocksteady and even several gospel albums. His powers as a live performer remain undiminished. In recent years he has worked with the 36-piece Mel-bourne Ska Orchestra and has also played at three of the annual London International Ska Festivals. In 2004 Trojan put out the most comprehensive Owen Gray anthology to date, a double CD called *Shook, Shimmy and Shake* showcasing the highlights of his career, but there remains a goldmine of deleted material that deserves being made available again to the wider world.

Owen Gray performing with Lester Sterling in London 2007
Photo by Adam Reeves

--A.R.

Owen Gray at the MBE award ceremony for his friend and fellow Alpharian Rico Rodriguez in 2013

Winston 'Sparrow' Martin

None of Alpha's remarkable musical success could have happened without its lineage of bandmasters, Alpha graduates who returned to the fold to dedicate themselves to keeping the tradition going. The current bandmaster in 2017 is Winston 'Sparrow' Martin, universally known as Sparrow. He is the longest serving bandmaster in the school's history, having sacrificed his music career at the behest of Sister Ignatius in 1988 to come and teach full time. A harrowing incident during his Alpha days profoundly affected his outlook on life. 'In 1951 I was in the junior home and there was a terrible hurricane. And there were three guys that died, one on my right and two on my left. And that piece of ceiling that fell on them didn't touch me and I always remember that,' Martin recounts wistfully. As is often the case with those who have stared their own mortality in the face, it has infused him with a sense of gratitude, humility and an unwavering commitment to his life's work and mission at Alpha . 'I always remember those three guys. I went and I look at them. Four of us is in the dorm sleeping in the same row. So I have a purpose. And when I look I see these three guys, out of sight, and I am still here. And I say, *Dear Lord*.'

Winston Alphonso Martin was born in 1941 and he says he came to Alpha Boys' School after 'being a little rude.' He remembers, 'I was a boy who would do things that sometimes a boy would do. During the week sometime I would stay away from school and go to the sea. The ship used to come in with the American sailors and they used to throw money and we would dive down. One day we went to dive and somehow a boy pushed me over the sea in my school uniform. So I went to my dad and he saw me coming with my books wet and everything and he said to me, "Winston, why are your clothes like that?" and I said, "Well daddy, rain was falling." He says, "Rain wasn't falling today." So I took off my clothes and put on my yard clothes. He took my clothes and taste it. He taste the salt water and I got a good whipping for that. A very good whipping, first of all by saying untruth, and for leaving school. So my mother said to him, "Look, we can't beat this boy so much. We have to find a place for him to go to school and stay there because if we keep him here he's going to be on his own way."' A neighbor who was aware of the beating expressed concern to his mother, which helped her make her decision. 'So my mother sent me to the country because she's from St Thomas.' Finding himself in the slower-paced countryside, Martin would skip school and go and play in bushes, picking mango, grapefruit and cane. Word soon got back to his mother in Kingston that he was playing truant so she came for him and brought him back to the city. It was then that Sparrow's parents took him to Alpha, but first they had to go through the proper authorities. 'So they went to a Catholic priest and he recommend me. But you have to report to the police. They took me to the police station about what I've been doing. They make an appointment for me to go see the judge. My mother gave her statement, my father gave his statement. I have no statement! He decided I would go to Alpha. Pure bad boy go to Alpha, that's what they say, so I got a bit scared. My mother and father brought me here on a bus. I was shown to an office and we met Ignatius, this tall, slim woman. She had on her glasses and I sat there and I look at her. She said, "Good afternoon, welcome," and they had a talk. I was about nine years of age. Sister asked my name and I told her my name and she said I was going to love it here and I would be a man someday,' he says.

Winston "Sparrow" Martin

Winston Martin joined the band under bandmaster Lennie Hibbert, Jamaica's great vibraphone player. He initially learnt trumpet but Hibbert had other plans. 'Dizzy Johnny Moore teach me the trumpet, because being a junior boy the senior boys have to help the juniors and I said I'll follow Johnny Moore's footsteps. But Lennie Hibbert came and said I should learn to play the drums, so I had to do both, I had to learn the trumpet and practice the drums also.'

Martin was inspired by the music all around him growing up in Kingston. He used to see black civil rights activist Marcus Garvey with his band playing and would go and stand by the drum section absorbing the rhythm. Even before the birth of the recording industry, Jamaica was a place infused with

Winston "Sparrow" Martin on drums with Carlos Malcolm & His Afro-Jamaican Rhythms, 1965

extraordinary musical sounds. 'They used to have mento people, Pocomania and revival singers and I loved to hear that. They had a group of people, the Bobo Tribe, it was run by Prince Emanuel. So I used to pass there and hear them singing and playing their kettle drums and things like that. I used to go to the Back-O-Wall where Mortimer Planno used to have his group as a little boy and listen to them.' Back-O-Wall was a notorious slum inhabited by Rastas that the government bulldozed to make way for what is now the Tivoli Gardens area.

Even now, Martin has a deep love for Sister Ignatius, the woman who took him in as a boy and later invited him to return as a teacher and work alongside her in the music department. It was Ignatius who gave him his nickname. 'She gave me the name Sparrow Martin. One day the rain was falling and she took her umbrella and she walk the grounds to see that all the boys are in the dorm. And I saw her coming and I decide to dodge. So I climb into a tree and I was up in the tree and came under the tree and she stand there and she says, "What will you do if you stay there and drown, you naughty little sparrow?" So I came down. She says, "Go to the dormitory and then I'll come there to you. So she came to the dormitory and she said. "If you go into the tree anymore you naughty little sparrow you will drown."

The Vagabonds in May, 1964 with Winston "Sparrow" Martin, standing in sunglasses on the left

And the boys in the dorm heard that and they started calling me Sparrow.' After graduation Martin gained employment, not in music but in engineering, although it wasn't long before music called him back. 'I started with a company by the name of Chin's Radio Service and fix Delco plant because in those days electricity didn't reach all of Jamaica yet so you have to have a Delco plant and I used to fix them, service them. But I say I really want to play my music and I got a hold of some Jamaican musicians and get a band

and start to play with them. I went to the Jamaica Military Band and I really wanted to have a steady income and I stayed there for quite a while.' In the

Sparrow in Lennie Hibbert Hall at Alpha

Photo by Davis Coome

Jamaica Military Band he played French horn, vibraphone, trumpet, drums and percussion. While still in the military he joined Jamaican soul and ska singer Jimmy James and the Vagabonds, with whom he later toured England. While in London Martin recorded some tunes with Jimmy James for Chris Blackwell. Returning to Jamaica he briefly joined the Sonny Bradshaw Quartet before moving on to the newly formed Carlos Malcolm and His Afro-Jamaican Rhythms. 'That's where I start doing my real drumming,' he says. With Carlos Malcolm he went to Nassau, Trinidad, Barbados, British Guyana and the US. Martin also formed his own big band The Swinging Sixteen, gigging around Kingston and Ocho Rios. He worked for Coxsone Dodd at Studio One on some of the label's early jazz excursions. As a drummer-for-hire, Martin played drums on The Wailers' 'Stir it Up' and for Lord Creator's 'Independent Jamaica.' His drums can be heard on American guitarist Eric Gale's acclaimed 1975 jazz-reggae fusion album *Negril.* He was also a member of the All-Star Band that performed for Sammy Davis Jr. on his visit to Kingston in 1963, and a member of Frankie Bonitto's and Val Bennett's bands. In the late 1960s he was briefly in an early line-up of the group Inner Circle. However, Martin says he felt he had a deeper calling beyond gigging and recording on the Kingston music scene. 'I said to myself that I would like to teach music. I would like to teach kids. So I went back to Trench Town and I got a sponsor and I started a school by the name of SSAMA, South St. Andrew Music Academy, sixty boys and girls there. There are a few of them who still play music all over the place. I got some instruments from the leader in that area.' In August 1987 he co-founded a studio with Jimmy Cliff's recording engineer, a man known as Shaggy. Only a couple of months after launching the studio he received a call from Sister Ignatius who had heard he was back living in Kingston. She wanted him to come and assist her with the band at Alpha, to fill the position of the previous bandmaster Jackie Willacy. 'So I explained to her that I am doing a little business. She said to me to leave that business alone and come to this business.' Martin tentatively agreed but told her he needed a couple of months to finish his work up until the year's end, which gave him some breathing space to think her proposition over. In the meantime, Martin sought advice from musician friend Babe O'Brien, who encouraged him to accept the job. Shortly after this, O'Brien contracted an illness and passed away. On his deathbed he had told his wife how right he felt it was that Martin should become bandmaster at Alpha. Hearing this helped Martin make his final decision and confirm with Sister Ignatius that he would indeed be coming in the new year. He's been there ever since. 'I could have really done other things, I could have travelled, I could have earned more money, but there is an inspiration through Ignatius and I remember the days with her, and she inspired me.' Martin's own days as a student at Alpha Boys' School, and his strong musical career touring with certain key bands, recording on crucial tunes, made him the perfect leader for

Sparrow leading his students in practice at Alpha 2013
Photo by Heather Augustyn

the next generation of musicians. What Sparrow is able to bring to his students though is something that cannot be chronicled in a resume of performances and accolades or measured in matrix numbers in a record catalogue. Sparrow is a leader by example, the ultimate motivator. One of his personal missions has been to ensure that boys are able to make a living from music once they leave the school. One of the stumbling blocks has always been the prohibitive cost of professional standard musical instruments which has meant that graduates sometimes have to work for several years to save enough money to buy a decent horn, in which time they may have lost their musical ambition and even some of their skills. He explains: 'Every band that you think of throughout Jamaica, there's always Alpha Boys. You have some band leaders come to the school and pay down on a boy. They say, "I want this boy to join my band" and pay down on him. So when he leaves school he goes to that man. Some time there are advantages and disadvantages. When he goes to that man he never get a proper pay, because that man have to buy him an instrument. So instead of getting his full pay, he gets small pay. But he has to work. Now if these guys have him own instrument then that man have to pay him his salary. You see what I'm trying to drive at? So that is my whole aim. So I tell them "once you have your discipline and you learn your music you have to leave with an instrument." So I am really on that.' His persistent calls to the worldwide community for assistance have led to many donations of instruments, enabling boys to hit the ground running upon graduating instead of having to save up for a year or two. Martin has seen the school go through many changes during his tenure, not least the changeover from a boarding school to a day school in 2015. Before Sparrow Martin, there had been a period where bandmasters had not stayed very long, maybe only a few months.

Sparrow Martin
Photo by Mary Fowles

'They couldn't manage the kids because these kids now who come to Alpha it's different from our days. These kids you have to have a lot of diplomacy with them. You have to deal with them very strong. They don't have the discipline of those guys before them. You have to understand that they are coming out of *hard* homes. These guys have reached a stage where they are exposed to so-called modern things. So we have to break them down and show them another road and say, "Listen, ya see that road? That road will take you to where ya doesn't want to go. But if ya take this road, you will enjoy a beautiful life.'

In 2007, Sparrow Martin was awarded a Bronze Musgrave Medal for his distinguished career in music, and in 2012 he was awarded at the Caribbean Community of Retired Persons Limited's Jamaica 50 Living Legacy Award for service to Jamaica since Independence. 'I used to do recordings and I left all of my musical life and it feels good,' he says. Bringing the next generation of musicians into the massive fold made by the legends of Alpha Boys' School in the past is a mission to which Sparrow has made a personal calling. He has formed a group called Ska Rebirth comprised of Alpha alumni that performs many songs composed by Alpha elders. 'We are starting a movement, one which will bring back the original sound of ska from its roots and home, Alpha Boys' School in Kingston, Jamaica, and spread it once again across the entire world, this is the real ska rebirth!!'

--H.A. & A.R.

Sparrow Martin leads Ska Rebirth during rehearsal in 2013

Photo by Heather Augustyn

Kenneth "Mutt" Davy

One half of the sound system duo known as Mutt and Jeff, Kenneth Davy was a graduate of Alpha Boys' School and a continued supporter of Sister Mary Ignatius Davies and her students. Mutt was Kenneth Davy and he named his sound system Mutt and Jeff after the popular comic strip of the day which featured a very tall character, Mutt, and a "half-pint" named Jeff. The comic strip was carried in the *Star*, one of the island's newspapers. Davy, who was over six feet tall, held the Mutt moniker, and Jeff was better known as Leighton Geoff, a short fellow with an appropriate last name.

Mutt and Jeff Sound System with Lennie Hibbert's Combo
Daily *Gleaner*, February 14, 1958

Davy attended Alpha Boys' School and was a skilled public speaker and debater. After he graduated, Sister Ignatius asked Davy to return to emcee various school events and presentations, such as plays, concerts, and sporting competitions. He did this all without the aid of any amplification, but around 1956 he purchased a microphone, a small amplifier, and two 12 inch speakers. He quickly moved into providing background music at these events and started hosting sound system dances at Alpha. As word of his entertainment skill spread, Davy began organizing dances outside of Alpha and he soon found the need to upgrade his equipment to meet demand. Davy worked his full-time day job in the Alpha Boys' School printery, directing the boys in the trade of setting type, inking presses, and printing books that were then bound in the school's bindery. With the blessing of Sister Ignatius, Davy's sound system upgrade was a project handled by the school's woodshop. The boys learned to produce a custom item under the watchful eye of Davy whose printery was adjacent to the woodshop and he would frequently leave his shop to help supervise the boys with their table saws, sanders, and hammers. The woodshop, like the printery and the pottery shop and the garden and the shoe shop, were not only areas of trade instruction for the boys. They were also revenue makers, as they still are today, helping to offset the operational costs of the school. Making custom items for customers was part of the school's operation, and part of training for the boys.

Davy was able to generate a decent amount of revenue from the sound system. Sets were advertised, "Mutt and Jeff Clear As A Bell," since Geoff frequently upgraded the system with parts from where he worked, Wonard's electronics and appliance store. Davy's wife Gloria supplied the soundsystem dances with her catering. When Davy decided in 1964 to leave the life of the sound system behind to spend more time with his wife and their eleven children, he sold his entire set, equipment and music, to Sister Ignatius who added the records to her already-large collection. Sister Ignatius had hundreds of 78 and 45 records in her collection—everything from classical music to speeches by Malcolm X—and she used this system to teach the boys about music, and to host events and dances for the school.

--H.A.

***Daily Gleaner*, February 14, 1958**

Ron Wilson

Learning to play the trombone as a member of the Alpha Boys' School Band, Ron Wilson became a member of the original Skatalites, though arguably not officially. He recorded in 1964 and 1965 for King Edwards as "Upcoming Willow and His Trombone and King Edwards All Stars." "Willow" was Wilson's nickname and these songs, "Jones Town Special," "Prime Minister's State," "Lon Chaney," and "Red China," featured Wilson on trombone in addition to members of The Skatalites. According to the Alpha Boys' School Radio bio, "The fact that Ronald Wilson led the band on these sessions was probably the reason for the name change." He also performed on the classic recordings, "Musical Workshop" with Baba Brooks for King Edwards, and on "African Queen" with Don Drummond, both for King Edwards. He also recorded "Lonely Man" for King Edwards, and he recorded for other producers as well, including Duke Reid as a member of Lynn Taitt and the Comets on the song "Tender Loving Care," Lloyd "Matador" Daley on the song "Repatriation Version II," and for Errol Dunkley on "Taga Special," to name a few.

In 1967 he led his own band, Ron Wilson and the Comets, performing at venues such as Club Havana, Mimosa Hotel, and Bill's Place. That same year, Ron Wilson and the Comets backed up 15 artists, including Desmond Dekker, and Stranger & Patsy, for street concerts celebrating the fifth anniversary of independence and the shows drew huge crowds. In July 1971, Wilson performed with Tommy McCook, Glen DaCosta, David Madden, and others for the Four Tops tour in Jamaica.

Daily Gleaner
August 26, 1967

Wilson continued to record as a solo artist, as well as with fellow Alpharian Tommy McCook. Over the years, Wilson appeared in The Upsetters lineup and he also recorded with King Tubby and Glen Brown, Gregory Isaacs, and Bob Andy, in addition to beginning his own label, Splendid Sound. In 1998, Wilson recorded the album *T. Bone* for Foxtail Records.

In the early 1970s Ron Wilson returned to the Alpha Boys' School Band where he taught with Lennie Hibbert. Tony Greene cites him as being one of his teachers. His Alpha Boys' School Radio bio states that he also, "Played in the Lester Sterling reformed Skatalites in 1978-80 and then with the Tommy McCook led Skatalites in 1988 and 1990. Ron appears in a Skatalites concert video from the Church House Inn, formerly of Providence Rhode Island. It was recorded on September 14, 1990 and released commercially. Ron became a music teacher in New York City Public Schools in the 1980s and taught for over 20 years."

--H.A.

Ron Wilson on left on tour with The Skatalites in 1989 with Manager Ken Stewart, Devon James, Lloyd Knibb, Lloyd Brevett, and Tommy McCook
Photo courtesy Ken Stewart

Trades at Alpha: Woodworking
Photo by Adam Reeves

Leslie Samuels

Tenor saxophonist Leslie Samuels found work, as many others did after graduation, with the Jamaica Military Band. He then performed with a number of popular bands during the late 1950s and early 1960s including Sonny Bradshaw, Kes Chin, and Carlos Malcolm, with whom he traveled to Nassau to tour. Malcolm explains how Alpha was always a good source of talent. He states, "The personnel of the original Carlos Malcolm and His Afro-Jamaican Rhythms were trained at Alpha Boys' School and the Jamaica Military Band. They read and interpreted music fluently. Oftentimes, while playing at engagements we would have requests for tunes that were not in the band's repertoire. I would disappear with sheets of music manuscript, sketch a simple arrangement of the requested tune in a quiet place like the 'john,' place the new music on each music stand while they were playing, indicate the new tempo of the piece and they would jump right into music that they had never seen before as if it were part of the standing repertoire. Winston Turner, Ozzie Lawson, Karl 'Cannonball' Bryan, Les Samuels were excellent 'first sight' readers and outstanding musicians."

Leslie Samuels with Carlos Malcolm and His Afro-Jamaican Rhythms, fourth from left

Malcolm says that he didn't go directly to Alpha to find Samuels, but that he came to Malcolm years later through another musician. Malcolm recalls, "I found Les an ideal, cooperative team player. I found him a capable musician who responded to instructions and listened to the other musicians with whom he played in order balance his input with the 'horn section.' Ozzie

Lawson, second trumpet, brought Les to me when the orchestra was experiencing a run of several players (including Roland Alphonso), who temporarily occupied the tenor saxophone position. I never shared much with Les off the bandstand, regarding his private life. My observations were that he was a private person who was did not volunteer information." Samuels appeared on Malcolm's *Space Flight* album with Alpharians Karl "Cannonball" Bryan and Winston "Sparrow" Martin, as well as Larry McDonald on congas, and vocals by Boris Gardner and Lascelles Perkins.

Samuels continued to perform after his tenure with Malcolm, and in July, 1971, Samuels backed up the Four Tops at the Regal Theatre along with Alpharians Tommy McCook and Dave Madden as well as Herman Marquis, Ron Wilson, Hansel (Smudge) Smith, Nemiah Bennett, and Egbert Evans. Samuels also performed sax with the Mystic Revelation of the Rastafari which is now a 10-piece unit. Samuels and bass drummer Sustan James are the longest tenured members of the band, though their playing as a group is sporadic.

While appearing as a featured speaker at an event in Kingston at the Jamaica Music Museum in February, 2017, Malcolm says he reconnected with Samuels after the lecture. "I began wending my way through the crowd, I was confronted by an old colleague in the company of another man. The other man said to me, 'Do you know who I am?' I took a long, careful look at the individual standing before me, then answered, 'I'm not sure…no.' He said, 'Don't you recognize your own tenor sax man?' 'Les?' I asked. 'Yah, man!' The shock of the moment reassured my respect for time and mortality. In our warm reunion, Les revealed that over time he concluded that he could no longer meet the demands of the saxophone and had to retire."

Leslie Samuels on right with Delfeayo Marsalis

--H.A.

Joseph "Jo Jo" Bennett

When it comes to the trumpet, some have a style that is brash and bold, more like a bugle, an announcement, a proclamation. Not Jo Jo Bennett. His expression of his inner spirit as communicated through his horn is smooth, warm, sincere. It is, like one of his songs declare, ten steps to the soul. Or even closer.

Joseph "Jo Jo" Bennett was born in 1940 in Kingston and came to Alpha by way of an orphanage associated with the school. He explains, "My mom [Mable Noble] took me to a children's home when I was two years of age, Maxfield Park Children's Home. It was a big family and mom couldn't really take care, so me and my brother went to Maxfield Park, but he was three years older than me and I was two when I went there. I had two brothers and two sisters. I didn't grow up with my mom and dad. I grew up at Maxfield Park and then I went to Alpha when I was 10. Alpha is home. There were about 400 or 500 boys there at the time. I had more than one mother. All the sisters were my mother. Growing up at Alpha I didn't really see my siblings and they didn't really visit me too often. One of the boys came to Alpha for a few years too but he wasn't in the band, and one of my sisters, they had a girls' school too, Alpha Girls School, and she went there too. I joined the band at 10 or 11."

Jo Jo Bennett at the Legends of Ska Concert, Toronto 2002
Photo by Greg Lawson

Like many other students in the band, Jo Jo started on a different instrument than he eventually made his own, but performing on other instruments extended his musical education. "I started on the drums because that's the one I choose, but there were so many drummers and the bandmaster, Reuben Delgado, said some of you have to change your instrument, so I change to the trumpet." This knowledge gave Jo Jo the ability to teach these instruments to other students at Alpha, as well as later in life when he started his own school.

Immediately after leaving Alpha at age 16, Jo Jo says he went to find work performing for tourists. "First I went on the north coast, Montego Bay, to go play at the hotels because in Kingston it was only record business. There was not many live parts in Kingston, so I went to Montego Bay and I played in a few hotels over the years, mostly American stuff really, for tourists. I did that about four or five years. After the hotels I played in the Military Band. I didn't want to get involved with the recording business in Kingston because I wasn't comfortable really. The owners of the recording studio, they tell you what to play and I didn't want to get involved with that. I was with the Military Band about four years and they wanted me to sign up for a couple more years but I didn't like too much military thing, you know? So I left and went back to the north coast and spent a few years there. I did a couple of months at the Tower Isle, and the Half Moon Hotel in Montego Bay and a few more hotels there," he says.

It was here on the north coast that Jo Jo was visited by the most popular bandleader on the island at the time who asked him to join their ranks, and he jumped at the chance. "Byron Lee came to Montego Bay with his band and he asked me if I could come join his band because his trumpeter was leaving his band to the states, so I said definitely. So after a few months I left Montego Bay to go to Kingston and joined Byron Lee & the Dragonaires. I toured with him in 1965 and I went back to Jamaica and start to tour with him in 1966 and 1967," says Jo Jo. But he was restless for something different, he says. Just as he wanted to stay out of the recording studios in order to spread his own wings, so too did he want to leave the country to see what the world had to offer. "In the meantime, I was really kind of planning to run away from Jamaica. I just wanted to get to the outside world, you know what I mean? That's when I decided I was going to go to Canada. I toured with him [Byron Lee] to the United States, but my vibes couldn't take to the Americans, so in '67 after the tour, I just board a Greyhound bus and head for Canada. When I reach the border, this immigration man ask why I am coming to Canada. I say I am just on a tour with Byron Lee & the Dragonaires and I'm just taking a likkle holiday, a break before I go back to Jamaica, but that wasn't the case!" he says, laughing. "And I'm still in Canada!"

Jo Jo settled in Toronto, like many other Jamaicans during this time. He found work at a place where Jamaican musicians on tour with the Jamaica Women Teachers Federation had performed a few years earlier. It was a little island away from the island. "I was playing at the West Indian Federation Club once a week. The owners asked me if I could put a band together so I said yes, but I would love to get some of those Jamaican musicians, so the owners said they would help with the papers. I gave him a few names, and after about three months they showed up at the airport. I called it Jo Jo and the Fugitives. We played mostly

West Indian music and one or two American songs. I did that for a few years and then the immigration caught up with me!" he says, again laughing. "We went to court and they said Mr. Bennett you have to leave the country. They said, Mr. Bennett, if you don't leave, we are going to deport you, and I didn't want that to happen. So I work at the club on a Saturday night and jump on the plane on Sunday morning. I was back in Jamaica about two years and in the meantime the club was working to get me back there, for the club's sake, they wanted the band. All of those guys I brought up, they apply for permanent residency and all of them got through, but me!"

During this time back in Jamaica, Jo Jo did make a number of recordings. He had made a few recordings as Jo Jo and the Fugitives in Canada that was distributed on Graeme Goodall's Doctor Bird label, and a few for Byron Lee, but in 1970 Jo Jo recorded a solo album for producer Harry Mudie called *Groovy Joe.* Articles in local newspapers called Jo Jo "Happy with a Hot Horn." His most notable song on this album, which was also released as a single, was "Leaving Rome," and instrumental ballad featuring a string arrangement. Soon though, Jo Jo was leaving Jamaica, again, to return to Toronto where he had grown his own roots, though some things had changed during his time away. "I got my traveling papers to come back to Canada and I came back, but I heard the club got burned down and one of the owners passed away, so the rest of the owners decided to just give it up."

But Jo Jo pressed on. He had performed with his band for years in Toronto, and despite not having a venue or an impresario, he still had his musicians. He says, "I still had my band there, taking gigs here and there, so we were still together so I can see and feel that I am onto something good, you know? So we all stick together." But touring around, not being at one location, eventually became a burden. "I was always on the road traveling and I get tired of the road, so I decide to start a music school in 1980 and I named the school Sattalite Music School, named after the famous Jamaican band The Skatalites. We were school-mates and so that's how I got the name." Jo Jo founded the school with Canadian musician Fergus Hambleton.

Jo Jo Bennett and Fergus Hambleton with the Sattalites

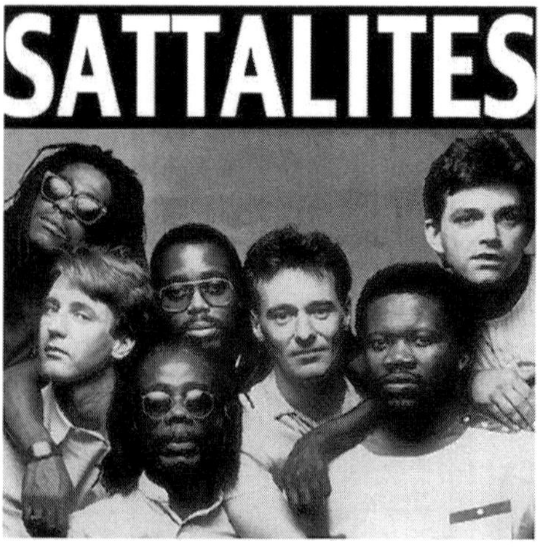

Jo Jo says that the school was successful and it led to the foundation of another band of the same name, the Sattalites. He says, "The school stick around for a few years and it taught all instruments because I can play them all, you know? Not for a living—my trumpet playing was my bread and butter, but I could fool with the piano, the bass, the drums, you know? I had about two or three other instructors and we taught all ages. The funny thing about it, most of the professionals that came to the school, all they wanted was to learn how to play the Jamaican music, the reggae music, how to get the guitar to go like that. And the drum and the bass, the offbeat, the second half of the beat. Some of us that put that school together start going on the road, operating outside, all over. The name was building and the school was building too."

The school eventually closed when Jo Jo says that the owner of the building raised rent and they were unable to afford the hike, though he continued to teach students at his home. The band, however, continued to be successful, even performing in Jamaica as the first Canadian band to play at Sunsplash in 1990. They also made a number of recordings and have won two Juno Awards and three Canadian Reggae Music Awards. They were called "Canada's UB40" by the *Montreal Gazette*, quite an accolade during the late 1980s. The band still performs regularly at Toronto's Orbit Room. "Even if I can't make it every Tuesday, the rest of the band still make it," says Jo Jo.

Personally, Jo Jo was married twice—once in Jamaica and once in Canada. He has eight children and his youngest daughter takes care of him in

Toronto. He says that Alpha is still near and dear to his heart. "That's my second home, or my first home. We were the instrumentalists," he says with a little pride in his voice. "Most of the players in the early times were boys of Alpha." In 1984, Jo Jo returned to Alpha to donate a number of instruments to the school in celebration of their 100th anniversary. "Let us give back something to Alpha," he said at the time. Jo Jo Bennett has devoted his life to making sure he has—a legacy of warm, soulful music.

--H.A.

Alpha music students in 2013 look at photos of successful Alpha Boys' School band alumni
Photo by Heather Augustyn

Glen DaCosta

Equally as comfortable with a clarinet, saxophone, flute, or oboe in his hand, Glen DaCosta is no stranger to the stage. Performing as a member of Bob Marley's horn section, as a member of the incredibly popular Zap Pow, as a decade-long member of the military band, and as a session player at numerous studios, DaCosta is a master musician.

Born in Trelawny in 1942, DaCosta says his mother moved the family to Kingston at an early age. "My mom came to Kingston pretty early, when I was three years old, so she could have a better life and find employment because in those days there was not much opportunity in the country. To see all of the bright lights was a treat for us because in Trelawny at night it's mostly peenie wally. That's a firefly. You see twinkling like lights. That was the most light we saw at night in those days. We went to a very intense inner city area, Chestnut Lane which is close to the Coronation Market and my mom would go there and sell anything she could put her hands on, just to make sure she could put food on the table for us. That was her main objective. She had four kids at the time, well five but one died shortly after birth unfortunately, Lennie was his name. We were all so sad because he lived for at least a year. He died from pneumonia," DaCosta says.

Life was hard for his mother who raised the children on her own. Unable to properly care for them, she sought help. She had no choice. "I came to Alpha from an orphanage, which is Maxfield Park Children's Home. Mom had more kids than she could manage and my dad was not there for us so she had to look out for what was best. She had to make sure we had some education but she couldn't afford it. She was having the kids so fast. She had to do menial things to survive and it was hard. I had to go at an early age of six, which was a little puzzling to me at the time, but I understood the situation after a while. She hardly even come to look for me because she had to be working seven days a week to take care of my other little brother because from him she wouldn't be parted. She wanted to hold on to him because he was the last kid she had, what we call wash belly," he says.

A number of boys who attended Alpha Boys' School began, like DaCosta, at Maxfield Park Children's Home. When they were 11 years of age they then attended Alpha. DaCosta says he was one of these boys. "I was at

Alpha Boys' School until I was about 17. I left in 1959. I went to Maxfield Home in 1948," he says. While at Alpha, like many others, he found a calling with the band rather than the other forms of vocational training available. He says, "I always loved music from when I was a little child. When I was at Maxfield Park I would hear the parties around, which we were not able to attend as kids. The music was appealing to me as a kid. I gravitated toward it very early. I always enjoyed listening to the band play and I would hide under the tree where they would play just to listen to band. Then one day Mr. Delgado caught me in the tree when I should be at the garden at the time. I didn't so much take to my agricultural part of my experience there. It wasn't really what I enjoyed. And Mr. Delgado saw me in the tree because my foot slip and shake a branch. He turned around and said, 'Aye, Zacchaeus, come down!' like in the Bible when Christ asks Zacchaeus to come out of the tree. So I came down and he said, 'What are you doing up there?' and I said, 'I'm listening to the music.' He said, 'You like music?' I said, 'Yeah.' He said, 'You want to play music?' I said, 'Sure, sir!' He said, 'What instrument you want to play?' I said, "Saxophone.' He said, 'I'm sorry but we have so much saxophone players, we don't need saxophone players right now, so what else you like to play?' I said, "Anything!' So he picked up a clarinet and said, 'If you get a sound out of it, you're in the band.' It took me about half an hour to get a sound from the clarinet! A guy was there teaching me how to blow it and once I get a sound he said, 'Okay, you have a tutor now,' so someone started teaching me then. I was about eleven-and-a-half years old then. We had Sparrow Martin, Nugent Clarke, Cedric Brooks was first clarinet. We had practice every day except for Sundays. We play a half day on Saturday. It was a good foundation for me."

After DaCosta left school, instead of following a career in music, he sought a career in electrical engineering, which was unanticipated, even for him. "When I was about ready to leave school, after six years of musical study, I was sent to an electrical engineering establishment, which was surprising to me. They thought I was suited for electrical engineering because I was one of the guys who was able to wire the entire compound. But I wasn't comfortable there. While I was there, all I was thinking about was music!" That job lasted only a short time, but DaCosta was forced to quickly find a job to pay his bills. He says, "I was working with a hardware store and I had to carry things on a bicycle to deliver, and it was fun for me, after leaving school, learning to be independent. The money wasn't much but I appreciated whatever I could get." Though his career may have taken him further astray from his personal interests than he would have liked, he was careful not to allow his social relationships do the same. He explains, "While I was working at the hardware store, I had friends who were close by who were brothers, who were considered bad guys at the time. They were actually fighting with the police. They were shooting at the police. They would ask me to come out with them sometimes when they are going out, but I say, no boy, and I would cook the food for them sometimes when they come back. I could have been ... they were charged for murder. They got life imprisonment, both of them," says DaCosta of his narrow escape from the rude boy life.

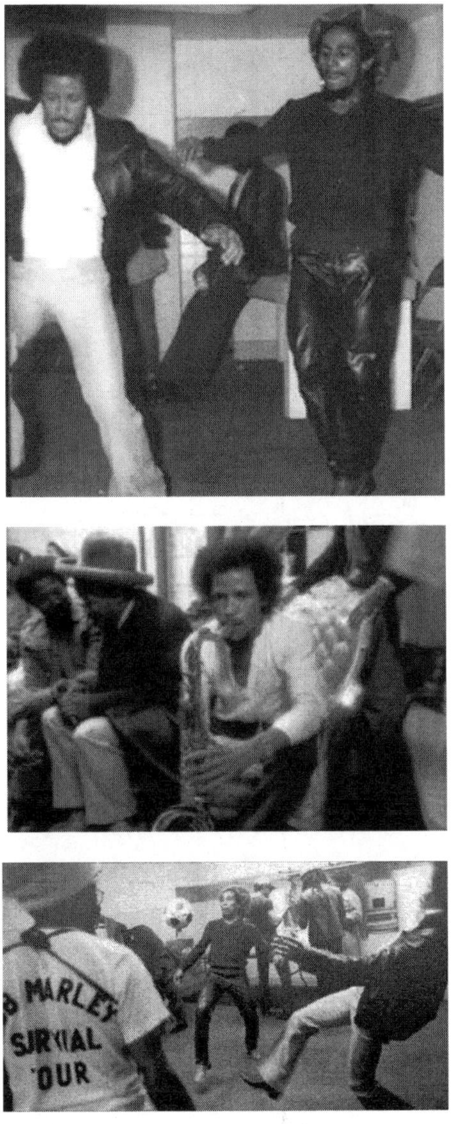

DaCosta on tour with Bob Marley

Soon, DaCosta found himself returning to what he loved best—music. "I started with the Jamaica Steel Band, which was the first steel band in Jamaica with a man who had a wine distilling establishment and I would wash the bottles and keep the place clean, and then he had a band, and that really excited me. A guy was teaching steel pan to the group, and another guy make the steel pans. They were from Trinidad and Barbados. I got chosen to play the lead pan because I had a little experience in music. We played for the float parade, the Marrakesh Hotel before it became the Playboy, and the Copa Cabana. That was a lot of fun for me, until I decided I wanted to play serious music. I had an opportunity to get a little saxophone that was leaking. I think it was from Alpha at the time. I used soap to patch it so I could get a sound from it," he says.

But washing bottles and playing a few gigs on the weekend wasn't satisfying enough for DaCosta. He chose to follow a route that many Alpharians select after graduation. DaCosta explains, "The West India Regiment Band, I went on my own because they weren't actually recruiting. This was 1961. They said they weren't recruiting, and plus I was too short. You had to be 5'8" and I was only 5'6". They said, 'Why you want to join the army?' It was my expression that 'I am willing and able and want to serve my country to the best of my ability' and they were impressed with my statement. They said, 'Okay, let us see what you can do,' so they got a clarinet, which I told them I played, and they thought I played well, and they gave me an academic test, and I remember they said, 'We have a little gentleman here who is quite determined to join the army and it is hard to turn him away. He is so ambitious and intelligent.' They said they won't get a uniform until about three months' time when they are recruiting. I say, 'No problem, sir.'

Advertisement from 1979

Finally I was admitted in the army and I was playing in my civvies! It was a great bunch of guys, well qualified musicians. After independence the name was changed to the First Battalion Jamaica Regiment. I always wanted to be a part of it. It was not only employment, but what I love to do the most." DaCosta served with the military band for 10 years.

At the same time, DaCosta also performed in the studio with a few local bands. "My first recording was about 1962. I was playing on a song, I can't remember the name of it, all I remember about that song was my solo, the first song I ever soloed on, and I remember it like it was yesterday. I was so proud of that because there were some legendary musicians like Tommy McCook, Roland Alphonso, the Lloyds [Knibb and Brevett], Raymond Harper was the trumpeter on that particular session, which was at a home studio, somewhere in the ghetto, I think it was Jah Jerry's studio, Jah Jerry was there too. When it came time to solo, Tommy and Alphonso say, 'Go ahead, blow yout, blow,' and I was so shocked, they wanted me to solo instead. It went, da dada da dum (sings the melody of "Feeling Fine"). And that was a clarinet solo. I'll never forget it. They used to have sound systems at the time and it was done for King Edwards. I remember hearing it on the juke box because our music was not played on the radio, which was absurd, you know? I was also playing with bands like Los Caballeros at the drive-in on Maxfield Avenue [Johnson's Drive Inn] and it was a big band and you have to read sheet music, so that was good training for me. I started venturing out with other groups like Lynn Taitt and the Comets who was a fixture in the rocksteady era. In the studio from time to time I was brought in, like Black Ark Studio with Lee Scratch Perry and Dynamic and there were so many studios we were going to. We were going

DaCosta, center on sax, with Zap Pow

to Federal for sure because my father actually build that studio for them. He was a construction builder and architect, Walden was his name. He was a genius. He built houses for the family," says DaCosta.

His musical career gained even more momentum when Glen reconnected with trumpeter and fellow Alpharian David Madden. "I was actually wandering down King Street one day," recalls DaCosta, "and I heard this marvelous music, so I said, 'Wow, where is this music coming from?' So I went upstairs, they had a little place there, they used to play on Sundays, and the music really caught me because it was so different from everything else that was happening. I like it when people explore and be spontaneous and just play from the heart. When I went and saw them there, I could just see myself in the lineup. And I said to them, 'Boy, if only there was a saxophone.' They said, 'You want to play that?' I said, 'Sure man,' they said, 'Okay, you're in.' Because they knew I was competent enough because I was used to playing in a group. I was so happy to be with Zap Pow, with all individuals being so proficient. I was an integral part of the music as well as the business."

Glen DaCosta

Exposure of his talents with Zap Pow led to further opportunity. "Zap Pow was one of the most prominent groups at the time," he explains. "We were making hits and we had one of the best horn sections in reggae music at the time. We were making hits like 'Mystic Mood' and Bob Marley heard about us. He wanted the best horns and he asked us to come along and he asked us to play on his records, so we started in about '73. Our first album was *Natty Dread*, then we went to England in '76 to do *Kaya* and *Exodus*. I didn't do the *Survival* album, I just did the tour which was recorded live. That was a treat, a highlight of my career, seeing how the world embraced Bob." Today, Glen DaCosta continues to perform from his home base in the state of Maine in the United States.

--H.A.

Cedric 'IM' Brooks

One of the most intriguing and original musicians to emerge from reggae is Cedric 'IM' Brooks, the tenor saxophonist who fused elements of Afrobeat, be-bop jazz, reggae, mento, rumba, calypso, disco and Nyabinghi into his own unique sub-genre. At a time when reggae music was pre-occupied with singing about Africa, Brooks Africanised the very music itself. He managed to re-define the boundaries of what can be called reggae, while staying true to the essence of Jamaican music. Like his fellow Alpharian Joe Harriott, Cedric Brooks opened himself up to a wider vision of global rhythm and sound and can be called a true pioneer of today's world roots music melting pot. He was deeply involved in Jamaican music for over fifty years, which included working on landmark recordings with Burning Spear, Bob Marley, The Heptones and many more.

Cedric Brooks in 1965 performing at Club 35 in Montego Bay

Born in Denham Town, a neighbourhood on the west side of Kingston close by Trench Town, Cedric Brooks grew up in a musical environment. The family home belonged to a senior member of the Salvation Army and was often used as a band rehearsal space. Cedric's uncle, Oswald 'Baba' Brooks, the great ska trumpet player grew up in the same household.

Brooks was sent to Alpha at the age of eight due to family financial constraints. He joined the band to study piano and clarinet under the guidance of bandleaders Reuben Delgado and Lennie Hibbert and showed early signs of musical promise. Upon leaving Alpha he took the familiar route of joining the Jamaica Military Band, touring Canada in 1961 while further developing his musical confidence. He visited the Wareika Hills Rastafarian community above Kingston where he spent time with the master percussionist Count Ossie, learning to play drums by staying up all night for extended Nyabinghi drum sessions. Count Ossie's camp was a place where many of the future innovators of ska and reggae would find their musical

Cedric 'IM' Brooks on sax with Rico Rodriguez, trombone, and Count Ossie and his drummers

expression, such as Rico Rodriguez, Don Drummond, Tommy McCook and many more. After this tour he joined the popular Jamaican group The Vagabonds, gaining regular work playing for tourists in upmarket hotels as well as the local nightclub scene. With the Vagabonds he first entered a studio and made a few records with them, for which he also did musical arrangements. After a three year stint with the band, he would later migrate to other key big bands of the day such as Sonny Bradshaw's Band and the Granville Williams Orchestra.

Brooks moved to Philadelphia in 1968 to further his musical studies at the Coombs College of Music. As well as getting to meet one of his heroes, Sonny Rollins, in Philadelphia he would connect with locally based cosmic jazz experimentalist Sun Ra and his band of otherworldly jazz mystics known as The Arkestra. Sun Ra headed up a kind of free-jazz commune, where the members lived a frugal monastic life together fully immersed in jazz and new philosophies of music. The impact of meeting this extraordinary ensemble of players would have a major impact on the course of Brooks' musical life. Sun Ra offered Cedric Brooks the opportunity to become a full time Arkestra member, but he was about to have a second child so returned to Jamaica. Talking about his time with Sun Ra, Brooks spoke on CLM TV saying, 'I met the group and at one time I was heading towards getting involved. The philosophy behind the group is really to create a new awareness, a new creativity based on the African culture itself. Of course all the music has some bearing with Africa but a group like Sun Ra emphasizes more of the traditional African music as the core of their musical evolution. Of course, it's in a jazz setting and jazz has been to the American community the freedom of expression of our people.'

Cedric "IM" Brooks and Rico Rodriguez

Brooks returned to Jamaica as Cedric 'IM' Brooks, a direct inspiration from his time with Sun Ra, who had encouraged him to embrace his African identity. 'IM' was an abbreviation of Imperial Majesty, referencing Emperor Haile Selassie and an assertion of his own calling to Rastafari. Again he immersed himself in the local music scene, working with Coxone Dodd at Studio One, where he would record some fine instrumentals as one part of Im and David with his old Alpharian friend trumpeter David Madden. At Studio One he helped with arrangements on several classic tracks including the majestic horn riff on Burning Spear's spookily atmospheric 'Door Peep.'

Having passed on the opportunity of joining Sun Ra's Arkestra, Brooks envisioned forming his own Jamaican equivalent, a Rastafarian community of drummers, musicians, dancers and artists where they could live as one and express their creativity together. The influence of Sun Ra really only went as far as the communal living, devotional, musical collective aspect, as Brooks's music bore no resemblance to Sun Ra's free-form be-bop jazz. Initially Brooks formed The Mystics with David Madden, fusing reggae and experimental jazz. Members of the group would soon merge with Count

Cedric "IM" Brooks from the cover of his *United Africa* album

Ossie's drummers to form The Mystic Revelation of Rastafari in 1971. The idea was to bring together Nyabinghi drumming with chanting, poetry, free-jazz and a back-to-Africa roots philosophy. The group's debut album *Groundation* was a three-disc epic and one of the most ambitious records ever made in Jamaica. It is a no-frills, lo-fi outpouring of spiritual devotion, causing the listener to feel like they are right there in the drum circle. Rough around the edges, the record has the purity and urgency of a field recording. Talking in an interview on CLM TV, Brooks explains his passion for drumming and its importance in the culture of Jamaica: 'The drum is the main African voice. The drum culture throughout Africa is really the main musical component, the main musical voice. I've been involved in a number of groups that use the drum as the basis, for example The Mystic Revelation of Rastafari. Of course, the drumming is a very important part of the Rasta culture because it is the thing that keep the chanting and the group collection when the groups meet, then the drumming is a part of the calling of the Rastafari community and that is of course because it really emphasizes the importance of the African culture.'

A further step towards Brooks' vision of a Jamaican-style Arkestra was Divine Light, a group Brooks formed in 1973, incorporating the Afro-beat sound of Fela Kuti, the township jazz of Hugh Masekela and the deep roots drumming of Count Ossie. It was around this time that Brooks stepped into a new role as lecturer at the African-American department of the Jamaican School of Music. He would later become head of the department. Through his work here Brooks recorded the album *From Mento to Reggae to Third World Music* for the Institute, a kind of audio-academic study of the development of grassroots musical styles in Jamaica. The group changed their name to The Light of Saba with the release their next album *In Reggae*, a continuation of the free-jazz reggae mash-up. Brooks also helped produce, arrange and play on the second album by The Mystic Revelation of Rastafari, *Tales of Mozambique*, another landmark recording. A return to Studio One with David Madden in 1977 produced an outstanding instrumental album, *Im Flash Forward.* Then in 1978 Brooks put a new band together consisting of up to 30 players to record *United Africa,* a gloriously cacophonous wall-of-sound reggae and Afro-beat experiment. At the end of the 1970s Brooks moved to New York City where his output slowed down as he studied to be a minster with the Ethiopian Orthodox Church, spending time living in Ethiopia. Speaking of his time in Ethiopia to CLM-TV, Brooks said, 'I was given the privilege through the Ethiopian Orthodox Church to go and study in Ethiopia so I got a really good glimpse of the Ethiopian society and a lot of the culture. I learned so much more about the general African cultures because almost all the other African cultures of the other parts of Africa, you can find some corresponding culture in Ethiopia. It was very interesting going to Ethiopia and it broaden mi scope, even musically.'

Brooks' musical work lessened over the next two decades, but he did find work as a session player and arranger, as well as joining Carlos Malcolm's California-based 20 strong ska and mento band, Zimbobway's King Kingston Orchestra. He became a full-time member of the The Skatalites after the passing of Roland Alphonso in 1999, injecting the band with his unique flavor, travelling the world playing to way larger audiences than he'd ever seen before and allowing many fans of his music to connect with him in person at long last. In 2002 he was honoured for his life's work at the Ocho Rios Jazz Festival. Host Dwight Wylie described him as 'the perfect blend of musician and educator.' After suffering complications from diabetes Brooks was admitted in an unconscious state to Bronx Lebanon Hospital in 2010. He was later moved to a care home in Queens where he remained in a semi-comatic state until the end of his life in 2013. He was honoured with several prestigious awards for his life's work. Firstly, an award by Caribbean Lifestyle TV at its gala and awards ceremony in Manhattan as part of Black History/Reggae Month celebrations. Then in June 2011 he was honoured with two proclamations by New York State Assembly at the Assembly House Floor in Albany, NY, both accepted by his sister Paulette Keise. One was from the Bronx New York State Assembly Eric Stevenson and another from Queens Congressman Gregory Meeks. A ceremony took place with many longtime friends and associates which Brooks was unable to attend due to his comatose condition. In 2013 shortly after his passing Brooks was given a posthumous Groovin' award at the 2013 Groovin' In The Park outdoor reggae and contemporary R&B festival in Queens, NYC.

Cedric Brooks
Photo by David Corio

--A.R.

David Madden

In April, 2016, Studio One reissued the album *Money Maker*, one of the rarest albums that was originally released in 1970. It was the first time that many audiences heard the sweet saxophone and trumpet melodies and harmonies of Im and David, Cedric "Im" Brooks and David Madden. The duo was together in this incarnation for only a few years, though they frequently played together on stage behind Bob Marley with their fellow Alpharian Glen DaCosta and in studio with Alpharian Vin Gordon. David Madden, like the others, would also have a successful solo career and was member of countless bands and studio sessions, thanks to his start at Alpha Boys' School.

Born in Kingston on January 6, 1943, Madden says he first became enamored with the trumpet after hearing it as a young child. "There was a little garden party in town, a little carnival thing, and there was a band playing and there was a guy blowing the trumpet, and I can remember I was about four or five at the time. I remember standing by the guy when he was playing this thing and I was fascinated by that. Every time I went away to eat an ice cream or that sort of thing I came back to that spot," he says.

It wasn't until Madden came to Alpha Boys' School that he had the opportunity to learn to play that same instrument he saw a man play at the carnival. He came to Alpha when he was about eight years old, he says, after Hurricane Charlie. He explains, "I hail from this little rural town called Garden Town. There was a storm in 1951 and my house was blown down and I was a product of the convent, Catholic. My mother was there but not my father. It was just my mother and my sister and me. The storm came, the house was blowing down. We went to the Sisters of Mercy convent. There was a little area there, you stayed there for about three weeks or a month or something like that. My mother couldn't deal with me and my sister, as it were, so she start by asking the sisters if they could board me in Alpha. They said yes and so this is when I came to Alpha. I was about eight at that time. When I came, I wasn't a ward of the state. I came because my mother asked if I could board for a while. It was a big melting pot of people. The saying was that Alpha was a bad school. People felt that kids who went to Alpha was because they were on the streets flinging stones or they were mixed up in this or that, but there were two kinds of persons in Alpha, some guys were ill mannered and others who were just ordinary guys who were here. I came to the junior home and I heard the band playing, marching. They asked if any of us juniors wanted to be in the band and I said yes. They asked me, 'Which instrument do you want to play,' and I didn't know what the instrument was called, I just pointed out the instrument I saw when I was four years old. I said, 'That!' They said, 'The trumpet?' I said, 'That's what it's called? Yes, I want to play that!' They gave it to me and after about two weeks of trying to get a sound out of it, there was a guy named Jo Jo Bennett who taught me and Johnny Moore. And after two weeks, no sound coming out of it. After the third week a sound came out and it was worse than a cow in a pasture! Terrible!" Madden says that he wasn't proficient on the instrument at first but after many years of practice he became better. "After about four years, people say to me, 'David, you still trying to do that thing?' I say yes. After about ten years somebody say, 'David, you are there.' After about 20 years, people start to say, 'You sound alright.' After about 40 years, people start to say, 'You are a wicked trumpeter,' and I say, 'Yeah!'" He was able to continue to play the trumpet after finding work with the military band and with groups and in studios throughout Kingston. "I went to Jamaica Military Band after Alpha. I was 16 when I left Alpha, I was in the army and I did three years there. I was going out trying to play with this group and that group, Lynn Taitt and the Comets, you name it, all

David Madden, back row left on trumpet, with Karl "Cannonball" Bryan and the Diamonds.

around the place. Then after the army I came out and went down to Coxsone Dodd where Bob Marley and all the other great Jamaican musicians were. And I started to play on a recording session here, recording session there, playing in this band, playing in that band, doing this, doing that, going around just like everybody else, learning to play, practicing, doing everything. And it worked out, after so many years. So I lift my heart to Alpha for that," he says.

David Madden, lower left, and members of Zap Pow, including Alpharian Glen DaCosta, top second from right

Madden was mentored by Jo Jo Bennett while he was at Alpha since the two were in the band at the same time, but he was also mentored by Johnny "Dizzy" Moore who was a few years older than him. Madden says of Moore, "When he used to get his paycheck from military band and he used to pass through school, he used to give me a penny and tell me to keep on blowing. When he was playing with The Skatalites, that was enough to guide me that this is what I should do. When I got the chance to talk to him he'd say, 'How are you coming, what are you doing now and he would say to practice and just keep going out there."

The band provided Madden with a way to earn a living, as well as the camaraderie of his fellow bandmates, some of whom he would perform with for the rest of his life. He remembers the good times with the band at Alpha. "One thing I can remember more than anything is we went to play out and we were going in a little truck, not a bus. And the side drum, one guy plays the side drum and one guy plays the bass drum. And we went to do this country gig and we were about 60 miles out and we get to the gig and we

Members of Zap Pow in 1972 with David Madden, second from right, and Glen DaCosta, far left

went to take the instruments out and we realize the side drum was not there. We looked everywhere for the side drum including, do you know, a flute case! We open the flute case to look for the side drum in the flute case! That's how desperate we were. We were not laughing at the time but afterward we laughed, looking in a flute case for a side drum!" he says, noting that they had left the drum back at Alpha.

Over the years, Madden performed trumpet for dozens of vocalists and groups including Ken Boothe, Dennis Brown, Gregory Isaacs, Bob Andy, Dawn Penn, Leroy Sibbles, The Heptones, Burning Spear, Beres Hammond, Stranger Cole, Culture, Derrick Harriott, Max Romeo, Johnny Osbourne, Sly & Robbie, Jimmy Cliff, and Yellowman. He also performed with fellow Alpharian Karl Bryan and his band, The Diamonds. Perhaps his most notable performances were with Bob Marley as a member of his horn section on tour and on record. Madden performed on Marley's *Natty Dread* along with Alpharian Glen DaCosta, as well as 17 other Bob Marley songs including "Rat Race," 'Buffalo Soldier," and "Is This Love." Marley was attracted to the horn section, of which Madden was a part, after hearing them perform with Alpharian Vin Gordon as Studio One's horn section, and in the band Zap Pow which formed in 1969. Zap Pow featured DaCosta as well as Dwight Pinkney, Max Edwards, Mike Williams, and Joe McCormack. They had a number of hits including, "Mystic Mood," which catapulted them onto the charts, and "This is Reggae Music" for Harry J. Later they were joined by a number of singers including Beres Hammond, Jacob Miller, and Bunny Rugs before they split up in 1979. Madden also performed and recorded with Alpharian Cedric "Im" Brooks, including a number of tracks on the Studio One album, *Money Maker*, as Im and David just prior to his departure for Zap Pow and Brooks' departure for Count Ossie's Mystic Revelation of Rastafari. Madden has also had a prolific solo career and he still resides in Jamaica.

Bob Marley, Rudy Mills, and David Madden

--H.A.

David Madden

A chalkboard in the Lennie Hibbert Music Hall 2015

Photo by Heather Augustyn

Tony Gregory

Billed as "Mr. Emotion" and "Mr. Soul," Tony Gregory's name is synonymous with romantic ballads. But his life didn't begin with such sweet songs of love. In fact, his family life was, as he describes it, "a very traumatic and sad affair." Tony Gregory was born in Kingston on June 21, 1946 and he had seven sisters and three brothers. He says that Alpha essentially saved his life. "I live all over Kingston really—Rae Town, all sort of places as a child. It was very depressing actually. I went to the school for the fact that my mother and father were no longer together and they had problems. There were two of us and the girl in Jamaica always have the opportunity to go and stay with someone else, but the boy have the problem. And when you have two people coming from the ghetto, as it were, it was difficult. So when your

Tony Gregory in school at Alpha, second from left

father didn't want to take you and your mother is very upset with the father and she didn't really want to keep you because you're holding her back, then you're left in limbo, and that was my case. No one really wanted to have the responsibility. So I was taken to courts, well they were taken to court because I was found on the roads, walking on the road and that was just too much.

And the court said, 'What are you going to do,' and they said we can't afford to take care of him and then they asked me what I would want to do and we lived close to Alpha Boys' School and I would go over sometimes and play with the boys and so there was a connection, so I just said, let me go there. I was very happy that I went there. At least I had some stability in my life, which I didn't have before. You had a bed and you could eat three times a day. You're around other boys and you can play games and it becomes a home. Of course you run around without shoes and get sores and if you do anything wrong you get lashings as well, but that is normal in schools like that. That was another time. That is something that may not take place today. It was just part of the system. But I was just living as a child and developing as a child. It was very strict. Whenever you're in a school run by nuns you have to adhere to that autocratic sort of development. I was in the Alpha Boys' School from age about six to 10," he says.

Tony Gregory at the age of 12 (far left) with Skitter & Bunny and Dobby Dobson (back center) before he won the all-island championship at the Ward Theatre in 1958

Gregory says he was on the receiving end of punishment at times because even though Alpha was now his home, he still ran away. He explains, "I absconded because I wanted to find my mother. There was a desire to see my mother. I did not see my parents at all. The others had relatives who would come see them on a Sunday and bring them a banana and shoes and I would stand there and see these people coming and there was no one to see me. I had this desire to see my mother. But Sister Ignatius was inspirational in all of this. She saw the potential in me, because I was messing around. She thought it would be good for me to pursue music. So that is a very important part of my life and I am forever thankful. She gave me a chance to get a scholarship to go outside of the school and I was a choir boy and I studied music and all this other stuff. I was not in the band, but I was in the choir at the cathedral [Cathedral Choir under Father Healey]. So it was really a college education I was getting at a young age. I had to pass quite a few tests to do that, so it was like going to St. George's but it was a separate entity which concentrated on music and choir. I learned the theoretical and also the practical side. It enabled me to pursue my dream, and that was to be a singer and to be a good musician. Alpha certainly gave me that chance, to do that. The sisters saw that there was something in me that needed to be extended. I used to sing all over the place and they heard that there was a little bit of a quality in my voice, so they gave me a chance."

Tony Gregory in 1961

Tony Gregory in 1962

Gregory says that his first chance to sing outside of the choir came as a result of being encouraged by his classmates. "What started my singing career was when we went to a film that was shown on a Saturday and all the kids from different schools came to that cinema, the Carib Theatre. The kids in the school, in my dormitory, in between the films they had a contest with Vere Johns and he broke a lot of singers, and I went on stage, pushed by my other classmates and I sang 'Somewhere Over the Rainbow.' That's the first time I ever sang outside of the choir, on my own, alone. I won the first place, a box of chocolates, and I'll never forget that. That started my career. He [Vere Johns] liked what I did and he invited me to the contests he had at other cinemas. I became professional at the age of 12 in 1958 after I won the all-island championship and then I was a vocalist with some big bands, one called Bertie King & His Orchestra," he says. He also made appearances at local cinemas which were broadcast live on the radio. He explains, "Between '58 and '60 they started a radio station called JBC which did live shows between films at the Regal Cinema. It was called Hit Parade Top 10 and you sort of do what's in the charts—songs you would just cover because most of them were just American tracks anyway, so they would find singers who would sing these songs, live on stage, which was live over the radio."

Tony Gregory in 1963

In 1960, Tony Gregory performed as a lead vocalist with Byron Lee & the Dragonaires. "I went to a dance that they were playing at, close to the cathedral, the rectory actually. I just asked to do a song and I went up there and do a song. Afterward I was asked if I wanted to sing with the band and I said I wouldn't mind and that's how it started. I stayed with the band for three years up until 1963 after touring with them and before that in 1960 I made my first single with the band. It was called 'Baby,' which I wrote as well. It was a 45 and the B side was 'Eileena.' It was sort of a rock and roll, ska-y type of song. Then I worked very intensively with a band, working on shows because Byron was also a promoter

From the cover of the album, *Tony Gregory Sings*

who brought in artists from the United States, acts at the time like Ben E. King, Ray Charles, and Sammy Davis Jr., they all came to Jamaica, so I had the opportunity, because I was with the band, to go on stage and sing on the shows with these people—Sam Cooke and all these, a big long line of rhythm and blues and soul acts that came out of the states. Exposure and experience," says Gregory.

After he left Byron Lee & the Dragonaires, Gregory performed with Kes Chin, the Vagabonds, Ernest Ranglin, Sonny Bradshaw, and Carlos Malcolm with whom he traveled throughout the West Indies, the Bahamas, and in South America. Tony Gregory recorded with a number of artists including Leslie Butler, the Soulettes, the Soul Brothers, Doreen Shaffer, and The Skatalites, all for Coxsone Dodd. "Most of the stuff that I recorded at Studio One, most of the musicians were The Skatalites or in a different set up there, but they all came together and worked at the studio on all of the acts. People like Jackie Mittoo, most of them, most of them played on my tracks," he says. Gregory also recorded a duet with Marcia Griffiths in 1965, also for Coxsone Dodd. "Marcia Griffiths made her first record with me, a song called 'You're Mine.' I had a hit called 'Baby Come On Home,' this was with Coxsone and Marcia wanted to sing then and she came, I think she recorded something with him but he wasn't too happy with it. He thought I would do a duet with her so she recorded 'You're Mine' which was a pretty big hit here in Jamaica. That was her first recording," he says.

Tony Gregory dancing the ska with the Mighty Sparrow in 1964, backed by Byron Lee & the Dragonaires

In 1966, Gregory migrated to Canada, though he continued to tour and in fact spent almost a year in England performing with Count Prince Miller and others. In 1971 he recorded the song, "Bouncing All Over the World," perhaps a nod to his experiences during this time. The song garnered much airplay in England where it was recorded, utilizing a 40-piece orchestra in the studio. In 1971, Gregory traveled to Germany to promote the B-side of that recording, a song called "I Love You So," and he says it was then, in 1972, that he decided to call Germany home—for the next 35 years. He says, "I got a lot of offers to write and produce. I did more contemporary pop music, not reggae and ska. I got into the publishing side of the business and that took up a lot of my time." Gregory also played behind the Iron Curtain, in the USSR, Romania, Hungary, and Czechoslovakia. Over the years he performed in Australia, Japan, Africa, and all over Europe. He recorded perhaps his most popular hit, "Gypsy Girl," in 1982 for Sonic Sounds and he moved back to Jamaica in the '90s to set up his publishing company, Sunland Music, and his entertainment company, Gregory Entertainment Limited.

Tony Gregory from the Alpha Boys Reunion Show in 2007
Photo by Adam Reeves

Tony Gregory continues to perform selectively at festivals and in Jamaica. He and his wife Nina call the countryside in St. Ann home and in 2012 he was awarded the prestigious Order of Distinction with Toots Hibbert and Courtney "Jackie" Jackson. "I think I have fulfilled all of my goals," he says.

--H.A.

Johnny Osbourne

A perennial favourite of sound systems the world over, Johnny Osbourne is truly one of the giants of reggae music. Born Errol Osbourne in 1948 and raised in Kingston, he is not generally associated with Alpha, perhaps because he appears to want to somehow distance himself from the place. His reluctance to give us an interview on the subject means little is known about his early childhood or his time at Alpha. His musical obsession was, like most working class Jamaicans, instigated by a love of going to the local dancehalls every week to hear fresh new sounds. 'From me born me know about sound system,' he told reggae bloggers and promoters Irish and Chin. 'I hear sound system from Duke Reid, King Edwards, Sir Coxsone, like those are the three prominent big sound, the big house of joy. Poor people couldn't afford a gramophone so everybody haffe listen a sound system.' Although, like many of the great Jamaican singers, it was in church where he learnt to sing properly. Coming from dire poverty, his mother arranged for him to attend Alpha because, 'She was poor. She couldn't watch me and work,' he told a panel hosted by reggae writer David Katz at the 2012 Reggae University at Rototom Sunsplash. Once at Alpha he joined the band and took up the trumpet but did not respond well to bandmaster Lennie Hibbert's teaching style. He told the panel, 'He had a weird way of teaching. Every mistake he'd hit you with drumstick. If it wasn't for his drumstick perhaps I wouldn't be a great singer today!' Throughout the late 1960s he used to attend auditions every Sunday at Studio One, which was situated conveniently close to his home. Every week he tried to hustle his way into the weekly open

audition, but most weeks he wouldn't even be allowed through the door, such was the nature of the competition. Speaking to Canadian reggae journalist and photographer Beth Lesser for a late 1980s interview for her fanzine *Reggae Quarterly* (*RQ*), Osbourne talks about those early days: 'To get into the studio you had to go through audition after audition after audition, every Sunday, audition. Come back every Sunday for two years.' Although his relentless hustling would prove fruitless at this stage, Osbourne did manage to set afoot in Studio One in 1967, albeit for an independently funded recording for producer Winston Riley. 'I used to sing for a little band called The Wildcats so what we did, the manager for the band got some money so we went to the studio and recorded our first song. It was "All I Have Is Love," done over by The Mighty Diamonds and Junior Delgado.' For the release Osbourne dropped the name Errol in favour of Johnny as a nod towards American crooner Johnny Mathis. In 1969 keyboard player Winston Wright noticed Osbourne's talent and brought him down to see Duke Reid with whom he recorded a full length LP, *Come Back Darling*, billed as Johnny and the Sensations. Although it is often assumed this was Osbourne's own band, this wasn't actually the case. 'I wasn't really a member of the Sensations,' he told *RQ*. 'But if some work was going on maybe I'd just sit down and sing with them. On my first album, *Come Back Darling* they sang all the harmonies. That's why it says Johnny and the Sensations, because we did all the work together.'

During this time the street violence in Kingston was boiling over. Extreme poverty combined with political unrest and the upsurge of 'rude boy' gangs made it an unhappy place, causing many Jamaicans to seek a more stable life in the US, Canada or England. On the very same day as The Sensations finished the last song on *Come Back Darling*, at the behest of his mother, Errol 'Johnny' Osbourne took a flight to Toronto, to join her and his siblings, where he would remain for the next ten years. 'I did the recording in the morning and then I had to catch the plane,' he recounts. The album cover featured a photo of Johnny boarding the steps of an Air Jamaica plane and a girl waving him farewell, although according to Johnny this was not his actual flight and the shot was taken at an earlier time (possibly early in the morning that same day). He recounted to Beth Lesser for *RQ*: 'It took my mother four years to convince me to come. She sent me the money and the passport about eight different times and I spent it. This was the last try, so I had to come 'cause she said if I turn out to be a bum it's not her fault, because she tried.' Once established in Toronto an entirely new life unfolded. With no real Canadian reggae scene to speak of, Osbourne decided to get things going himself. After drifting through a few different bands eventually he formed his own band Black Magic with Carl Henry and Patrick Thompson, playing crowd-pleasing US soul tunes from the WBLK (US soul station) top 40, 'sliding reggae in between top forty material like Earth Wind and Fire.' Osbourne finally made his mark a few years later when he formed Ishan People, one of the first ever reggae bands in Canada. 'We played reggae in clubs where reggae had never

Johnny Osbourne from the cover of *Come Back Darling*

been heard before.' The band's brand of catchy, funky roots reggae had a mass appeal and attracted the attention of a major label, GRT. They released two highly polished LPs, *Ishan People* (1977) and *Roots* (1978) as well as three singles—including a neat version of Bob Dylan's 'I Shall Be Released.' Ishan

Johnny Osbourne in Waterhouse in 1985
Photo by Beth Lesser

People stayed together until 1979 when internal differences in the band caused them to break up. 'GRT didn't know about reggae, they didn't research reggae at all. I think it was a company that wasn't really interested in reggae. David Clayton-Thomas (singer with Blood Sweat and Tears) was the one who was interested because he was the one who heard us and signed us up,' he told *RQ*. Around the time of the split, GRT went bankrupt and the Canadian phase of Johnny Osbourne's career came to an abrupt end.

Having developed his skills as a singer and performer, Osbourne was ready and primed for his next major challenge. Now aged 31, he returned to Jamaica as a confident, seasoned professional, for what he aptly calls 'my second coming.' The days of fruitless, demeaning Sunday auditions were long behind him. Making Studio One his very first stop, he was welcomed warmly through the door by Coxsone Dodd where he immediately began work as a Studio One artist in his own right. Going straight back to Studio One after all that rejection as a youth was like completing unfinished business. 'Until I could get a foot in the door there I didn't feel I had fulfilled my musical purpose,' he told the Rototom panel. 'I went back and did some records. I figured I knew my potential, my capability and I felt I had too much locked up inside I'm not getting out,' he recounted to *RQ* magazine. 'So it's like I took a big slice out of my life. Ten years! And after ten years I start to realise I sound like I was fourteen again.' His first songs were 'Forgive Them' and 'Jealousy, Heartache and Pain,' showcasing Osbourne's mature, soulful vocals and paving the way for what would be one of his defining moments. They began recording new vocals over some dusty vintage Studio One riddim tapes (to the uninitiated: the riddim track is the underlying structure of a reggae song—drum, bass, guitar and piano. It is the reggae equivalent to the word *groove*. A big part of reggae culture is that riddim tracks will get used multiple times by producers to give them fresh interpretations and to milk each riddim economically for everything they are worth. Also, it's fun to jump around to something that sounds both familiar and different). This would form the basis of Osbourne's only ever Studio One LP, *Truth and Rights*. Not only is this record one the best albums ever to come out of Studio One, but *Truth and Rights* is simply one of the greatest reggae records ever made. The album's message of peace, love, redemption and devotion was Osbourne's response to the desperate political situation in Jamaica he had returned to, although he maintains that it was never a political record. Drawing heavily on the vocal styling of great US soul singers like Al Green and Bobby Bland, Osbourne's voice appears to float over the music and his understated, impassioned delivery of every single song shows an artist reaching for the sublime and finding it each

Johnny Osbourne from the cover of the *Warrior* album

and every time. The title track is an evergreen sound system classic that never goes out of style and is one of the most reworked songs in all of reggae. It wasn't apparent back then what *Truth and Rights'* legacy would become, but demand over the years has seen it re-pressed numerous times and over the decades it has reached the status of an all-time classic, revered by serious reggae fans the world over. Unlike so many artists who bear grudges towards Coxsone Dodd for the usual lack of payment, Osbourne speaks highly of the man. 'Studio One I think is the reggae college. You can't go wrong. You get a name and you're on the open road,' he told *RQ*. 'What I like about Coxsone, he will not put a man on record unless he knows you have potential. If it don't sound good he won't put it on record because he want you to hear what you have.' Osbourne gave a surprise revelation to the Rototom panel, that he had in fact recorded a second album at Studio One singing over some old riddim tapes featuring master drummer Count Ossie. Unfortunately Coxsone lost the tapes and it will forever remain one of the great lost reggae albums.

Never one to stand still, having made his statement as a deep soul-reggae singer, Osbourne threw himself headlong into the emerging sounds of the day. Having grown up in the dancehall, sound system was in his blood and he now set his sights on conquering it. First out of the gate was the *Folly Ranking* LP. Recorded with Prince Jammy while still working on *Truth and Rights*, its title track provided his first big hit in the dancehall. Later that year he made 'Ice Cream Love' and 'Fally Lover' for Henry 'Junjo' Lawes, at which point Osbourne's career went stratospheric. He went on to become one of the defining reggae artists of the 1980s, releasing dozens of hits, many of which have stood the test of time, most notably 'Water Pumping,' 'Yo-Yo,'

Johnny Osbourne, center, with Jennifer Lara and Coxsone Dodd

'Murderer,' 'Purify Your Heart,' 'On The Right Track,' 'Hill,' 'We Gonna Rock It Tonight (Dub Plate Playing In The Ghetto)' and the almighty 'Buddy Bye Bye' set to the 'sleng-teng' riddim which had only just exploded out of King Jammy's studio, tearing up the rule book and turning reggae on its head.

Johnny Osbourne in Chicago 2015
Photo by Heather Augustyn

'Buddy Bye Bye' ranks alongside a select handful of tunes such as Tenor Saw's 'Ring the Alarm,' Dawn Penn's 1990s re-recording of 'No, No, No,' Sister Nancy's 'Bam Bam' and Barrington Levy's 'Under Mi Sensi' – universally loved songs which DJs the world over who don't necessarily even specialize in reggae know they can throw down at some point in a session and can be sure to set any dancefloor on fire when played at the right moment. In an interview with *Reggae Directory*, Osbourne explains the song is about the dancehall crowd shouting out for a 'rewind,' where the selector lifts the needle off the record and starts the track anew. 'Buddy Bye Bye is a way of calling an "encore." Where I get it from, it's from the original folk songs. 'Cause I used to listen to them original folk songs and the slaves used to sing them songs: (mimics a call-and-response) "de-be-de-be-de-be-do-*uh-uh*," that answering thing. So it's in the people and their spirit. So that buddy-bye it's simple like that, it's a participation song and buddy-bye is just a figure of speech for "encore," saluting the song. You go, "blo,blo,blo,blo!" and that means, "Salute, bring it back (rewind the track)." But actually, buddy-bye wasn't really what I was saying. It was "put it by." So "put it by number one," I'm saying, this is so good I want you to put it by number one!'

Osbourne left Jamaica for a decade or so, disappearing from sight for a time, but in 2012 he returned to Jamaica for Tony Rebel's Rebel Salute festival for what he describes as 'my third coming!' Since then Osbourne has been touring all over the world, enjoying his status as one of the true heritage acts from the classic reggae era. 'I have no regrets where my career is concerned,' he says. 'My voice is like vintage wine, it gets better with age.' In 2001, Osbourne's song 'We Need Love' from the *Truth and Rights* LP was featured on a double LP compilation *100% Dynamite* by London-based label Soul Jazz Records. The package was groundbreaking in both its blend of dancefloor-orientated, funky reggae and in its iconic vintage-style cover design. By having only a few tracks on each side it appealed to DJs of all persuasions and has gone on to become the label's biggest ever selling record and a must-have item in any self-respecting DJ's collection. The inclusion of 'We Need Love' introduced Osbourne to a new generation of dancers and listeners, acting as an entry point for the more curious musical explorers into his wealth of recorded material.

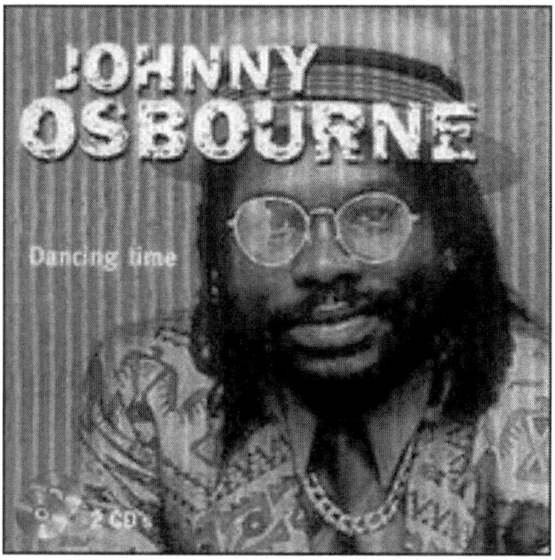

--A.R.

'Floyd' Lloyd Seivright

Out of the ashes of the British ska revival—all but dead for over five years, came a fresh burst of ska bands in London around 1987, sounding less punky and more jazzy and soulful than the 2Tone ska groups had been. At the forefront of this new evolution was South London's The Potato 5, headed up by the charismatic vocalist 'Floyd' Lloyd Seivright. Also a multi-instrumentalist and producer, Seivright brought an authentic Jamaican feeling to The Potato 5's fat brassy ska sound and for a couple of years they ruled the London ska scene.

Floyd Lloyd Seivright

Born in 1948, Seivright originated from a rural farming community called Brown Town in Liberty Valley, situated in the parish of St Ann's, where he had eleven brothers and sisters. When his father left to live in London, Seivright went to live with his maternal grandparents. Unsettled in his new home, he ran away from home on several occasions, until eventually the social services stepped in. 'Due to unhappiness I ended up at Alpha which was good for me in more ways than one. Yeah, it was blessed,' he says. Joining the school aged eleven, he studied music under bandmaster Lennie Hibbert, forming a lifelong friendship with the vibraphone and percussion maestro that would later see them performing in the same bands and ultimately Seivright would produce some of Hibbert's final recordings.

A close encounter with Emperor Haile Selassie I of Ethiopia made a big impact on Seivright while on his fabled visit to Jamaica in 1966, where frenzied crowds followed the Emperor wherever he went. The Alpha band played for Selassie in the stadium in Kingston and it was Seivright who sang vocals for him. 'We were honored to be right in front of him, representing the school, welcoming him and all those things. The band played some "yard" music and calypso.'

Floyd Lloyd Seivright

Seivright formed a strong bond with Sister Ignatius, becoming one of the privileged boys who she would send on errands to the record shops into downtown Kingston to buy tunes to play on her sound system. 'Sister Ignatius was a special woman, very special. And she would call early in the morning and say, "We're gonna have showers and get ready, and I have a list for you." And I would get my pocket money and a list of songs to choose, whatever was happening at the time, for her parties. She used to put on parties to raise money. She keep parties, garden parties and indoor parties. I'd go downtown right to the heart of it, from Prince Buster's to Randy's and I'd go up to Tropical Plaza and them places, depending on what the song is. If it's Don Drummond or The Skatalites it's downtown.' Seivright would act as selector, spinning the tunes, but was also involved in organizing the garden parties and dances as well as booking artists to come and play, such as Derrick Morgan. 'You used to have a garden party for your year, everybody, his group is there,' he says. 'She put on some food, get the sound system, and the place packed out, all boys and dem girlfriends, a great feeling. She raise money to buy equipment for the band or something else.' Seivright was nominated as head boy of Alpha for two years and would help out with some of the administrative duties in the school office. He was also granted the privilege of being allowed up into Ignatius' dwellings. 'Not many people get to go in their quarters and see what they eat and all dem tings, but I was allowed to Alpha upstairs. She say, "Lloyd," and she have special food for me at the top, deh.' After Don Drummond's murder trial he would sometimes travel with Sister Ignatius, driven by a school driver to visit Drummond's mother followed by a visit to see Don who was incarcerated in Bellevue Mental Hospital. 'You know where the Gleaner company is, his mum lived behind there on Love Lane. And she [Ignatius] would jump in the car and go down there to see if his mum is alright. We would often end up at Bellevue with some food to cheer him up.' After leaving Alpha in the late 1960s Seivright started his musical apprenticeship singing with his mentor Lennie Hibbert's group.

Floyd Lloyd Seivright

By 1969, Seivright had left the island for England to seek musical opportunities, but the environment was competitive and not always friendly. 'In England there were people who were Jamaican and to other Jamaicans they were not allowed in with open arms, we have to prove ourselves.' Seivright cut a few singles for various British producers under his own name, starting with a gospel-reggae single 'Mary's Boy Child' (eight years before Boney M), a single called 'Yo Yo' and a couple of offerings for Trojan Records' subsidiary label Horse. Seivright also wrote songs and produced, notably for a band called Rastafari who released only one single, a heavy funk tune called 'Funky City.' He wrote 'Soulful Lover,' a single for Earl George and provided a song called 'Sweet Lady' for The Mighty Diamonds for their Virgin Frontline LP *Planet Earth.*

Seeing what was happening to his fellow artists, it became clear to Seivright that reggae artists were being ruthlessly exploited by the music industry and so he decided to help by starting his own music publishing business in 1976, Tropic Music, to look after the interests of Jamaican artists. 'Overall I started the business because they weren't taking us seriously in

England in the early reggae days.' It is a business that he continues to run today. 'Us in England, we weren't treated with a lot of respect, they treated stars in reggae at that time like a joke and so I would seek out whatever avenues I can to take care of the publishing and all that side of the business in whatever way I can help other people, which I do. I point them in the right direction.'

In the mid to late 1970s Seivright sang vocals in an American big band called the Salt Lake City Jazz Band, 'playing jazzy swing, reggae and ska.' With them he toured Switzerland, France, Germany and Holland. Then in 1978 he signed a recording contract with EMI and recorded an LP, *Better to Laugh Than to Cry*. He continues to have a working relationship with EMI, providing incidental music for TV and film. He is their 'go-to guy' when a screen writer or producer demands something with a Caribbean flavour, whether Barbados, Trinidad or Jamaica.

Seivright helped found the British reggae and disco band Red Cloud who he sang with for the first half of the 1980s, releasing the albums *Sweet Lady*, *Painted Faces* and *Red Cloud In Dub*. But it was in The Potato 5 where Seivright really took London by storm, playing to packed venues around the capital and beyond. Initially he had helped the band out with their sound, providing some Jamaican studio 'riddims' to get them a more authentic sound. First he was invited to do his own solo piece with them and he ended up joining the band on a full-time basis. With them he recorded the LP *Floyd Lloyd And The Potato 5 Meets Laurel Aitken*, which is considered one of the all-time greatest ska albums. One side

features Seivright, the other has Laurel Aitken. It was possibly the first post-1960s ska record to really emulate the jazziness of The Skatalites, paving the way for a whole new generation of authentic-sounding jazz-influenced ska bands all across Europe, the US and in Japan.

Despite the band's success and his popularity as the singer, there were problems with a racist element among some of the skinheads at the gigs. The original late 1960s skinhead movement in England had been a multi-cultural affair with an obsession with ska, rocksteady, early reggae and US soul music labels like Motown and Stax. In the late 1970s the movement got hi-jacked by a racist element who supported the far-right National Front party and who couldn't quite equate their love of black music with a love of black people. This nastier element among the skinheads would sometimes make Seivright feel he was in an unsafe situation up on stage. It was stress he didn't need and it eventually led to his decision to leave The Potato 5. He continued with writing and production, eventually returning to live in Jamaica, where he resides today. He has produced a big band ska album for his close friend Ernest Ranglin called *EB @ Noon*, and he looks after some of Ranglin's business affairs while also managing the royalties of Lennie Hibbert's music, notably on the song 'Rose Len' which was sampled by Miss Dynamite. He has also been working on a double LP with Ernest Ranglin, due for release at the end of 2017.

Floyd Lloyd Seivright, left, with the Potato 5

--A.R.

The baobab tree that once stood at Alpha Boys' School, called the Dibby Dibby Tree or Monkey Tambourine Tree
Jamaica Journal, July 1978

Uriah Johnson

Trombonist Uriah Johnson idolized Sammy Davis Jr. for his showmanship, and so he set out to become the same style of performer, according to the *Star Newspaper* which ran a feature on the young musician on October 7, 1966. "I would like to be perfect where music is concerned," he said. Johnson came to Alpha from Maxfield Park Children's Home. Upon graduation from Alpha he found work with the Virtues in 1963. "This young and very talented 18-year-old musician," says T.W. in the *Star*, "has a great future ahead in the musical world, as clearly depicted in the manner with which he blows his horn.... He had always loved music, and was greatly inspired to pursue it further by the regular concerts given by the Jamaica Military Band at the [Maxfield Park Children's] Home. But Maxfield Park did not have the facilities for teaching him music and so he went to Alpha Boys' School where he got his musical education under the tuition of that well-known vibraphone player, Lennie Hibbert."

Uriah Johnson
Star Newspaper, October 7, 1966

"After eight months' residence with the Virtues, he migrated to the Cavaliers for a one-year sojourn and it was while playing with the Cavaliers that he was discovered by Vikings' manager Winston Chin Quee. Young Johnson has a lot of plans for himself, his main ambition is to become a Davis-type showman and one can say that he has certainly gone a far way, as in addition to playing trombone, he also plays the trumpet and even the drums too, accompanying his renditions with his youthful 'Satchmo voice. If you want further proof as to this young man's ability, then hop along to any Vikings performance and see for yourself," T.W. writes.

Uriah Johnson

Johnson went on to record for producer and soundsystem operator Lloyd "the Matador" Daley in the late 1960s, and in the early 1970s he recorded for Hopeton Lewis at Dynamic Sounds, produced by Byron Lee and Winston Blake. Not much is known of Johnson after this period and it is likely he immigrated and is still alive today since he has a presence on social media.

--H.A.

Vincent Gordon 'Don Drummond Jr.'

Alpha produced many great trombonists, but three of them are closely linked as a kind of trombone movement in their own right, each playing their own distinct take on a rootsy, bluesy style with a 'natural mystic' kind of feeling. Vin Gordon forms one third of this trio of trombonists alongside Rico Rodriguez and Don Drummond and between them they should be rightfully acknowledged for giving the world the Alpha Boys trombone sound, emulated by reggae and ska trombonists worldwide.

Vin Gordon

Vincent Gordon was born in Kingston's Jonestown district on 4th August 1949, sharing a birthday with another great horn player, Louis Armstrong. He grew up in the slums of Trench Town and went to Alpha from the age of five to fifteen and has been working in music more or less continuously for the five decades since. He is perhaps Jamaica's most prolific trombonist, and was right in the eye of the hurricane for reggae's most creative periods, having played with every important name in the business. Gordon studied tuba (or 'blow-bass' as it called in Jamaica) and upright bass under the guidance of Alpha bandmaster Lennie Hibbert. Upon leaving Alpha his first engagement was with the Salvation Army Band but as demand for tuba players was virtually non-existent, Gordon took up the trombone and taught himself this highly complex instrument by sheer determination. The tuba has similarities with the trombone which smoothed the transition. 'It's very easy to leave from the blow-bass to play the trombone,' he says. 'You get a rounder, better, sweeter sound because you read the music the same way. They are in the same clef, the bass clef. All I had to do was learn the positions and there I go!' The trombone differs from other brass instruments because you have to find the notes by ear as you move the slide, requiring discipline and skill to master. For Gordon to teach himself as a teenager and to evolve into a world-class player is truly remarkable and may partly be to his years immersed in Alpha's music program, but as much down to his own determination and passion. 'This instrument is one of the hardest instrument in the world. This instrument is a *technical* instrument, the trombone. Ya have to build a sweet tone. Ya can't play this thing too loud, loudness doesn't work. But if ya play it sweet and soft and you can spell your phrases, like speaking proper English, it will be so… *level!'* (Level: patois meaning pleasant, nice, easy).

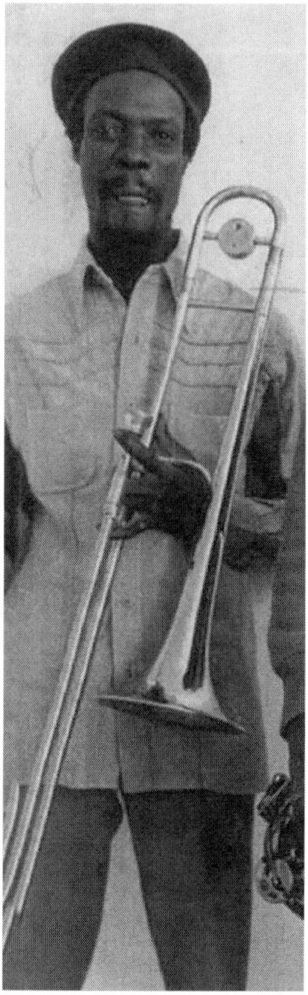

Vin Gordon

Gordon's youthful talent was recognised by Skatalites sax man Roland Alphonso who in 1964 invited him down to Studio One to record his first ever session. It was to prove an auspicious occasion as there he would have his first encounter with nineteen year-old Bob Marley, who a decade later would call on Vin Gordon to play on some of his finest works. 'I was fifteen years old when I did my first session for Studio One. I think the song was called, um, "Rude Boy Train," Wailers, with Headley Bennett, deh. 'Cause Roland Alphonso discovered me down in Trench Town deh and he took me up by Studio One. It was alright, everybody like it, Coxsone like it.' Alphonso later gave him his first solo on The Wailers' 'Jailhouse.'

Vin Gordon spent the 1960s playing in some of the key bands which birthed the new evolving sounds of rocksteady and reggae. For a brief period he played live shows in the original line-up of The Skatalites. 'I started playing with The Skatalites at a street dance in Wellington Street. That must have been around 1964.' With the birth of rocksteady he played in Tommy McCook and The Supersonics as well as Studio One's house band The Soul Brothers led by Roland Alphonso, which later became The Soul Vendors, then later Sound Dimension. Gordon's trombone sound can be heard on countless tracks during the rocksteady era, adding depth and richness to everything he played on, many of which are considered part of the foundations of Jamaican music.

Headley Bennett and Vin Gordon

Vin Gordon's trombone sound was initially so similar to Don Drummond's he was given the nickname Don Drummond Jr, which he is credited as on dozens of record sleeves. He is also widely known as Trommie. Coxsone Dodd even hoodwinked the public into believing three tunes Gordon played on were by Don Drummond: 'Heavenless,' 'Real Rock' and 'Valley Princess.' Vin Gordon was not yet an established name, whereas a Don Drummond tune would always sell well. Both 'Real Rock' and 'Heavenless' were rocksteady and early reggae, respectively. Since Drummond was incarcerated in Bellevue Mental Hospital by early 1965 just before the dawning of the rocksteady era they could only be Gordon's. 'I did "Heavenless" as a little boy in Studio One and Coxsone Dodd say Don Drummond play it. He put it on his album. He told me that it's a mistake he made.' Despite Dodd's reputation for not paying musicians and generally making them feel dispensable, Gordon speaks highly of him. 'Coxsone was a good man, to me at least. People say he was a bad man, but he gave me a lot of encouragement. He didn't give me money, but he did encourage me. He bought me a trombone to give you an example. Without Coxsone, nobody would know Vin Gordon.'

'Real Rock' was later reworked into Willie Williams' 'Armagideon Time,' the 'riddim' being one of the most re-used and instantly recognisable in the entire history of reggae. A decade later it was given a punky-reggae treatment by The Clash as the B-side to their single 'London Calling.' Gordon recalls making the tune: 'That was just a rhythm that Jackie Mittoo made up. Just a straight B flat to A flat two-beats-to-the-bar rhythm. Jackie Mittoo was the kind of guy that anything you play he could find an instrumental out of it. So he just give me the part to play, "bap-bap-bap-baaaam-bam!" But the solo deh, I did it. But it was only a trial because I was so young, in taking the first solo in my life. Not really one of my first recordings, but one of the first instrumentals that I had a chance to play maybe a sixteen bar solo or something.'

Drummond obviously had respect for his namesake, as he made sure a message was passed on to Gordon via Drummond's close friend Seedie who had been visiting Drummond in Bellevue Mental Hospital. Seedie worked in Randy's record store on North Parade and one day Gordon was dropping off some records and Seedie told him that Drummond had wanted him to know that he was doing OK. A seemingly small gesture, but something that might have an impact on a young musician whose role model has lived through a tragedy, and whom Gordon must have known he may never see again.

Yet another classic in the reggae canon, The Abyssinians 1969 Rastafarian hymn, 'Satta-A-Massagana' had a crisp, Far-Eastern sounding horn arrangement to reflect the Amharic song title and the name of the band, which is the original name for Ethiopia. Played by Gordon and saxophonist 'Deadly' Headley Bennett (who did the song's horn arrangement), the song has become such a huge part of reggae history that it is considered to be the country's unofficial reggae national anthem, popular in both the dancehalls and the churches of Jamaica. Gordon remembers that the then unknown Abyssinians sneaked into Studio One at seven in the morning without Coxsone's knowledge because the lead singer Donald Manning's brother was Carlton from Carlton and The Shoes who were having hits at Studio One at the time and so Carlton had the keys to the studio. Later Coxsone found out and demanded studio hire fees. Gordon attributes the time of day to the session's success, because they were buzzing on being up so early recording and perhaps the fact they were doing it illicitly added to the excitement. Dodd refused to release the track because he saw no commercial potential, so the band released it on their newly formed label, Clinch. Not only is 'Satta-A-Massagana' one of the first roots reggae tunes according to The Abyssinians' Bernard Collins, it is also one of the foundations of dancehall and dub, with the slow 'toasting' version on the B-side, 'Mabrak,' a sparse drum and bass workout pointing the way towards the DJ culture. It was one of the first-ever records made in this style.

With hindsight Gordon reflects on this time and how oblivious he and his fellow musicians were to what timeless music they were making. 'As a featuring horns specialist, they put you there an' you playin' the tunes when you was young. You play "Real Rock" an' dem song, but it's not your songs. It's not your album. At that time you was so young and you did it because you were in practice. You didn't care about watching it. You didn't know how great you was, so it didn't matter. Now when you listen back, you say, "Oh my God, if I knew!"'

Moving on to the 1970s and Gordon finds himself again at the heart of the action in Kingston, working with the top studio bands of the day such as The Revolutionaries at Channel One, The Aggravators for Bunny Lee, Black Disciples for Jack Ruby, The Upsetters for Lee Perry at his Black Ark Studio, The Professionals for Joe Gibbs, The Intimidators for Tappa Zukie and Sound Dimension at Studio One. Between them, these in-house bands provided the backing for just about every great artist of the day; attempting a list would be pointless, maybe better simply to ask who *didn't* Vin Gordon play with?

In 1974 Bob Marley was looking for horns players for his forthcoming album *Rastaman Vibration* and so he turned to his old comrade from ska days at Studio One. 'Bob needed a special horn section. Bob know me from Studio One time. He wanted a permanent horn section, so I know two guys by the name of David Madden and Glen DaCosta. They play very sharp, crisp horn, yuhknow? So Bob say, "Can you find two guys?" We used to work for a guy named Harry Mudie and these guys, they're into the business, to do the timing and get the music straight and everything. I call 'em and work together and Bob like the way they work.' So began his time as The Wailers' trombonist, touring and recording with them up until 1979. Gordon was at Marley's house at 56 Hope Road on December 3rd 1976 when the failed assassination attempt by armed thugs took place, two days before a huge concert called Smile Jamaica. At the moment of the break-in, Gordon was rehearsing for the show with the other members of The Wailers. 'We had been practicing one night for a show and they come and shoot up the place. And the first song we'd been playing was 'So Jah Seh,' because Family Man (Aston Barrett) said we gotta open the show with a sorta ganjaman song (laughs!) and we just start playing that opening and then *poi, poi, poi!* (makes gunfire sound). And we just pile up in the bathroom. And so I went over to England, I feel so cheesed off, man.'

In fact the entire Wailers entourage de-camped to England, where Marley lived in self-imposed exile. It was here that they recorded both the *Exodus* and *Kaya* albums, to which Gordon contributed greatly, playing on such tracks as 'Natural Mystic,' 'Guiltiness,' 'Exodus,' 'Kaya,' 'Running Away' and 'Misty Morning.' In late 1999 *Exodus* was declared 'album of the century' by *Time Magazine*, giving Gordon the status of having played on one of the greatest records of all time.

With Jamaica in throes of a blood-thirsty civil war leading up to the elections in 1978, Bob Marley and The Wailers returned to Jamaica for the One Love Peace Concert, like a messianic second coming. The political tension was fraught and the bloodshed on the street was reaching terrifying proportions. With all this as a backdrop along with the previous year's assassination attempt on Marley, the Wailers were walking into a potentially deadly situation. It would have been easy for a rogue gunman to fire at the stage in a massive open air show. Video footage of the show stands testimony to the electrifying atmosphere that night, with lightning and thunder thrashing and clashing over the stage, culminating in the moment the iconic photo was taken of Marley holding aloft the two hands of political foes Prime Minister Michael Manley and his opponent Edward Seaga. Vin Gordon was up there on stage looking out at as the crowd went into a frenzy.

By the end of the 1970s, still living in England, Gordon was invited to join West London roots reggae outfit Aswad, alongside fellow Jamaican hornsmen Michael 'Bammi' Rose and Eddie 'Tan Tan' Thornton. Aswad needed to inject some authentic Jamaican vibes into their distinctly British sound and the Aswad horn section did exactly that, becoming a kind of legend in their own right within a legendary band. In 1979 Aswad lead singer Brinsley Forde took the starring role of Blue in the film *Babylon*, a gritty backstreet story about sound system culture and police brutality in Brixton, south London. Blue's Lion Soundsystem crew buy a hot 'dubplate special' fresh from Jamaica from an underworld importer for their upcoming sound clash with rival sound Jah Shaka. The dubplate featured in the soundclash scene was 'Warrior Charge' by Aswad, a groundbreaking instrumental recorded in London showcasing the trombone sound of Vin Gordon. 'The instrumental on "Warrior Charge" was really my arrangement,' he says. Gordon claims Aswad named the track after the intense look on his face while playing his solos. 'Warrior Charge… when they see the look in my eyes man, they see the warrior … with the charge! Two trombone solos were required because it was a trombone melody. It was a trombone player who make the melody, two beautiful trombone melodies.' *Babylon's* climax is a

Vin Gordon
Photo by David Corio

tense scene at the Jah Shaka vs Lion soundclash, with 'Warrior Charge' on the turntable and Blue toasting on the mic as Gordon's trombone tears the place up, just moments before the police storm the building. A huge success in the dancehalls, 'Warrior Charge' sent a clear message back to Jamaica that British roots reggae is the real deal. Another of Gordon's signature tunes made with Aswad was 'Love Fire,' the dub of which was a soundsystem favourite and was picked up by Dennis Brown who used the rhythm on his 1983 hit 'Promised Land.'

Vin Gordon London 2007
Photo by Adam Reeves

Since leaving Aswad in the mid-1980s Gordon has recorded and toured with artists such as Alpha Blondy, Justin Hinds and The Dominoes and The Wailers Band. In 2003 he finally went full circle and joined The Skatalites as a full-time member for five years where he found true freedom of expression as a musician. On his time with the greatest ska band of all time he says, 'The best thing that ever happened to me was to play with an instrumental band. That's the best thing in my life.' Rather than providing horns for a singer or group, now he could really let rip and show audiences just how far he could push his instrument. After The Skatalites, Gordon continued to develop his career as a solo artist. He regrouped the 1970s Wailers horn section with Alpharians Glen DaCosta and David Madden to record a critically acclaimed solo LP *Gordon In De Garden*. Now based in Paris he records and tours with his Real Rock Band. He keeps on pushing forward: 'When I was young, about seventeen or eighteen years old, I fell in love with this instrument and I've lived with that love, that passion ever since. You just live your music!'

--A.R.

Jackie Willacy

Trumpeter Jackie Willacy was one of those rare few who was both a student at Alpha, as well as a bandleader, and it was as the later that he made an impact on many lives, and not just musicians. In the early 1950s, Willacy began his career on the stage playing jazz. He quickly drew the attention of critics who recognized his talent despite the large pool of skilled musicians. The *Daily Gleaner*, December 10, 1961 offered a review from a jazz "jam session" at the Regal Theater. The article stated, "There were some more top drawer moments.... It was an exhilarating set that offered spirited solos by [Monty] Alexander, a young pianist with a lot of up and come, Carlos Malcolm and Jackie Willacy." For Willacy to be singled out, along with Monty Alexander and Carlos Malcolm, demonstrates the level of proficiency Willacy had on his trumpet.

Jackie Willacy (left) with Leslie Butler piano, Steven Lanz bass, Billy Deans drums, and Larry McDonald tumba, and Janet Enright center on guitar

Daily Gleaner, May 25, 1962

In 1962, Willacy performed with the Janet Enright Combo with guitarist Janet Enright, Leslie Butler on piano, Steven Lanz on bass, Billy Deans on drums, and Larry McKenzie on tumba. According to the *Jamaica Gleaner*, Willacy was part of a group of musicians who performed an important show on September 9, 1962. The newspaper states, "Mickey O'Bryan promotes a benefit show at the Regal cinema house in Cross Roads, St Andrew, to purchase a new trombone for jazz star Don Drummond. The best of the best jazz musicians, including Cecil Lloyd, Ernest Ranglin, Carl McLeod, Billy Cooke, Thaddy [sic] Mowatt, Tommy McCook, and Jackie Willacy, share the stage as Don thanks the artistes and the audience with a selection of tunes such as, 'Mr. Wonderful,' 'Skylark' and 'Cherokee.'"

Jackie Willacy

A number of years later, Willacy again drew attention from critics. Journalist James Carnegie in the March 1970 *Jamaica Journal's* article, "Notes on the History of Jazz and its Role in Jamaica," wrote of Willacy that he was "an excellent trumpeter who has somehow not made the mark he deserves." Carnegie wrote the article in the context of jazz worldwide, so his opinion that Willacy was being underestimated demonstrates the ability Carnegie identified in Willacy. Also that same decade, in 1977, Willacy played at the Stage One Theatre in the Sheraton Kingston Hotel in New Kingston as the house band with Harold Butler, Calvin McKenzie, and Lennox Gordon.

Over the years Willacy also performed trumpet on recordings for Audley Williams, Cynthia Schloss, and Ernest Ranglin, and he performed flugelhorn on Beres Hammond's album, *Soul Reggae*, as well as trumpet along with Alpharian David Madden. He also composed songs for the band Happiness Unlimited, and a career highlight came in 1979 when he performed trumpet on Bob Marley & the Wailers' album *Survival*. Willacy also led his own ensemble that played at locations around Kingston throughout the 1980s with fellow Alpharian Cedric Brooks.

At the same time that Willacy demonstrated his own talents on the stages and studios of Jamaica, he also turned his attention to the next generation of musicians. In the late 1970s he taught at the Jamaica School of Music, and from 1984 until 1988 he was bandmaster of the Alpha Boys Band. Alfred Poyser was a student at Alpha Boys' School at the time that Willacy led the band, coming to the school in 1981 at age four and entering the band to learn the clarinet at age six. Poyser says, "To us students, Mr. Willacy was an expert at music. One thing he definitely instilled in us was discipline and self-worth. The words 'I can't' did not exist with Mr. Willacy. To him, 'I can't' meant 'I can, but I am not prepared to try.' It was better to try and get it wrong than never to have tried at all. If we tried and couldn't get it right, Mr. Willacy would take us individually, ascertain our weak points, and help us to reach our strengths. Mr. Willacy didn't take kindly to time wasting but he would always be there for anyone who wanted to learn music. If you showed an interest, Mr. Willacy could make you a star. I was performing at the age of eight years old, and I was reading music fluently at this age. Don't ask me how Mr. Jackie Willacy did it, but he got us to read music fluently at such tender ages. I remember being able to transpose and play from sight reading music. Mr. Willacy was a sharp dresser who always maintained a calm personality. He never boasted and he never looked down on us orphans. He was a perfect father, teacher, and friend. When Mr. Willacy left Alpha it broke the hearts of every member of the Alpha Boys Band and most of the other students of Alpha Boys Home. He influenced me so much

Jackie Willacy

that I became a music teacher and taught up to teachers-college level, before becoming a vice principal at high school level. If it had not been for Mr. Jackie Willacy I would not have achieved the feats I achieved in music education. I will forever be grateful to Alpha Boys' Home and Mr. Jackie Willacy."

--H.A.

Alpha's main mode of transportation for today's Alpha Boys Band

Photo by Heather Augustyn 2017

Leroy 'Horsemouth' Wallace

At The Music Room studio complex set in an old South London library, during a break from rehearsals in the run-up to the February 2007 Alpha Boys' School one-off reunion show, drummer Leroy 'Horsemouth' Wallace perches behind a red drum kit. Shouting out over the noise of his drums he takes us on a guided tour of the rhythms that make up reggae, offering up his own commentary on each style through ska, rocksteady and various phases of reggae including the 'rockers' style he helped to pioneer. You couldn't wish for a more authentic lesson in reggae drumming—Horsemouth's drum sound is stamped all over some of the greatest reggae ever made. He has been an essential component in the elite core of studio musicians who made up the beating heart of reggae during its heyday. On meeting Wallace in the flesh it becomes glaringly apparent why he is known universally—even to the nuns at Alpha—as Horsemouth. While wanting to be completely respectful to someone who has brought so much enjoyment to the world, you cannot help but be drawn to the fact that his mouth does look quite a lot like that of a horse, especially when he talks. Seeing as his name is so well-known, many reggae fans will have wondered about his name so let's just get this matter cleared up before we go on: Horsemouth is called Horsemouth because he has mouth like a horse. While it might seem a tad harsh that he should have this quirk forever highlighted, it's fairly commonplace in Jamaica for people to get nicknames after their physical appearance or behavior traits. Horsemouth has made it his own by making his nickname an essential part of his charismatic persona. His brethren address him as 'Horsey,' and several times I heard the phrase 'straight from the Horse's mouth' bandied about. Playing up to his own mythology, at one point during our drumming lesson, Wallace gives a loud, proud horse's 'neigh,' followed by yelling over the noise of his drums, 'YES—HORSEMOUTH, TRUE ORIGINAL COMING FROM ALPHA!' The 'Horsemouth' persona was immortalized in fine style when Wallace took the starring role in the 1978 cult reggae movie *Rockers*, playing himself alongside a stellar cast of the reggae royalty of the day.

Leroy Wallace was born in 1950 and found himself in Alpha aged seven as a result of a brutal domestic incident. Living without a father around, his mother was working hard to keep him by selling fish. At this stage it was just him and his mother, although she later had eleven more children. As Wallace himself explains, an unfortunate attempt by his mother to discipline him for stealing turned ugly and led to him being taken away from her and into the care of the Sisters of Mercy. 'I went there for childcare protection from my mum. I used to take her money. I take her threepenny, thruppence from her windowsill. She used to hide a lot of threepennies on her window sill and I used to take them off. I was maybe six, seven years of age. Just me and my mum live alone, no dad, so real reckless. She used to sell mackaback fish, very good with dumpling and yam. That's how she used to make her money to send me to school.' It appears that the young Leroy's behavior upset his mother to the point where she lost complete control of any sense of what was good for both her child or herself and her calculated brutality would change the course of his life forever. Wallace recounts the story: 'But one day she get fed up of me taking her thruppence. Because she went to a shop, in those days ya have a trust thing at the shop. So weekends when she stop by the shop she say, "how much I do owe you?" And he say, "You owe me $20 plus your son take three penny." She say, "What? I didn't tell him… I give him money to go to school." When I went home she give a good whipping. She get so bad maybe she get emotional. She tell me to make up a big fire. And she put my hands in the fire. That's how I end up in Alpha, for childcare and protection.' The severe burning of young Leroy's hands did not go unnoticed by a neighbour, who duly reported the incident to the police, although Wallace believes this may have been more because this particular neighbour bore a grudge against his mother rather than out of care for the child. Like so many Alpharians, Wallace takes a philosophical view of how severe circumstances

Leroy 'Horsemouth' Wallace

led to him being saved from an entirely different kind of destiny and has no illusions about the kind of person he would have become without the school's intervention. 'I went to Alpha because my mum burn up my ten fingers and I give thanks to my mum because if she didn't do that I would be a big t'ief (thief) around the place, yuh know wha' I mean? If I don't go to Alpha, yes, I would be somebody dangerous.'

Leroy Wallace was taken into Alpha in 1957. He recalls his arrival as 'very chaotic. I went to the juniors' home. When ya pass the bump in the road, ya know ya past the border. I was very excited because I never seen so much kids. There was some big guys there to beat ya up because I was small in those days.'

The junior home at Alpha, where Horsemouth once resided, is no longer used since the school is now strictly a day school

Photo by Heather Augustyn 2017

Wallace would watch the band practicing with awe and fascination and he wanted to get closer to the action. Sister Ignatius refused to consider him for the band despite his many requests to her. Frustrated and angry at being left out, Wallace set out to prove a point by annoying the Sisters with his own renegade drumming and hoping to draw attention to his musical potential. He had soaked up his family members' drumming played at Pocomania rituals, a Jamaican folk tradition, and the young boy was determined to make a noise with it.

'I used to ask Sister Ignatius to get me in the band, but she never get me in the band. So I used to get some big metal drums and beat them (shouts) "BOOM! BOOM! BOOM!" Because I used to hear my grandma play drum in her church, Pocomania. So I have an experience of Poco drum and Junkanoo,' he recounts. 'I used to play this tin pan … I use those willow trees as a brush on the drum and she sit there reading her Bible.' (Pocomania is a Jamaican spiritual tradition that harks back to pre-slavery Africa and Junkanoo is a frenzied street parade involving costume and masks and a hypnotic drum and fife band). Wallace's plot turned out to be successful, but not without having to make a formal application to demonstrate his seriousness. 'Sister saw me play the drum and I was annoying to her, and she called me and said, "Wallace you wanna be in the band?" I say, "yes." I have to write her a good letter, put it in the chapel. You wanna get in the band ya gotta write her a good letter and put it somewhere she can see.' No other Alpha boy we interviewed has mentioned making a written application, so this may be something employed for boys whom the sisters had dubious expectations of to see if they would step up to the plate.

Joining the band taught Wallace about rhythmic structure of a wide variety of musical styles. Those formative years of disciplined musical drill enabled him to be much freer and expressive later on as a reggae drummer. Such strong rhythmic foundations gives rise to the kind of confidence needed to develop one's own unique sound, and so Wallace was able to help develop a rhythmic sub-genre within reggae, the era-defining militant 'rockers' sound, generally credited to Sly Dunbar, which dominated reggae at the tail end of the 1970s. Wallace explains how formally learning classical and jazz helped him to become one of the most in-demand reggae drummers. 'It's orchestration. It help you to play bossa nova, bolero, cha-cha-cha, calypso, merengue. We play all Latin sounds, Cuban, Central America. And Jamaica have its own sounds like Junkanoo and Pocomania, those are things that we bring from Africa, our ancestors bring all those things to Jamaica here. So when we are in the ghetto, Trench Town or wherever we come from and we listen, those things en-trance us. But what I learn from Alpha is bigger. It expand my vocabulary in music and I love that. It give me an advantage right now as a drummer. Right now I can go and play on a tour and play music that these youths can't play, because of this experience in Alpha.'

An Alpha band practice session would often attract quite a crowd from the surrounding areas according to Wallace. Locals would gather to watch and listen, creating a sense of excitement and occasion for all involved. Even some of the Rastas used to come down from the hills to hear the Alpha Boys play. 'Count Ossie and all those people used play in the mountains nearby Alpha and everybody comes around Alpha to listen to the Alpha Boys Band to get knowledge of music, because when we play in those days you can hear the band all around, Up Park Camp, South Camp Road, Allman

Town, neighbours nearby ya can hear Alpha Boys band. When we play we look at our fence and it's full of people listening to the band.'

Wallace learnt ways to make a living at Alpha which would support him before he could make a living from music. 'These people, they grow me, they give me a trade, they have twenty one trade shop in the school. I got three trades, tile making, music and I used to work in the printery. I used to work in the government office printing passports for everybody in Jamaica.' Wallace shares the same humble love and gratitude towards Sister Ignatius as

Leroy 'Horsemouth' Wallace in *Rockers*

A still from Rockers, courtesy Cherry Kaoru Hulsey, Blue Sun Film Co.

so many other Alpharians. 'I go to bed and I dream about Sister Ignatius a lot of times. She was like a mother, like an angel mother that just appeared to me in my life. And she was good, she taught me a lot of discipline too. I was here there and everywhere. 'Cause leaving ya mother from six or seven they have to discipline me, and for me it was good.' The anger he carried about his childhood was hard to control and led to much rebellious behavior.

Horsemouth in *Rockers*
A still from *Rockers*, courtesy Cherry Kaoru Hulsey, Blue Sun Film Co.

In the mid-1970s a twist of fate came Leroy 'Horsemouth Wallace's way that would be life-changing. Independent movie director Theodoros Bafaloukos came to Jamaica with the intention of making a reggae documentary, but somehow struck upon the idea of making a feature movie with the stars of the day playing themselves. Rockers contains elements of the Robin Hood fable of stealing from the rich and giving to the poor, combined with elements of the 1948 Italian neo-realist classic *Bicycle Thief*, the storyline transposed from depress-sion-era Rome to 1970s Kingston. Horsemouth plays himself as a hustler distributing records around Kingston on a motorbike. His bike gets stolen and Horsemouth loses his livelihood. We are then taken on a journey through Kingston's ghetto underworld as our hero searches for his treasured bike. Short on storyline but rich in cultural atmosphere, *Rockers* captures the spirit of the moment and is about as close as you can get to hanging out in Trench Town with your favourite reggae artists. Gregory Isaacs, Jacob Miller, Burning Spear, Big Youth, Dillinger and Kiddus-I all make appearances and we also get to see the inside of Harry J's studio. *Rockers* has reached near mythical status and is arguably a more raw, authentic and honest movie than *The Harder They Come.* Horsemouth is proud of his acting achievement, although naturally he wishes he made more money from it.

When it comes to Horsemouth's musical credentials a full list might take up a couple of pages, but his works include drumming for Ken Boothe, Hugh Mundell, Kiddus-I, The Abyssinians, Half Pint, Justin Hinds, Mikey Dread, Prince Far-I, Yabby-U, The Royals, Sugar Minott, Dennis Brown, Burning Spear, Earl 16, Dillinger, The Gladiators, Horace Andy, Tony Tuff,

Rita Marley, Hugh Griffiths, I-Roy, Bunny Wailer, Augustus Pablo and Bim Sherman—and that's just the tip of the iceberg. He worked for most of the major studios including Joe Gibbs, Studio One, King Tubbys and Channel One.

Leroy 'Horsemouth' Wallace is above all else a Rastaman. Against all odds he became one of Jamaica's greatest and most prolific drummers of all time. Alpha gave him music, but Rastafari gave him knowledge of self. 'There's another school we call *overstanding*,' he declares. 'Understanding is what they taught us in school, *overstanding* is this knowledge of searching of your spirit and what you know is the truth. So when you have that overstanding you can move along and do what *you* wanna do, you are very free in your mind because the way we were brought up is that people tell us what to do. You finally find yourself in a position when it's like ya don't know where you are. So you got to have this overstanding of knowledge of things to come into this presence of knowing yourself.' Straight from the Horse's mouth, you can't argue with that.

--A.R.

Leroy Wallace on his home drum kit above, and outside his home in Spanish Town, right

Photos by Davis Coome

Albert "Apple Gabriel" Craig

Under the cover of darkness, the field slaves, house slaves, children, gathered with their sticks and torches, set the cane on fire and retreated into the mountains where the bush gave them refuge. Here they ambushed their attackers, warning their brothers and sisters across the mountain with the call of the abeng. They were warriors—fierce, ruthless, organized, and smart. They were undefeatable and today their most zealous leaders are national heroes. These are the Maroons, and their blood runs thick in the veins of Apple Gabriel, decendent of this rebellious and conquering people.

Apple Gabriel is, like his Maroon ancestors, a fighter, defensive against attack, but as he will also tell you, he was made to be this way. He has had a hard life. He has been a sufferer in many ways, including during his days at Alpha, about which he does not mince words. Apple Gabriel's days on this earth have been tough. But despite his warrior shell and words he throws like stones at his foe, Apple Gabriel is a kind and strong man, a funny and smart man, a creative and productive man, and he is a hell of a musician.

Apple Gabriel was born as Albert Craig, the youngest of 10 children. "My great grandparents were white. My great grandfather was General Brumfield, a British military officer in Jamaica in 1906. I was raised by my mother and my grand aunt Kate, a white woman. My mother used to have a big grocery shop and a bar and was doing good. My mother's white grandparents were wealthy and they had acres and acres of land in Clarendon and they produce a lot of stuff with dozens and dozens of workers with trucks coming in to chop the cane and pick the ackee and the fruits and everything," he says. But soon, the promise of a bountiful life changed when Craig was just a toddler. "That's when I got the polio, when I reach 3 ½ years, I got the polio."

The *Jamaica Gleaner* on December 21, 2014 reported on the polio outbreak in Jamaica, saying, "It's a part of Jamaican history which is not often recalled.... The outbreak in the 1950s was severe.... For most children around the island it was very difficult to access treatment because they didn't know what it was; vaccines were not available. It was new to the island and there were no symptoms. People were simply fine one day, and by the next morning they couldn't walk or they couldn't breathe." There were two outbreaks—one in 1954 and one in 1957. Craig contracted polio during the second outbreak in 1958 after playing in a nearby river. Polio is a waterborne virus. "I was playing in the river and that's how I got polio. My mom take me to the river and I'm playing in the water, looking at the tadpoles swimming and we went back home. In the morning, I get sick overnight. I always wake up early, but in the morning I couldn't wake up when the cock crow. She keep shaking me to get up and when I woke up, I start crying but I couldn't move. When she lift me up to make me stand up, I fell on the floor, and that's when she realized something was wrong with me. She put me back on the bed and took off all of my clothes to check my body and that's when she saw my right leg was shorter and smaller than the left one. She said when she touch it, it feel ice cold. All this happen at night when I was sleeping, it shrink down my muscle," he says.

The Daily Gleaner

POLIO EPIDEMIC CONFIRMED

Beware flies, dirty hands and food

12 CASES, 3 SUSPECTS IN CORPORATE AREA

FRESH ATTACK LAUNCHED IN GUATEMALA

***Daily Gleaner*, August 4, 1955**

Though his mother tried a variety of bush remedies, his leg continued to get smaller. When nothing worked, two weeks later she took him to one of the island's three hospitals where the doctor diagnosed him with polio. Apple was quarantined at the hospital and then sent with other patients to Mona Rehabilitation Center until Jamaica received Jonas Salk's vaccine and the virus disappeared. "They were testing the vaccine on us. They sweat us out with heated blankets like fire on us on aluminum tables. I was a guinea pig. I was only 3 ½ but I can see it like it was yesterday. There were babies dying all around me, but God keep me alive," he says. It was here, as one of the first shipments of patients to Mona Rehab, that Apple met two other victims of the polio epidemic, Cecil "Skelly" Spence, and Lascelle "Wiss" Bulgin after they arrived months later. Apple would go on to form the group Israel Vibration with Skelly and Wiss. Other notable musicians who contracted the polio virus throughout the world during the outbreaks of the late '40s and '50s include Ian Dury, Joni Mitchell, Judy Collins, Donovan, Neil Young, Steve Harley, and Gene Simmons.

Craig took the name Apple early in his life, but Gabriel came later and was given to him by Haile Selassie's grandson. Both have biblical significance, and the Bible was an important part of Apple's life at Mona, though he says he was always a spiritual person. "My mother told me I was born as a prophet. After a while she became a spiritual healer and had a church and did spiritual healing. She was very powerful and she was called a "Mother," which means spiritual healer. My mother told me I have the spirit of a leader. I asked her to read me and she told me I am going to be a great leader in the world and that millions of people are going to follow me as a prophet." Such a maternal expectation on a child may cause anxiety or feelings of inadequacy in others, but not for Apple Gabriel who wears his mother's premonition as a badge of honor, a revelation of love, a blessing. He knows it will be fulfilled, and in many ways, it already has.

Apple Gabriel

While at Mona, Apple's grandfather died and the family became embroiled in estate disputes, leaving his mother fighting for her share of 16 acres of bauxite land worth millions of dollars that was left to her in her grandfather's will. Apple says that his mother was cheated from her inheritance, it was stolen from her by a greedy family, and as a result she became depressed and she lost her businesses. Apple's father disowned Apple when he was just six years old, unable to accept his son's handicap and blamed Apple's mother for the misfortune.

After a few years at Mona Rehab, Apple was transferred to the Salvation Army children's home called The Nest which sent him to an able-bodied school called Swallowfield School where he nurtured his love for music, teaching himself to play piano by watching his teacher perform at lunchtime. He wrote his first song for his childhood love when he was just 10 years old. But Apple says he was also teased relentlessly by the able-bodied children, and so he fought back. "They made my life a living hell." The

Salvation Army administration at The Nest punished him for fighting back by withholding food and putting him in isolation. They didn't investigate why Apple fought back—to retaliate being bullied because of his handicap. "The students hit me on lunchbreak in the school yard. When the bell rang and everybody went back to their classes, I asked to use the bathroom and instead of going, I went into their classes and hit them over the head. The woman who was in charge of The Nest, the brigadier, never investigated why these fights took place in school. Instead she put baking soda in my wound to punish me and it turned black after months. She was an evil Dutch woman from Holland. She sent me to walk three miles to the clinic after it get so bad. She didn't want to use the children's home van so the medical people at the clinic could not identify where I was coming from and who was doing this to me. She was covering up the abuse. The doctor said, 'Oh my God, what happen to your leg,' and I told him the woman at the Salvation Army childrens' home put baking soda on my sore,' and he said, 'You don't put baking soda on a sore.'" Out of the brigadier's fear of being investigated, she transferred Apple to Alpha Boys' School. "This is how I end up at Alpha. It was a youth detention center for bad and runaway children. They send me there in 1967 in the middle of the year. I was 12 ½ going on 13. It's a prison for kids. They have jail there, they lock us up, with bars on the windows and you have to sleep on the concrete. It was cold at night," Apple says.

He says that he rejected the nun's attempts at indoctrination, which frustrated administrators, and so he was denied his requests. "They have trade shops in there including the printery shop, that is what I love, and the music class. I wanted to join the band and play keyboard. The bandmaster said I was brilliant and he want me in the band, but the nun wouldn't allow me to be a part of the band, so I wanted to learn printery and they reject me again. They put me in the damn tile shop. I said hell no, the hell with this shit, so I quit going. Then they put me in the woodworking shop and I curse out the teacher and I leave. I am very sensitive to dust. It's not my line of work, but all of this was done to hurt me. They get mad at me now." Apple says that this is when he experienced a side of Alpha that many have either never seen, or those who have rarely talk about. "The head staff, big men who walk around with big strap and things and he slap me with the strap and I curse him out. I say if you do that to me again, I'm going to be the last person you do that to. You don't beat with a strap. I was in the big dining room and I feel blam! Right across my back! The same man come and hit me with the strap. I took up my breakfast and the hot cup of tea and I throw it in his face and I walk outside of the dining room and he come out and I hide behind the door and the Maroon spirit rise up in myself. I broke two bottles and with the pieces I am ready to stab him. I say if you think you're bad, come out here. I told you not to put your hands on me again. They go and call the nun and I tell them to go back to Italy with your brainwashing stupid shit. Everything just come out of my mouth. I ain't no damn Catholic, I ain't no damn slave, I'm not into your program, fuck that program. They put me in the jail for seven days. Another time I tell the staff to go suck his bomboclaat ass because he hit me with a strap and the nun come now with a little plate, a saucer, with three scotch bonnet pepper in it and told me I must eat the peppers to burn the bad words out of my mouth. She got seven big boys to hold me down over a bench to force me to eat the peppers. When they hold me down, I bite down on their flesh, I become a vampire now, I want to taste blood. Seven boys I bite them up. Every one of them have to go to the medical when I'm done with them, and I look at that nun and I say, 'Fuck you, you nyam that pepper!' She turn red, I tell her if she approach me again I'm going to take that and stuff that in your fucking mouth and rip up your bomboclaat face. I was like a mad man. After that they put me in the senior center. Out of revenge they send me down to the garden, and I am handicap, how am I supposed to walk with a damn bucket of water? To punish me worse they put me in with the garbage dump where they dump the garbage. So they make me shovel the garbage through mesh to get

Apple Gabriel

fertilizer. It was a dump full of scorpions. We call it the scorpion pit in Alpha. That was the worst punishment. And that's when I start to plan to run away. I'm not staying in that place."

Officials at Alpha today say there is no record of Apple Gabriel having ever attended the school. But Albert Malawi confirms that Apple did indeed attend and the two were friends. "Yes, we were at Alpha. He was in the junior home part. Apple was there. How dem don't have his record?" Malawi asks, in disbelief. Apple says he remembers that his friend Malawi had a nickname at Alpha—Turbit—which Malawi confirms. "Perfectly right. Dat shows we were together because when we are getting beating, we nuh cry. We tough like turbit fish," says Malawi. Apple says he thinks his missing record is because Alpha wants to "hide the mistreatment they have done." As a result, he ran away. "The nuns never called the police to bring me back. I was the only one no police try to bring back. They never had an experience like me, they were facing a Maroon!" He had no immediate plans when he ran away from Alpha, but he dreamed of a better life. "I used to go up and sit in a tree out on the playfield and sing and play this pan as a drum. I used to look at the planes flying overhead, leaving Palisadoes Airport, and I say, 'One day, one day, I am going to be on one of those planes going to America.' I decide I'm leaving this place today. I climb through the fence and I just hit the damn street, at 13 years old, went straight to downtown and never look back. My 14th birthday I was on the street as a homeless sleeping on the sidewalk in downtown Kingston."

While on the street, Apple met many people, including rude boys and musicians. He was a beggar, wiping car windows at stoplights for change, asking shop owners at Bruce's Patty at Crossroads for a patty or two. "That's one of the places where I used to hustle." Though he took up with his mother again for about a year in 1970 after living on the street for three years, she had been living with another man who wanted Apple to help clean his hog pens and he refused because he was becoming Rastafari and didn't eat pork. "He threw me out." Apple was 16 and he started sleeping in the Hope Riverbed for months. His mother brought him food so he could survive and broke up with the man, unable to stand the way he treated her son. She moved to Rockfort and Apple moved with her in an area with his cousins. "We were all family inside that yard, 7 St. Patrick Road at the foot of the

Wareika Hill, and people come out and play domino and smoke some chalice pipe. It was a gathering yard, island style, and my mom didn't like that kind of gathering I'm involved with, with the Rasta. She said I couldn't stay around because my Rasta ways was clashing with her spiritual vibes. I was 17 and my mom threw all of my clothes over the fence!" he says, laughing.

Apple Gabriel

Apple went back to Mona Rehab in search of the rights that were given to him by the government as a victim of polio. "I rode my bicycle all the way up to Mona Rehab. There was an open bush with cows, donkeys, horses, goats and it was government property. I hide my clothes there and live there for years in that bush. I went up there for help because John Golding and Sammy Henriques who ran the rehab were obligated to help me and set me up with a job and live. They live like two gods. They were rich, millionaires. I told them I need help because my mom signed papers for you to help me. I was a spokesperson for the people in Mona Rehab because I snuck in the office and read all the papers and I knew our rights. I want to see if I can still get the help I can get my parents sign up for, but I went as a Rasta, and they did not like that shit. But I start to sleep and eat on the compound and I need help, I need a job, and they say if I stop preaching Rasta we will help you but I have to stop preaching the Rasta thing, but I said to John Golding in his office, 'What does my religion have to do with the obligation you have to give to me by law?' They call the police and I said I am going to live inside this damn institution and the police said this man is right, you people owe him that obligation to rehabilitate him. It is his right to be here."

Apple met up again with Skelly, who was his best friend from three years old, and Wiss, who both grew up in the institution. Apple says he read the Bible to Wiss and Skelly so soon they too were associating with the Rasta culture. "Every day I used to sit in the bush at Mona Rehab in a big big open land, bush land, and Skelly and Wiss come with me and we sing and sing and sing and every evening we make a likkle audience and people passing by in the bush used to clap at the end of the song and encourage us, so we became known in the whole area as the three Rasta handicap who sing." Because Apple used to play piano every day at the Theological College with Donald Manning, lead singer for the Abyssinians, and all the students knew him, he was asked to perform at a college party, their first performance. Apple named the group Israel Vibration. Apple played piano while all three sang.

"By this time now we join the Twelve Tribe people and we do stage shows for them and everyone come to see the three handicap. We were the headliner. A lot of people join Twelve Tribe because of we. This was the first time in history this sort of thing rise up. This guy named Hugh Booth, me and him were close bredren, and he own a sound called JahLoveMuzik and he take us to a studio and he produce us. We made Skelly lead vocal first because he cannot sing back vocal. He sing a song we call 'Why Worry' and two other songs." Apple says that though there were many other artists with Twelve Tribe, they all left because "it wasn't real, it was fake people. Take the money and feed them big belly, jump in their fancy car and leave us standing there. Bob was a member, Dennis Brown was a member, Jacob Miller was a member and Gad Man [Vernon Carrington], the leader of Twelve Tribe, treat us ghetto dreads all worse than the light-skin dreads. Bob was angry and said it was racist and he left Twelve Tribe and make a song call, 'Running Away.' He was telling the Twelve Tribe people about the divide in the organization and the favoritism show to the light-skin dreads over the black dreads. He was angry over it and that's why he left Twelve Tribe. Bob sit down and tell me he wrote that song and record it, he said, 'I have to sing about this shit.' After they left, we left. We lick them like Bob, by singing the 'Same Song,' and the first album we put out also called *Same Song*. Twelve Tribe was full of hypocrisy."

Israel Vibration then recorded with Tommy Cowan and his newly developing Talent Corporation, but Apple says they left there too after a short time because of conflicts with Inner Circle who was also with Cowan. "There was a conflict between Inner Circle and Tommy Cowan because of us. We were number one and the band become jealous and they take the original tape for 'We Are the Rasta.' To this day that tape was never found. It was a different mix from the album and it was revenge so they could be the front line again for Talent Corporation. It wasn't Jacob Miller. Me and Jacob was best friends. It was the other guys and they were jealous and because we were handicap they look down on us."

Israel Vibration's Apple Gabriel (center), Skelly (left), and Wiss (right)

They next went to Tuff Gong because Bob Marley hired Tommy Cowan who produced their second album, backed by the Wailers band. "Five of us start Tuff Gong Distribution in Jamaica—Israel Vibration, Nadine Sutherland, Rita Marley, The Melody Makers, and Bob Marley himself, five of us. We start Tuff Gong Distribution in Jamaica. Then Bob have a radio show called the Tuff Gong Package and every Saturday Bob have a one hour show on JBC Radio and they only play the five of us music, emceed by Errol Thompson, the number-one disc jockey then. All this was going on and I'm still sleeping in bush on the property alongside the Mona Rehab, and I also slept at the Island House after Bob bought it when it wasn't fixed up or anything yet. That's where Bob and the band used to rehearse every weekend. Family Man was living in the back. It wasn't Tuff Gong yet. We did the album called *Unconquered People* and Bob love it. We was Bob's favorite singing group in Jamaica. It was the Wailers who played all the backup on the album, all the rhythm section dem."

Apple did have his childhood dream realized when he boarded a plane to come to America in 1979 for a sold-out show in New York, returning again in 1981 for another sold-out show. "We did a show in Manhattan at Negril Club and that was the last show that Bob Marley came to before he died. He sit right at stage side and give us juice. He do his show the next night with the Commodores and he collapse on stage. He never come back. But *Billboard* magazine interview him, the last interview Bob make to the world, he said if God take away this illness from me, the only group I would produce is Israel Vibration, I'll take them on every tour with me. These are the words of Bob Marley."

Apple Gabriel

In the subsequent years, Israel Vibration toured the world and sold out shows everywhere they went—all over Europe, North America, and South America. But Apple says that the band was torn apart due to division within the group which he believes was fostered by their manager, Doctor Dread, who he accuses of stealing money from the group—money from the shows, merchandise, and music sales. Despite what Doctor Dread has written in his book, Apple says he did not walk off the stage during a performance and quit the group. "That's a damn lie," he says. Instead, Doctor Dread sent Skelly and Wiss on tour with the Roots Radics without Apple. He heard about it through a friend who called him from Germany, wondering why the trio was now a duo.

"After the group break up, a lot of things happen to me," he says, noting the death of one of his three children. He has also moved a number of times, but he continues to write music from his home studio in Atlanta and he has had a successful solo career. "I could put out 50 albums back to back, right now, but I have no investor. I never stop writing. I never stop making music. I'm the fountain of music, I can't dry up!"

--H.A.

Leroy Smart

One of the most eccentric and flamboyant characters in reggae is undoubtedly the singer Leroy Smart, the man who branded himself 'The Don' of reggae music. For 40 years he has maintained an invincible aura of bad-boy ghetto swagger and flashy charisma, producing a wealth of both roots and lovers material. His impassioned, brooding and sometimes even desperate sounding tenor voice is comparable to reggae singers like Junior Byles and even Keith Hudson in its ability to reach into the dark corners of the soul, giving the impression of purging himself of deep-seated, gut-wrenching emotion. He was given a shout-out by The Clash in the opening verse of their 1978 reggae crossover hit 'White Man (In Hammersmith Palais)' after lead singer Joe Strummer saw him as part of a reggae package show at a west London music venue: *Midnight to six, man / For the first time from Jamaica / Dillinger and Leroy Smart / Delroy Wilson, your cool operator.*

Smart was born in 1952 but due to losing his parents by the age of two, was placed in the social care system, firstly Maxwell Park Children's Home then followed by Alpha Boys' School at the age of twelve. At Alpha he learnt drums under bandleader Lennie Hibbert, but he also sang in the school choir, which helped develop his self-assured vocal style. As well as singing, Smart claims to have learnt dancing but it's not clear which style of dancing was taught at Alpha back at that time. As with all Alpha Boys he undertook a trade, in Smart's case shoemaking.

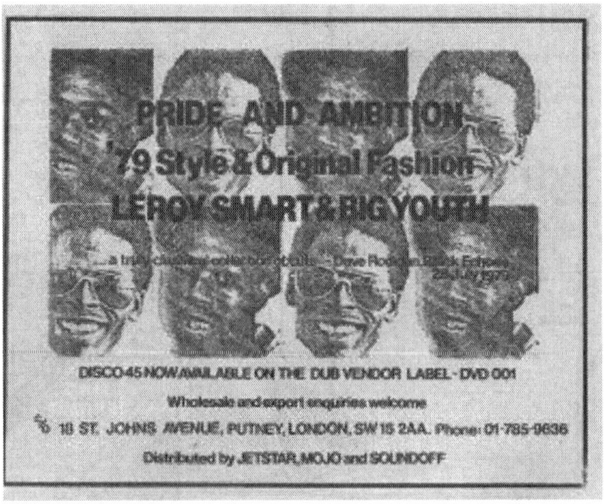

Speaking to Seb Carayol for *The Hundreds* music blog at The Dub Club in Los Angeles in 2015, Smart discussed his early life circumstances. 'I'm an orphan. Right now I still don't know no father, no mother, no brother or sister. Nobody from where

I was born. Only God is my guidance, and only God helped me through and gave me this break. Coming up was a struggle, I got misled in the ghetto. It's none of us fault. It's happened to many rappers, many stars, everybody. Because of the struggle with poverty.' Smart's ability to elevate himself from extreme poverty to reggae royalty is down to his own talent, resilience and determination, but without the dedicated care of the nuns at Alpha who knows whether Smart would have found his way. 'Alpha Boys' School is a school of the nuns—the Catholic people,' continues Smart. 'They respond with the people that are orphaned and people that have no way out, no family to take care of them. It's a blessing school, because they help a lot of orphaned just like myself, you know?'

Leroy Smart in 1983
Photo by Beth Lesser

Smart left Alpha aged sixteen and started supporting himself through a series of menial jobs such as hotel work and construction work. Having no place to call home meant that he would often sleep at whichever building site he happened to be working at. He harboured a burning passion to become a singer and would spend hours listening to the radio every day, dreaming of becoming a rocksteady singer like Alton Ellis. Smart would spend increasing amounts of time hanging out in the ghetto yards of Kingston, where he would come into contact with other singers and musicians every day. His first single came in 1968, 'So Mean to Me,' a strong blast of fast *kerchanga*-style early reggae that was in full flow at that time. Smart did not go unnoticed by the producers of the day as he took the mic to sing at sound system dances such as Tippertone, but it took another four years before he scored his first hit, 'Pride and Ambition' for producer Gussie Clarke, one of Smart's signature songs.

In 1972 he approached producer Jimmy Radway at Dynamic Studios and pleaded with Radway to write a song for Smart to record. Radway responded by penning 'Mother Liza' which was backed by the swampy horns of Bobby Ellis and Richard 'Dirty Harry' Hall, a slow, moody skanker with Smart's tormented voice sounding like he could emotionally crack at any moment. Expressing this kind of smouldering anguish was to become Smart's trademark and a string of strong hits followed. His key breakthroughs of this period include 'Ethiopia' for Joe Gibbs, 'Ballistic Affair' for Jo Jo Hookim at Channel One Studio, 'God Helps the Man' and 'Trying To Wreck Up My Life' for Bunny 'Striker' Lee, 'Keep On Trying' for Big Youth and 'I Am The Don' for Henry 'Junjo' Lawes. This latter record, released in 1983 asserted his status as ruler of the Kingston scene in a fairly typical piece of ghetto self-aggrandizing boastfulness that over the decades Smart has become renowned for. He explains, 'Don is an exclusive name that the world has chosen and given me. I am a professional dancer. I am a hitmaker. When I dress, I am one of the most outstanding dressers on the stage, on television. So I came up with a song in the early days called "I Am The Don," and right away people said, "Yes, that's The Don. He looks like a Don, he dances like a Don. He sing hits like The Don." Many others

Leroy Smart
Photo by David Corio

claim that they are The Don but people don't choose them as no Don. They say Leroy Smart is the real Don.' Surely, a mission statement fit for a ghetto superstar. In 1981 Smart took a break from Kingston life, perhaps as a reprieve from the relentless violence at this time which forced so many to

Leroy Smart
Photo by David Corio

leave. He relocated to California where he did some shows and also undertook some formal voice training. Upon his return to Kingston in 1982 his coaching immediately paid off with a string of hits showcasing his newly emboldened voice, including 'She Love It In The Morning,' 'Stop Criticizing' and 'All My Love,' firmly staking his claim as a major force in the revolutionary new digitized dancehall.

Leroy Smart always moved with the times, embracing new styles as reggae has constantly re-invented itself. He has perpetually made his presence known in the charts and in the dancehalls. Smart has recorded a staggering 350 singles and released over 35 albums for many of Jamaica's greatest producers and his own self-produced material for his Worldwide Success label. He continues to tour and perform at home and around the world.

--A.R.

Albert Dixon, AKA Albert Malawi and Ilawi

One could be forgiven for confusion over the identity of the man named Albert Russell Dixon. As one of Jamaica's original roots reggae sound system selectors he is known simply as Ilawi, although his original name as a selector was Turbot, like the fish. As a roots reggae drummer, percussionist and singer he goes by the name of Albert Malawi. As a member of the Rastafari sect Twelve Tribes he is known as Naptali. His birth certificate carries an incorrect name altogether. 'Me 'ave a 'ole 'eap o' name,' he says. 'My father name Victor Dixon, my mother name Gwendoline Jackson.' As a baby his mother's family insisted he take on his mother's family name. 'When them ready to register me, they give the name to the post mistress and say 'write down Jackson.' It seems the post mistress got confused when filling in the relevant documents as to whether he was Dixon or Jackson and accidentally registered him as Johnson. 'I go wid it,' he says. 'It's the post mistress make the mistake. But as Rastafari we have many names. Right now me is Naptali and Ilawi and Malawi.' The songwriting credits on his singles are listed as A. Johnson, the incorrect name given on his birth certificate.

Born in 1953 in the parish of St. Andrew's, Johnson entered Alpha in 1966, having previously attended four other approved schools. Exactly why he was sent there is unclear. 'I don't know why, it was not for any crime, it was as I say, for the power of the Almighty, from me walk in a straight line, guided. I never join gang, I never hurt people, I never fling stone, yuh un'erstan' me?' From an early age he was drawn towards music and was experimenting with percussion long before starting at Alpha, inventing homemade drums from whatever he could find.

Ilawi selecting on the Jah Love Muzik Tour of England in 1982

Sister Ignatius once again demonstrated her uncanny ability to see a child's potential and invited Albert to audition for the band. 'I don't know what happened but they send me to Sister Ignatius. She saw something within I.' Initially allocated the French horn, the instrument was not one he would connect with because, he says, 'it never have that meditation.' Lennie Hibbert, his bandmaster, 'instruct me to go on the drums.' Under the name Ilawi, Johnson would go on to become one of Jamaica's most beloved sound system selectors of all time and it was Ignatius that set him out on that path. For reasons unknown to him, he was invited by Sister Ignatius to learn how to operate her famed sound system. 'I was instructed how to play the amplifier and turntable. That's where I start playing sound, he explains. 'I started out at Alpha playing the sound every Saturday.'

Upon leaving Alpha, Johnson found work in the library at The University of the West Indies and it was here that he met someone who had a link to music, leading to him joining the 30-piece Y. de Lima's Blue Diamond Steel Band from Trinidad, which included some members of the Twelve Tribes of Israel sect. After a while this band divided into two separate calypso groups, one of which was called Advocate, which Malawi joined because this was where the Twelve Tribes members went into. Later Malawi and others left to form The Twelve Tribes of Israel Band. This new band would provide musical backing for some of the emerging roots reggae artists of the era, notably Fred Locks' *Black Star Liner*, a much revered roots reggae LP. 'That's the first album I play drum on.' Malawi would play drums for Sugar Minott on the song 'Roll River Jordan' and on early some Dennis Brown Studio One tunes, including a cover of US singer Bobby Russell's 'Little Green Apples' and a cover of Cuban mambo artist Oswaldo Farrés' classic, 'Perhaps.' He also provided drums for Carlton And The Shoes, The Ethiopians and Augustus Pablo. In the late 1970s he played in The Black Roots Band (not to be confused with British reggae band Black Roots) backing Sugar Minott and also The Gaylads, Rankin' Dread, Tony Tuff, Rankin' Joe, Sammy Dread and Michael Palmer. Malawi played on three as yet unreleased Bob Marley demo tapes, including 'Babylon Feel Dis One' and 'She Used To Call Me Dada'

Ilawi from his MySpace page

both available to hear on YouTube. With The Twelve Tribes Band he provided backing on albums by The Visionaires, Little Roy and Israel Vibration. Recording as Albert Malawi he released a handful of highly regarded devotional Rastafari 45s, including 'Children Of The Emperor,' 'Mercy Of Jah,' 'Ethiopia Land' and 'Jah Is Sweet,' the originals of which are prized collector's items although some have seen re-issue.

As Ilawi, he began selecting on a sound called JahMikMuzik operated by Twelve Tribes member Mickey 'Jah Mik' Mowatt. Another Twelve Tribes sound system was called Sounds of Love operated by Earl 'Jah B' Belcher. When Mowatt immigrated to the USA in 1976, the two sounds merged as JahLoveMuzik, managed by Jah B. This new expanded operation became the leading roots sound over the following decade, featuring Ilawi as selector and Brigadier Jerry as its headline DJ. 'I am the original and only selector with Jah Love,' he says. 'Me a one of the first selector who play cultural sound in Jamaica. We play all the people at the time who are sending messages.' Ilawi and DJ Brigadier Jerry stand tall as iconic figures in Jamaican sound system culture. 'Me and Brigadier are the worker, the teacher and the preacher and the selector, we are the ones doing all the work while they are in their bed. Collecting money for the dance.' Jah Love had a special theme song, 'Tell Them About Jah Love,' which would always be the signal for Brigadier Jerry to step up to the mic. 'We play that song over forty years. That is the song Ilawi always play. We set a pace and we set a trend,' says Malawi.

The skill he developed as a young boy operating the Alpha sound system would serve him well when operating a big rig for crowds up 6,000 people. A massive bass-heavy reggae sound system requires a high level of technical expertise and constant sound monitoring. Each tune played needs skillful balancing to get the best out of the speakers and to prevent it sounding rough. Knowing which tunes to play is an intuitive skill learnt through trial and error. Keeping a crowd bubbling all night is the selector's special art and requires a total belief in the music they play. 'I start my thing from Alpha so me know about sequence of music and volume, and me know about when sound too loud, and me know when ya outta key, if ya sharp or

too flat,' says Malawi. With pride he recounts how Bob Marley, through his association with the Twelve Tribes, would frequent JahLoveMuzik dances. 'I man Ilawi are the only selector in the world who bring Bob Marley in the dance seven times. The last time Bob Marley came to a dance was at Golden Spring Community Centre in '79/'80. In St. Ann in the country. It was a Twelve Tribes dance. Run by a daughter named Sister Doreen it was her dance and Bob Marley was coming through the gate in a khaki suit. And a guy come down to me at the control tower and say black out the sound becau' the next sound called Socialist Roots told me to stop and let that sound play. They were about a mile away. And the guy just take out a gun and mash up the turntable needle wid it. The bredren heard the music stop play. The man fire a shot and run out and a man get shot.' Fortunately nobody was hurt.

Malawi's musical talent has been handed down through his daughter Kerida, a conscious roots singer and DJ who performs under the name Hempress Sattiva. 'It's an energy within the family,' says Malawi proudly. 'Mi daughter so powerful, she's unconquerable'—a reference to her 2017 debut album, *Unconquerebel.* 'There is no other artist in her category, or inna the reggae business yuhknow?' Reflecting upon his legacy as a selector and his impact on sound system culture in Jamaica, Malawi summarizes, 'For me is a man who a 50 years inna dance, from me 13 me a selector, from me at Alpha, at 12, 13, 14. 'Nuff work, 'nuff night work, don't get no sleep, just try to make people happy, teaching in the night, I and I was stylin' through the night, teaching and educating yuhknow wha' I mean? And that generation is still about the place right now, very much alive.'

--A.R.

Vernal Kelly, AKA Charlie 'Eskimo' Fox

Reggae drummer Vernal Kelly, better known as Charlie 'Eskimo' Fox, is one of the lesser-known Alpha musicians, but his left-field rhythmic experimentation forms a cornerstone of one of the most intriguing and influential British musical evolutions, the London-based On-U Sound collective, headed by visionary sonic wizard Adrian Sherwood. Perhaps because his musical schooling did not come directly from Alpha as he was never in the band, Fox has not generally been associated with the Alpha tradition.

Born Vernal Oliver Kelly, he enrolled at Alpha aged nine but his musical schooling began much earlier, through participating in marathon all-night Kumina, Nyabinghi and Pocomania drumming sessions, Jamaica's surviving African traditions. Speaking with an otherworldly, hypnotic quality Fox explains his rural heritage. 'I'm coming from the hills where we are a Kumina player. My family background, they all play Kumina music, Nyabinghi music. So my birth-ful up-springing is actually from there. I wake up with those family around playing drums, playing music consistently, 24/7. Sometime it carry on for one week straight,' he explains. 'It was a strong musical connection coming from there long before I went to Alpha.' There would be no formal training other than basic rhythmic guidance from spiritual elders in the community and a shared family experience of living and breathing the power of the drum. 'As a child then, I had this beautiful opportunity to grow up around it, to get into the spirit of it, long before I even got the chance to see a conventional drum kit. I grew up playing

rhythms on rocks and stones and creating wooden boxes with their own tones and vibration.' The young Vernal Kelly was already so strongly steeped in music and rhythm that just being in that environment, hearing the band practice every day, he maintains, was inspiration enough without feeling a need to join the band. He prefers to see his musical influence from Alpha as more of an absorption of its unique essence, the discipline and austerity as well as the camaraderie. Maybe learning in such a classical way would have smoothed out the rawness of his talent. Certainly, his music is not typical of Alpha musicians, but he maintains that he is an Alpha musician through and through. 'Alpha is inside me. As soon as I woke up in the Alpha home I would hear the hornsmen blowing, the drummer man doing his thing, the nuns chanting. So immediately, you'd wake up with this feeling "What is that beautiful sound? Where is it coming from?" I was around sound and intense vibes every day. It leaves you with an impression that those are your aspirations too.' One of his closest friends at Alpha was also somebody who also made it as a musician without joining the band, Winston Foster AKA Yellowman. Fox says Foster was vulnerable to bullying when he first arrived because of his albino skin pigmentation and so he took him under his wing. The pair formed a strong bond, but as Fox was older it was he who would leave school first. 'He was like my everyday friend, and walkin' away from your everyday friend it's like ya feel like some of ya missing.' Upon leaving Alpha, Fox came almost straight away to join his parents in England. The sudden change would have a devastating emotional impact as almost overnight he left the nuns, his Alpharian friends and the tropical sun behind and found himself in a freezing cold and unfriendly London. 'That was a broken moment, the heart breaking then. But

Vernal Kelly, AKA Charlie 'Eskimo' Fox

Photo courtesy Kishi Yamamoto

that heartbreak help my development to become a serious drumming player.' To see him through this unsettled time his parents bought him his first drum kit, enabling him to channel his feelings into something constructive. His early training in African percussion made Fox a natural kit player and he was soon offering his skills as a session player on the London reggae scene. 'I was very, very busy at that time. We worked on many sessions that often we didn't get credited. It didn't matter to us at the time though, because we weren't aware of what we were all working towards in any wider sense, we were just working.' It was during this time that he was given his new name, Eskimo Fox. The cold in London was such a shock to the young Vernal Kelly, he would always be seen in a fur hat and a big heavy coat. 'So people just said to me, "man, you look like an Eskimo!" So I just stuck with that name.'

In the early 1970s he joined Dove Rocks comprising the cream of the young reggae musicians of the day, including future members of west London roots reggae band Aswad such as Brinsley Forde and Angus 'Drummie Zeb' Gaye to whom Eskimo would serve as a drum mentor. They became the touring band for major Jamaican singers including Dennis Brown, Gregory Isaacs, Ken Boothe, Dillinger, Trinity, Delroy Wilson, Jimmy London and many more. After one particular show, Fox was approached by the then teenage reggae obsessive Adrian Sherwood, who informed him of his plans to launch a studio and label. Heavily influenced by the experimental dub of Lee Perry and King Tubby, Sherwood gathered a diverse collective of musicians from both reggae and post-punk to work on an array of musical projects that would point the way to the future for bass-heavy electronic dance music. On-U Sound brought together reggae, dub, funk, post-punk, industrial music and electronica with a series of interlinked projects, all stamped with Sherwood's unique production sound. Creation Rebel were one of the first acts to be

Vernal Kelly, AKA Charlie 'Eskimo' Fox
Photo coutesy Kishi Yamamoto

produced by Sherwood. Eskimo Fox was one of its drummers and contributed to their cinematic sci-fi dub opus *Starship Africa.* This spacious, psychedelic bass and drum workout would form the template of much of On-U Sound's output for the next 15 years. Kelly became a mainstay of the On-U family. His unique drum style shaped the sounds of bands such as African Head Charge, Singers and Players, New Age Steppers, Noah House of Dread, Dub Syndicate and Mark Stewart and The Mafia. He even features on the front cover of Singers And Players' LP *Leaps and Bounds.* The drum track would always be a key element of On-U Sound recordings. 'In the early days I focused a lot on roto tom, syn drum and timbale tones. I used to tune it to my own sound hearing and I'd listen carefully for the *sharpness* of sound. I love the richness, the sharpness of the acoustic drum kits, but then things started to move in the direction of electric percussion. So ultimately I love a fusion of the two, both acoustic and electric.' This approach would culminate in Fox's involvement with African Head Charge. Formed after a chance meeting with percussionist Bonjo Iyabinghi Noah, who observed Fox's drumming performance intently at a show at Dingwalls live music venue in Camden Town. He told music writer Greg Whitfield, 'It all happened one night down at Dingwalls in Camden Town. Bonjo was in the audience watching me playing, watching me closely, so instinctively I played to him. So after the gig I went over to have a word with him and we start to talk and he told me he was a percussion player too. You want to know about those early African Head Charge records? Those were extreme, extreme records. In those days I was concerned with sound mixing and development of ideas. I like to go into that whole motion. I was crazy about it.' African Head Charge would be the perfect platform to showcase his Pocomania, Jonkanoo and Kumina influences. The band fused psychedelic, industrial-sounding dub with African and Nyabinghi drumming

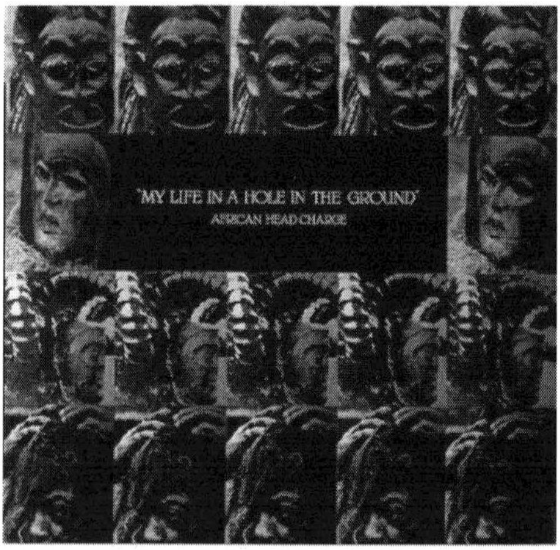

and chanting, overseen by Sherwood's radical approach to mixing. 'Regarding the intensity of sound on those early African Head Charge albums, to tell you the truth I cannot maintain that vibe for too long, because it's *too* extreme. It takes you overboard. But as a fresh listening thing I can really relate to all those early African Head Charge records. Those sounds were original vibrations. One thing's for sure, you'd always get something original out of

our corner,' he says. Listening back to the early AHC albums they are nothing short of astonishing, some of the most bizarre and fascinating records ever made. Although like Fox himself says, you can't listen for too long because it's just too extreme. Fox was also a member of New Age Steppers, featuring Ari Up, former vocalist with female punk band The Slits and also roots singer Bim Sherman with whom Fox had a strong friendship until Sherman's sudden death in 2000. New Age Steppers produced three outstanding LPs for On-U Sound. In 2004 *Nattorius*, the first solo LP by Eskimo Fox was released by On-U Sound. It is a largely instrumental set in the tradition of On-Sound style and is the culmination of his life's musical journey. He told Greg Whitfield, '*Nattorius* is a combination of two words, 'notorious', because On-U Sound albums have always been notorious, and the concept of 'nah tarry here' which is a spiritual perspective on life. Because you know, living in this physical form, in this earthly realm, we are all just passing through.'

Fox sees his entire approach to music-making as a way of channeling his spirituality and sums it up succinctly: 'That spiritual approach to music is deep within me. Spirituality has a powerful touch and music without spirituality is nothing. It's a natural thing. Many think this way, but few have the chance to express through the medium of an instrument, to express that goal. It's a spiritual freedom and it's a very deep thing within me and it has always been with me from an early age. Spirituality and spirituality *within sound* has always been with me. Within. I will make it live with me for now and forever.'

--A.R.

Band practice at Alpha
2013
Photos by Heather Augustyn

Winston 'Yellowman' Foster

Bob Marley's passing in 1981 left a giant vacuum in Jamaican music. Without Bob leading the way, what would happen to the music? While there were plenty of great roots reggae artists spreading their message of love, hope and redemption, what reggae needed most was a new superstar to take the stage. Few could have predicted that rather than another sage-like, charismatic figurehead exuding mysticism and righteousness, the next big thing to explode out of the tiny island would be a hilariously funny, lewd albino show-off calling himself Yellowman. Spearheading the new 'dancehall' style of reggae, Yellowman's message appeared to the more po-faced to be just salaciously bragging about his sexual prowess and relentlessly boosting his own ego by asserting his greatness. He seemed the complete antithesis of all that Bob had stood and worked for. To the consciously-minded roots rebels who had been both spiritually, culturally and politically galvanized by Rasta philosophy, Yellowman and the new dancehall style might have looked for all the world like the beginning of the end for reggae music. But as Bob Marley himself once sang, what goes around comes around, and after a decade of reggae serving as a spiritual voice for the dispossessed and oppressed people—not just of Jamaica but the entire world—maybe the time had come, at least for a while, to get back to the good-time escapism that the sound system operators had started 25 years earlier.

Born Christian Winston Foster in 1956, Yellowman's story reads something like a movie script. Found as a newborn baby inside a plastic bag by a garbage collector in a dumpster, literally thrown out like domestic waste because of his albino skin pigment, Foster would spend his entire childhood in children's homes. 'All my yout'ful life I grow up in orphanage home, starting with Maxwell Park then I go to Swift Purcell, that's in St Mary then after that Alpha was the other school I go to,' Foster explains. 'I don't know my family. I don't know my parents. No mother, no father, no sister, no brother, no uncle, no aunty, all I know is the people that grow me, like Sister Martress, Sister Ignatius and Sister Aloysius.' As if being abandoned at birth was not hard enough, Foster would face extreme prejudice for being a 'dundu' as those with albino pigment are derogatorily called in Jamaica, something quite socially unacceptable back in the 1960s, viewed with hostility and otherworldly superstition. At Alpha, Foster was met with unkindness by the other boys from day one. 'Well, the first day it was rough, I get beat up by the other kids, so it was very rough. I get a lot of tease and jeer and all type o' name call like *dundus*, *red mulatto*, *whiteman*, yuh know? All type o' name, but all those things I leave behind because those are the kinda things that make me strong up til now.' At meal times the boys would refuse to sit with him, then in the school room too, Foster would find himself sitting alone. Fellow Alpha boy Vernal Kelly (AKA drummer Charlie 'Eskimo' Fox) was a year older than Foster and saw he was vulnerable to bullying so was charged by the Sisters with the responsibility of keeping an eye on him and making sure he was not taken advantage of. He could tell that Foster's larger-than-life appearance and charisma would one day lead to something. 'We didn't know nuttin' about dundus, but he was a person who was true,' says Kelly. 'I recognize him from the day I met him and we spending time together, as a great talented person and I know that along the line if I'm not even there I know that he will come to play a role of importance.'

Yellowman in 1983
Photo by Beth Lesser

Yellowman's stage act is full of bouncy athletics, a continuity of the playground clown persona he developed at Alpha as a survival technique. If he could entertain and make the others laugh, then he could avoid the torment of being bullied and ostracized. His clowning would often lead to beatings from Sister Ignatius who was unimpressed by his often dangerous antics. 'I was an acrobat, I used to walk on my hand, and flick over backwards, I used to jump off the housetop to the ground, but I used to get a lot of

Yellowman
Photo by David Corio

flogging from her for that because she think that I was crazy.' Kelly also remembers this side of Foster's personality. 'He teach me to walk on my hands, backflips. He was like a circus personality. Anything you want him to do in circus he could do it. He could walk on his head and t'ings like that. Break up his body in all different ways, spin his eyes. But the ones who was his friend like myself, we was there to make sure that no one take liberty of him and I was one of the members of that gang, yuh know?'

Regardless of the harsh punishments Foster still has a deep love and reverence for Sister Ignatius. She was the one who would take him aside and try and build his confidence, even though she would call him by one of the names the other kids called him. 'She helped me because she talk to me. She used to call me Whiteman, though and she say, "Whiteman, please don't let anything stand in your way, especially when it wrong. Do your best and keep on doing it just as long as you're doing good and people will always give you respect." And that's what I getting now, yuh know? Because if I did stop I wouldn't get the respect.'

Foster would be on the receiving end of a lot of beatings at the mercy of the nuns as well as being locked in a broom cupboard for extended periods. Rather than harbouring resentment for such brutal treatment Foster seems accepting and understanding, perhaps because without the care of the nuns at Alpha he knows he wouldn't be where he is today. 'I used to spend time in "lock up," which was a dark room, because I used to give some trouble. I used to curse a lot of bad words to the people who in charge. They treat me good, better than a prison.' He goes on to justify Alpha's hardline approach: 'They're right, Alpha is a Catholic School, a Christian school. They don't stand for dirt, and they don't stand for wrong. Everything they do is right, even when they flog me they flog me for my own good and my own right. So I agree with them. When I was younger it never look that way. Now that I grow older and see the importance of the music, I said to myself everything they do and say is right. It's for my own good and I'm benefiting.'

Although Foster did not join the band, he did have a job packing instruments away and used to sing with the band sometimes as they played, but possibly more like taking an occasional impromptu turn. Winston Foster describes how his career as a DJ chatting on the mic started in his days at Alpha, helping out Sister Ignatius at her famed parties. (DJing in Jamaica means rapping or chatting rhythmically over records, what the Jamaicans call 'toasting,' while the one who chooses the records to put on is the 'selector'). Ignatius would be operating the turntable playing her favourite ska, jazz, reggae and R&B tunes and sometimes Foster would rap over the instrumental 'versions' on the B-sides to keep the party swinging. 'It was the time that Sister Ignatius started operating the sound system. I used to DJ, because first she play the vocal and then she play the version. And I would sing over the version, yuh know? Sister Ignatius would work the turntable, the sound. Actually, that's where I start in the dancehall.' It is interesting to note that both the King of the Dancehall and one of Jamaica's most beloved soundsystem selectors of all time, Albert 'Ilawi' Malawi, both started out alongside Ignatius on her Mutt and Jeff soundsystem. Her status as the Godmother of Jamaican Music is undisputed, but it seems Sister Ignatius' influence reaches right into the beating heart of sound system culture—an astonishing achievement for a white Roman Catholic nun.

After Alpha, Foster met with further prejudice when trying to hustle his way into the music business since no studio operator would allow him through the door on account of him being albino. The situation was the same in the dancehalls as he was never allowed near a microphone due to extreme cultural prejudice against his pigmentation. 'I remember they used to discriminate against me in the dancehall, because on a show we used to pass mic to mic and whenever me pass the mic, dem either take it and put dem rag over the mic or dem kerchief. I guess you coulda call it scorn,' he recounted to Kavelle Anglin-Christie of the *Jamaica Gleaner* in 2005.

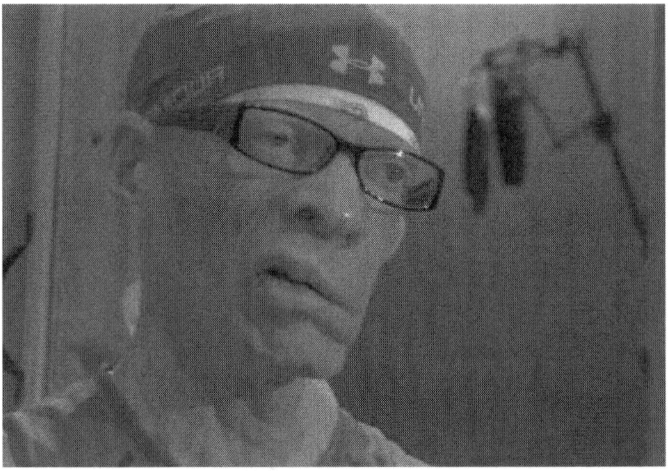

King Yellowman at a studio in Kingston
Photo by Davis Coome

But a surprise win at a talent show would be the turning of the tide for Foster and heralded the emergence of a new reggae star. 'I heard about Tastee's talent contest and I go and do the concert and it was off-the-hook. And from there—soundsystem, dancehall. Start follow sound like Gemini, Virgo, Stirgath, Aces, Black Scorpio, Jammies, Peacemaker, Jack Ruby's, Studio 54.' As a result of Foster putting himself in the limelight, the ingrained cultural attitude towards albinos began to change. He told Anglin-Christie, 'Is only when me come out that people like me started to show up, because them used to hide away from shame. But before the Tastee competition me used to go round to different producers to voice, but them used to run me away because them never believe inna me, or because of my skin colour them feel seh man like me cyaan do nuttin'.'

Yellowman's ability to effortlessly ride a rhythm with his lyrics was what made him such a compelling artist, combined with outrageous lyrics full of sexual innuendo, with tunes like 'Them A Mad Over Me.' Traditional reggae critics spurned this new style, calling it 'slack.' 'I don't call it slackness. I call it entertainment,' he told Mel Cooke of the *Jamaica Gleaner*. But Jamaica was still recovering from a civil war and the dancehall in the early 1980s provided the perfect release from the pressure of the previous decade. Those who criticise dancehall, even today, forget that both ska and reggae were born out of the sound system culture. Ska *is* dancehall music. Toasting over records goes back to the early ska dances, with DJs like Sir Lord Comic and Count Matchuki bringing a vaudevillian, pantomime element to proceedings. With dancehall, DJing simply developed into the main source of entertainment. Despite accusations of being sexist and derogatory towards women, it was not so much the men but the ladies who would go crazy at Yellowman shows. They lapped up all the bedroom braggadocio and turned Foster into the most unlikely of sex symbols.

In 1982 things really exploded for Yellowman. After the release of his debut LP *Mister Yellowman* for UK label Greensleeves, he was in such high demand that by the end of the year he had released ten albums, including *Jack Sprat, Duppy Or Gun Man, Just Cool, Live At Reggae Sunsplash* and *Them A Mad Over Me.* His prolific output earned him a Guinness World Record for the most albums recorded by an artist in one year. The release of two live albums and a couple of lesser ones that did not make the Guinness list, meant that in actual fact he had released fourteen albums that year, working with producers such as Joe Gibbs and Henry 'Junjo' Lawes. Yellowman paired up with fellow sound system DJ Fathead to release a run of five albums as Yellowman and Fathead, starting with *Bad Boy Skanking.* He also performed and released records with two other albino dancehall artists, Purpleman and King Mellow Yellow. Another breakthrough album was 1983's *Zungazungagazungazeng*, the title track of which was an international hit and remains a party favourite all around the world.

Yellowman became the first dancehall artist to sign a major recording deal with US label Columbia in 1984. Although he was never to repeat 1982's extraordinary level of vinyl output, his LP *King Yellowman* for Columbia outsold all of his previous 20 albums combined. Foster's rise to international stardom suddenly made it cool to be 'yellow' for the first time ever in Jamaica and greatly improved the perception, acceptance and quality of life for those with albino pigmentation in Jamaica. 'When I come out in the music business, all albino come out of the woods, everybody. Ya have albino is doctor now, ya have albino is police, ya have albino is nurse. They in all type a field, in the music field. That's because of King Yellowman, the King of Dancehall,' Foster says proudly. Yellowman took Jamaica by surprise in 1985 by having a hit with his cover version of Fats Domino's 'Blueberry Hill' proving he could sing as well as talk. In a similar vein he had a hit with his take on 'I'm Getting Married in the Morning' from the musical *My Fair Lady* and later he did it again with 'I'm Getting Divorced in the Evening.' Foster even incorporated a cover of his hero Elvis's 'Are You Lonesome Tonight' into his routine, which he sang in tribute to an audience in Las Vegas.

Back at Alpha, the Sisters made their disapproval of Yellowman's lyrical 'slackness' known. 'When I come out with the X-rated stuff, they used to send people from Alpha to talk to me, and they say that this is not the way we used to do it in Alpha Boys' School, they used to distance themselves away from that until I start clean it up a bit in the 1990s. They never fascinated with the rude stuff.' The school's disdain was made clear when Sister Ignatius refused to have him take part in a fundraising concert for the school, even though he would have been the biggest draw. 'When they used to keep concert there, she said she won't have me on the concert, so I never do concert there. But I did do a lot of charity concert in Madison Square Garden at that time and the charity go to Alpha Boys' School, so that was a good thing.' However, it seems it wasn't personal, as Ignatius was quite happy to be taken for a spin around the school compound in Yellowman's flashy new

Yellowman
Photo by David Corio

Volvo Coupe when he came back for a visit. 'I just give her a round-the-school drive, down to the convent and down to the school, and she enjoy.' Yellowman did indeed appear to be cleaning his act up briefly in the mid-1990s. Having released the bawdy *In Bed With Yellowman* LP for UK label Greensleeves, he followed it a year later with *Prayer* on Ras Records, which appeared to be heading in a more conscious direction. However it was business as usual only a year later, with the release of *Yellowman's Good Sex Guide*, although to be fair he has mostly since steered clear of the kind of slackness of his early years.

At the height of Yellowman mania in 1983, Winston Foster was given a diagnosis of skin cancer on his face and even worse, was given just three years to live. He was operated on and the cancer went into remission. The cancer reappeared in his jaw, meaning he would have to have part of his jaw removed to access the tumour. The operation would give him a permanent disfigurement, twisting his face asymmetrically.

Although Yellowman's presence in Jamaican dancehall seemed to wane, he kept on putting out music and touring the world despite a lack of interest back home. 'I released songs on the international market and when me say international, me nuh mean like America and Europe. Me mean like me target places like Israel, Japan, the Asian market and dem place deh,' he told Anglin-Christie. He was one of the first reggae artists to play live in Israel and he toured East Germany before the wall had come down.

It has been said that Yellowman is the second most famous reggae singer in the world because if you ask people on the streets of countries in Africa or Latin America or in North America to name two reggae artists, they will always mention Bob Marley first, followed by Yellowman. He has massive followings in both Japan and Nigeria. His influence extends not just to dancehall but he has also been hugely influential in hip-hop and has been sampled, quoted and name-checked by artists such as KRS1, Biggie Smalls, Tupac Shakur, Ice Cube, Junior Mafia, Joe Buddens and Dead Prez as well as making a guest appearance with Run DMC on their song 'Roots Rap Reggae.' Yellowman continues to perform around the world with the Sagittarius Band and has to date released over 65 albums and 150 singles.

--A.R.

Tony Greene

An important part of Alpha's philosophy is about bringing routine into the lives of boys who may have not known much stability before. By instilling self-discipline the school strives to produce young men who are able to face the challenges of making their way in the outside world, which can be especially tough in Jamaica. Saxophonist Tony Greene explains: 'Everything is here for you to choose from, the discipline is there, school is there for you to go to learn to read and write probably not to the level where you can get a masters, but to learn to help yourself. But if you don't like music you can learn printery, you can learn tailoring, you can do woodwork, you can plant food. Everything is here, the discipline is here to teach you how to get around, how to have manners and everything, how to get along living with people.'

Tony Greene at one year old

Born in 1957, saxophonist Tony Greene entered Alpha in 1969 at the age of twelve and stayed for five years until 1973. He believes Alpha saved him from a bleak future. 'Well, I was a rotten boy and I used to do a lot of things that wasn't pleasing and it's my personal belief I'd probably be in prison or six feet six under.' This last statement was a recurring sentiment among Alpharians we interviewed. Greene was referred to Alpha having been expelled from a previous school for unruly behavior. By his own admission he was too much for them as he would steal and skip school and generally be difficult. 'In the 1960s, they used to leave milk and bread outside the doors and every little bad kid woulda just come by and just grab that off and eat and drink and throw away, go to the seaside and have fun, abscond from school and t'ing. Anything you say, as a kid I used to do. And I get expelled from a school in Calabar. And in those days ya couldn't just go back into a school so I was recommended to come to Alpha.'

In particular, it was the guiding hand of Sister Ignatius that enabled him to find his direction after he absconded from Alpha early on. Ignatius seemed to have an uncanny way of seeing the greatness inside boys that the mainstream system would have overlooked and she passionately believed that their so-called wayward behaviour just needed reining in and channeling into a creative, fun and dynamic discipline such as music. Tony explains how absconding led to his lifelong journey with music. 'From the first day I came here I ran away. My mother took me back to Sister Martress, and she have twelve lashes for me. But when I was walking down, Sister Ignatius say, "Don't beat him, leave him alone." I can remember it clearly. And she say "Ya have to behave yourself you know, and get something going. It was a Thursday and the following day, Friday, after school I stop and see the guys they used to practice under the shed out deh, which was actually a refectory where we eat only. I just stand out there watching them play them instrument, fascinated by how they get some sounds outta it. Then Sister Ignatius came around and saw me. She said, "What you doing out there, ya not going to school?" And she turn to me and say, "Do you like it?" And I say, "Yes." I didn't have a choice as whether to say yes, jus' to save me from getting some beatin'. She tell Martress, "From Monday he's in the band." And that's where it all start.' Greene clearly remembers that first day in the band room. 'Most of my friends used to play clarinet and drum. So when I come in on Monday morning, they say, "What you want to play?" I say "drums." They say, "We have enough drummer already." So they put me on E-flat clarinet. And the first day in the band I learnt a G scale.'

Greene later switched to the instrument he made his name from, the saxophone, becoming proficient on tenor, alto and soprano sax. Looking back, he believes part of Alpha's success for turning out so many great musicians lies in having old boys coming back to work as bandmasters. By returning their musicianship back to the school, it completed a circle of learning and success that they could clearly see they were part of. 'The majority of teachers are Alpha boys, and that's one of its secrets, that keeps it all going. They come back and introduce their teaching back into the school and keep that tradition going. It's the same method from when it start.'

After Alpha, Greene spent six years in the Jamaica Military Band, where he was able to continue developing his own unique style while earning

Tony Greene with the Jamaica Military Band in 1975

some money and gaining the confidence needed to work in the fiercely competitive Jamaican music industry. It's an obvious next step for many Alpha boys especially as they may have become accustomed to the discipline and routine of life in an institution so it offers a smooth transition and keeps them on a steady path. 'At my time in Alpha a lot of guys go on to the military band,' he says. 'I guess it was like a safe job for them to go on to do. Ya get three meal a day, somewhere to live and somewhere to sleep. So it give ya a beautiful start, yuh un'erstand?'

Upon leaving the military, Greene started working with the Bare Essential Band led by Errol Lee. They worked the hotel circuit on Jamaica's North Coast, playing ska, rocksteady, reggae, calypso and R&B, covering hits of the day for tourists. At the same time he was doubling up playing for the Sonny Bradshaw Seven, another safe haven for Alpha boys nurturing their craft and getting their careers up and running. According to one web source, his first foray into the recording studio was for King Tubby, allegedly on a Jackie Paris tune. Soon he was fully in the game, working the studios around Kingston such as Harry J's, Aquarius and Joe Gibbs. His reputation as a rock solid hornsman would eventually lead him to joining The Roots Radics Band led by bassist Flabba Holt and drummer Style Scott, one of the foundation backing groups of late 1970s and 1980s reggae. With Roots Radics, Greene worked both live and in the studio with reggae greats such as Yellowman, Eek-A-Mouse, Gregory Isaacs, Michael Prophet, Israel Vibration and many more.

By the mid-1980s another foundation stone of reggae beckoned, that of Lloyd Park's We the People Band, who backed Dennis Brown on his epic world tours. 'I've been to the four corners with him,' Greene says. As part of

We The People he would again tour with many of reggae's foundation artists notably The Mighty Diamonds, Alton Ellis, John Holt and Leroy Sibbles.

Tony Greene in 1986
Photo by Beth Lesser

Also during the 1980s, Greene would begin a strong working relationship with Joseph Hill of Culture with whom he would embellish his solo LP *Lion Rock*. Greene joined the freshly invigorated Studio One backing group the Soul Defenders on some successful US and European tours with Hill, helping to re-energise his career at a time when dancehall had taken hold as the primary musical force. In 1986, Culture reformed and Greene laid down the horns for their well-received comeback LP *Culture in Culture*. Also during this fertile period he teamed up with deep roots singer Ijahman Levi for three much loved albums, *Tell It to the Children*, *Africa* and *Lily of My Valley*, with Greene's sublime horn arrangements adding to the music's mystical, soul-searching atmosphere.

Tony Greene at the Alpha Boys Reunion Show 2007
Photo by Adam Reeves

Tony Greene found expres-sion as a solo artist in the 1990s, with eight largely self-produced reggae instrumental LPs including *Groovin' Sax*, *Square From Cuba*, *Evolution*, *Mean Greene* and *Blessed*. He continues to record reggae as well as occasionally working with Jamaican jazz artists.

Like so many Alpha grad-uates, Tony Greene feels a depth of gratitude to the way Alpha shaped his destiny and being an Alpharian is as much a part of his identity as is being a musician. 'Ya have to know where ya comin' from to know where ya going,' he muses, 'and Alpha is where I'm coming from.'

--A.R.

Osbert Maddo, AKA Papa Madoo

The influence of Alpha Boys seems to permeate every corner of Jamaican music. It was at a major turning point in the evolution of reggae culture that one lesser-known Alpharian played a crucial part. While Yellowman stole the limelight for the new 'slackness' era of dancehall in the early 1980s, it was several years earlier that the late Osbert Maddo and his crew started spicing up the dancehall with bawdiness and vulgarity. At a time when preaching roots and culture was the order of the day, the singer known variously as Madoo, Papa Madoo and Bionic Singer, along with his compadres General Echo and Colonel Flux, decided that the way forward was to put a smile on people's faces with preposterous boasting, teasing and salacious innuendo. Their platform was the Stereophonic Sound System at The Bionic Lawn (hence the name Bionic Singer), owned and operated by Leon 'Big John' Johns. Speaking to dancehall tape collector (cassettes recorded direct from the sound desk at dancehalls known as 'yard tapes') Dave Brown from Boston in November 2011, Maddo discussed his earliest musical influences as being the appearance in his home of a record player, suggesting that Maddo may have come from a relatively comfortable background to have been able to afford such a luxury item. 'My mother is a woman who always buy the records, dem. I remember a time come in Jamaica when we start have stereo. So she had a stereo which was musically two little eight inch speaker, a turntable where you can put a bunch of records on it and it fall as one done, an' it fall and automatically play the next. So my mother now used to sing the songs and it impressed me how she know the lyrics. So all this motivate me so at a young age,' remembers Maddo. He recalls an incident in the early 1960s when he illicitly attended a local party. 'I was about five at the most, one night I sneak out of my house, I had on my pyjama, I put my pants on over my pyjama, sneak out of the window to go down to the dancehall, because there was a band playing there. Now the band that was playing was

Osbert Maddo

Winston Grennan. See, Winston Grennan, he grow up with my mother, like he grow up on my grandfather's property, they rent it from us.' Grennan was an influential ska and reggae drummer and band leader sometimes attributed with developing reggae's 'one drop' drum pattern and who in the 1980s became a founding member of Kid Creole and the Coconuts. Witnessing this family friend entertaining the crowd made some kind of impact on him. 'From that point on I started doing things at school like elocution and poetry. I start to do my recital, this is where it start breaking me into the crowd. And I'm always a very shy person,' he says, seemingly expressing surprise at himself, although the world of entertainment is full of quiet, shy types who seem to burst out of themselves once on a stage.

Initially Maddo attended Rennock Lodge School but we have no information about how and why Maddo was transferred to Alpha or whether he benefitted from its musical program, however he seems to have been encouraged to develop his performance skills there. He told Dave Brown, 'So, I went to Alpha primary school, a Catholic school and here again they throw me into elocution contest where I do a lot of poetry recital, ya know wha' I mean? So what happened next, they started putting out the lyrics of the songs in the newspapers which was making things easier, my mother used to cut out the lyrics. I realised lyrics are coming together so I start singing the songs with the lyrics dem, just as a fun thing, everybody was doing it.' In his late teens, after his time at Alpha, Osbert attended Excelsior High School, where he would organize school fundraising events, putting together bands comprising local musicians and getting up on stage to sing. Often he would cover songs by Philadelphia soul group The Stylistics. 'People know me as kind of a Stylistics kinda singer because I sound just like that guy.' As a youth in the 1970s he would attend the sound system dances around East Kingston such as Sir Stanford, Sir Norman, Arrows and Phase One. Maddo was hugely influenced by one of the freshest new Jamaican singers of the day Horace Andy, who shot to stardom with a soaring vibrato sounding unlike anything heard before in reggae (and possibly anywhere else on Earth!). A lot of young singers would emulate stars like Pat Kelly, Ken Boothe and Alton Ellis. 'But nobody could sing like Horace Andy at that time, so when I cover Horace Andy song nobody could believe it was me not Horace Andy,' Maddo says of one of his early sound system performances. Indeed, there is a great similarity between the two singers' reedy, youthful tenor voices and Maddo was one of many, starting with Wayne Jarrett who adopted Andy's unique style. It was one night in 1977 that everything changed, when he and his friends dropped into the Bionic Lawn to hear Stereophonic Sound, featuring DJ Welton Irie on the mic. Back then a DJ would often stay on the mic all night without passing it up to anyone else, so they would be the star of the show. Also, singers were not a feature of sound systems, it was purely DJs 'toasting' over the mic—reggae singers could only be heard being backed by a band at a live music show. Papa Madoo was about to change all of that. His friends were forever encouraging him to have a go on the mic when they went out. 'They was always like, "'Doo, why don't you go over and say something, you sound better than the people who are on the mic over there." And I wouldn't do it, I'm just not interested like that. One of these days they forced me.'

Writing on his own MySpace page, Maddo recounted how his career accidentally kicked off: 'Long before Stereophonic we transformed Sir Stanford into Stylistics (my favourite singing group at the time). I was always singing but only did it in public under pressure from my friends in school or

at home who were very encouraging. It all started when my brethrens from Wareham Rd, Michael and Scarely (R.I.P.) decided that we should stop at Stereophonic Lawn and check up on Donovan our homie who was working for Stereophonic, when Scarely approached Welton (Irie) and dare him to give me the mic. I sang a few songs and Welton Irie was blown away especially when I covered Horace Andy's (my favourite singer) "Skylarking." I was asked to perform the following weekend. The rest is history.' Allegedly he just stopped everyone in their tracks, by working the lyrics into the 'riddims' in a combined singing and chatting style. His fresh approach started to pull in the crowds, which greatly pleased the owner Big John.

Maddo further recounted on his MySpace page: 'When Welton went to Gemini I decided to stay with Stereophonic. Flux and I covered the dances until Echo (the late General Echo) came along. Welton Irie went to record for Joe Gibbs who heard me on one of the dancehall tapes, they ask me to come to the studio. They immediately record me in the middle of a Dennis Brown session. They ask me what kind of style that was, I told them it was my dancehall style because I was singing lyrics that was suited to both styles (singing and DJ). Robbie Shakespeare and Leroy Palmer of HomeT4 were always encouraging me to go to the studio instead of singing in the bathroom, where people would stay outside the window to make their request. I remember one day before school (Excelsior) Robbie took me to Randy's recording studio downtown. I was very impressed that he wanted to record me but time was running out, I had to get on the twenty seven bus to school.' It was in the Dennis Brown session that he cut the tunes 'Yuh Jamming So,' 'Joe Grines' and 'Landlord.'

Maddo continues: 'The first song, "Jamming So" had them laughing so hard that D. Brown told me it was certainly going to be a hit song. Now all of my dancehall fans were familiar with this hit song, then out of nowhere our dances started exploding. The fans in the country sides all over Jamaica started turning out in full force. I was the only singer they knew before and after and the only one who would perform on a disco. The only way they could see other artist would be to go to Kingston or one of the cities to see them with a band.... I was different. I brought the music to them.'

Osbert Maddo

When Welton Irie moved on to work at Gemini Disco it was Papa Madoo and Colonel Flux (as selector) who held it down until joined later by General Echo. Echo was the one who brought in the slackness at Stereophonic and heralded in a whole new style of DJing. Up to that point everybody had been working the style of U-Roy and Big Youth, but Echo brought the comedy factor and virtually invented the 'rub-a-dub style' overnight. The sparring sessions between General Echo and Papa Madoo became a huge draw and have gone down in dancehall mythology as some of the greatest of all time. A run of singles were released on various labels such as 'King In The Ring,' 'Coming From Town,' 'Give Me Your Love,' 'Have You Ever Been To Heaven' and 'Meet Me By Jah River.' He also released some twelve inch disco mixes with both Trinity and General Echo.

1980 saw one of the greatest tragedies in reggae history, the notorious Halfway Tree Killings, a police execution which shocked the entire country. On 22nd November, General Echo, Stereophonics owner Big John and selector Colonel Flux were going to get an amplifier checked over by a sound system builder named Denton. They were pulled over by police on Derrymore Road and for reasons still unknown, were all shot dead. The incident has never been satisfactorily investigated or resolved. The effect on Osbert Maddo must have been devastating. He released the single 'Bite Di Dust' as a tribute: 'Me sitting on mi bed wid a mi radio a' mi head/Mi hear di news come over say di General dead/ A likkle after me t'ink a rumour dem a spread/but dem full him up a lead… now di General dead.' Other tribute records followed, notably Clint Eastwood and General Saint's *Tribute to General Echo* which asks the question, 'Madoo, a wha' ya gon' do?'

An LP of Papa Madoo's singles appeared in 1981 called *Rock With Papa Madoo* although he claimed this was a bootleg. A second album, *You Turn Me On* produced by Tony Shabazz was released in 1982. The same year Maddo left the dancehall scene and permanently relocated to the US where he raised his family. Much to the confusion of the reggae world, his brother, known as Hugh Hugh Madoo started performing and recording. Producers were more than happy to capitalize on his name and reputation as a heavyweight dancehall singer by promoting dances and listing records as Madoo. As the two brothers looked and sounded very similar, the wider public assumed they were one and the same person. It wasn't until Osbert returned in 1984, disgruntled at the confusion, that the pair agreed that the younger brother would insist on being called Hugh Hugh—first utilized on a release by Prince Jammy that year. Often it was just abbreviated to UU Madoo. Osbert Maddo later said that he'd never met anyone apart from those actually in the music business who had the faintest idea which one was which or were even aware at all that there were in fact two different Madoos!

Site of Bionic Lawn and Stereophonic Hi-Fi
Photo by Dave Brown

Having retired from the business for many years, in 2015 Papa Madoo was approached by London-based reggae label Cubiculo Records to voice a riddim by a producer called Casio Love. Madoo instantly loved the riddim and agreed to work with them to make his long overdue comeback record. According to a statement by Cubiculo, Maddo was so excited to be back in business and eager to start pushing the tune in the US that he would call them every day asking to be sent the final mix. On the very same day that they sent him the finished tune they were shocked to receive a message to say that Osbert Maddo had passed away earlier in the day at his home in Bangor, Maine after a history of heart problems. Released on a twelve inch single as 'Hear Mi Name Call' by Casio Love featuring Bionic Singer, the record became Cubiculo's tribute salute to him and a percentage of its profits went to support his wife Janet and their youngest son.

--A.R.

Tafane Buchsaecab

Having an on-stage jam session with three founding members of The Skatalites must be some kind of dream-come-true for any serious ska musician, but that's exactly what Tafane Buchsaecab's journey through Alpha led him to. At just 17 years of age while still a pupil at Alpha he had a rare opportunity to spar with the masters, Tommy McCook, Johnny 'Dizzy' Moore and Roland Alphonso at a nightclub in Kingston. For a boy orphaned from birth who'd spent his entire childhood in the care system, rubbing shoulders with ska's founders inspired him to take his music as far as he possibly could, ultimately leading Buchsaecab to become a full-time professional player.

Tafane Buchsaecab was born in 1977. He spent his early years in Maxfield Park Children's Home and was sent to Alpha along with his brother to give him the opportunity to learn a professional trade. He joined the band aged 13 initially on trumpet, although his heart was always on the saxophone.

Tafane Buchsaecab

Growing up in the care system taught him survival skills and Buchsaecab adapted well to life at Alpha. 'I wasn't a saint but I always knew how far to go,' he says. 'I'd bend the rules but I never break them. I learnt that early from children's home, and my days at the children's home. I was a popular kid and a bright kid, so I knew how to get away with stuff and I knew when to push and when to not, so I just transferred that at Alpha, knowing how to get through without the punishment.' Buchsaecab displayed a natural aptitude for music and early on was given the chance to perform his first ever solo piece at the Ward Theatre, the classic Irish ballad 'Danny Boy.' 'Believe me, I was so nervous that I was shaking and all that shaking came across the instrument and became a natural vibrato at the time. From the first three notes that I played of the song, the place just went wild! I just flew through the rest of the song and I'm not sure how it finished or what happened. It was something to remember.' Speaking about Sister Ignatius and how in tune she was with contemporary jazz Buchsaecab recounts another story involving the same Irish ballad a year or so later. At the opening ceremony of the brand new school band room Lennie Hibbert Hall, he played 'Danny Boy' as a solo piece again. 'When I finished she came over to me and said, "You did a great, great rendition of that song. You should go and check out the recording of that by Sil Austin." She was on it, she always know what was happening, y'know? I never forget that and every time I play "Danny Boy" I always remember the conversation we had about it.' He left Alpha in 1995 and soon joined a band named Alpha Sonics with players from the same Alpha generation as him, headed by Sparrow Martin on keyboard and trumpet which took them to Cuba for the 14th World International Youth Festival. Buschaecab spent time playing with the Sonny Bradshaw Big Band and performed alongside the singer dubbed Jamaica's First Lady of Jazz, Myrna Hague. In 2007 he got his first big engagement, touring Europe in Jimmy Cliff's band and the first time playing to massive audiences. 'It's an experience that you would never trade and my first show with Jimmy Cliff was on my birthday in Wolfsburg, Germany,' he recounts. 'I felt like I'd arrived.'

Tafane Buchsaecab

After a stint with Ky-Mani Marley, Buchsaecab now plays with Bunny Wailer's touring band. He also works as a session player and enjoys supporting new talent. He's worked on material by Ras-I, Runkus and Roots Underground as well reggae-soul singer Jack Radics. Buchsaecab has plans to build a name as a solo artist and is working on his first album which has a strong mento and ska influence. 'I want to leave behind a legacy for all that I've been given, for Alpha and the foundation that is set, it can only go one way and I've got to add to all of that rich history of music. So that's one of the things I want is a legacy to leave behind.'

--A.R.

Nicholas Laraque

Jamaican flute players have been surprisingly lacking in their abundance since the lightness of the flute can work to perfectly counterbalance reggae's heavier rhythmic elements. Nicholas Laraque brings a bright, polished sound to both flute and soprano saxophone and has built a reputation as one of Jamaica's hottest players. Born in the country parish of St. Mary in May 1976, his father placed him in Alpha in 1985 due to his reckless behavior and seeming lack of focus. 'At school I was getting in fights and all o' that. I abscond school, I didn't go to school and all those things so it was quite a mess.' Upon hearing the Alpha band, Laraque knew that it was a calling for him and worked hard to behave himself so that he might get selected. Initially he played clarinet, but a life-changing inspiration came from an unlikely source. A builder named Mr. Dermott who was doing some re-construction work on the school buildings was playing a cassette by French classical and jazz musicians Jean-Pierre Rampot and Claude Bolling—*Suite For Flute And Jazz Piano Trio*, a bestselling album of the day fusing baroque and modern swing. Laraque recounts: 'When I heard the flute it just grabbed me. I was like, wow, I love this sound! Shortly after, the flute player for the band died, this guy called Gary Simms. He passed away, and I was kinda close to him. So I says to myself I would like to journey on what he started. I loved the way he played the flute and I said, wow, I'd really love to do what he was doing. So he kind of pushed me.'

Nicholas Laraque
Photo by Natty D Photography

After graduating from Alpha, Laraque signed up with the Jamaican Regiment Band. This band is different from the military band that many Alpharians served time in, because as well as music it actually involves regular army duties like patrolling and guarding. The band would play in parks, churches and often in embassies. Laraque was offered the opportunity to go on a one year course at the Royal Military School of Music in Twickenham, West London. Here he completed his grade eight music theory and practical, gaining a distinction. The college offered him the chance for further study but the Jamaican army insisted he return to his country to serve out his contract. It was while at Twickenham that he was introduced to the music of Kenny G and immediately went out and bought himself a soprano saxophone and taught himself how to circular breathe. Back home he impressed his peers greatly with his new-found talent. He soon joined a brand new group, The Jamaican All-Stars, put together by Alpha bandmaster Sparrow Martin and featuring seasoned players Johnny 'Dizzy' Moore on trumpet, Sparrow on drums, Skully Simms on percussion and Justin Hinds on vocals. He would tour Europe with them on army leave. Towards the end of his tenure in the army he was given leave to tour but at the last minute the army recalled him due to an upcoming State visit by the Queen. 'I already had the ticket and all o' that, so I said, "I'm sorry, I'm going." I went and when I came back they lock me up,' he laughs. 'They lock me up in the army prison deh. I did the tour and when I came back that's when the army hold on to me and lock me up because they said I wasn't supposed to go because they have all these parades coming up. I did a month deh.' A month in solitary confinement wasn't so bad he says. 'I had my flute there, so I just play my flute.' Since leaving the army Laraque has worked as a session player with Jah Cure, Pressure, Turbulence, Richie Stephenson, Etana and Iba Mahr. He joined Beres Hammond's touring band in 2005, then in 2009 he joined Stephen Marley's band and presently juggles between the two. Laraque's as-yet untitled debut solo album is released in 2017. --A.R.

Nicholas Laraque
Photo by Natty D Photography

Denver Smith, AKA 'Feluké'

Bearing the musical torch for a future generation of Alpha Boys is one of Jamaica's rising new reggae artists, the hugely talented singer, songwriter, composer, producer, multi-instrumentalist and master percuss-sionist Denver Smith AKA Feluké. His life story is an inspiring example of how Alpha manages to successfully turn around the fortunes of those who otherwise would have been left by the wayside, slipping through the system's net and possibly into oblivion. Despite his eloquence, charm and infectious dynamism, Feluké truly comes from the street. Having run away from home aged ten, he spent four years surviving as a homeless boy on some of the toughest streets in the world, until taken into the care of the Sisters of Mercy at Alpha.

Born in Montego Bay in 1977, Smith's early life was tumultuous. His mother abandoned him while he was very young to live in the US and he would not see her again until he was 27. Smith was placed in the hands of a pastor, who looked after him until his mother's regular maintenance payments eventually dried up. The pastor then delivered Smith to live with his father, a chef, who was now married with a child. The move proved to be highly traumatic as Smith says he was the victim of some severe physical and emotional abuse by his father. Even at this age he already knew he wanted to be a musician, despite his father's insistence that he follow in his footsteps into the catering trade. He recounts, 'All I know is that the abuse was unbearable. So at ten years old I just leave and decided to find my way to music.' Smith says that he was never reported as officially missing and since he was being looked out for by various locals, he managed to stay off the radar of the social services for four years. 'I used to

Feluké

Feluké

sleep literally on the side of the road. I used to get looked after and taken in by certain people for short periods, then would be on the streets again, often working as a street sweeper,' he remembers, without the faintest hint of self-pity. All the while he was living on the street, he still attended a church and pursued his musical ambitions by playing drums in the church band. Smith would hustle to make money by selling banana chips and 'bag-juice'—fruit juice sold in a tied plastic bag. After getting mixed up in some trouble aged 14, he then came to the attention of the social services, who had no idea of his existence. His father had moved away and could not be located so the authorities recommended Smith to enroll at Alpha. 'I had a choice, I could either stay on the streets and turn out to be nothing or go to Alpha. I chose Alpha.'

Denver Smith entered Alpha in 1991 and immediately felt at home. 'The nuns were like fabulous parents to us. We didn't miss anything. They treated us like they were our own parents. They gave us all the love we need, we couldn't complain about lack of love. You could sit and talk to them about anything.' One of Alpha's much loved nuns, Sister Maria Goretti, a native of New Zealand, became like a mother-figure to him. 'She was a fabulous woman,' he says enthusiastically, 'She loved each and every boy like her own child. And she always tell us, "You're mine, you're my children." When you were rude, we could see the disappointment.' On joining Alpha, Smith had a broken wrist so was unable to play music, but soon made his musical talents known among the staff and was spotted by one of the nuns, who recommended him for the band. 'Sister Goretti started recognizing my musical abilities. She saw me knocking stuff and making up a drum kit from steel pan. She took me to see (bandmaster) Sparrow Martin.' He auditioned as a drummer, but Martin saw his potential and wanted to challenge him, so gave him a crash course in bass playing, becoming proficient on some basic ska and mento tunes in just a couple of weeks. He then moved on to trumpet and in a relatively short time was out with the band playing gigs. This initial success was cut short when Smith was diagnosed with sickle cell disease, a genetic condition of the red blood cells which is particularly common in Afro-Caribbean peoples. He was admitted to St. Joseph's hospital for a course of treatment and close monitoring. Sickle Cell is a lifetime disease and once diagnosed, one has to accept that specialist treatment will always be a part of your life. While he had to give up the band for a while, Sister Ignatius made sure he didn't lose his interest. 'She decided to put me in the choir to keep me close to music. I still practiced my drumming.' The regime at Alpha helped Smith to be independent, to know how to care for yourself and for others. 'The nuns trained us in their way to be humble. We had to clean the bathrooms, sweep the corridors, sweep the places that we walk, clean the room where we slept in, spread the beds, there was no servant there for us, the only thing someone did for us was cook. We wash our own clothes, spread our bed, wash our sheets, we did everything ourselves. So at the end of the day, you leave school knowing how to take care of yourself and your family.'

Feluké

Smith's way out of Alpha is a little different. He was determined to leave the school and launch a musical career. Aged around seventeen his close school friend Huntley McCulskey told him he was auditioning for a performing arts ensemble called Ashé that specialized in singing, acting, dance and drumming. Dance was something that Smith had always loved. 'There used to be a lot of dancing competitions in Alpha and I would often win. Dancehall type styles, like bogle, tattie, heel-and-toe, limbo, whirl-a-dance.' Smith asked Sister Ignatius if he could attend too. She seriously questioned his motives but once she was convinced he was serious about it she allowed him to attend. Both he and Huntley passed the audition, but there were further complications. 'Sister Ignatius was still very protective over me because of the sickle cell,' he says. Ashé required them to pay a fee to be a part of the group. 'When Sister heard that, she said, "No, no, no, no, no, NO!" I had a couple more years in the book. She said, "I'm not going to let them take your hard earned money that you've worked so hard for to be part of a company. If they want you, they should pay you!"' he says, laughing at how formidable she was. 'So when Huntley went the following Wednesday they asked for me, but Huntley said that Sister was not going to send me because I have to pay for it and the money that I'm saving up is for my future. And she's not going to allow me to spend that on the company. So they said, "No, no, we'll take him." So Huntley came and told Sister but she insisted that they come and speak to her.' Smith heard nothing and assumed that he had missed his opportunity. But two weeks later, he was in class and someone told him that Sister Ignatius wanted to see him, which generally meant a boy was in some kind of trouble. To his surprise he saw two members of the Ashé troupe in discussion with Sister Ignatius. She negotiated on his behalf with them that he be paid a wage while working with them. He soon started moving between training at Ashé in the evenings and studying his curriculum at Alpha, developing his songwriting abilities and his percussion skills as well as writing his first ever song for one of their plays. 'The transition from Alpha to Ashé was God-sent,' he says. 'Because it was the same sort of institution, with protectiveness of the kids as Alpha. They motivate you to be the best, just like our system motivates you to be the best. Ashé had that same thing that they instilled in us. They always tell us, "You can do this, you can do this."' Problems arose when repeatedly he would arrive at the school gates at one in the morning after intense training sessions since the gates were officially locked at midnight. Ashé was constantly apologising on Smith's behalf and so in 1994 Sister Ignatius allowed him to leave Alpha early to go and be a full-time member of Ashé, on the condition that they help him out with paying his rent and bills in his newly found accommodation.

After a couple of years performing and touring with Ashé, disaster struck. Smith had met a girl and fell in love with her. He thought that the feeling was mutual, and she soon moved in with him. He went away on a tour, leaving her in charge of the home. 'I left my life savings with her but when I came home the whole lot was empty. I lost everything, I lost the house I was living in, I lost everything. So I started living on the streets again. And I had to start over.' It was while he was living on the streets that Smith was introduced to a man who would become his great mentor and change his life forever. A friend of his in the music business, Dwight Bancey saw how bad his situation was. 'He just looked at me and said, "You want to start touring?" I didn't believe him, and he called reggae sax maestro Dean Frasier who said I should come to the audition. He knew of me, but he wanted to see me in a band setting. I got the job right away and he just groomed me into who I am today as a percussionist.' At the age of 25, Smith found himself touring the US, Europe and Africa with Frasier. 'The first time I went in my hotel room, I cried. Same thing with Ashé, the first time Ashé took me on a plane, I cried. Because I never, ever knew I would be able to be on a plane and I never know I could make this into a job where I could makc a living from this.' Frasier took him under his wing. 'In terms of fine tuning my craft it was Dean Frasier. He carry me to my first music store and got me buying all my instruments. He showed me how to spend my money!' Smith also became a percussionist for reggae and jazz drummer Desi Jones. He joined a band called Zinc Fence with a couple of Ashé members and a couple of Alpha Boys (not to be confused with the Chronixx band of the same name, which came later). After playing with Zinc Fence, Smith started working as a percussionist with Luciano then Jimmy Cliff, Damian Marley

Feluké

and Stephen Marley. He became a musical director for Kyamani Marley, Jah Cure and Etana and played on Stephen Marley's Grammy winning album *Revelation Part One: The Root of Life* and the acoustic re-recording of Marley's Grammy winning LP *Mind Control*. He worked as a co-producer for Jah Cure and wrote a song for his Grammy-nominated album *The Cure*. One of his reggae heroes Jimmy Cliff invited Smith to do some recording with him and he worked on the promotional tour for Cliff's acclaimed 2012 LP *Rebirth*, produced by Tim Armstrong from US punk band Rancid. He has also worked with German reggae superstar Gentleman, playing percussion on his MTV Unplugged album and has also played with dub poet and cultural firebrand Mutabaruka. A self-produced solo LP entitled *Musically Disturbed*, under the name Denver D was released in 2012 on his own label, DDM music. It received positive praise but did not sell well. Smith has since changed his name to the more rootsy-sounding Feluké, a Nigerian word, meaning 'in the hands of God.' In 2016, under his new name he travelled as a solo artist to Belgium for the first time where he was well-received.

Smith returns to Alpha often and gets involved with the music side of things there. He works voluntarily as a motivational speaker in schools around Kingston, sharing his remarkable story to try and show young people that anything is possible if you put your mind to it. As Feluké he has been working with producer Riff-Raff (Lamar Brown) on an EP. The record fuses reggae, jazz, pop and R&B and features guest artists Kymani Marley, Gentleman, Jesse Royal and Runkus. Feluké says the EP is the culmination of all his life's experiences. It was due to be released in March 2017, a few weeks after our interview with him. However in April 2017 we learned the shocking news that Denver Smith had been diagnosed with the stage four colon cancer. A successful crowd funding campaign was launched to raise finances for him to travel to Mexico to get the kind of specialist treatment unavailable in Jamaica. In May the *Jamaica Star* reported that he was responding well to the treatment and was due to fly back home.

--A.R.

The Alpha Boys Reunion Show 2007

Photos by Adam Reeves

Karl Bryan, Headley Bennett, Vin Gordon, and Sparrow Martin

Lester Sterling, Rico Rodriguez, and Vin Gordon

Tony Gregory and Sparrow Martin

Sparrow Martin directs the grand finale of the show.

About the Cover Artist—Jean-Christophe Molinéris

The Sound of Colour

In my life as a painter, often I am confronted by the bridge between painting and music, and yet musicians regularly describe their sounds as colourful melodies. Listening to music we can be transported to magical worlds, where emotions are transformed to images. Painting, like music, is pure emotion. It is the link between the real and the imaginary, the path transcending the void.

It is in this void, between of overflowing life and inner emptiness; within the rhythm of form, the force of the stroke, and the smooth and colorful touches, the artists' brush lays layer on layer upon the canvas, tranforming his creative consciousness from the abyssal depths of his soul.

Then there is the model, his life, merging with the artist, whereby the two become one, more than the sum of their parts, and oftentimes much much more; living and reliving together and filling the space between.

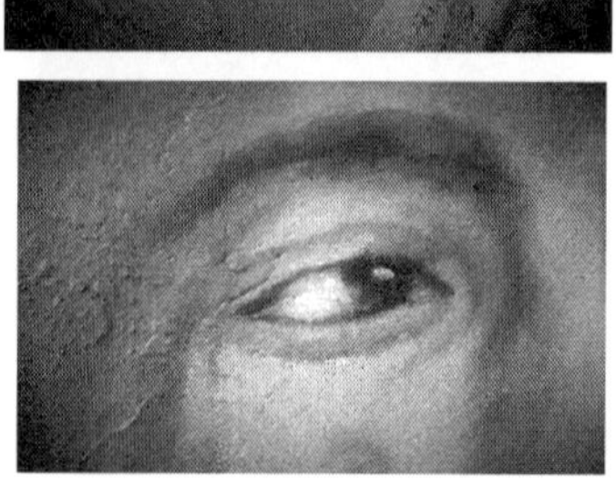

Suggested Listening

By Adam Reeves

As mentioned previously, for instant gratification alphaboysschoolradio.com broadcasts 24/7. Rather than attempting any kind of comprehensive discography, which could easily extend to hundreds of pages, this is a suggested listening guide to take you closer to Alpha's musical legacy. For the more obsessive of our readers, we suggest heading over to discogs.com where a simple search will show you the most complete list of releases to be found anywhere on the internet with links to available copies from individual dealers at competitive prices.

Many of the earlier Alpharians were never recorded and some of them recorded so much music it can be overwhelming to know where to start. These pages offer an entry-level guide for those wanting get their feet wet and then perhaps get a little deeper. Such a list will never satisfy everyone, so this is in no way the be-all-and-end-all of any artist's output. Although Alpharians are to be found playing on thousands of LPs and 45s, we have honed in on albums where they are credited as featured solo artists, with the most readily available editions rather than rarities. We have included some of the original vinyl editions also for the keen collector. We have also invited some leading reggae authorities to pick their favourite Alpha-related records. Although many of the titles listed have been deleted and are only available on the second hand market, they are not impossible to track down.

Alpha Albums

Music In Education: Alpha Boys' School 1910-2006. Label: Trojan Records (cat. TJCCD179), UK/US, 2006. UK reggae stalwarts Trojan put out this nicely packaged CD to honour the life and work of Sister Ignatius. Featuring jazz, R&B, ska, rocksteady and early reggae, it features solo work by 24 different Alpharians.

Come Dance With Me, CD, 2002. Collaboration between Alpha Boys' School and Studio One, featuring the school band with Sister Ignatius and Coxone Dodd taking care of production. Recorded at Studio One in the year before Ignatius' passing and with her voice introducing songs, which range from

ska, calypso, bolero and Jamaican folk songs. This is the one and only release by the Alpha school band.
Studio One Scorcher Volume One, 3 x vinyl LP (cat. SJR LP67), CD (cat. SJR CD 67) UK, 2002, re-issued 2017. *Studio One Scorcher Volume Two*, 2 x vinyl LP (cat. SJR LP143), CD (cat.SJR CD 143), UK, 2006. Soul Jazz Records. Available to download direct from Soul Jazz.
Soul Jazz are the UK licensees for Studio One re-issues and these two volumes of instrumentals give good representation to the work of Alpha boys as they define the sound of Jamaica's greatest studio. Volume One has a deeper, harder edge and includes an astonishing eight minute funky, dubby re-edit of The Skatalites' 'Cleopatra Ska', re-titled 'Shocker's Rock.' It also features the 12 inch extended mix of Vin Gordon's 1968 hit 'Heavenless'.

Individual Alpharian Solo Releases

Dizzy Reece

Mosaic Select. Label: Mosaiç (cat.MS-011). Triple CD overview of Reece's career. Limited edition US release (5000 copies), 2004.
Five Classic Albums Plus Bonus Tracks (cat.RGJCD350). Label: Real Gone Jazz. Four CD box set of digitally remastered LPs dating mostly from the 1950s. Includes Blues In Trinity, Star Bright, Soundin' Off, A New Star, Progress Report.

Joe Harriott

Killer Joe! Birth Of A Legend, CD (cat.GSCR 020). 2 x CD compilation. Label: Giant Steps, UK, 2007.
Joe Harriot, *Three Classic Albums* (cat.RGJCD499). Label: Giant Steps, UK, 2015. Two CD compilation of remastered albums, *Southern Horizons* (1960), *Free Form* (1962), *Abstract* (1962).
Joe Harriott Double Quintet, *Indo Jazz Fusion*, LP Label: Columbia (UK edition), Atlantic (US edition), CD re-mastered Atlantic (Cat.WPCR-27924), 2014.

Wilton 'Bogey' Gaynair

Blue Bogey, vinyl LP (cat.Tap25). Label: Tempo, 1959, UK. Re-issued on vinyl and CD by Atelier Sawano, Japan, 2009.
Africa Calling. Original vinyl release 1960. Re-issued on CD, Label: Candid, UK 2006.

Sonny Grey
Skippin', vinyl LP (cat. Mai 9). Label: Numero, France, 1974.
Sonny Grey, Dextor Gordon, Georges Avanitas, *Paris Concert* vinyl LP, (cat. Ger41), Label: Futura, 1974. Re-issue: Vinyl LP and CD by Futura, France, 2009.

Tommy McCook (see also The Skatalites)
The Sannic Sounds Of Tommy McCook,), CD and vinyl (cat.DSR 004). Label: Dubstore, 2015, Japan.
Reggae In Jazz, vinyl LP Originally released 1976, Eve Records (cat.EVLP 5004). Re-issue: vinyl LP (cat.PSLP 81), CD (cat.PSCD 81), Label: Pressure Sounds, UK, 2013.
Dubbing With Horns, vinyl LP (cat.EVLP 5004), CD (cat.JRCD043), Label: Jamaican Recordings, UK, 2011.

Cook With McCook, CD (cat.LCK DM), Label: Disc, Jamaica, 1999.
Blazing Horns: Tenor In Roots, CD (cat. BAFCD 044), 2 x Vinyl LP (cat.SVLP393), Label: Blood And Fire, UK, 2003.
Pleasure Dub, Original vinyl release on Treasue Isle, 1976. Re-issue: CD (cat. PSCD63), vinyl LP (cat. PSLP63). Label: Pressure Sounds, UK, 2009.

Bobby Gaynair
Black Jack , CD (cat.SHM 0201193), CD, Label: Shuttle Music, Germany. Date unknown.

Harold McNair
Fruit And Nut, CD (cat. CDSML8494) Label: Vocalion, UK, 2012.
Affectionate Fink, vinyl LP (cat.ILP 926). Label: Island, UK, 1965. Re-issue: CD, Japan, 2016.

Lennie Hibbert
Creation, vinyl LP (cat.SOL 0015). Label: Studio One, Jamaica, 1969. Re-issue: CD, US, 2000.
More Creation, vinyl LP (cat.SOL. 1119). Label: Studio One, Jamaica/US, 1971.

'Deadly' Headley Bennett
35 Years From Alpha, vinyl LP (cat. On-U LP14). Label: On-U Sound, UK, 1982. Re-issued on CD (cat. On- U CD 0014), UK 1999.

Eddie 'Tan Tan' Thornton
Third World All Stars, (also ft. Rico Rodriguez), *Rebel Rock*, original vinyl LP (cat.TWLP 103), Label: Third World Records, UK, 1975. Re-issue: vinyl LP (cat. PS LP 78), CD (cat.PS CD 78), Label: Pressure Sounds, UK, 2013.

Bobby Ellis
Tommy And Bobby (with Tommy McCook), vinyl LP (cat. ATLP 1004), Label: Attack, UK, 1974.
Bobby Ellis And The Professionals Meet The Revolutionaries, vinyl LP (cat.TWS 921), Label: Third World Records, UK, 1977.
Bobby Ellis And The Crew, *Shaka*, vinyl LP, (cat. Da 102), Label: Dub Lab, US, 1984.
Tommy McCook And Bobby Ellis, *Blazing Horns*, vinyl LP, (cat.GMLP 002). Label: Grove Music, UK, 1977.

Don Drummond (see also The Skatalites)
Jamaica Jazz From The Workshop, vinyl LP (cat. SOLP 1140). Label: Studio One, Jamaica, 1962. CD (SOCD 1140), Studio One, 1994.

In Memory of Don Drummond, vinyl LP (cat. CSL 02), Label: Studio One, Jamaica/UK 1969.
Greatest Hits, vinyl LP (cat.TI LP 004), Label: Treasure Isle, UK/Jamaica 1969.
100 Years After, vinyl LP, (cat. SOL 1114). Label: Studio One, Jamaica, US, date unknown.
Reggae Jazz Attack, (second CD is Rico Rodriguez LP *Rico's Message*), 2 x CD (cat.CDVAL 130-2), Label: Charly Records, Germany 2000.
Don Cosmic, vinyl LP/CD, Label: Studio One. US, 2017.

The Skatalites

For an overview of The Skatalites 1960s material, the following compilations showcase their work at Top Deck, Treasure Isle, Studio One, King Edward's and Randy's.
Ska-Boo-Da-Ba (Sounds From Top Deck Vol 3), CD (cat. WESM 518). Label: Westside, UK, 2003.
Phoenix City, 2 x CD (cat.TJDDD160). Features the best of their recordings for Duke Reid at Treasure Isle). Label: Trojan 2004, UK. US release (cat.06076-80453-2).
Foundation Ska, 2 x CD and 2 x vinyl LP (cat. SOR 006). Label: Studio One, US, 2017.
Kingston 11, vinyl LP (cat. KECD 07). Label: King Edwards, UK, 2005.
Rollin' On, CD (cat.KECD 09). Label: King Edwards, UK, 2010.
The Skatalites And Friends At Randy's, CD. (cat. VPCD 1497). Label: VP, US, 2016.
Some key post-1960s Skatalites releases:
African Roots, previously released in 1976 as *The Legendary Skatalites* (US) and *Rebirth* (Jamaica). CD/vinyl (cat. GRO-LP 009). Label: Grover, Germany, 2016.
Stretching Out, Live At The Blue Monk Jazz Gallery, 1983, 2 x vinyl LP (cat.RUSLP 8312). Label: ROIR, US, 2007.
Herb Dub, Collie Dub, vinyl LP (cat. FASTLP 008), Label: Motion, UK, 2001.
Rolling Steady, The 1983 Music Mountain Sessions. CD/vinyl LP (cat. FASTLP008). Label: Motion, UK 2007.

Return Of The Big Guns, CD/vinyl (cat. UICY-76889). Label: Island, Japan, 2014. Earlier versions released 1984 and 1999.
Ska Voovie, CD (cat.45009). Label: Shanachie, US, 1993.
Hi-Bop Ska, CD (cat. 45019). Label: Shanachie, US, 1994.
Bashaka, CD, (MRCCD 1029). Label: Marston Recording Company, US, 2000.

Rico Rodriguez
Trombone Man, Anthology 1960-'71, 2 x CD (cat. TJDDD222). Label: Trojan, UK, 2004.
Man From Wareika, vinyl LP, (cat. ILPS 9485). Label: Island, UK 1976, UK. Original US release (cat. BN-LA819-H). Label: Blue Note 1977. Re-issued on CD, (cat. UICY-76902). Label: Island, Japan 2014.
Roots To The Bone, CD (cat. RRCD 54).Features seven tracks from *Man From Wareika* and seven rare singles and B-sides. Label: Mango/Island, Europe, 1995.
Man From Wareika Dub, by Ghetto Rockers, vinyl LP (cat. ILPS 9485, Pre-LP1). Label: Island, 1976, UK. CD release (cat.UICY-76903) Island, Japan, 2014. 180g vinyl LP re-release, (cat. 535 179-8, PRE 1), Europe, 2014.
Jama Rico, vinyl LP (cat.HR TT 5006). Label: Two Tone, UK, 1982.
Wareika Vibes, vinyl LP (cat.JAMUKCD008), Label: Jamdown, UK 2006.

Lester Sterling (see also The Skatalites)
Bangarang, vinyl LP (cat.ECO 15). Label: Pama, UK 1969.
Sterling Silver, CD (no cat. Number). Label: Echo, USA, 2002.

Johnny 'Dizzy' Moore (see also The Skatalites)
Live And Love, CD and vinyl LP (cat. JAHCD19). Label: Buffy, Canada, 1998.

Owen Gray
Shook, Shimmy And Shake: The Anthology, 2 x CD (cat.TJDDD188). Label: Trojan, UK, 2004.
Owen Gray Sings, vinyl LP. Label: Island. UK/Jamaica, 1960.
Forward On The Scene. LP. (cat.TSL 103), Label: Total Sounds, Jamaica. UK release (cat.TWLP 4). Label: Third World, 1975
Dreams of Owen Gray, vinyl LP (cat. TRLS 150). Label: Trojan, UK, 1978
Battle Of The Giants (with Pluggy Satchmo), vinyl LP (cat.STLP 1010). Label: Echo, 1990, UK.
Fire And Bullets, vinly LP (cat.TRLS 139). Label: Trojan, 1977, UK.

Ron Wilson
T-Bone, vinyl LP (cat. FRLP 5946). Label: Foxtail, US, 1998.

Jo Jo Bennett
Groovy Joe (With Mudie's All Stars), vinyl LP (cat.TBL 133). Label: Trojan/Moodisc, 1970, UK.
The Sattalites, vinyl LP (cat. AXS 525). Label: Axe, Canada, 1985. CD re-issue (cat.SGR) CD 41015), Label: Solid Gold, Canada, 2002.
The Sattalites, *Reggaefication,* CD (cat. SGR-CD-41017). Label: Solid Gold, Canada, 2003.

Glen Da Costa
Mind Blowing Melody, vinyl LP (cat. TDWD 11). Label: Third World Recordings, UK, date unknown.
Zap Pow (with Alpharian David Madden) *Revolution,* vinyl LP (cat. TRLS 130). Label: Trojan, UK, 1976.
Zap Pow, *Now,* vinyl LP (cat. VULP 004), Label: Trojan, UK, 1976. CD re-issue (cat. CP 4015). Label: Culture Press, France, 2002.
Last War, The Best Of Zap Pow, CD (cat. TJCCD375). Label: Trojan, UK, 2007.

David Madden (see also Zap Pow)
Going Bananas, vinyl LP (cat. 8147). Label: LMS Jamaica, 1983.
Reggae Trumpeter, vinyl LP, (cat. None). Label: LMS, Jamaica, 1998.
Cyber Charged Ska, CD (cat. none). Label: Large, Medium and Small Music, Jamaica, 1997.

Cedric Brooks
The Mystic Revelation Of Rastafari, *Grounation,* 3 x vinyl LP (cat. ND 0001). Label: New Dimension, Jamaica, 1973. Re-issue: CD (cat.2X604), Retro, Europe, 2007. Re-issue: 3 x vinyl LP (cat. DSR LP 007) and CD (cat. DSR CD 007), Dub Store, Japan, 2016.
The Mystic Revelation Of Rastafari, *Tales Of Mozambique,* vinyl LP (cat. DY 3358). Label: Dynamic Sounds, Jamaica 1975. Re-issue: 2 x vinyl LP (cat. SJR LP325) and CD (cat. SJR CD325). Label: Soul Jazz, UK, 2016.

Cedric 'IM' Brooks And The Divine Light Of Saba, *From Mento to ReggaeTo Third World*
Music, vinyl LP (cat. 001). Label: Doctor Bird, Jamaica, 1973. Re-issue: CD (cat.VP 4118). Label: 17 North Parade, US, 2008.
Cedric 'IM' Brooks And The Divine Light Of Saba, *The Magical Light Of Saba*, 2 x vinyl LP/CD compilation (cat. vinyl: HJRLP4, CD: HJRCD4). Label: Honest Jon's, UK, 2003. Re-issued on vinyl, 2008.

IM Flash Forward, vinyl LP (cat.SOL 00330). Label: Studio One, Jamaica, 1977.
United Africa, vinyl LP (cat. ARCO LP 009). Label: Water Lily, Jamaica, 1978. Re-issued on CD (cat. none). Label: Wait A Bit, Jamaica, 2001.
Cedric Brooks & Mystic Revelation Of Rastafari, *One Truth*, vinyl LP (cat. VILP 0010) Label: Visions, UK, 1980.

Tony Gregory

Tony Gregory and Family Child, *One More Time*, vinyl LP (cat.2396 104). Label: Finger, Polydor, Germany, 1973.
Comin' On Strong, vinyl LP, (cat.FL-LP00), Label: Frontline, Jamaica, 1986.

Johnny Osbourne

Johnny Osbourne and The Sensations, *Come Back Darling*, vinyl LP, UK (cat.TTL-29), Jamaica (cat.LP-3300). Labels: Trojan (UK release), Techniques (Jamaican release), 1970.
Truth And Rights, vinyl LP (cat.SOLP-0132). Label: Studio One, Jamaica/USA, 1979. Re-issued CD with bonus tracks (cat.11661-7840-2), Label: Heartbeat, USA/UK/Europe, 2008.
Folly Rankin', vinyl LP (cat.JAM 1000). Label: Jammy's, UK/US, 1980. Re-issue: vinyl LP (cat.VPGSRL7002). Label: Greensleeves/VP, UK 2013.
Fally Lover, vinyl LP, (cat.GREL 12). Label: Greensleeves, UK, 1980. Re-issue: Greensleeves vinyl LP, 2013.
Yo Yo, vinyl LP (cat.A1-002). Label: Arrival, Jamaica, 1982.
Never Stop Fighting, vinyl LP (cat.GREL 38). Label: Greensleeves, UK, 1982.

Water Pumping, vinyl LP (cat.GREL 61). Label: Greensleeves, UK/US/Canada, 1983. Greensleeves vinyl re-issue, UK, 2015.

Rub-A-Dub-Soldier, vinyl LP (cat.J005). Label: Jammy's, Jamaica, 1985.
Rougher Than Them, vinyl LP. Label: VP (cat.VPRC 1048), US, 1989, 1992. Also available on Vine Yard (cat. VYDCD 8), UK, 1989, 1995.

Floyd Lloyd Seivright
Better To Laugh Than To Cry, vinyl LP (cat.STLP 1016). Label: Vista Sounds, UK, 1982.
Red Cloud In Dub, vinyl LP, (cat.STLP 1009). Label: Released on both Echo and Vista Sounds, UK, 1982.
Floyd Lloyd and Potato 5 Meet Laurel Aitken, vinyl LP (cat.LP GAZ 001). Label: Gaz's Rockin' Records, UK, 1987. Re-issue: Grover Records (cat. GRO-CD 045), Germany, 2000.

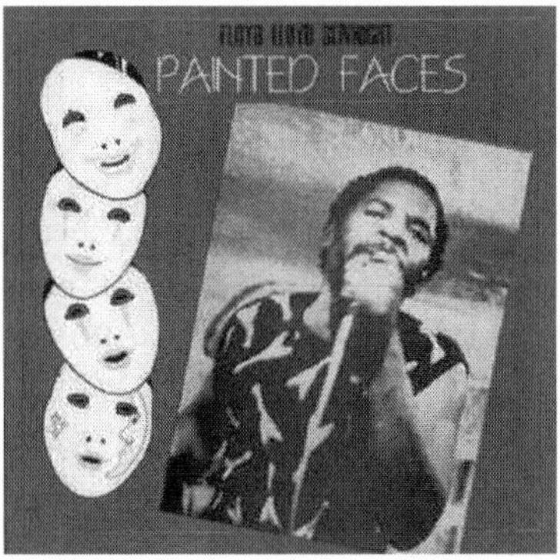

Painted Faces, with Red Cloud, vinyl LP (cat.PPC 0024). Label: Tropic, UK, 1987.
Tear It Up: The Ska Album, vinyl LP (cat. CD TROPIC 008). Label: Tropic, UK, 1997. US labels: Tuff Gong International and Tropic (both cat.54198-2), 1997.
Village Soul, (featuring Alpharians Lennie Hibbert, Eddie 'Tan Tan', Rico Rodriguez and Leroy 'Horsemouth' Wallace), CD (cat.PIC 009). Label: Tropic, US, 1997.

Leroy 'Horsemouth' Wallace
Horsemouth, *Original Armageddon Dub* (also featuring Alpharians David Madden, Headley Bennett and Vin Gordon), CD (cat. CDSO 01). Label: Stable One, US. Recorded 1978 but not released until 2000.

Rockers, Original Movie Soundtrack, compilation. Vinyl LP/CD (cat.ILPS 9587). Label: Island/Mango. Over 30 editions released worldwide since 1979.
Burning Spear, *Marcus Garvey*, vinyl LP (cat.ILPS 9377). Label: Island, UK, US, Canada, Europe, Japan, 1975. Over 30 editions available. The dub version of the *Marcus Garvey* LP is *Garvey's Ghost,* vinyl LP (cat. ILPS 9382). Label: Island/Mango, UK, US, 1976.

Apple Gabriel

Israel Vibration, *The Same Song,* vinyl LP (cat. TCL 1001), Label: Top Ranking, Jamaica/US copy (cat. 3218), 1978. Over 25 editions worldwide.
Israel Vibration, *Unconquered People,* vinyl LP (cat. none). Label: Tuff Gong, Jamaica, 1979. CD re-release (cat.VPCD2028). Label: VP, US, date not known.
Israel Vibration, *Apple Vibes,* CD compilation (cat.RAS 3331). Label: RAS, US, 2000.
Israel Vibration, *This Is Crucial Reggae,* CD (cat. 06076-89941-2). Label: Sanctuary, US, 2005.
No Racism, CD (cat. none), Label: Royal, US, 2002.
Another Moses, vinyl LP, CD (cat.RAS 3245), Label: RAS, US, Netherlands, 1999. Re-release, CD (cat. NTCD625), Nocturne, France, 2004.

Teach Them Right, CD (cat. HB#CD 20662), Label: Heartbeat, Europe, 2010.
Groundation with Apple Gabriel and Don Carlos, *We Free Again.* 2 x vinyl LP (cat.SBR034) CD (cat.SBR033). Label: Soulbeats Records, France, 2013.

Leroy Smart

Superstar, vinyl LP (cat.none), Label: Hot Stuff, Jamaica, 1977. CD re-issue: (cat.CM2149). Label: Planet Vibe, France, 2006.
The Very Best OF Leroy Smart, vinyl LP (cat.none). Label: Channel One, Jamaica, 1977. CD re-issue: (cat.JJ-CD-033), US, date not known.
Dread Hot In Africa, vinyl LP (cat. BS1004LP). Label: Burning Sounds, UK, 1977. CD re-issue: (cat. MKS15). Label: Makasound, France, 2007. Vinyl re-issue: (cat.BSRLP987). Label: Burning Sounds, UK, 2016.
Disco Showcase (featuring The Mighty Diamonds), vinyl LP (cat.none). Label: Gussie Roots Sounds, Jamaica, 1979.

She Love It In The Morning, vinyl LP (cat. GG 031). Label: GG's, Jamaica, 1983. Album also known as On Top vinyl LP (cat.LP 003). Label: Live And Learn. US, Canada, 1983.

Vintage Classics, CD (cat.RASCD 3163). Label: RAS, US, 1995.

The Don Tells It Like It Is, compilation, CD (cat. KSLP045), vinyl LP (cat.KSCD045). Label: Kingston Sounds, UK, 2013.

The Very Best Of Leroy Smart, CD (cat. LSCD-100). Label: VP and WWS, US, date not known.

Albert 'Ilawi' Malawi

Many of Ilawi's sessions as a sound system selector are lovingly archived and can be downloaded free of charge at www.whocorkthedance.com/jahlovemusic.html

Charlie 'Eskimo' Fox

Nattorius, CD (cat. ON-U CD 0089). Label: On-U Sound, UK, 2004.

African Head Charge, *My Life In A Hole In The Ground,* vinyl LP (cat.ON-U LP 13). Label: On-U Sound, UK, 1981. CD re-release 1999, UK. Vinyl re-issue 2016.

African Head Charge, *Environmental Studies* (cat.ON-U LP19). Label: On-U Sound, UK, 1982. CD re-release 1997. Vinyl re-release 2016.

African Head Charge, *Environmental Holes And Drastic Tracks,* 5 x CD deluxe box set, (cat. ONUCD134). Label: On-U Sound, UK, 2016.

Singers And Players, *Leaps And Bounds,* vinyl LP (cat. BRED 58). Label: Cherry Red, UK, 1984. Re-issue on CD, 1991 and on vinyl, 2006.

Singers And Players, *War Of Worlds* (cat.ONUCD134). Label: On-U Sound, UK, 1982. Re-issue on vinyl and CD, UK, 2015.

Creation Rebel/New Age Steppers, *Threat To Creation,* vinyl LP, (cat.B RED 21). Label: Cherry Red. Re-issued on CD (cat.CDM RED 21), date unknown. US CD re-issue, Label: Anthology, 2014.

Creation Rebel, *Starship Africa,* vinyl LP, (cat.ON-U LP 8/4DLP1). Label: 4D Rhythm/On-U Sound, UK, 1980. CD re-re-issue (cat.ON-UCD1017), On-U Sound, UK, 2011.

Dub Syndicate, *Pounding System,* vinyl LP (cat. ON-U LP18). Label: On-U Sound, UK, 1982. CD re-issue, UK/Europe, 1998.

Vin Gordon

Sound Dimension, *Roots Dub,* vinyl LP (cat.none). Label: Studio One, Jamaica, date unknown. Re-issue: CD (cat.SO CD 50153). US, date unknown.

Sound Dimension, *Jamaica Soul Shake Vol. 1*, CD (cat.SJR CD 127), 2 x vinyl LP (cat. SJR LP127). Label: Soul Jazz, UK, 2006.

Sound Dimension, *Mojo Rocksteady Beat,* CD (cat.SJR CD 173), 2 x vinyl LP (cat. SJR LP173). Label: Soul Jazz, UK, 2007. Re-released 2017.

Burning Spear Live, vinyl LP (cat.ILPS 9513). Label: Island, UK/Europe/US/Canada, 1977. Re-released on CD, date unknown.

Way Over Yonder, vinyl LP (cat.JGML 6042). Label: Joe Gibbs Music, US, 1980.

The Melody Moods Of Vin Gordon, vinyl LP (cat.MMLP008). Label: M&M Music, UK, 1989.

Gordon In De Garden, CD (cat.001). Label: Masaya, France, 2008.

Vin Gordon And The Real Rock Band, *Heavenless* (cat.RGRLP003). Label: Roots Garden, UK, 2016.

Lee Perry And The Upsetters, *Musical Bones* (featuring Vin Gordon and Bobby Ellis), vinyl LP (cat.DLP 6000). Label: Dip, UK, 1975. Re-issue: CD (cat.JLCD 5002), Label: Justice League, UK, 1997.

Babylon Movie Soundtrack (compilation), vinyl LP (cat.CHR 1294). Label: Chrysalis, UK/France/Germany/Spain, 1980. Re-issue: CD, 2005 (cat.5843212), UK, 2005.

Osbert Maddo (Papa Madoo)

Rock With Papa Madoo, vinyl LP (cat.DMLP 1084). Label: Darace, Canada, 1981.

Best Of Madoo, vinyl LP. Label: Techniques (cat.none) and also on Black Rose (cat. DMLP 1084). Jamaica, 1980.

You Wanna Turn Me On, vinyl LP (cat.none). Label: Sonic Sounds, Jamaica, 1982.

Several of Papa Madoo's live DJ sessions for Stereophonic Hi-Fi can be played for free at the online archive Who Cork The Dance? www.whocorkthedance.com/stereophonic.html (scroll down the page to find the Madoo sessions).

Yellowman

Them A Mad Over Me, vinyl LP (cat.LPJJ-060). Labels: J&L, Channel One and Hit Bound, Jamaica, US, 1982. Re-issue: CD, US, date unknown.

Duppy Or Gunman, vinyl LP (cat.VPRL 1009). Label: Northworld Recordinds, UK, 2012.
Label: Jah Guidance, Jamaica, 1982. Re-released on vinyl LP 2010. Re-issue: vinyl LP, Label: VP, US, 2010.
Mr. Yellowman, vinyl LP (cat.GREL 35). Label: Greensleeve, UK, 1982. CD release (cat. GREWCD35), 2001, UK. Re-issue: vinyl LP, UK, 2014.
Zungguzungguguzungguzeng! Vinyl LP (cat. GREL 57), Label: Greensleeves, UK/US/Canada, 1983. Re-issued on vinyl LP and CD, 2009.
King Yellowman, vinyl LP (cat.GREL 57). Label: Columbia, US. Epic/Sony, UK (cat.40 25922). 1984. Re-issued on CD (cat. NW0039CD
Reggae Legends, compilation, 4 x CD (cat.VP2395). Label: VP, US, 2008.
Young, Gifted And Yellow, compilation, 2 x CD plus DVD recorded live at Reggae Sunsplash 1988 (cat.VP5003). Label: VP, US, 2013.

Most Wanted, compilation, CD (cat.GRELCD606). Label: Greensleeves, UK, 2007.
Yellow Fever, compilation, CD). Label: Trojan, Europe (cat.TJACD 201), US (cat.TJACD 201) 2004.
To hear the excitement of Yellowman at the height of his powers on Jack Ruby Hi-Power Sound System there are some archive sound system recordings at Who Cork The Dance? www.whocorkthedance.com/Jackruby.html

Tafane Buschaecab, Nicholas Laraque and Feluké
Unit 3, *In The Fields,* CD (cat. BF 0062). Label: Born Free, US, 2013. Three of Alpha's newer generation of musicians featured in this book all feature on this album.

We invited a handful of authorities on Jamaican music to select their favourite Alpha-related records. Here's what they came up with together with some of their comments. Release details are only included on titles not listed above.

David Corio, reggae photographer

The Mystic Revelation of Rastafari, *Grounation.* Cedric Brooks' band along with the veteran Count Ossie produced this triple vinyl or two CD raw masterpiece of a nyabinghi session. One of the best examples of what the legendary grounations in the Warreika Hills sounded like.

Johnny Osbourne. *Truth And Rights.* Classic Studio One rhythms with Johnny Osbourne's sing-jay vocals make this one of the must have records in reggae. The deluxe CD edition on Hearbeat Records has extra previously unreleased tracks and mixes.

Jimmy Radway & The Fe Me Time All Stars, *Dub-I,* (cat.PSLP 61). Label: Pressure Sounds. Featuring Alpharians Tommy McCook, Vin Gordon, Bobby Ellis, Cedric Brooks and many of Kingston's other finest musicians performing heavy dubs over simple productions. This highlights the exquisite horn players that Alpha Boys' School produced. There is a short vocal by Leroy Smart on a version of 'Mr Smart'.

Diggory Kenrick, reggae flautist and producer of *I Am The Gorgon*, documentary on Bunny Lee

Tommy McCook, *Brass Rockers,* vinyl LP (cat.TSL106). Label: Total Sounds, Jamaica, 1976. Re-issue: Vinyl. Label: Jamaican Recordings, UK, 2010. McCook never sounds better than backed by the Aggrovators and mixed by King Tubby.

Burning Spear, *Marcus Garvey.* As well as featuring Alpharians Vin Gordon and Bobby Ellis, the drumming of Leroy 'Horsemouth' Wallace is truly amazing throughout this album.

Aswad, *New Chapter Of Dub,* vinyl LP (cat.ILPS 9711). Label: Island, UK, 1982. Vinyl and CD re-issue on Island/Mango, UK/Europe, 2013. Aswad's horn section featured Vin Gordon and Eddie 'Tan Tan' Thornton. Vin was central to so many Jamaican recordings, but it's great to hear his influence on British music here. The high point was probably 'Warrior Charge' but this LP features the amazing 'Dub Fire', the version to 'Love Fire' and Dennis Brown's 'Promised Land'.

John Masouri, reggae journalist and author of *Steppin' Razor: The Life of Peter Tosh*
IM and Dave, *Money Maker*, vinyl LP (cat.none). Label: Studio One, Jamaica, date unknown.
Tommy McCook & Bobby Ellis, *Blazing Horns.*
Rico Rodriquez, *Man From Wareika.*

Noel Hawks, reggae writer and album compiler
The Very Best Of Leroy Smart, Channel One.
An excellent selection of Mr Smart's seventies recordings for Channel One that includes 'Ballistic Affair' and 'Badness Don't Pay' and an excellent re-cut of his 'Pride And Ambition' signature tune.
Yellowman and Fathead, *Live At Aces,* vinyl LP (cat.VPRLP 1011). Label: Jah Guidance, USA, 1982. The first ever LP to be recorded live in a dance capturing King Yellow at the height of his popularity, generating the type of excitement that had previously vanished into the balmy Jamaican nights.
Cedric I'm Brook, *IM Flash Forward.*
A showcase for the saxophone artistry of Cedric Brooks over a selection of classic Brentford Road rhythms including The Abyssinians' 'Declaration Of Rights' and Horace Andy's 'Skylarking'.

Steve Barrow, co-author of *The Rough Guide To Reggae*, former head of Blood And Fire_Records and lifelong reggae collector
Steve recommends three jazz and three reggae albums.
Dizzy Reece, *Blues In Trinity,* vinyl LP (cat. NY BN 40061). Label: Blue Note, US, 1958.
Alphonso Son 'Dizzy' Reece left Jamaica in 1948, led sessions for the Tempo label in London, contributed the score to the Ealing Studios thriller 'Nowhere to Go," before cutting this definitive hard-bop set for Blue Note with trumpeter Donald Byrd. Proof, if any were needed, that the top Jamaican jazzmen could shine brightly on the world stage.

Joe Harriott Quintet And Sextet , *Southern Horizons,* vinyl LP (cat.JLP 937). Label: Jazzlands. UK, 1960. Although perhaps better known for his celebrated free-form sets, here Harriott delivers a throughly enjoyable hard bop set for the US Riverside label subsidiary Jazzland, fronting an excellent group that includes trumpeter Shake Keane, bassist Coleridge Goode and pianist Harry South.

Harold McNair With Ornette Coleman's Sidemen, *Affectionate Fink,* vinyl LP (cat.ILP 926). Label: Island, UK, 1965. Re-issue: CD, Japan, 2016. McNair recorded a wide range of music, ranging from folk-rock with Donovan, through easy listening and into jazz. Here he displays his talent over the formidable rhythms of bassist David Izenzon, drummer Charles Moffet, both with Ornette Coleman and the excellent English pianist Alan Branscombe.

Tommy MCook, *Best Of Tommy McCook and The Skatalites,* CD (cat. 11661-7716-2). Label: Heartbeat, US, 1999. Another excellent Heartbeat CD, this time with no vocal cuts, so the focus is squarely on McCook on a selection of ska tracks, only a few anthologized elsewhere, but the superb sound quality here is the clincher for this recommended set. Plenty of lesser-known cuts too.

Tommy McCook, *Hot Lava,* vinyl LP, (cat.TWS 920). Label: Third World, UK, 1977. This is perhaps the best of several albums Tommy recorded for Bunny Lee in the mid-1970s, as Tommy is well featured over a selection of dubbed-up Aggrovators rhythms. One of the many standout tracks is a version of the 'Riding West' theme, first recorded in the 1950s by the US R&B band of 'Billy Hope', here dropped onto a leisurely Sly Dunbar rhythm track.

The Revolutionaries, *Revolutionary Soundscat,* vinyl LP (cat. JJ-LP-034), 1976. Re-issue: CD (cat. JJ-CD-034). Label: Channel One, Jamaica date unknown. Pivotal set featuring the Channel One studio group, with Tommy McCook leading the horns. The group delivers a set of new versions of old Studio One rhythms, which really shook up the whole reggae world in the mid-1970s and this set remains a definitive example of the 'rockers' rhythm.

Sean Flowerdew, leader of ska and reggae outfit Pama International and host of the annual London International Festival Of Ska
The Wailing Wailers, self-titled album, vinyl LP (cat. S1001). Label: Studio One, Jamaica, 1966. Re-issue: vinyl and CD, US/Jamaica, 2016. This is where Bob Marley, Peter Tosh and Bunny Wailer started out. Blistering ska and soul ballads inspired by The Impressions and backed superbly by the Studio One house band starring Alpha legend Johnny 'Dizzy' Moore.

Rico Rodriguez, *That Man Is Forward,* vinyl LP (cat.CHR TT 5005). Label: Two Tone, UK, 1981. Re-issue: CD and vinyl, 1998. Label: Reggae Retro Records, UK, 1198.
Could have picked any Rico album. The man transcended the generations. I've gone for one I grew up with. *That Man Is Forward* is a masterclass.

Cedric 'IM' Brooks, *The Magical Light of Saba.* Label: Honest Jon's.
Wonderful artwork, brilliantly forward thinking music. Cedric 'IM' Brooks came with true world music ahead of its time.

Tony Rounce, senior A&R representative at Ace Records
Owen Gray, *Owen Gray Sings.* To my knowledge, this is the first non-jazz album to be issued anywhere in the world by any Alpharian. Its' also the first album to be issued in Jamaica by a local artist singing R&B, shuffles, ballads and music other than calypso or mento. Owen is still going strong nearly 60 years after its release. Not currently available in its original format, but I hear that it will be soon.
Tommy McCook and Glen Brown, *The Sannic Sounds Of Tommy McCook, AKA Horny Dub*, vinyl LP.
Bobby Ellis And Tommy McCook, *Green Mango.*

Lambros Fatsis, lecturer in sociology and criminology at the University of Southampton and reggae collector/selector for Boulevard Soundsystem
Joe Harriott and Amancio D' Silva Quartet, *Hum Dono,* Label: Vocalion
Harriott paired up with guitarist Amancio D'Silva to create a mystical, deep jazz sound.

The Skatalites, *The Legendary Skatalites In Dub* (Motion Records).
This record captures the band in a somewhat different light mixed by the dub pioneer King Tubby. An irresistible album which fuses the instrumentations of the ska era with experimentations in dub.

Vin Gordon and The Real Rock Band, *Heavenless, vinyl LP (cat.RGRLP003).*
Label: Roots Garden Records, UK, 2016._
Heavenless showcases Vin Gordon's fine musicianship not in the past but in the present, produced by Brighton-based Roots Garden label and mixed by and in the unique style of Nick Mannasseh.

David Katz, author of *People Funny Boy: the Genius of Lee 'Scratch' Perry* and *Solid Foundation: An Oral History of Reggae.*
The Skatalites: *Ska Authentic: Presenting The Ska-Talites, Volume 2*, vinyl LP (cat.JBL 113). Label: ND Records, Jamaica, 1965. CD re-issue on Studio One (cat.SOCD 0907). Jamaica, 2001. Various vinyl re-issues are available, but cat. and country of issue are unknown. Contains Don Drummond's 'Rain Or Shine,' one of his most dramatic compositions, and Tommy McCook's 'Cow and Gate,' a melodious blast of proto-ska that retains a rhythm and blues backbeat.

Various: *Rock Steady Beat:Treasure Isle's Greatest Hits,* vinyl LP (cat.101/2). Label: Treasure Isle, Jamaica, 1968. CD re-issue (cat.JET SET 44 418-2). Label: Jet Set, France, 1998. Vinyl re-issues (cat.101/2 and DSK 3506). Label: Treasure Isle, Jamaica, dates unknown. A collection of ace rock steady and related material that highlights Tommy McCook's crucial role as bandleader and arranger at Treasure Isle, following the breakup of The Skatalites. Without Tommy's guidance, rocksteady would not have made such an impact and Jamaican music clearly would have taken a different course.

Cedric 'IM' Brooks, *United Africa,* 1978. Brooks' cosmic saxophone explorations are given the full big-band treatment on this exceptional LP. The seven minute version of 'Satta-A-Massagana" is intensely astounding, and the whole programme is guided by Brooks' wide-ranging musical vision.

Yellowman: *Jack Sprat,* vinyl LP (cat. none). Label GG's Hit, Jamaica, 1982. CD re-issue as *Life In The Ghetto* (cat.TASSA 7003). Label: Tassana, USA, 1990. Yellowman changed the shape of reggae with his hard-edged, risqué sing-jay style, pointing towards the coming prominence of dancehall. The *Jack Sprat* album did not receive as much widespread distribution as other popular titles of the same era, but is no less captivating, showcasing the diverse subject matter and fluid style of his humorous toasts.

The door leading out of the Lennie Hibbert Music Hall
Photo by Heather Augustyn

Acknowledgments

Heather Augustyn

I would first like to thank all of the individuals who have shared their stories with me. You opened up your lives, your spirits, to a complete stranger, entrusting me with personal and intimate memories and feelings and believed that I oculd somehow retell these stories with accuracy and emotion, and for that I am deeply grateful. More than that though, you connect with me, bonded with me, exposed your heart and I am profoundly thankful and return that love tenfold. I consider you family.

I would also like to thank my family close to home—my husband Ron, and our boys Sid and Frank—for allowing me the time to research, interview, and write, late at night, early in the morning, all day long. Thank you for indulging my constant conversations on all subjects related on Jamaican music. To my mom, for instilling in me a love of learning, from reading to adding coins. To my father, for introducing me to the music of Bob Marley, on 8-track. To my brother for a shared love of music and an analytical ear. To my sister-in-law Liz, and a mutal respect as mothers and scholars.

Thank you to Roberto Moore for your constant guidance, feedback, corrections, illucidations, research, expertise, and your own contribution to this book. Let it be the beginning of all your work to come. We all need your historical chronicles. To Charlotte Simkle and Julianne Lee, for opening your home and heart to me. Your hospitality and friendship are important to me.

Deep gratitude and love to Carol Biel for the gift of critical thinking, the art of argumentation, and a passion for world events and culture, in addition to teaching me to write. Without you, I would not be me.

To Dr. Kevin Stein and Dr. James Ballowe at Bradley University, and Richard Jones at DePaul University for developing my voice and supporting my work. To my mentors and colleagues at Purdue Northwest, for the support of my research and scholarship.

To Dr. Donna Hope, Dr. Carolyn Cooper, Dr. Sonjah N. Stanley Niaah, Herbie Miller, Dr. Clinton Hutton, and Garth White, for devoting your lives to Jamaican culture and scholarship so those of us who humbly walk your path may see with bright eyes. David Rodigan, your enthusiasm is contagious.

To the people of Jamaica, for allowing me to fall in love with your music and your culture. Respect.

Finally, to the students and staff at Alpha Boys' School and Alpha Institute, for allowing me to tell the story of a few who have walked your hallowed ground. May I offer just a small glimpse of the immense energy that has been transferred over these 137 years to each trumpeter, trombonist, or tailor in ways that are both tangible as well as invisible and unknown.

Acknowledgments

Adam Reeves

All the Alpharian musicians who kindly shared their personal stories, this book would not be possible without you. It has been an honour to be entrusted with your inspirational life stories.

My amazing partner Peta for supporting me patiently and kindly throughout every stage of this book.

My brother Mark for helping me discover reggae in the first place.

Heather Augustyn for her unwavering belief in this project and for encouraging us both to keep going with it.

Milton and Susan Moore and the Alpha Old Boys Association (UK Chapter) for ongoing support and allowing access to film the re-union show and carry out interviews. This book would not have happened if you had not said 'yes' to me all those years ago.

Ben Cole and Alice Ross for assistance with phase one of this journey.

Daniel Junge and Davis Coome for re-igniting my fire with this story.

Jane Wilkinson for general kindness.

The following people I would like to thank for being forthcoming with their support and generosity in allowing access to photographs and archive material or helping to link me up with people: Beth Lesser, Adrian Sherwood, Laurence Cane-Honeyset, David Corio, Cherry Kaori Hulsey, Karen Hanrahan, Dave Brown, Jayman (Who Cork The Dance?), Edward 'Tan Tan' Thornton, Ray Hurford, Graeme Durham.

The following for their enthusiastic contributions for Suggested Listening: John Masouri, Steve Barrow, Noel Hawks, Lambros Fatsis, Sean Flowerdew, Tony Rounce, Diggory Kenrick and David Corio.

David Rodigan for kindly writing an introduction.

And finally I would like to thank my late mother, Vivienne Silver-Leigh, an amazing person who never understood why I liked reggae but would have loved to have seen this book.

Bibliography

Alpha Boys' School Radio. "Johnny Osbourne." alphaboysschoolradio.com

Augustyn, Heather. *Don Drummond: The Genius and Tragedy of the World's Greatest Trombonist.* Jefferson, NC: McFarland, 2013.

-----. *Ska: An Oral History.* Jefferson, NC: McFarland, 2010.

-----. *Ska: The Rhythm of Liberation.* New York: Rowman & Littlefield, 2013.

-----. *Songbirds: Pioneering Women in Jamaican Music.* Chesterton, IN: Half Pint Press, 2014.

Barrow, Steve. "Ska Boo-Da-Ba. Top Sounds from Top Deck." [CD booklet]. London: Westside, 1998.

-----. Headley Bennett interview. Palm Pictures, mid-1990s.

Bennett, Headley. Interview with Heather Augustyn, March 7, 2011.

-----. Bennett, Headley. Interview with Adam Reeves, Feb. 10, 2007.

Bennett, Jo Jo. Interview with Heather Augustyn, Feb. 7, 2011; March 10, 2017.

Bowen, Winston. Interview with Heather Augustyn, Apr. 30, 2017.

Bradley, Lloyd. *Bass Culture.* London: Penguin, 2000.

-----. *This Is Reggae Music: The Story of Jamaica's Music.* New York: Grove Press, 2001.

Browne, Dalton. Interview with Heather Augustyn, Apr. 30, 2017.

Bryan, Karl. Interview with Adam Reeves, Feb. 10, 2007.

Buchsaecab, Tafane. Interview with Adam Reeves, April 17, 2017.

Butler, Leslie. Interview with Roberto Moore, July 30, 2017.

Carayol, Seb. "Don't Test: Leroy Smart Is the Real Don of Jamaican Dancehall." *The Hundreds*, Feb. 23, 2015.

Chang, Kevin O'Brien and Wayne Chen. *Reggae Routes: The Story of Jamaican Music.* Philadelphia: Temple University Press, 1998.

Chinenjan, Nate. "Blasts From the Bebop Past of an Elusive Trumpeter." *New York Times*, Jan. 9, 2007.

Clifford, Allen. "Dizzy Reece: From In to Out." *All About Jazz*, Mar. 7, 2006.

Craig, Albert. Interview with Heather Augustyn, March 22, 2017; March 29, 2017.

DaCosta, Glen. Interview with Heather Augustyn, July 22, 2016.

Ellis, Bobby. Interview with Daniel Junge, March, 2012.

Enright, Janet. Interview with Heather Augustyn, June, 24, 2013.

Farrier-Mba, Margaret. Interview with Heather Augustyn, Apr. 25, 2017.

Farrier, Miriam. Interview with Heather Augustyn, Apr. 26, 2017.

Foster, Winston. Interview with Daniel Junge, March, 2012.

-----. Interview with Adam Reeves, July 25, 2007.

Gaynair, Anne. Interview with Heather Augustyn, Nov. 25, 2016; Dec. 5, 2016.

Gaynair, Bobby. Interview with Heather Augustyn, Nov. 27, 2016; Nov. 28, 2016.

-----. Interview with Roberto Moore, July 24, 2017.

Gordon, Vincent. Interview with Adam Reeves, Feb. 10, 2007

Gray, Owen. Interview with Adam Reeves and Daniel Junge, March, 2012.

-----. Interview with Adam Reeves, Feb. 10, 2007.

Green, Jeffrey. *Swing from a Small Island: The Story of Leslie Thompson*. London: Northway Publications, 2009.

Greene, Tony. Interview with Adam Reeves, Feb. 10, 2007.

Ismay, Sammy. Interview with Roberto Moore, June 14, 2017.

-----. Manuscripts 1958, 1960.

Daily Gleaner. Numerous articles accessed at Jamaica-gleaner.com.

Harris, George W. "BET YOU'VE NEVER HEARD OF…Sonny Grey: At the II Festival Internacional De Barcelona 1967." *Jazz Weekly*. Aug. 8, 2016.

Heining, Doug. "Will the Real Joe Harriott Please Stand Up?" *All About Jazz*, Apr. 10, 2012.

Ianna, Tim. "Jamaica All Stars (Johnny 'Dizzy' Moore & Noel 'Skully' Simms." Rebelbase.be. Feb. 2005.

Johnson, Albert. Interview with Adam Reeves. Apr. 28, 2017.

Johnson, Howard. *Reggae Nashville: Deep Roots Music Vol. 1-3*. MVD Visual, 2007-2008.

Katz, David. *Solid Foundation: An Oral History of Reggae*. London: Bloomsbury, 2003.

Kelly, Vernal. Interview with Adam Reeves and Daniel Junge, March, 2012.

Keyo, Brian. Sterling Silver, liner notes, 2001.

King, Herman. Interview with Heather Augustyn, March 29, 2011.

Laraque, Nicholas, Interview with Adam Reeves, Apr. 7, 2017.

Lesser, Beth. Johnny Osbourne interview. *Reggae Quarterly*, issue #3.

-----. Leroy Smart interview. *Reggae Quarterly*, Vol.1, No.3, 1983.

-----. Johnny Osbourne interview *Reggae Quarterly*, Vol.1, No.3, 1983.

"The Light of Saba: The Magical Light Of Saba." Honest Jon's Records. honestjons.com.

Little, Sister Mary Bernadette. *You Did It Unto Me*. Cincinatti: Beyond the Trees, 2013.

Maddo, Osbert. Reggae-Vibes.com.

-----. Reggaepedia.com.

Malcolm, Carlos. *A Personal History of Post-War Jamaican Music: New Orleans Jazz, Blues to Reggae*. Canada: Pewter, 2017.

Martin, Winston. Interview with Heather Augustyn, June 15, 2011.

-----. Interview with Daniel Junge, March, 2012.

-----. Interview with Adam Reeves, Feb. 10, 2007.

Miller, Herbie. "Blue Bogey at Fifty." *Jamaica Journal*, Vol. 32, 2009.

Möeller, Donna. Interview with Heather Augustyn, Feb. 22, 2017.

Morgan, Derrick. Interview with Roberto Moore, 2014.

-----. Interview with Heather Augustyn, June 5, 1997; Feb. 25, 2011; March 17, 2017.

Music Sheet, March 25, 1955, p.4.

Nasralla, Ronnie. *Lessons to Learn*. Booksurge.com, 2008.

O'Neill, Tim. "A Conversation with Original Skatalites's Tommy McCook." *Reggae Report*, Vol. 12, 1994.

Perrone, Pierre. "Obituary: Sister Mary Ignatius Davies." *The Independent*, March 3, 2003.
Peter-I. Interview with Bobby Ellis." Reggae-Vibes.com.
-----. Interview with Lester Sterling, Reggae-Steady-Ska.com, 2013.
Porter, Christopher. "Dizzy Reece: Progress Report." *JazzTimes*, Oct. 1, 2004.
Ranglin, Ernest. Interview with Heather Augustyn, July 18, 2017.
Reggae Directory. Johnny Osbourne interview, Youtube.
Robertson, Alan. *Joe Harriott: Fire In His Soul*. London: Northway Publications, 2012.
Robinson, Greg. "The Skatalites: Playing the Jamaican Sound." *Windplayer*, No. 51.
Rodigan, David. "Interview with The Skatalites." Capital Radio London, 1984.
Rodriguez, Rico. Interview with Adam Reeves, May, 2013.
Seivright, Floyd. Interview with Heather Augustyn, Apr. 17, 2017; May 11, 2017.
Simpson, Charles. Interview with Heather Augustyn, Jan. 6, 2014.
Slim, Mohair. "Interview with Johnny 'Dizzy' Moore." Niceup.com, May 11, 2000.
Smith, Denver. Interview with Adam Reeves, March 2, 2017.
Star Newspaper. Numerous articles accessed at the National Library of Jamaica archives.
Sterling, Lester. Interview with Adam Reeves, Feb. 11, 2007.
Swing Magazine. Numerous articles accessed at the National Library of Jamaica archives.
Thornton, Edward. Interview with Adam Reeves and Daniel Junge, March, 2012.
-----. Interview with Adam Reeves, Feb. 11, 2007.
"Tribute to Osbert Maddo, AKA Bionic Singer." Cubiculo Records Soundcloud.
Wallace, Leroy. Interview with Daniel Junge, March 2012.
-----. Interview with Adam Reeves, Feb. 11, 2007.
Whitfield, Gregory Mario. Interview with Vernal Kelly, Uncarved.org, 2004.

Index

C

D

I

J

K

L

M

N

U

V

W

X

Y

Z

About the Authors

Heather Augustyn is the author of *Ska: An Oral History*, McFarland, 2010, with a foreword by Cedella Marley which was nominated for the ARSC Award for Excellence; *Don Drummond: The Genius and Tragedy of the World's Greatest Trombonist*, McFarland, 2013, with a foreword by Delfeayo Marsalis; *Ska: The Rhythm of Liberation*, Rowman & Littlefield, 2013; and *Songbirds: Pioneering Women in Jamaican Music*, Half Pint Press, 2014. Forthcoming books include *Dragon: The Story of Byron Lee, Ambassador of Jamaican Music*, and *Move On Up: Stories of America's Soul* for young adults. She is a continuing lecturer of composition in the English Department at Purdue University Northwest where she also directs their writing center, and she has been a correspondent for the *Times of Northwest Indiana* since 2004. She is also a regular guest blogger for *Wax Poetics*. Augustyn and her husband, Ron, live in Chesterton, Ind., one hour outside of Chicago, with their two boys, Sid and Frank.

Adam Reeves has been a lifelong devotee of the music of Jamaica and loves to showcase its greatness by spinning his favourite tunes at any opportunity to a packed dancefloor—something he has been doing for over fifteen years. He has previously worked as a massage therapist, having studied Tui Na, a 4000-year-old system of Chinese massage which he adapted to build his own business addressing stress in the workplace. He later trained as a magazine journalist and wrote features and news for the UK's leading Natural Products industry journal. In an even earlier incarnation he studied footwear design and manufacture and co-ran a small bespoke handmade shoemaking operation in Sheffield. He is a co-producer of a forthcoming documentary on Alpha Boys School, directed by 2012 Oscar winner Daniel Junge. Adam is also an animal carer and has lost count of the number of dogs he has taken care of. He lives with his partner Peta in Brighton, UK.

Praise for *Alpha Boys School: Cradle of Jamaican Music*

The Alpha Boys' School is at the roots of the explosion of Jamaican music which has circled the world, starting in the late fifties and still evolving right up to today. There are only three countries whose popular music is played all over the world—American music, British music, and Jamaican music. We owe maximum respect and thanks to the Alpha Boys' School for its contribution to this fact.

Chris Blackwell, founder of Island Records

The Alpha Boys School has produced more major musical talents than any other Jamaican institution, with legendary faculty led by pugnacious Sister Ignatius who had her own legendary sound system. The rambunctious history of the school is now revealed in its fullness by the tireless research of Heather Augustyn and Adam Reeves in a book filled with riotous and rootical ramblings in its hallowed halls.

Roger Steffens, author of *So Much Things to Say: The Oral History of Bob Marley*

A significant history of popular Jamaican music has been documented by this book. It tells how monumental Alpha Boys' School has been and is without parallel. The testimony of the Alpharians interviewed bears witness to this, as their revelations are insightful and deep. Coming through the narrative is the towering humanity of Sister Ignatius.

Dermot Hussey, on-air host, SiriusXM Satellite Radio

The story of the Alpha Boys' School is a tale of amazing love and care, the transformation of young lives, and the creation of the music for which Jamaica is known across the world. To understand the development, reach and power of Jamaican popular music is to understand the legacy of Alpha and its impact on Jamaica's creative community. Alpha's story must be told and retold.

The Honourable Olivia Grange, CD, MP, Minister of Culture, Gender, Entertainment and Sport, Government of Jamaica

Under the auspices of the benign taskmistress that was Sister Mary Ignatius Davies, Kingston's Alpha Boys School was the seed-ground for much of Jamaica's very greatest music. Among its alumni were Rico Rodriguez, Cedric Brooks, Vin Gordon, Eddie 'Tan Tan' Thornton, Joe Harriott, Harold McNair, and Leroy 'Horsemouth' Wallace. Alpha was an extraordinary educational establishment that literally saved the lives—and directed the first steps of their careers—for many of these artists. There was never a school like it.

Chris Salewicz, acclaimed music writer

The progressive role played by Alpha in Jamaican music history can never be underestimated. From the days of Jamaican jazz stars like Bertie King, Joe Harriott, Dizzy Reece, Harold McNair and Wilton Gaynair, through the ska period of Don Drummond, Johnny Moore and Tommy McCook and into the period of roots reggae and dancehall with such prominent artists as Leroy Smart and Winston 'Yellowman' Foster, Alpha has provided stability, schooling and musical skills to generations of young men, who owed their success to this wonderful institution.

Steve Barrow, former director of Blood and Fire Records and author of *The Rough Guide to Reggae*

"These are some of my boys," said Sister Ignatius proudly, gesturing towards the portraits lining the walls. It was my first visit to Kingston's famed Alpha School, and looking back at us were some of the most gifted and influential musicians that Jamaica has ever produced—all of whom learnt their craft at Alpha, and would make timeless contributions to ska, rocksteady and early reggae music. This invaluable book is the first such tribute to these pioneers, many of whom came from deprived backgrounds, and also those who taught and encouraged them.

John Masouri, reggae journalist and author of *Steppin' Razor: The Life of Peter Tosh*

It is impossible to overstate the importance of Alpha Boys School. By providing opportunity to young talents who wouldn't normally have access to musical instruments and training, Alpha vastly enriched the culture within Jamaica, and by extension, the world. Simply put, without Alpha there wouldn't be Jamaican music as we know it. Respect is due to Alpha for a gift that is as immense as it is immeasurable, and continues to this day.
Beth Lesser, reggae photographer and author of *Dancehall: The Rise of Jamaican Dancehall Culture*

Alpha was formed in 1880 and from that time until now, every musical event that come out of Jamaica, Alpha Boys were involved with it, either playing in a band or production. Alpha is the backbone of Jamaican music today.
Tony Greene, Alpha graduate, formerly with the Roots Radics Band and We the People Band

26791673R00221

Printed in Great Britain
by Amazon